Responses to Crime

VOLUME 4

Dispensing Justice

Lord Windlesham

CLARENDON PRESS · OXFORD
2001

OXFORD
UNIVERSITY PRESS

Great Clarendon Street, Oxford OX2 6DP

Oxford University Press is a department of the University of Oxford.
It furthers the University's objective of excellence in research, scholarship,
and education by publishing worldwide in

Oxford New York
Athens Auckland Bangkok Bogotá Buenos Aires Cape Town
Chennai Dar es Salaam Delhi Florence Hong Kong Istanbul Karachi
Kolkata Kuala Lumpur Madrid Melbourne Mexico City Mumbai
Nairobi Paris São Paulo Shanghai Singapore Taipei Tokyo Toronto Warsaw

and associated companies in Berlin Ibadan

Published in the United States
by Oxford University Press Inc., New York

First published 2001

British Library Cataloguing in Publication Data
Data available

Library of Congress Cataloging in Publication Data
Data available

ISBN 0–19–829844–7
ISBN 0–19–924741–2 (pbk.)

1 3 5 7 9 10 8 6 4 2

Typeset by Hope Services (Abingdon) Ltd.
Printed and bound in Great Britain by
T. J. International Ltd, Padstow, Cornwall

RESPONSES TO CRIME

Volume 4

To dispense justice fairly and efficiently and to promote confidence in the rule of law.

Foreword to *Criminal Justice System Business Plan, 2000–01*: The Attorney General, Home Secretary, and Lord Chancellor

To dispense, with justice; or, to dispense with justice.

Geoffrey Hill, *The Mystery of the Charity of Charles Péguy*

Preface

'DISPENSING Justice' is the fourth instalment of my work on *Responses to Crime*. Like its predecessors, this final volume identifies and comments upon the political origins and Parliamentary history of criminal justice legislation and administrative change over a relatively short span of time. The close of the twentieth century saw the transition from eighteen consecutive years of Conservative Government to the Labour Government which took office after the general election in May 1997. The advent to power of New Labour, after a long and arduous period of internal reform and modernisation, led to radical changes in the administrative structure and presentation of policies designed to reduce crime. Yet once the novelty had worn off, and the pace slowed down, it became apparent that the thrust of many of the actual policies, whether novel or inherited, had changed far less than had been hoped for by penal reformers and other sources of liberal opinion.

Post-1997 the real division over penal policy was not to be found in the attitudes of the two main political parties; still less in the personalities of the successive Home Secretaries. Both Michael Howard and Jack Straw shared authoritarian instincts. Deeper, below the surface of party politics, was the clash between the authoritarians and the experts. On most issues relating to crime in the late 1990s a large majority of the politicians, Labour and Conservative alike, were demonstrably authoritarian in outlook. There were, of course, exceptions on both sides, but that the prevailing culture in the elected House was authoritarian few would doubt. On the Government benches sensitivity to popular opinion was enhanced by the interplay of two factors: an increasingly strident tabloid press, and consciousness of the role of MPs as elected representatives. A sympathetic awareness of the plight of many of their constituents living on housing estates, where the quality of life was dramatically diminished by offending and disorderly behaviour, was a powerful and wholly legitimate influence.

Generally insulated from these pressures, and the demands of party politics, are the experts. Their essential contribution to public policy is to ensure that libertarian values are not swamped by authoritarian populism either in the making of policy or in its interpretation. That there should be tension between these two forces is inevitable, and arguably healthy in a democratic system. But neither should predominate. The relationship calls for constant assessment and a facility for periodic adjustment.

High levels of crime have led to political imperatives that are essentially reactive. In the background, and sometimes the foreground, of virtually all criminal policy-making the necessity is recognized of presenting decisions and objectives in terms designed to be perceived as tough by the general public. In recent years the primacy accorded to effective presentation has come to dominate the orientation of criminal policy at every stage from inception to implementation. In this way the strains of populism merge with, and reinforce, authoritarianism.

If initiation of legislative change is almost exclusively in the hands of ministers and their advisers, scrutiny is the province of Parliament. In the House of Commons elected in 1997 the Labour majority was so large that the Government seldom experienced difficulty in getting its measures accepted. The partial reform of the composition of the House of Lords, by which all but ninety-two of the hereditary peers were displaced, unexpectedly resulted in a sense of its greater legitimacy. Lacking an overall majority, ministers had to work hard to convince a sometimes sceptical, and on criminal justice issues often well informed, House of the merits of their proposals.

Outside Parliament the most important source of non-authoritarian influence is the judiciary. The Home Secretary normally consults the Lord Chief Justice on any significant proposals for change in the criminal law, or the powers of the sentencing courts. The communication channel is not one-way. Successive holders of the office have used their access, sparingly but effectively, to intervene either privately or publicly on such controversial issues as mandatory sentencing, the mode of trial, and enforcement of community penalties. All are described in this book. Yet it is not only the judges who have the task of upholding the rule of law and all it stands for. There is a wider libertarian responsibility to ensure that these values should never be subordinated to political advantage whenever the system of criminal justice is modified in response to authoritarian concerns.

For the second time in the four volumes of *Responses to Crime*, this book includes a descriptive account of one aspect of the criminal process in the United States. Whereas in Britain the aim of successive governments has been to curb the growth in public spending on legal aid, civil as well as criminal, in America it has been the reverse. Rights granted by the Constitution to defendants in criminal trials have been diminished by the lack of financial resources. For nearly four decades since the landmark case of *Gideon* v. *Wainwright* in 1963, the courts and much of the legal profession have been struggling to make a reality of the constitutional idealism which it embodied. There is still a long way to go.

WINDLESHAM

Brasenose College, Oxford
April 2001

Acknowledgements

The subtitle of this volume, *Dispensing Justice*, derives from the two frontispiece quotations. In giving permission to reprint the brief, but telling, extract from one of his finest poems, Geoffrey Hill remarked that such a use confirmed his belief that poetry is an art of public significance. The contrast is apt between his precise use of words and punctuation, and the 'overarching aims' of the ministerial mission statement. 'The Mystery of the Charity of Charles Péguy' is included in Geoffrey Hill's *Collected Poems*, first published by Penguin Books in 1985.

As with the previous volumes of *Responses to Crime* the many extracts from Government publications, Hansard reports, and other Crown and Parliamentary Copyright material, including official ministerial correspondence, are reproduced with the permission of the Controller of Her Majesty's Stationery Office. The Home Office, the Lord Chancellor's Department, the Law Officers' Department, and other organizations, public or private, have also supplied a wealth of information without which the book would be much the poorer. The use made of the material is entirely the responsibility of the author.

Researching a book of this sort over a period of years places a burden on the Library staffs who help in tracking down source material and references. The House of Lords is exceptionally fortunate in the quality of its reference librarians. Among those who have been of particular assistance during the preparation of this volume are Caroline Auty, Dr Isolde Victory, and Parthenope Ward. For legal research Glen Dymond has co-operated with many inquiries.The Public Bill Offices of both the House of Commons and House of Lords have also supplied factual information. At Oxford the Bodleian Law Library and the Codrington Library of All Souls College have first-rate collections and helpful staff; I have made regular use of both.

As to policy, I have benefited from the advice and expertise of a retired senior Home Office official, Sydney Norris. With a background in criminology and long experience of policy-making, administration, and financial control, at the Prison Service Headquarters as well as the Home Office, Syd Norris has been an intermediary between the insiders and a commentator from the outside. Once again, David Faulkner and Bill Bohan have contributed guidance and insights on various aspects of the formulation and execution of policy, as they did for the previous volumes. Since May 1997 I have been afforded interviews with the Home Secretary, the Lord Chancellor, and the Chairman of the Youth Justice Board, as well as being in periodic correspondence with them and other ministers. While seldom winning a point against him in debate, I record my admiration for the exceptional forensic skills of Lord Williams of Mostyn, first as Minister of State at the Home Office, and then Attorney General, in the Parliament of 1997–2001. Part of Chapter 8, on the enforcement of community penalties, was first published in the *Criminal Law Review* [2000] Crim. L.R. 661, and is reproduced with the Editor's permission.

None of those who have helped by making comments on the Chapters, or providing information, should be identified in any way with the contents of the book or the opinions expressed. In addition to those named above, I wish to acknowledge the advice and information provided by Lord Allen of Abbeydale, Professor Andrew Ashworth, Lord Bassam of Brighton, Lord Belstead, Professor Vernon Bogdanor, Paul Cavadino, John Croft, Sir Iain Glidewell, Paul Hayter, Robert Heard, Professor Roger Hood, Colin Roberts, Roger Smith, Professor Nigel Walker, Dr Rhodri Walters, Lord Warner, Nigel Whiskin, and Dr Richard Young. The statistical details contained in Tables 5–8 and 13–16 were provided by Clerks in the Public Bill Offices of the House of Commons and the House of Lords. Above all else is my gratitude to my secretary, Patricia Spight, who for more than a decade has prepared my books for publication. Her industry has been matched only by her patience. Thanks are due also to Anna Rayne for her meticulous copy-editing of both Volumes 3 and 4 of *Responses to Crime*.

Part of the cost of my research for Chapter 6 was again met by a grant from the Andrew W. Mellon Fund at the University of Oxford. Many people helped with my inquiries in the United States, and two in particular contributed not only valuable guidance, but opened doors that otherwise would have remained closed. They are Frank Sullivan, a Justice of the Supreme Court of Indiana, and Jonathan Lippman, Chief Administrative Judge of the State of New York Unified Court System. Judge Lippman's Executive Assistant,

Antonio Galvao, deserves especial thanks for arranging so many useful appointments. Gratitude is also recorded to Professor Adele Bernard, David Cook, Robert Dean, Judge JoAnn Ferdinand, Daniel Greenberg, Professor Philip Heymann, Dean Norman Lefstein, Professor Mark Moore, Leonard Noisette, Professor Ellen Schall, Robert Spangenberg, Christopher Stone, Cheryl Sullivan, and Jeremy Travis.

Contents

List of Tables

1

High Tide: Mandatory Sentences, 1995–7

I

The Conservative Party Conference in 1995 was held at Blackpool. Each Autumn the party faithful assemble in large numbers at a seaside resort, Brighton being the preferred location in the South and Blackpool in the North of England, to participate in a familiar and comfortable ritual. This is the moment for constituency workers to hear, and maybe to meet, leading members of the Parliamentary party. For an unbroken sequence of sixteen years the Conservatives had been in power. As Prime Minister until November 1990, Margaret Thatcher, and John Major after her, had deployed all their rhetorical skills in making an uplifting appeal at the end of the conference to send the delegates back to their constituencies fortified to keep the Tory flame burning bright for another year. In such speeches it was the tone, the appeal to traditional values, and the style of leadership, rather than the detailed content of government policies, that was paramount. Other ministers also concentrated on raising the spirits of the audience, a favoured tactic being to pillory the policies of the Opposition parties.

Although decisions on policy might be outlined in general terms, it was rare for ministers to use a party conference platform to announce specific changes calling for legislation. But as Home Secretary for two and a half years[1] Michael Howard had already shown himself to be a non-conformist. Unlike most of his predecessors holding the same office in Conservative governments, who had viewed the ordeal of addressing the annual conference with apprehension,[2] Howard saw it as an opportunity to be grasped. Where

[1] Michael Howard was appointed Home Secretary on 27 May 1993, having previously served as Secretary of State for Employment, 1990–2, and for the Environment, 1992–3. It was a rapid ascent.

[2] See the memoirs of two long-serving Conservative Home Secretaries: *The Whitelaw Memoirs*, Arum Press, London, 1989, p. 196, and *The Art of the Possible: The Memoirs of Lord Butler*, Hamish Hamilton, London, 1971, p. 201. William Whitelaw was Home Secretary, 1979–83, and R. A. Butler, 1957–62.

they had been uneasily aware that the more vociferous among their audiences could be counted upon to articulate the extremes of populist punitiveness, with such contributions being euphorically received, he sensed that these primal instincts could be harnessed, and turned to advantage.

Consciously or otherwise, Howard was able to exploit some little-known features of ministers' speeches at party conferences. First there is the convention that no minister may announce a government policy initiative that would call for additional funding without prior clearance from the Treasury. In 1995 this covered any proposals creating spending requirements beyond the time span of what had been agreed in the annual Public Expenditure Survey. But the pressure of events, the shortness of the time-scale, and the allure of the political dividends sought combine to make this restraint hard to enforce as rigorously at the party conference season as at other times. There is also some relaxation in the orthodox process of collective policy-making. The full routine of consultation at official level between the sponsoring department, the Treasury, and other departments of government in advance of approval by the appropriate Cabinet Committee may not be possible. A minister may be tempted to announce a policy that has implications for other departments after what he regards as consultation, but which they regard as little more than preliminary discussion.

The drafting of a party conference speech unveiling new policies is a composite process in which civil servants and political advisers both have a role.[3] The input of non-partisan departmental officials, however, inevitably risks being overshadowed in the heady atmosphere of a party conference when the objectives are primarily party political. The promotion of the speech in the media is in the hands of party spokesmen rather than government press officers, although the relevant department needs to be prepared to answer inquiries about the practical implications.

[3] The respective roles of political adviser and civil servant in the preparation of a ministerial speech to the Conservative Party Conference are well described by Douglas Hurd in his novel, *The Shape of Ice*, Little, Brown and Co., London, 1998. Before joining the Government as a Minister of State at the Foreign and Commonwealth Office in 1979, later becoming Secretary of State for Northern Ireland (1984–5), Home Secretary (1985–9), and Secretary of State for Foreign and Commonwealth Affairs (1989–95), Douglas Hurd had been Political Secretary to the Prime Minister, Edward Heath, 1970–4. He was created Lord Hurd of Westwell in 1997.

Even allowing for these tolerances, Howard's unexpected conversion to mandatory minimum sentences of imprisonment for repeat offenders in his conference speech came as a complete surprise to virtually all of his ministerial colleagues. The verbatim extract of the crucial passage, cited in full below, conveys the tenor of a rhetorical performance of great power. If the language seems emotive the characteristics of the audience at which it was aimed should be kept in mind.

I am acutely aware of how strongly many people feel about one particular problem. Sentencing. Today I want to set out radical, new proposals to tackle this problem. I want to hear views on this from the judges. From the police. And, yes, from the British people. And then I will act.

First, release from prison. It comes too soon. A robber receives a sentence of two years. He's out in one. A rapist receives a sentence of nine years. He's out in six. Automatically. No matter what. Every one. That can't be right. It makes a mockery of the courts. It sends the wrong signals to criminals. And it outrages the victims. I propose to end it. Model prisoners should get a little time off for good behaviour. Everyone else should serve their sentence in full. And five years should mean five years. It's time to get honesty back into sentencing. Time to back the courts. And time to send a powerful message to the criminal. No more automatic early release. No more release regardless of behaviour. And no more half-time sentences for full-time crimes.

Secondly, serious violent and sexual offenders. The maximum sentence for these crimes is life imprisonment. But these offenders don't always get life. Even if they offend again and again. Unless they do get life they have to be released at the end of their sentence. Regardless of the risk they pose to the public. The risk of offending again. The risk of destroying another life. Take a real life example. A rapist. Sentenced to seven years. He was out after four. Three years later he raped again. This time he was sentenced to twelve years. And he was out after eight. Even though the prison authorities thought he was unstable and disturbed. They had no choice. It's the law. That can't be right. I believe it must change. There is a strong case for saying that anyone convicted for the second time of a serious violent or sexual offence should receive an automatic sentence of life imprisonment. They would only be released when they no longer posed a risk to the public. And if they continued to pose a risk, life really would mean life.

Third, burglars and drug dealers. Burglary is a foul crime. It defiles people's memories. It creates a terrible sense of violation. And it destroys peace of mind. For many there is the awful fear that the burglar will return to strike again. It really is a crime of violence. The same is true of the dealers in hard drugs. They prey on the young, the lonely and the vulnerable. They deserve long stretches in prison. And they ought to receive them. In some cases they do. But sometimes they don't. If prison—and the threat of prison—are to work effectively, there's a strong case for greater certainty in sentencing. For stiff minimum sentences for burglars and dealers in hard drugs who offend again and again and again. I will tell you now, some people won't like it. They'll say it's too tough. I've got a simple answer. If you don't want the time, don't do the crime.[4]

Howard's Blackpool speech in 1995 stands out as a landmark in English penal history. It was far more significant than an ephemeral rhetorical triumph, cheered to the rafters of the vast hall, and earning him a standing ovation that lasted for four minutes, the longest of the week.[5] There can be no doubt that he identified correctly, and manipulated shrewdly, the 'something must be done' strain of frustrated opinion that too many convicted criminals were let off lightly by the courts. However ill informed the general public might be about the level of sentences actually imposed for specific offences,[6] the overwhelming volume of popular support for stiffer sentences was demonstrated by the proportion of respondents who agreed with the proposition that 'too many convicted criminals are let off lightly by the courts'. As measured in surveys reported in the *British Social Attitudes* series, the positive response rate rose from the already high total of 79 per cent to 86 per cent between 1990 and 1994.[7]

We should pause to note that when such emotive terms as 'stiffer sentences' and 'let off lightly' were eliminated and replaced by more neutral wording, the calls for greater punitiveness were muted. In response to an alternative statement that 'courts should give longer sentences to criminals' only 61 per cent in the 1994 survey agreed, i.e. some 25 per cent below the proportion responding positively to the more evocative wording.[8] Even so, 61 per cent was ample to verify the political assumptions made about underlying attitudes towards the punishment of offenders. Irrespective of party loyalties, the research also indicated widespread public support for the Home Secretary's declaration, from an earlier party conference platform in 1993, that the criminal justice system had been tilted too far in favour of the criminal and against the protection of the public.

[4] *Conservative Party News*, 478/95, 12 Oct. 1995, pp. 9–11.

[5] *The Daily Telegraph*, 13 Oct. 1995.

[6] See M. Hough and J. Roberts, *Attitudes to punishment: Findings from the British Crime Survey*, Home Office Research Study No. 179, Home Office, London, 1998.

[7] R. Tarling and L. Dowds, 'Crime and Punishment', in *British Social Attitudes*, 14th Report, Ashgate Publishing, 1997, pp. 197–214 at p. 209.

[8] Ibid., pp. 209–10.

Although a general election was not far off, and could not be delayed for more than about eighteen months, Howard's dramatic switch in policy cannot be dismissed simply as pre-campaign posturing. The motives of leading politicians are always likely to be more complex. Ever since becoming Home Secretary he had been at pains to reject what he regarded as the negativism implicit in the prevailing attitude that nothing could be done to check the apparently irresistible rise in crime and lawlessness, and the feeling that society was powerless in the face of it. He insisted that more severity in sentencing would contribute to a reduction in crime through the incapacitation of habitual offenders for longer periods of time, and the creation of a generally deterrent effect. The need for better protection and security was the keynote throughout.

His message was designed to reassure a fearful and uncomprehending public, so generating a greater measure of confidence in the effectiveness of the criminal process and the maintenance of law and order. It was not an ignoble aim and was one that had been pursued by other ministers who had preceded him, as it was to be by his Labour successor at the Home Office. But the overtly simplistic solutions, put forward with such vehemence and in disregard of so many contrary factors, exposed Howard to charges of cynical opportunism. Other voices, less strident but backed by practical experience, were either ignored or shouted down when some of the likely outcomes were pointed out. In this sense, his announcement can be likened to a strike of lightning, momentarily illuminating an overcast landscape in brilliant relief, but leaving behind a scene of destruction which would take years to repair.

Away from Blackpool the adverse reaction was immediate. Lord Taylor of Gosforth, the Lord Chief Justice,[9] who had received advance notice of the contents of Howard's speech, was forthright in condemnation. Acting with a rapidity which showed that politicians were not alone in practising the skills of news management, Taylor issued a statement later the same day which ensured that his strictures were reported simultaneously with Howard's proposals:

> Long sentences, sometimes very long sentences, are necessary in some cases to protect the public. But I do not believe that the threat of longer and longer

[9] Lord Taylor of Gosforth, previously a Lord Justice of Appeal, 1988–92, was appointed Lord Chief Justice of England in April 1992. He resigned on grounds of ill health on 2 May 1996, and died from cancer on 28 April in the following year at the age of sixty-six.

periods of imprisonment across the board will deter habitual criminals. What deters them is the likelihood of being caught, which at the moment is small.[10]

While Taylor made no criticism of the police, who had to do their best with the limited resources they were given, he questioned whether anyone believed that a professional burglar, who knew he had at most only three chances in twenty of being caught, would be deterred by the possible addition of six months, or even two years, to his sentence. As to the proposals for mandatory minimum sentences, judges already disliked the mandatory life sentence for murder as it prevented them from being able to match the sentence to the severity of the crime. He continued:

There are maximum sentences of life imprisonment for rape and drug trafficking, and fourteen years for domestic burglary. Judges apply this framework conscientiously, but must be free to fit the particular punishment to the particular crime if justice is to be done. Minimum sentences are inconsistent with doing justice according to the circumstances of the case. Instead of limiting judicial discretion by introducing unnecessary constraints on sentencing, the police should be provided with the resources they need to bring criminals before the courts in the first place.[11]

At the start of the following week *The Times* published a letter to the Editor from myself about the relevance of American experience across three columns at the head of the Letters page.[12] It was hard to believe that the Home Secretary and his advisers should have overlooked the fact that, of all the populist-inspired panaceas to have afflicted the administration of justice in the United States, none had resulted in greater unintended effects than mandatory sentences of imprisonment, of which 'three strikes and you're out' was the latest and most conspicuous example.[13] The federal prisons were so overloaded with inmates serving lengthy mandatory sentences for relatively low-level offences of buying and selling harmful drugs that in the previous year Congress, with some reluctance, had enacted a 'safety valve' permitting a relaxation in penalties for the least culpable drug offenders who met certain conditions.[14] In California, the breeding ground of three strikes, a broad version of the policy had

[10] *The Times*, 13 Oct. 1995. [11] Ibid. [12] *The Times*, 16 Oct. 1995.

[13] For an account of the origins of the three strikes sentencing policy and its initial impact in California, see Windlesham, *Responses to Crime*, Vol. 3, Clarendon Press, Oxford, 1996, pp. 246–58.

[14] Ibid., pp. 267–9.

been adopted precipitately which had dislocated the entire system of criminal justice, and for a time brought the processing of civil disputes to a standstill in parts of the state where judges and courts normally hearing civil cases were redirected to criminal cases. In jurisdictions throughout the United States plea bargaining had transferred power from judges to prosecutors who determined the offence for which the offender was sentenced, and hence the penalty. Far from being 'radical' new proposals, as Howard had claimed at Blackpool, his policies were discredited old ones.

II

While the officials at the Home Office were grappling with the task of translating the sweeping statements of the political platform into workable legislative proposals, and assessing the implications in terms of prison resources and cost, a consortium of twenty-eight organizations, some of them in the public sector such as the National Association of Probation Officers, the Association of Chief Officers of Probation, the Prison Officers' Association, and the Prison Governors' Association, together with all of the main penal reform groups, carried out its own analysis. When the report was published in December 1995[15] it drew attention not only to the defects of mandatory sentencing, already roundly condemned by the Lord Chief Justice and other members of the judiciary, but also to the consequences of the fine sounding slogan 'honesty in sentencing', a term plagiarized from the American version of 'truth in sentencing'.[16] The aim of both was the same: to bring the amount of time spent in prison closer to the length of the sentence passed in court. If carried out to the full, this would mean the virtual elimination of early release mechanisms such as conditional release and the various forms of parole.

The criteria for eligibility had been changed several times since the inception of the parole system by the Criminal Justice Act 1967.[17] The essential feature retained throughout, although unmentioned by

[15] *Sentencing and Early Release: The Home Secretary's Proposals*, Penal Affairs Consortium, London, December, 1995.

[16] See Windlesham, *Politics, Punishment, and Populism*, Oxford University Press, New York, 1998, pp. 153–5.

[17] See Windlesham, *Responses to Crime*, Vol. 1, Clarendon Press, Oxford, 1987, pp. 251–6.

Howard, was that all prisoners released on parole, and after the implementation of the Criminal Justice Act 1991, all prisoners released from sentences of twelve months to four years, were subject to an initial period on licence, subject to specified conditions and supervised by the Probation Service, with the sanction of recall to continue to serve their sentence in prison in the event of breaches of conditions or further offending. Research commissioned by the Home Office indicated that prisoners released on parole had markedly lower reconviction rates than would have been expected of prisoners with similar records of criminal offending and personal characteristics. There was also a reduction in the gravity of later offences.[18] The Penal Affairs Consortium, drawing on the well grounded experience of the Prison Service representative organizations, argued that removing or diminishing significantly the possibility of early release would take away a powerful incentive for good behaviour and induce a sense of hopelessness, particularly among long-term prisoners. The result would be to 'increase the risk of indiscipline, riots, violence and hostage-taking in prisons'.[19]

Critically important as these considerations were, estimating the potential effect of the proposals on the size of the prison population exercised Home Office officials more than any other factor when advising ministers on the immediate and future practicalities of implementing the new policies. In the Autumn of 1995, partly resulting from a more punitive sentencing environment introduced by Howard's 1993 conference speech, when he coined the phrase 'prison works' in terms of general deterrence and protecting the public, and also from some statutory and other changes,[20] the prison population was already at an ominously high level. Table 1 shows the escalation which had taken place over the previous two years in the average population in custody, of both sentenced prisoners and those on remand awaiting trial or sentence, amounting to a total of 51,047 for the calendar year 1995. This figure represented an increase of nearly

[18] D. Ward, 'The Validity of the Reconviction Prediction Score', Home Office Research Study No. 94, Home Office, London, 1987.

[19] 'Protecting the Public: Comments on the White Paper', Penal Affairs Consortium *News Release*, 19 July 1996, p. 2.

[20] The Criminal Justice Act 1993 modified aspects of the Criminal Justice Act 1991 and coincided with a greater use of custody both by the Magistrates' courts and the Crown Court. The Criminal Justice and Public Order Act 1994 increased the maximum sentence length for juveniles from one to two years, and relaxed the requirement of pre-sentence reports for those aged eighteen and over. Home Office, *Prison Statistics England and Wales 1995* (Cm. 3355), HMSO, London, 1996, pp. 2 and 5.

6,500 over the comparable figure of 44,566 for 1993. The prison population had climbed steeply in the last three months of 1995, reaching an all-time high of 52,540 in November.[21] Twelve months later, when the impact of Howard's Blackpool speech on sentencing decisions in the courts had accelerated the existing upward trend, the monthly total for November 1996 had risen to 58,126.[22]

The responsiveness of the prison population to political interventions in the decade 1986–96 is graphically demonstrated in Table 2. The presence of factors other than sentencing should not be disregarded in tracking the sharp increase from the low point in 1993. More cars on the roads had led to more motoring offences, some of which resulted in prison sentences. Thefts of and from motor vehicles had become commonplace. Delays in bringing cases before the courts meant more persons remanded in custody awaiting trial or sentence. Changing attitudes towards the use of imprisonment for women and younger age groups of offenders also had begun to have an effect. But none of these factors were significant enough to account for the rate of increase. The only consistent underlying cause was the way in which the punitive policies and actions of government were directly reflected in the escalating size of the prison population.

This was the unpromising background for the urgent forecasts that now had to be made. Shortly after the new sentencing regime

Table 1. *Total population in custody: annual averages 1991–5*

Year	Prisoners under sentence	Prisoners on remand	Non-criminal prisoners	Total in custody
1991	35,440	10,157	300	45,897
1992	35,419	10,090	308	45,817
1993	33,318	10,674	574	44,566
1994	35,797	12,357	640	48,794
1995	39,057	11,375	615	51,047

Note: The 1996 total in custody was 55,281, rising to 61,114 in 1997

Source: Home Office, *Prison Statistics England and Wales, 1995*.

[21] Ibid., p. 13.

[22] Home Office, *Prison Statistics England and Wales 1996* (Cm. 3732), HMSO, London, 1997, p. 14.

Table 2. *Prison population: political interventions 1986–96*

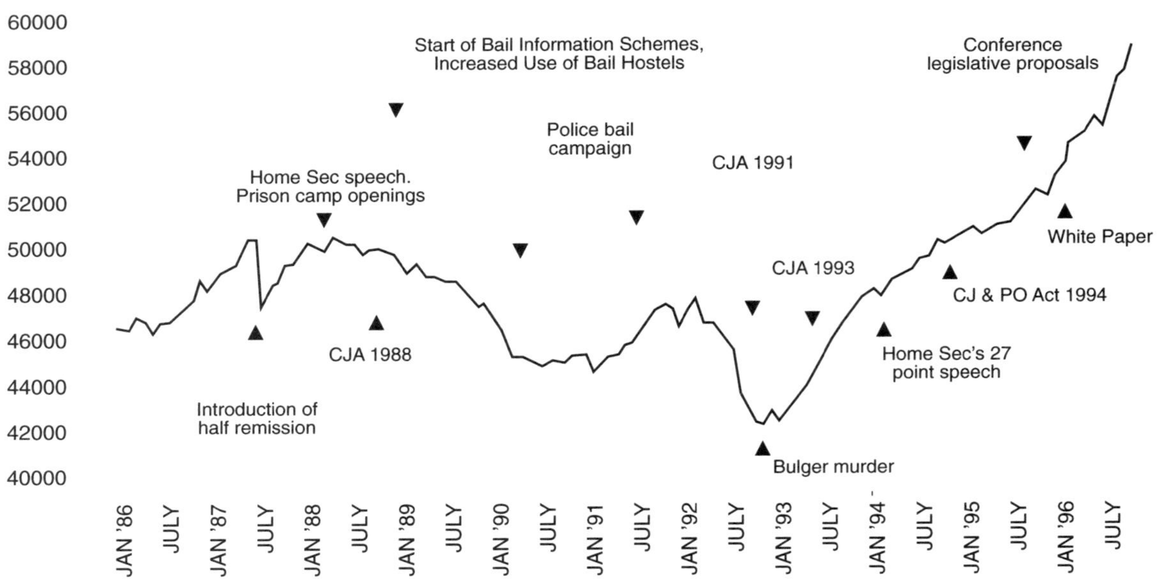

Source: *Prison Statistics, England and Wales*, 1996; Cm. 3732, HMSO, 1997.
Notes: 1. CJA = Criminal Justice Acts.
2. CJ&PO = Criminal Justice and Public Order Act, 1994.

was announced the first informal estimates by the Home Office of the likely scale of the increase in the population in custody were in the range of 15,000 to 21,500 extra prisoners. After carrying out detailed calculations on the effects of restricting early release, the Penal Affairs Consortium concluded that, taken as a whole, the Home Secretary's proposals would increase the prison population by a number nearer to 30,000 than to 20,000. To accommodate so many additional prisoners without increasing prison overcrowding would require the building of forty-eight new prisons the size of HMP Dartmoor.[23] If, in passing sentence, the courts were to reduce the length of custodial sentences to compensate for the abolition of parole and the changes in the rules on early release, the pressure of numbers would be eased. Such an outcome had no part in Howard's conference speech, although it was included in the subsequent White Paper.[24] Yet in the light of the harsher climate engendered by the 'tough on crime' proposals, it was improbable that the judiciary would be willing to incur the odium of reducing the length of sentences to levels which would risk exposing them to public censure for being over-lenient.

Even if relatively low estimates were adopted as planning assumptions, the rapid growth in the prison population was already causing severe practical problems. Ministerial colleagues could not easily be persuaded to provide unrestricted funds for prison construction, and in any event it was doubtful that enough new prisons could be completed in time to contain the incoming tide. Caught between these unwelcome realities and a highly publicized commitment from which there could be no going back, the Home Secretary had no alternative but to accept a phased implementation, taking account of the maximum financial resources that could be negotiated, and watching out for any indications of favourable changes in trends that might come to the rescue.

Nothing had been said about timing in the conference speech. A timetable allowing for the earlier implementation of those proposals likely to have the smallest effect on the prison population, followed at

[23] Penal Affairs Consortium, *Sentencing and Early Release: The Home Secretary's Proposals*, *op. cit.*, p. 6.

[24] Chapter 9, headed 'Honesty in Sentencing', stated that sentence lengths could be reduced in one of two ways: by a Practice Direction if the Lord Chief Justice decided that it was appropriate to issue such a Direction, or by a specific statutory provision. Home Office, *Protecting the Public: The Government's Strategy on Crime in England and Wales* (Cm. 3190), HMSO, London, 1996, p. 43.

a later stage by those requiring the largest expansion in prison places, offered the most plausible solution. Thus when the White Paper, *Protecting the Public*, was published in March 1996 it forecast a phasing in of the new mandatory penalties, and a phasing out of parole for determinate sentence prisoners. The automatic life sentence on second conviction for serious violent and sex offenders, and mandatory minimum sentences for drug traffickers having been convicted twice before of similar offences, were not expected to have a significant early effect on the prison population. The number of cases was relatively small, and such offenders tended to receive long custodial sentences already. Implementation could follow soon after the enabling Bill was passed by Parliament. Assuming Royal Assent in April 1997, a realistic date for the implementation of these provisions would be October 1997.[25]

The proposed mandatory minimum sentence of three years' imprisonment for offenders aged eighteen or over who were convicted of burglary or aggravated burglary of a dwelling, having been convicted previously of similar offences on two or more separate occasions, was of a different dimension. The anticipated effect on the prison population was so great that it was not possible to attempt to implement the change until an expanded building programme had supplied many more places. The requirement that the first and second qualifying convictions should be incurred after the relevant section of the Act had come into effect would allow a short breathing space before the full demand for additional places would be felt. The overall resource implications, however, compelled Howard to accept the unavoidable necessity of delaying the implementation of the three-year mandatory minimum sentence. He committed himself to the intention that the provision should be brought in by October 1999, well after the latest date for the next general election. The 'honesty in sentencing' parole reforms would also be postponed.

III

This was the background to an estimate in the White Paper that the prison population would increase by around 10,800 in the year 2011–12.[26] Allowing for a small operating margin, even this more

[25] Home Office, *Protecting the Public: The Government's Strategy on Crime in England and Wales* (Cm. 3190), HMSO, London, 1996, p. 55, para. 13.7.

[26] Ibid., para. 13.8.

distant target would call for some twelve new prisons to come on stream at a rate of one or two each year from 2001–2 onwards, amounting to 9,600 new places. An additional 3,000 places would be provided by 2001–2 as a result of constructing extensions at existing establishments and rebuilding and re-opening two existing prisons, making a total of 12,600 new places. It was intended that the new prisons should be provided through the Private Finance Initiative (PFI). Their cost, together with the recurring current costs of the new houseblocks and rebuilt prisons, was estimated to reach a peak of around £375–£435 million by 2011–12. There would also be resource implications for the courts, legal aid, the Crown Prosecution Service, and the Probation Service, although these would not take full effect until around 2009–10.[27]

Making forecasts and planning assumptions for the prison population is a hazardous undertaking at the best of times, let alone when there has been a sudden and profound policy change. In the mid-1990s, statistical projections based on recent or longer-term historical trends were regarded as the best guide available for planning assumptions.[28] These provided a band of possible future populations of varying probability, with the band widening as the projection extended into the future. Planning assumptions were then made within this band, on the basis of which the need for resources could be determined. The process allowed scope for argument about the quality of the projections, the planning assumptions to be chosen, and the cost implications that derived from them. The Treasury was typically sceptical of high projections and argued for low planning assumptions, while the Home Office usually insisted that the prudent course, if overcrowding and disorder in the prisons were to be averted, was to accept the higher planning assumptions. The situation following the Home Secretary's policy announcement would have been reflected in the bargaining tactics. Home Office officials must have been anxious not to exaggerate the risks of the highest projections being realized, since that might seem to postpone implementation indefinitely.

[27] Ibid., para. 13.9.

[28] In 1999 the Home Office conceded that, in forecasting the prison population, past trends might not be the best guide for future change. No projection between 1990–4 had forecast the rapid rise which had occurred since 1995. Instead a new methodology was developed for making long-term projections of the prison population. It used a flow model of offenders into and out of prison and allowed for changes in court sentencing policy to be predicted. Home Office *Statistical Bulletin*, 1/99, 20 Jan. 1999, pp. 2 and 10.

Treasury officials, on the other hand, might well have been concerned that the likely population numbers, and therefore the full costs of the policy, should not be understated.

The effect of the Private Finance Initiative would be to delay the full cost impact, since the design and construction costs were to be carried by private sector contractors and recovered through charges over the lifetime of the contract, commencing only when the new facilities were completed and brought into use. Although the 'build first and pay later' method held out the prospect of some financial relief in the short term, the Government's estimate that the cumulative effect of the new proposals when implemented would be an increase in the prison population of around 10,800, at an eventual recurring annual cost of £375–£435 million, still seemed too low to most informed observers on both counts.

Despite the scepticism with which they had been greeted, these estimates were repeated in the Explanatory and Financial Memorandum when the Crime (Sentences) Bill was published on 24 October 1996. One component of the calculations seemed particularly dubious. This was the assumption made in the White Paper that the deterrent effect of mandatory sentencing on those likely to incur the new penalties would reduce the demand for prison places by 20 per cent. When pressed to explain the basis for this assumption the Home Secretary replied there was research evidence showing that both the certainty of imprisonment and the severity of the prison sentence had a deterrent effect on offending, citing studies by Beyleveld (1980), Lewis (1986), and Burnett (1992). Exactly what the deterrent effect would be was a matter of judgment. But targeted measures of this sort had not been tried elsewhere, and the Government believed that a strong deterrent would achieve a reduction of about 20 per cent in relation to offenders who would on re-offending be liable to a mandatory penalty. No allowance had been made for the deterrent effect the proposals might have on other offenders, such as first-time burglars.[29]

[29] Reply by Baroness Blatch, Minister of State at the Home Office, to a Question for Written Answer tabled by the author asking the Government to give the factual and statistical basis for the assumption in Chapter 13, para. 4, of the White Paper (Cm. 3190). *Parl. Debates*, HL, 571 (5th ser.), col. WA 110, 25 Apr. 1996. The Home Secretary made the same claim when introducing the White Paper to the House of Commons. *Parl. Debates*, HC, 275 (6th ser.), col. 402, 3 Apr. 1996.

Within weeks Professor Beyleveld, the author of the most substantial of the studies cited,[30] repudiated the claim in a television interview.[31] He was astonished by what the Home Secretary had said. It was a complete misrepresentation of what he had written. At no point in his book had he made any assertion to the effect that increasing the severity of sentences would decrease the crime rate, or would act as a deterrent to crime. The Penal Affairs Consortium published his denial, together with an extract from a paper by another of the authorities, Dr Ros Burnett,[32] which also disputed the use made of her findings. To these corrections the Consortium added a neat quotation extracted from the 1990 edition of the Home Office's own handbook for sentencers, *The Sentence of the Court*:

> The inference most commonly drawn from research studies is that the probability of arrest and conviction is likely to deter potential offenders, whereas the perceived severity of the ensuing penalties has little effect.[33]

IV

In the twilight of the long period of Conservative ascendancy, Howard's imprint was so strong that the role of punishment overshadowed the public debate on crime in 1995–6. Nevertheless his White Paper ranged more broadly. In addition to sentencing it set out practical policies designed to: facilitate crime prevention and greater police effectiveness, help young people to resist drugs and reduce the health risks of drug misuse, address the needs of victims, and implement some of the remaining recommendations of the Royal Commission on Criminal Justice, which had been set up in

[30] *A Bibliography on General Deterrence Research*, Saxon House, Farnborough, 1980. In 1996 Deryck Beyleveld was Professor of Law at the University of Sheffield. See also his article on 'Deterrence Research and Deterrence Policies', in A. von Hirsch and A. Ashworth, *Principled Sentencing*, Northeastern University Press, Boston, 1992, pp. 77–92; second edition by Hart Publishing, Oxford, 1998.

[31] *On the Record*, BBC Television, 16 June 1996.

[32] Then Head of the Probation Studies Unit, Centre for Criminological Research, University of Oxford.

[33] Penal Affairs Consortium, *The Crime (Sentences) Bill*, Feb. 1997, pp. 19–20. For a later study of the effects of deterrence on criminal offending, see *Criminal Deterrence and Sentence Severity: An Analysis of Recent Research*, University of Cambridge, Institute of Criminology, Hart Publishing, Oxford, 1999. The report is cited in Chapter 8 of this volume.

1991 and reported two years later.[34] In two areas at least, some glimpses of the basic principles of justice could be detected.

The first was a reservation, attributed to the Lord Chancellor, Lord Mackay of Clashfern.[35] During the ministerial consultations to prepare the legislation necessary to give effect to Howard's undertakings at Blackpool, Mackay had been anxious to preserve the ability of sentencing judges to deal justly with particular cases. In an on-the-record interview he said he had ensured that a reference designed to continue the exercise of discretion 'in exceptional circumstances' was incorporated so that judges could escape what he saw as a restriction on their ability to match punishment and crime.[36]

In the version ordered to be printed by the House of Commons on 24 October 1996, the first three clauses of the Crime (Sentences) Bill required the court to impose a life sentence on persons aged eighteen or above who were convicted for the second time of certain serious sexual or violent offences (Clause 1); to impose a custodial sentence of at least seven years on persons aged eighteen or above on conviction of a class A drug trafficking offence, having had two or more previous convictions for similar offences (Clause 2); and to impose a custodial sentence of at least three years on persons aged eighteen or above on conviction of an offence of domestic burglary, having had two or more previous convictions for similar offences (Clause 3). To each of these clauses an identical qualification was appended: unless the court was 'of the opinion that there are exceptional circumstances which justify its not doing so'. The prefix 'genuinely', which had been incorporated in the White Paper references, was omitted. Whenever a court did not impose the prescribed sentence it would have an obligation to state in open court what the exceptional circumstances were.

When introducing the Bill on Second Reading in the House of Commons on 4 November 1996 Howard made clear that he intended the reference to 'exceptional circumstances' to be interpreted narrowly.

[34] The Royal Commission on Criminal Justice, chaired by Viscount Runciman of Doxford, reported in July 1993 (Cm. 2263).

[35] Lord Mackay served as Lord Chancellor for ten years between 1987 and 1997, the longest continuous term in the twentieth century. His predecessor, Lord Hailsham of St Marylebone, served for two terms as Lord Chancellor, 1970–4 and 1979–87, making a total of eleven years and nine months overall. Lord Mackay had previously been Lord Advocate of Scotland, 1979–84; a Senator of the College of Justice in Scotland, 1984–5; and a Lord of Appeal in Ordinary, 1985–7.

[36] Interview with Frances Gibb, Legal Correspondent, of *The Times* on 5 Nov. 1996.

The only example he gave of an exceptional circumstance justifying the passing of a sentence shorter than the minimum length was if someone appearing before a court had given the police exceptional help which had enabled a number of other serious criminals to be brought to justice.[37] The controversy over 'exceptional circumstances', or a more precise version of mitigation, as preferred by the judiciary, of specific circumstances which would make a mandatory sentence of imprisonment 'unjust in all the circumstances', was to continue until the final stages when the Bill was passed into law hurriedly before the dissolution of Parliament in March of the following year.

Another proposal raising considerations of procedural justice was the automatic life sentence on second conviction for a serious sexual or violent offence. Since life imprisonment did not mean incarceration for the remainder of the natural life of the convicted offender, but for an indeterminate period, the critical issues were how the initial term was set, and at what point in the future, and by whom, it was to be extended or terminated. The convoluted and irrational development of the life sentence since the 1960s is described in considerable detail in the second and third volumes of *Responses to Crime*.[38]

Mindful of the need to conform to the case-law of the European Court of Human Rights at Strasbourg if further challenges were to be averted,[39] the Bill left both these decisions in the hands of the sentencing court, or of a body with sufficient judicial characteristics to enable it to be regarded as court-like for the purposes of the Convention on Human Rights,[40] and therefore not part of the executive branch of

[37] *Parl. Debates*, HC, 284, cols. 914–15, 4 Nov. 1996.

[38] Windlesham, *Responses to Crime*, *op. cit.*, Vol. 2, chapter 7, 'Life Imprisonment: A Sentence Nobody Can Understand?', pp. 308–46; and Vol. 3, chapter 9, 'Life Sentences: The Defects of Duality', pp. 331–82.

[39] In the case of *Thynne, Wilson, and Gunnell* v. *United Kingdom*, (1991) 13 EHRR 666, the European Court of Human Rights had found the United Kingdom to be in violation of Article 5(4) of the Convention which defined the lawfulness of both the original and continued detention. The result was the enactment by the Westminster Parliament of new procedures for setting the tariff and the release of discretionary life prisoners after their tariffs had expired, in Section 34 of the Criminal Justice Act 1991. The Section did not apply to mandatory life sentences for murder.

[40] Article 5(4) of the European Convention on Human Rights states that 'Everyone who is deprived of his liberty by arrest or detention shall be entitled to take proceedings by which the lawfulness of his detention shall be decided speedily by a court and his release ordered if the detention is not lawful'. In *Thynne, Wilson, and Gunnell* three British prisoners who had received discretionary life sentences succeeded in their claim that no judicial procedures had been available to them to determine the continued lawfulness of their detention after the expiry of the tariff period nor, in two of the cases, the lawfulness of their re-detention following release on licence and recall to custody.

government. When passing sentence at the conclusion of the trial, the judge would prescribe in open court a minimum term of imprisonment that must be served for the purposes of retribution and general deterrence, colloquially known as the tariff. Release would not follow automatically on completion of that term, but would depend on a satisfactory assessment of the risk of re-offending. An initial review, and subsequent reviews as required, would be carried out by a panel of the Parole Board presided over by a judge at which the prisoner would be present, with a right to be legally represented, and to be given the reasons for the Board's decision within a specified period of time.

Once the Parole Board had directed release the Home Secretary would be obliged to give effect to its decision. Those who were released would be on life licence, to a known address, under initial supervision by the Probation Service, and subject to recall at any time. Ministers would play no part in the process. In this way, although the new life sentence would be automatic, the procedures attached to it were analogous to those applicable to discretionary life sentences, rather than to the mandatory life sentence for murder.

V

The opening shots in the Parliamentary campaign against mandatory sentencing came, not from a politician, but from the most senior criminal judge in the country. The interlude between Howard's conference speech in the Autumn of 1995 and the appearance of the White Paper in the following Spring had done nothing to abate the strength of the Lord Chief Justice's objections. If anything, Taylor's opposition had intensified as he reflected on the injustices that would result from fettering by primary legislation the ability of a sentencing judge to take account of all the circumstances of the offence and of the individual offender. Any inhibitions he might have had about the propriety of using his high judicial office to make a public assault on a policy of the elected Government were dissipated by the realization that his own time was running out. An inoperable brain tumour had been diagnosed, causing him to announce that he intended to retire prematurely on health grounds. While still holding the office of Lord Chief Justice, however, he decided it was his duty to inform Parliament directly of the grave consequences which he believed would follow if the Government's sentencing proposals were to be given statutory effect.

Taylor's last speech in the House of Lords, and his most eloquent, was on 23 May 1996. In opening a debate which he initiated to call attention to the White Paper, *Protecting the Public*, he did not mince his words:

Never in the history of our criminal law have such far-reaching proposals been put forward on the strength of such flimsy and dubious evidence. The shallow and untested figures in the White Paper do not describe fairly the problems the Government seeks to address. Still less do they justify the radical solutions it proposes.[41]

Taylor emphasized that his opposition did not arise from any entrenched views on government policy; still less, despite press suggestions to the contrary, from personal animosity toward the Home Secretary. His main concern was centred on minimum sentences 'which must involve a denial of justice'.[42] What he described as the palliative of 'genuinely exceptional circumstances', which had not featured in the original proposals, clearly had been added to mitigate the manifest injustice of the policy. He continued:

Simply to provide an 'escape clause' for the most extreme cases of injustice will not do. It may give some reassurance and comfort to those concerned by the enormity of the provisions as propounded, but the result would be the worst of both worlds. Judges would not be bound to impose minimum sentences willy-nilly. They would be left with some discretion in exceptional cases. But what is an exceptional case? If the escape clause is construed restrictively it will have little effect. That is what happened when suspended sentences were confined to exceptional cases. They became in effect a dead letter. If, on the other hand, the escape clause is construed more broadly, it will be said that the judiciary is driving a coach and horses through the provisions of the Act and thwarting Parliament. More fundamentally, the proposal subverts the function of the court, which is to sentence according to the justice of each individual case, not to see whether it can be accommodated within a narrow exception and otherwise to take a sentence off the shelf.[43]

Further criticisms were deployed on the Conservative benches by Lord Carr of Hadley, a former Home Secretary,[44] and by three former

[41] *Parl. Debates*, HL, 572, col. 1025, 23 May 1996.

[42] Ibid., col. 1026.

[43] Ibid.

[44] Robert Carr was Parliamentary Secretary, Ministry of Labour and National Service, 1955–8; Secretary for Technical Co-Operation, 1963–4; Secretary of State for Employment, 1970–2; Lord President of the Council and Leader of the House of Commons, April–November 1972; Home Secretary, 1972–4. He became a life peer in 1975.

Ministers of State at the Home Office: Lords Carlisle of Bucklow, Elton, and myself. Three experienced QCs: Williams of Mostyn and Baroness Mallalieu for Labour, and Lester of Herne Hill for the Liberal Democrats, added their voices in unqualified support of Taylor's strictures, as did the Earl of Longford[45] and Lord Donaldson of Lymington, a former Master of the Rolls.[46] More moderate in tone, but still critical of mandatory sentencing, were the other judicial speakers: Nolan,[47] Cooke of Thorndon,[48] and Lowry, the latter being a former Lord Chief Justice of Northern Ireland.[49] To the Bishop of Birmingham[50] the Government's proposals seemed fatally flawed by their narrowness of focus and preoccupation. Although the White Paper contained a chapter on the prevention of crime, he commented that its approach was focused on response rather than prevention; on response primarily in terms of punishment; on punishment primarily in terms of imprisonment; and on imprisonment primarily as containment. Such a scheme of things was unbalanced.[51]

A fresh element was injected into the debate by Lord Belstead, who spoke with authority both as the current chairman of the Parole Board and as a former Conservative minister and Leader of the House.[52] He confined his comments to the proposals which would

[45] Chancellor of the Duchy of Lancaster, 1947–8; Minister of Civil Aviation, 1948–51; First Lord of the Admiralty, 1951; Lord Privy Seal, 1964–5 and 1966–8; Secretary of State for the Colonies, 1965–6; Leader of the House of Lords, 1964–8. Joint Founder: New Bridge for ex-prisoners, 1956, and New Horizon Youth Centre, 1964. Author and penal reformer.

[46] Judge of the High Court of Justice, Queen's Bench Division, 1966–79; President, National Industrial Relations Court, 1971–4; Lord Justice of Appeal, 1979–82; Master of the Rolls, 1982–92.

[47] Judge of the High Court of Justice, Queen's Bench Division, 1982–91; Presiding Judge, Western Circuit, 1985–8; Lord Justice of Appeal, 1991–3; Lord of Appeal in Ordinary, 1994–8. Chairman, Committee on Standards in Public Life, 1994–7.

[48] President, Court of Appeal of New Zealand, 1986–96 (Judge 1976–86); Life Peer, 1995.

[49] Judge of the High Court of Justice (Northern Ireland), 1964–71; Lord Chief Justice of Northern Ireland, 1971–88; Lord of Appeal in Ordinary, 1988–94.

[50] Rt Rev Mark Santer: Principal, Wescott House, Cambridge, 1973–81; Area Bishop of Kensington, 1981–7; Bishop of Birmingham, 1987–.

[51] *Parl. Debates*, HL, 572, *op. cit.*, col. 1053.

[52] Parliamentary Under-Secretary of State, Department of Education and Science, 1970–3; for Northern Ireland, 1973–4; and at the Home Office, 1979–82. Minister of State: Foreign and Commonwealth Office, 1982–3; Ministry of Agriculture, Fisheries, and Food, 1983–7; Department of Employment, 1987–8. Deputy Leader of the House of Lords, 1983–7; Leader of the House and Lord Privy Seal, 1988–90. Paymaster-General and Minister, Northern Ireland Office, 1990–2. Chairman of the Parole Board, 1992–7. Lord Lieutenant of Suffolk, 1994–.

end parole for eligible prisoners serving determinate sentences, saying that in aiming to achieve what was described as honesty in sentencing the Home Secretary was 'in grave danger of jeopardising the main aim of the White Paper', which was summarized in its title, *Protecting the Public*.[53] Belstead reminded the House that selective parole was a system which provided an incentive for a prisoner to reduce the risk of re-offending. It also provided a mechanism for managing risk by supervision in the community after release. Although risk assessment remained a very uncertain science, research studies showed that parole could break a pattern of offending, and that parolees re-offended much less frequently than prisoners who were not paroled.

All that was now due to change. Reports assessing risk were to be discarded in favour of a mechanical system of adding up days earned by good behaviour of inmates when in prison. Good behaviour while in custody, however, was no predictor of good behaviour on release. The White Paper proposed that all long-term and short-term prisoners should be swept up into one huge remission scheme, which would mean that about 25,000 prisoners each year would be eligible for earned early release, depending on their co-operative behaviour while in prison. Special licence conditions, for example non-contact with the victim or victim's family, or a condition not to engage in work or other activities which might bring an offender into contact with likely victims, were important in terms of protecting the public. If prison governors, with all their existing responsibilities, were expected to decide on special licence conditions in the future, they could find themselves writing some 25,000 licences each year, and considering the reports on which conditions should be based. Moreover, how would recalls to custody for breach of licence conditions be handled in the future? Belstead was deeply concerned that the proposals for honesty in sentencing had not been thought through, and could result in affording less, rather than more, protection for the general public.[54]

With only a sprinkling of support from backbench speakers on the government side of the House in the later stages of a long debate, the Lord Chancellor had an unenviable task in replying to what had been said. After paying a sincere and generous tribute to Taylor, and assuring all those who had spoken that their remarks

[53] *Parl. Debates*, HL, 572, *op. cit.*, col. 1046.

[54] Ibid., col. 1048.

would be carefully studied and noted, Mackay had no alternative but to fall back on a rehearsal of the reasons already advanced for the policies described in the White Paper. As might be expected from such an accomplished advocate, it was skilfully and courteously done, but he was unable to provide any novel or convincing arguments that were likely to satisfy the Government's critics.

VI

One of the statistics in the White Paper which had attracted Taylor's ire was a table showing the number of convictions in the Crown Court and Magistrates' courts, and average sentence lengths, for burglary of a dwelling.[55] The figures had been calculated on the basis of a sample of 2,164 offenders of all ages convicted in 1993 and 1994. Taylor objected that part of the sample related to the period before 23 August 1993, when sentencers were prevented by the Criminal Justice Act 1991 from taking account of previous convictions or of any other offences save the most recent. To criticize the judges for not imposing custodial sentences on convicted burglars with numerous convictions at a time when judges were prevented by statute from taking previous convictions into account was, in Taylor's words, 'wholly unjustifiable'.[56] Moreover, even on the basis of such a 'partial and tainted sample' the table did not bear out the inference that the courts were soft on burglars and that mandatory sentences were required as a remedy. In the Crown Court 59 per cent of burglars had received a custodial sentence for their first offence; 71 per cent for their second offence; and 75 per cent for their third or subsequent conviction.

This example illustrated the difficulties which the civil servants had to face. The policy had been decided upon before any supporting evidence had been produced. It had been proclaimed on a highly visible public platform, and widely reported: there was no going back. In preparing a White Paper it was the task of the draftsmen to find whatever persuasive arguments they could. There had been no opportunity to evaluate responses to a discussion paper, for there had been none, nor any prior consultation with the main interested parties. For instance, Lord Carlisle of Bucklow, a former

[55] *Protecting the Public*, *op. cit.*, Fig. 11, p. 52.
[56] *Parl. Debates*, HL, 572, *op. cit.*, col. 1027.

senior ministerial colleague[57] who was chairman of the committee which had carried out an exhaustive review of the parole system in 1987–8, and on whose report the current system of early release was based,[58] was invited to meet the Home Secretary for a discussion only after the publication of the White Paper. His reply to the invitation left no room for doubt as to the strength of his objections:

> I am sorry to have to say that I consider that the sentencing proposals are unjustified, illogical and ill thought through. I believe that in practice they will lead to injustice in individual cases and a far greater increase in the prison population than you anticipate.
>
> I am opposed to mandatory minimum sentencing for all the reasons that are well known to you. I would add that so far as the chapter on drug dealers is concerned, I believe it is totally unnecessary. All people who traffic in any substantial way in drugs already receive severe sentences. I believe that the only people likely to be affected by these proposals are the rather pathetic drug addicts who supply small quantities of drugs to their 'friends' merely so as to try to feed their own addiction.
>
> I am equally opposed to the extension of automatic life sentences. I see nothing in the White Paper which in any way justifies these proposals . . .
>
> I note it is your clearly stated intention that Judges should take these changes into account and that therefore you do not expect an increase in the period of time offenders serve in prison. That means, as you will appreciate, that all sentences, including those for burglars and violent offenders (other than those covered by the mandatory provision) will have to be reduced by at least one third.
>
> Is that really what is intended and do you believe it is achievable? In the Parole Review, we did not believe that it was and I must say that I remain of that view.[59]

The only answer to such forceful criticisms was that the proposals set out in the White Paper were rooted in political conviction, not in practical experience or impartial evidence.

Embarrassing as it was for Michael Howard to find his plans so roundly castigated in the House of Lords, by the higher judiciary, and by some of his former colleagues, he knew that power lay elsewhere.

57 Mark Carlisle, a QC and Recorder of the Crown Court, was Parliamentary Under-Secretary of State, 1970–2; Minister of State at the Home Office, 1972–4; and Secretary of State for Education and Science, 1979–81. Chairman, Criminal Injuries Compensation Board, 1989–2000. Created a life peer in 1987.

58 Review Committee on the Parole System in England and Wales, *Report* (Cm. 532), HMSO, 1988.

59 Letter of 22 April 1996 from Lord Carlisle of Bucklow to the Home Secretary. Extracts quoted with permission.

Provided he could count on the government whips securing a majority in the House of Commons for his Bill, he would get his way. But it would not be plain sailing. He was aware that some recently retired ministers, now on the back benches, were harbouring doubts. One of the most outspoken was Sir Peter Lloyd, who had been a junior minister at the Home Office with responsibility for the prisons from 1989 to 1994, and was soon to become chairman of the influential Parliamentary All-Party Penal Affairs Group. There were also rumours that the support of two former Home Secretaries, Douglas Hurd and Kenneth Baker, could not be guaranteed on the sentencing issue. The Government no longer had a majority over all other parties combined, and the probability was that the Liberal Democrats and Welsh Nationalists would oppose the Bill outright. The Ulster Unionists were unpredictable and might not be present when votes were needed. That left the Labour Party in a strong position.

The Parliamentary arithmetic meant that although the Labour Opposition with Liberal Democrat help might not be able to defeat the Bill in the Commons, they could well be successful in obstructing its passage for long enough to ensure it had not completed all its stages by the time a general election was called. But what would be the electoral implications of resisting greater severity in the sentencing of repeat offenders? Even before Tony Blair became Leader of the Opposition, Labour had been painstakingly positioning itself so that it could mount a credible challenge to the Conservatives as the party of law and order. Research and fieldwork alike had established that many of the people most at risk of victimization were living in such traditional Labour strongholds as inner-city housing estates. Policies had been developed to counter neighbourhood disorder and anti-social behaviour, as well as the high volume of criminal offending by young people.

The origins of Labour's platform on crime and the causes of crime, as set out in its Manifesto for the 1997 general election, belong to a later chapter. In the last months before that long-awaited moment, it was inconceivable that the Labour Party leadership would allow a tactical Parliamentary decision to jeopardize its overall objective of regaining power after so long. No one could have been surprised when, following a fractious debate on the floor of the House of Commons on 4 November 1996, the Crime (Sentences) Bill was given a Second Reading by a majority of 149 to 23 votes. Minutes before, a Liberal Democrat reasoned amendment declining to give the Bill a

Second Reading had been defeated by 165 votes to 25.[60] In both votes the Opposition Front Bench and the overwhelming majority of Labour MPs abstained.

For close observers the main interest lay not so much in the ritual party political exchanges between Howard and Straw in their opening speeches, but in the signals of dissent on the Government's own benches. Not only Hurd, Baker, and Lloyd expressed reservations, but also a quintessential Tory loyalist, Peter Brooke, who had been Party Chairman as well as Secretary of State for Northern Ireland, and had held a string of other ministerial appointments.[61] He was the son of a past Conservative Home Secretary[62] and the brother of a senior judge.[63] His City of London and Westminster constituency represented the Central Criminal Court, the Royal Courts of Justice in the Strand, two of the Inns of Court, and the Law Society's offices. As a result, he was well aware that the Government and the judiciary were in conflict, and that made him uneasy. Consequently he approached the legislation with a 'whiff of agnosticism' and a 'tinge of scepticism'.[64] Unusually for such a senior Parliamentarian, Brooke volunteered to serve on the Standing Committee to consider the Bill in the hope that it might help to overcome his reservations. Baker was more explicit in his criticism, stating unequivocally that without the exceptional circumstances provision the first three clauses of the Bill would be unacceptable.[65]

The two weakest points in the Government's plans, the over-reliance on deterrence and the expectation that the judges would reduce their sentences in the new regime to take account of the abolition of parole, were fully exploited in Lloyd's speech. He did not agree that longer sentences were especially effective deterrents, nor that criminals were calculators who examined the tariff before acting. Common sense and bitter experience contradicted that 'convenient

[60] *Parl. Debates*, HC, 284, cols. 1004–07, 4 Nov. 1996.

[61] Parliamentary Under-Secretary of State, Department of Education and Science, 1983–5, Minister of State, 1985–7. Paymaster-General, HM Treasury, 1987–9; Chairman of the Conservative Party, 1987–9; Secretary of State for Northern Ireland, 1989–92; and for National Heritage, 1992–4.

[62] Henry Brooke, later Lord Brooke of Cumnor, Financial Secretary to the Treasury, 1954–7; Minister of Housing and Local Government and Minister for Welsh Affairs, 1957–61; Chief Secretary to the Treasury and Paymaster-General, 1961–2; Home Secretary, 1962–4.

[63] Sir Henry Brooke, Judge of the High Court of Justice, Queen's Bench Division, 1988–96; Lord Justice of Appeal, 1996–. Chairman, Law Commission, 1993–5.

[64] *Parl. Debates*, HC, 284, *op. cit.*, col. 951.

[65] Ibid., col. 941.

assumption'. Criminals rarely weighed the consequences of anything, especially persistent offenders, who had been through it all before, some many times, and against whom the measures in the Bill were particularly directed.[66] He echoed Hurd in arguing that changes in offending behaviour depended not only on the length of a sentence but on what happens to inmates while they are in prison and, equally important, how well they are supervised on release. As to the prospects for reductions in sentences, Lloyd doubted if the judges would oblige the Home Secretary. He continued:

> They know that, under the new arrangements, most offenders will not be considered at risk or be supervised as well as they are at present. They will feel the need to restore appropriate differentials between sentences. They will find it difficult to cut every three-year sentence to 18 months or so, in the face of public expectation that the new law means longer inside and taunts from the media and others that they have gone even softer. I have a great respect for judges, but I doubt whether they will remember exactly what sentence they would have imposed before the law was changed.[67]

VII

With no more than minor amendments made in the Standing Committee, the Crime (Sentences) Bill returned to the Commons chamber in the New Year for Report Stage and Third Reading. On 13 January 1997 three successive Labour amendments were defeated on divisions. They aimed to provide extended periods of supervision for violent offenders sentenced to four years' or more imprisonment; to require the Secretary of State to establish court psychiatric assessment schemes; and to provide for the Court of Appeal to issue sentencing guidelines covering all of the main criminal offences.[68] In each division the Government maintained comfortable majorities varying between forty and sixty votes. More controversial was the issue of exceptions from mandatory sentencing, which was the main subject of debate two days later. This time

[66] *Parl. Debates*, HC, 284, *op. cit.*, col. 955.

[67] Ibid., col. 956.

[68] Sentencing guidelines already existed for many of the more serious criminal offences. They included most sexual offences (rape, unlawful sexual intercourse, incest, indecent assault, and buggery); drugs offences involving class A and class B drugs; robbery, theft, and benefit fraud; public order offences (riot, violent disorder, and affray); and explosives offences. *Parl. Debates*, HC, 299, col. 750 WA, 27 Oct. 1997.

the sponsors of an amendment to substitute the phrase 'in the interests of justice' for 'exceptional circumstances' as the grounds for not imposing a mandatory sentence did not include the Labour Opposition.

Instead, a cross-party alliance had been forged by Elfyn Llwyd (Plaid Cymru), Alex Carlile (Liberal Democrat), and Sir Peter Lloyd (Conservative). Llwyd, the mover of the amendment, had sat on the Standing Committee in place of a Liberal Democrat member. The debate was well informed, on the whole dispassionate, with impressive although contrasting speeches by Lloyd and another Conservative, Sir Ivan Lawrence, Chairman of the Home Affairs Select Committee. Lloyd earned warm tributes from the Deputy Leader of the Liberal Democrats, Alan Beith, who said he had rarely heard a complex case deployed so brilliantly,[69] and also from the Minister of State at the Home Office, David Maclean,[70] when he replied to the debate.

Lawrence put the matter succinctly, remarking that the heart and soul of the Bill was minimum sentences, and that the issue was whether judges should have a wide or a narrow gate to pass through if they wanted to avoid the consequences of minimum sentences.[71] Taylor had already made abundantly plain the opposition of the higher judiciary to minimum sentences, arguing that they were inconsistent with a court doing justice according to the circumstances of each case. It was understandable that judges should be distressed at the thought that their discretion should be curbed, and want as wide a gate as possible. Had he been a judge he might have thought the same. But, claimed Lawrence, who was a QC and Recorder as well as being a long-serving Member of Parliament, lawyers and politicians thought in different ways. His experience in politics told him that the Government was right to introduce minimum sentences, and that in doing so they were reflecting the wishes of the people. The people were entitled to have their wishes respected, and they believed that the sentences passed on some persistent professional offenders, whether drug traffickers, burglars, or violent criminals, had been inadequate to protect them.[72]

[69] *Parl. Debates*, HC, 288, col. 381, 15 Jan. 1997.

[70] Parliamentary Secretary, Ministry of Agriculture, Fisheries, and Food, 1989–92; Minister of State: Department of the Environment, 1992–3; Home Office, 1993–7.

[71] *Parl. Debates*, HC, 288, *op. cit.*, col. 384.

[72] Ibid., col. 385.

Set against this frankly stated view, which was to carry the day with a large majority on the Conservative benches, and lay behind the Labour tactic of keeping as many as possible of their own supporters on the sidelines, was the concept of justice. If the purpose of a criminal sentence was to punish a convicted offender in proportion to the gravity of the harm done, and if this purpose was to have primacy over all other considerations, then the case for retaining flexibility in sentencing powers was unanswerable. But if the interests of the individual were to be regarded as secondary to the welfare of a wider community, the answer might be different.

At the end of the debate the 'interests of justice' amendment was defeated by an overwhelming majority of 35 votes for and 266 against.[73] All but a handful of Conservatives who joined Lloyd in the Aye Lobby voted against, while the Labour Party, also with a small number of exceptions, abstained once again. The Liberal Democrats then voted against giving the Bill a Third Reading, this time without allies except for one Welsh Nationalist and a single Labour renegade.[74] Challenged by Howard to explain the approach of the Opposition to the Bill overall, Straw replied evasively that no decisions would be made until the Bill was in its final form. At present it was a moving, shifting target. It had been changed before and might well be changed again in the Lords. Labour was not going to block the Third Reading.[75]

Earlier in the afternoon, during the debate on exceptional circumstances, Lloyd had ruminated that it would be doubly satisfactory if the interests of justice amendments were made in the Lords. The Labour Party would then see the undemocratic second chamber that it wanted to replace doing the Opposition's proper job for them, while the Government, who wanted to preserve the present Lords as a revising chamber, would be obliged to accept its revisions. He added mischievously:

> Perhaps that is our subtle Home Secretary's grand design: to demonstrate the usefulness of the other place as it is presently constituted, while giving a powerful incentive to the judiciary to turn its collective mind more thoroughly to matters of sentencing, . . . so enabling him to accept gracefully a suitable amendment.[76]

[73] *Parl. Debates*, HC, 288, *op. cit.*, cols. 399–401.

[74] Ibid., cols. 427–8. Dennis Skinner, Labour MP for Bolsover since 1970. The number voting for the Third Reading was 229, with 21 against.

[75] Ibid., col. 426.

[76] Ibid., col. 381.

2

The Inheritance: Mandatory Sentences, 1997–9

I

The peculiarity of British constitutional arrangements, pending any further instalments of Lords reform, permits some of the most senior members of the judiciary to play an active part in the legislative process. The Lords of Appeal in Ordinary are at the pinnacle of the judicial system. For more than a century they have constituted the final court of appeal on points of law of general public importance.[1] Up to ten Lords of Appeal in Ordinary are usually appointed from the ranks of the Lords Justices of Appeal who sit in the Court of Appeal or, very occasionally, direct from the High Court bench. In addition, two senior Scottish judges, and more recently one from Northern Ireland, may be appointed, bringing the total up to a statutory maximum of twelve.[2] Besides the Lord Chancellor, former Lords of Appeal in Ordinary, former Lord Chancellors, and the holders of certain other high judicial offices who are peers are also entitled to sit as Law Lords. The Judicial Pensions and Retirements Act 1993, which came into force in 1995, lowered the age of retirement of new Lords of Appeal in Ordinary from seventy-five to seventy. It also provided that no one except the Lord Chancellor may sit judicially to hear appeals in the House of Lords beyond the age of seventy-five.[3]

[1] The Appellate Jurisdiction Act 1876 provided for the appointment of up to four qualified persons as Lords of Appeal in Ordinary to sit in the House of Lords and assist the Lord Chancellor in hearing appeals. During their lifetime Lords of Appeal would have the rank of Baron, but the title would not descend to their heirs. They were thus the first life peers.

[2] The authorized maximum is set by the Administration of Justice Act 1968, Section 1, as amended by the Maximum Number of Judges Order 1994 (S. I. 3217).

[3] Information Sheet No. 8, 'The Judicial Work of the House of Lords', Journal and Information Office, House of Lords, Oct. 1996. This document contains a useful summary of the historical origins of the appellate jurisdiction of the House of Lords at pp. 10–12.

The holders of the offices of Lord Chief Justice of England, who presides over the criminal division of the Court of Appeal, and the Master of the Rolls, the head of the civil division, are often created life peers if they are not already members of the House of Lords. In the changes that followed Taylor's resignation, Sir Thomas Bingham, then Master of the Rolls, was appointed as Lord Chief Justice and to a life peerage, taking the title of Lord Bingham of Cornhill.[4] Lord Woolf, a Lord of Appeal in Ordinary, succeeded him as Master of the Rolls.[5] Their appointments were announced from 10 Downing Street on 24 May 1996. Both men were regarded as modernisers who had supported many of Lord Mackay's initiatives to reform the legal system, and it was he who had recommended their names to the Prime Minister. The choice of Bingham was unusual since he had limited previous experience in the criminal courts, either at the Bar or on the Bench. His particular expertise lay in the fields of civil and commercial law, and he had taken an active part in the development of judicial review of ministerial actions by the courts.

The rapid growth of judicial review, seen by some on the political Right as restricting the proper freedom of action exercised by a Government answerable to an elected Parliament, had been remarked on in the course of the Commons' debates on the Crime (Sentencing) Bill. At Westminster and beyond there was some apprehension that the promotion of two of the most liberal-minded senior judges could lead to attempts to extend the range of judicial scrutiny of executive action still further. One member of the Bar Council, a QC who did not want to be named for political reasons, was quoted as saying:

> Labour has never appointed a Lord Chief Justice—they have all been appointed by Conservative administrations. The irony is that Bingham and Woolf are absolutely the people Labour would have appointed had they been in power.[6]

[4] Judge of the High Court of Justice, Queen's Bench Division, and Judge of the Commercial Court, 1980–6; Lord Justice of Appeal, 1986–92; Master of the Rolls, 1992–6. Leader, investigation into the supply of petroleum and petroleum products to Rhodesia, 1977–8; conducted inquiry into the supervision of BCCI, 1991–2.

[5] First Treasury Junior Counsel (Common Law), 1974–9. Judge of the High Court of Justice, Queen's Bench Division, 1979–86; Presiding Judge, South Eastern Circuit, 1981–4; Lord Justice of Appeal, 1986–92; Lord of Appeal in Ordinary, 1992–6. Conducted inquiries into prison disturbances, 1990–1, and access to justice, 1994–6. Chairman, Lord Chancellor's Advisory Committee on Legal Education, 1986–91.

[6] *The Financial Times*, 25 May 1996. The prescience of this comment, as well as the strictly non-political character of judicial appointments, was borne out four years later

Although sitting on the cross-benches, and abstaining from any party-political affiliation, the Law Lords contribute to debates on a wide range of public policy issues. These include matters relating to the administration of justice, on which they speak with special authority. However, they speak not only in general debates, such as the motion to take note of the Government's sentencing proposals initiated by Lord Taylor when he was still Chief Justice, but also on legislation. On occasion the Law Lords (the description conventionally used to describe the various categories of judicial peers) can and do seek to influence legislation by putting down amendments, speaking, and voting in the same way as any other peer in receipt of a Writ of Summons. Generally they are cautious about how far it is proper to go, being aware that the doctrine of separation of powers is not a complete nullity, and that the House may have to rule on the lawfulness of some aspect of the legislation in the future. The opposition to the legislative changes made in the Criminal Injuries Compensation Scheme in 1995, and the subsequent challenge in the courts which later reached the House of Lords in its appellate capacity, was a salutary example of the difficulties of walking the tightrope.[7]

In 1999 the judicial functions of the House of Lords were reviewed by the Royal Commission on the Reform of the House of Lords. The pragmatic conclusion reached was that as long as certain basic conventions continued to be observed there was 'insufficient reason to change the present arrangements'. Indeed, the Commission saw some advantage in having senior judges as members of the legislature where they could be 'made aware of the social developments and political balances which underlie most legislation'.[8] Soon after his appointment as Senior Law Lord in the following year, Bingham implemented a recommendation of the Royal Commission that the Lords of Appeal should:

> set out in writing and publish a statement of the principles which they intend to observe when participating in debates and votes in the second chamber and when considering their eligibility to sit on related cases.[9]

when Lord Bingham was appointed as Senior Lord of Appeal in Ordinary and Lord Woolf as Lord Chief Justice by a Labour Administration. See Chapter 8 below.

[7] See *Responses to Crime*, Vol. 3, pp. 451–76. The appeal was *R.* v. *Secretary of State for the Home Department, ex parte Fire Brigades Union and Others* [1995] 2 AC 513.

[8] Royal Commission on the Reform of the House of Lords, *A House for the Future*, Cm. 4534, The Stationery Office, Jan. 2000, p. 6, para. 26.

[9] Ibid., Recommendation 59, p. 95.

In response, Bingham made a formal statement on the floor of the House a few months later.[10] Being mindful of their judicial role, he said, the Lords of Appeal in Ordinary considered themselves bound by two general principles. The first was that it would not be appropriate to engage in matters in which there was a strong element of party-political controversy. Secondly, Lords of Appeal in Ordinary should bear in mind that they might render themselves ineligible to sit judicially if they were to express an opinion on a matter which might later be relevant to an appeal to the House. They would continue to be guided by these broad principles. It was impossible to frame rules to cover every eventuality. In the end it must be for the judgement of each individual Lord of Appeal to decide how to conduct himself in any particular situation. Clearly stated as these principles were, they applied only to current Lords of Appeal in Ordinary and not to retired ones, or to other retired senior judges who had been made peers. This sub-category included such formidable personalities as the retired Lord Chief Justice, Lord Lane,[11] and Master of the Rolls, Lord Donaldson of Lymington.[12] Although no longer sitting judicially, they too spoke from the cross-benches in the Lords and were generally thought of as coming within the designation of Law Lords.

Three years before the adoption of these self-imposed inhibitions both Bingham and Woolf had taken part in the debate at Second Reading of the Crime (Sentences) Bill in the House of Lords on 27 January 1997. They were supported by one current and three retired Law Lords: Hope of Craighead,[13] Ackner, Oliver of Aylmerton, and Donaldson of Lymington. Although, as Master of the Rolls, Woolf was at the time primarily occupied with civil, rather than criminal law, he had conducted a high-profile inquiry into prison disturbances at the start of the 1990s. This had resulted in the publication of a seminal

[10] *Parl. Debates*, HL, 614 (5th ser.), cols. 419–20, 22 June 2000.

[11] Lord Lane had been a Lord of Appeal in Ordinary before his appointment as Lord Chief Justice of England in 1980. Lord Mackay of Clashfern had also served as a Lord of Appeal in Ordinary 1985–7 before becoming Lord Chancellor in 1987.

[12] Judge of the High Court, Queen's Bench Division, 1966–79; President, National Industrial Relations Court, 1971–4; Lord Justice of Appeal, 1979–82; Master of the Rolls, 1982–92.

[13] Until the end of September 1996 Lord Hope had been Lord Justice-General of Scotland, the Scottish equivalent of the Lord Chief Justice of England. Previously he had been Dean of the Faculty of Advocates, 1986–9.

report,[14] and encouraged him to maintain a continuing interest in the workings of the penal system.

Any expectation that Bingham would be more conciliatory than Taylor toward the Home Secretary's sentencing plans was quickly dispelled. Although of a less extrovert personality, he did not hesitate to confront the Government with a measured analysis of the adverse consequences of their sentencing proposals. While agreeing with the Minister of State, Baroness Blatch, who had opened the debate, that current levels of crime were a source of acute and proper public concern, there were three ingredients of the Bill which caused him, and those of his senior colleagues outside the House whom he had consulted, profound anxiety. They were: the proposal to shorten remission and abolish parole for prisoners serving determinate sentences; the proposal to impose automatic life sentences in certain specific cases; and the proposal to impose mandatory minimum sentences on repeat burglars and drug dealers.[15] These provisions, Bingham forecast, were likely to have a profound effect on the lives of those to whom they apply, and on the administration of justice. That in itself was not an argument against them, but it was necessary to test each of the proposals by asking four questions:

> Will it be just? Will it serve to reduce levels of crime or increase the protection of society? Will it be cost effective? Will it work in practice?[16]

In his judgment, the measures conspicuously failed to pass all four of the tests. Then followed a devastating analysis of the abolition of parole and the mandatory provisions of Clauses 1–3. The vice of the latter proposals, he declared, lay in their 'indiscriminate, scattergun nature'.[17]

Bingham's speech, all the more persuasive because of the quiet and reasoned manner of its delivery, was followed immediately by a trenchant retort from one of the most populist of Margaret Thatcher's cabinet ministers, and one of its most formidable debaters. Lord Tebbit[18] opened by saying that it must be the shortest straw

[14] *Prison Disturbances April 1990*, Report of an Inquiry by Lord Justice Woolf (Parts I and II), Cm. 1456, HMSO, London, 1991.

[15] *Parl. Debates*, HL, 577, col. 984, 27 Jan. 1997.

[16] Ibid.

[17] Ibid., col. 988.

[18] Norman Tebbit was Parliamentary Under-Secretary of State, Department of Trade, 1979–81; Minister of State, Department of Industry, 1981; Secretary of State for Employment, 1981–3, and for Trade and Industry, 1983–5; Chancellor of the Duchy of Lancaster and Chairman of the Conservative Party, 1985–7. Seriously

anyone could draw in a Parliamentary lifetime to rise to speak in support of a Bill so comprehensively attacked by no less a figure than the Lord Chief Justice. His speech had been not only that of a distinguished judge, but also of a great advocate. The question Tebbit had to ask himself, however, was why it should be, if Bingham was right in all he had said, that not only the general public outside Parliament believed that something akin to the Bill was needed, but that such a large majority in the House of Commons should have reached the same conclusion.[19] Tebbit said that while he understood the resentment of some judges at receiving Parliamentary guidance, it was a two-way street:

> . . . there are a number of us in politics who have at times resented the extension of the doctrine of judicial review in the way that has happened in recent years. At any rate, as a result of those happenings, especially that of judges speaking so much in public outside this House, I find myself, having almost all of my life regarded it as entirely improper for politicians to criticise the judicial conduct of judges, now doing so; and not too infrequently, I fear, in my role as a tabloid journalist. In my life, not just as a journalist or as a politician, but as a private citizen, I find the public are more confused and concerned about sentencing policy than any other aspect of criminal law. I do not believe it is enough for the noble and learned Lord the Lord Chief Justice to imply that it is the business of other people to explain to the public at large what judges are doing as regards the way in which they sentence; I believe that is not least the responsibility of the judiciary when they speak on these matters, and preferably in this House rather than outside.
>
> I believe the Bill addresses the concerns of ordinary men and women in the street. In that respect it will help to stem what I fear is a growing loss of respect for the Bench in our country today.[20]

II

Although the Crime (Sentences) Bill received an unopposed Second Reading in the Lords, the seven-and-a-half-hour long debate clearly established which of the provisions would be contested most strongly in the later stages. Speaking from the Opposition Front Bench, Lord

injured by a bomb attack on the Grand Hotel, Brighton, during the Conservative Party Conference in 1984. Life peer, 1992.

[19] *Parl. Debates*, HL, 577, *op. cit.*, col. 990.

[20] Ibid., col. 992.

McIntosh of Haringey[21] reminded peers this was the thirty-fourth criminal justice bill since the Conservative Government had come to power in 1979. That was equal to the entire number of criminal justice bills introduced by any Government between the years 1900 and 1979. The House should beware of thinking that in some strange way the quantity of legislation was equivalent to its quality. The truth was that the amount of legislation was evidence, not of the success of the Government's law and order policies, but of their failure. Since 1979 recorded crime had doubled.[22] McIntosh pointed out that in the Commons the Labour Party had supported the mandatory life sentence for a second violent crime. Its approach to the mandatory determinate sentences would be to revise, and not to wreck, the Government's proposals. In the search for non-wrecking amendments the Opposition would be considering the desirability of adding further explanatory wording to the phrase 'exceptional circumstances' in Clauses 2 and 3 of the Bill.[23]

The Leader of the Liberal Democrat peers, Lord Rodgers of Quarry Bank, a veteran Labour Minister in the past,[24] was not so accommodating. He was disappointed by the Labour Opposition's agnosticism or neutrality towards the central core of the Bill. He dismissed it peremptorily as:

> a bad Bill with few redeeming features, foolishly conceived, wrong in principle and deceptive in its relevance to the real fight against crime.[25]

Later in the debate, Lord Belstead, not a man given to hyperbole, repeated the solemn warning he had given in Lord Taylor's debate the previous year that the probable outcome of the abolition of parole and early release of prisoners would be to increase the risk of

[21] Andrew McIntosh was a Labour member of the Greater London Council, 1973–83; Opposition Leader on Planning and Communications, 1977–80, and Leader of the Opposition, 1980–1. Created a life peer in 1982 and an Opposition spokesman in the House of Lords, 1985–97; Deputy Leader of the Opposition, 1992–7; Deputy Government Chief Whip, 1997–.

[22] *Parl. Debates*, HL, 577, *op. cit.*, col. 975.

[23] Ibid., col. 978.

[24] William Rodgers, a Labour MP 1962–81, was one of the founders of the Social Democratic Party in 1981 and a member of its original joint leadership of four Labour ex-ministers. Previously he had been a junior minister at the Department of Economic Affairs and the Foreign Office, 1964–8; and Minister of State: Board of Trade, 1968–9, HM Treasury, 1969–70, Ministry of Defence, 1974–6; Secretary of State for Transport, 1976–9. Life peer, 1992. Leader of the Liberal Democrats in the House of Lords, 1997–, and Chairman of the Advertising Standards Authority, 1995–.

[25] *Parl. Debates*, HL, 577, *op. cit.*, col. 980.

their re-offending. In his view, the substitution of a prison-based scheme of remission for good behaviour whilst in custody would be 'a disastrous move for public safety'.[26]

In a well attended Committee of the Whole House on 13 February the Government suffered its first and, as it turned out, only defeat on the Bill. After a full debate, a New Clause moved by McIntosh was inserted at the start of the Bill, preceding the provisions for the mandatory life sentence and the minimum custodial sentences for repeat offences of drug trafficking and domestic burglary.[27] The aim was to ensure that a measure of judicial discretion should be retained, while accepting a presumption in favour of the mandatory sentences applicable to the other two categories of offender. The justification offered for different standards was that the automatic life sentence would be subject to judicial input at the start, in that the tariff would be set by the sentencing judge, and that it would be for the Parole Board, and not the Home Secretary, to decide when it was safe to release the prisoner after the expiry of the tariff.

In the form in which it reached the House of Lords, the Bill qualified the mandatory requirements of the first three clauses by stating that the court should impose the prescribed sentences unless it was of the opinion that there were exceptional circumstances which justified it in not doing so. Where the prescribed sentence was not imposed, the judge would need to state in open court what the exceptional circumstances were. The Government's view that the phrase 'exceptional circumstances' should be construed as narrowly as possible was already on record. The wording had been added at the initiative of Mackay, and formed no part of Howard's original scheme. During the consideration in the Commons, and from judicial sources, it had become evident that exceptional circumstances would not include such factors as good character, youth, an early plea of guilty, or contrition, whether taken separately or in combination.

The Lords' amendments, sponsored by Lord Carlisle of Bucklow as well as by Labour and Liberal Democrat front bench spokesmen, would allow judges, when considering whether it would be appropriate not to impose the prescribed penalties, to have regard to specific circumstances which related either to the offences or the offender. This provision applied to both the mandatory life sentence and the minimum custodial sentences. To the latter category only was added

[26] *Parl. Debates*, HL, 577, *op. cit.*, col. 1019.
[27] *Parl. Debates*, HL, 578, col. 332, 13 Feb. 1997.

a further condition: that the specific circumstances to which the court should have regard included any which would make the prescribed custodial sentence 'unjust in all the circumstances'.

If the device of two separate tests, one cumulative to the other, was complicated, and the drafting not easy to follow, the intention was clear enough. 'Exceptional circumstances' was a phrase already familiar to the sentencing courts, and the probability was that unless amended it would be interpreted narrowly, so reflecting the intention of Parliament incorporated in the legislation, as well as existing case-law. The amendment would allow a wider range of circumstances to be taken into account, including any which would make the imposition of a mandatory minimum custodial sentence unjust in all the circumstances.

The notion of justice, and the widespread sense in the Lords that unless changed the wording of the Bill would inevitably lead to cases of injustice, meant that this was a non-party-political issue well suited to a revising chamber. In the debate on the exceptional circumstances amendment the Lord Chief Justice spoke for the judiciary when he said that sentencing judges did their best. They weighed what they perceived to be all the relevant factors: the interests of the public; the legitimate interests of the victim; the protection of other potential victims; and the interests of the defendant. They were not always right. If they passed sentences which were excessively severe, the Court of Appeal existed to correct them. If the sentences were unduly lenient, the Attorney General could refer them to the Court of Appeal for review. Rules of thumb did not provide an answer because the passing of a sentence was not a mechanical task. Bingham ended with a plea that the courts be given the power to decline to pass sentences which were offensive to the professional and moral consciences of judges. Surely, he protested, that was not asking too much.[28]

In the division, two hours after McIntosh had begun his opening speech, 352 peers voted. In support of the amendment was an unprecedented trio of the current Lord Chief Justice and both of his immediate predecessors, Lord Taylor and Lord Lane.[29] They were joined by ten other Law Lords, both serving and retired. From the Conservative benches there was the ex-Lord Chancellor, Lord

[28] Ibid., cols. 341–2.

[29] Lord Chief Justice of England, 1980–92. For an account of his influence in the development of penal policy, see *Responses to Crime*, Vols. 2 and 3.

Hailsham of St Marylebone, and four other ministers in previous Conservative administrations. Against making any changes were a large majority of those who took the whip on the government side of the House, supplemented by a few cross-benchers. The outcome was uncertain until the last moment. Then the result was announced: 'Their Lordships divided: Contents, 180; Non-Contents, 172'.[30] The amendment had been carried by eight votes.

III

If the second important change made in the Lords was less dramatic, it was more extensive in its effect. Part II of the Bill put the Government's concept of 'Honesty in Sentencing' into legislative form by proposing to abolish parole for determinate sentence prisoners and to replace it by a system of early release for good behaviour. A prisoner's sentence was to be reduced by up to six days every two months if his or her behaviour met 'the prescribed minimum standard', and by not more than a further six days every two months if their behaviour exceeded that standard. This would mean that a prisoner could earn a maximum of 16 per cent remission of sentence for good behaviour. The balance of 84 per cent of the sentence that must be served in custody was remarkably close to the 85 per cent requirement of the 'Truth-in-Sentencing' incentive grants in the United States, whereby a large part of the federal funding for state prison construction and expansion was linked to the elimination of parole and acceptance of the policy that persons convicted of violent crimes should serve not less than 85 per cent of the sentence imposed by the court. While this was by no means the only manifestation of American antecedents in Howard's approach, it was one of the most visible and tenaciously defended.

In his capacity as Chairman of the Parole Board, Belstead had been in close contact with Home Office ministers ever since the publication of the White Paper. Behind the scenes discussions had taken place to convince officials at the Home Office and Prison Service that public safety would be jeopardized by the abandonment of conditional release in favour of real-time sentencing. As an alternative to the Government's proposals, Belstead tabled a New Clause which

[30] *Parl. Debates*, HL, 578, *op. cit.*, cols. 359–61.

would have retained the opportunity for a single parole review at the three-quarter point of a sentence for prisoners serving four years or more. If granted parole, the prisoner would be supervised for the remaining 25 per cent of sentence, which was exactly the time allocated for supervision under the Government's scheme, and which ministers claimed to be an advance on the current supervision periods. Under the New Clause, if a prisoner was refused parole it would still be possible to qualify for days of earned early release for good behaviour.

The New Clause concentrated attention on the desirability of preserving three crucial advantages of the existing system. The first was the assessment of the risk of re-offending before any discretionary early release was contemplated. The second was to retain a facility to impose licence conditions during a released prisoner's period of supervision in the community. The third was to preserve a system enabling immediate recall in the event of further offending, or of behaviour likely to result in the commission of further offences. During the second day in Committee on 18 February 1997 the Minister of State, Baroness Blatch, acknowledging that she had held two 'very constructive meetings' with Belstead and Carlisle, indicated that the Government was willing to reflect on the 'entirely legitimate' arguments that had been put forward, and to consider how best to reconcile the principle of honesty in sentencing contained in Part II of the Bill with the likelihood that an important element of public protection would be lost if parole were to be abolished.

At the Report stage, the Government brought forward its own amendments.[31] The compromise was that all prisoners sentenced to three years' imprisonment or more should not be eligible for earned early release, but instead should be able to apply to the Parole Board for release at the five-sixths point in their sentence if their behaviour warranted it. That was the equivalent of the maximum discount they would have been able to accumulate under the early release scheme. The Parole Board would then carry out an assessment to determine whether it was safe to release a prisoner and, if satisfied on ground of risk, would set conditions for post-release supervision. The Home Secretary would have a duty to release a prisoner if recommended by the Parole Board to do so. The period of supervision would be 25 per cent of the original sentence. Since, unlike the existing scheme, the

[31] *Parl. Debates*, HL, 579, cols. 847–8, 18 Mar. 1997.

time spent under supervision in the community was not part of the original sentence, the prisoner would not be subject to recall to custody for breach of the terms of the licence. Instead, breaching the conditions of a release supervision order would be an arrestable offence. Although Carlisle, with support from the Liberal Democrat benches, wanted to go further and tabled an amendment for Third Reading to substitute parole at the three-quarter point of the sentence, rather than five-sixths, this final attempt to limit an inevitable increase in the prison population was overtaken by events.

IV

Earlier in the day scheduled for the Report stage of the Bill, 18 March 1997, the Leader of the House, Viscount Cranborne, unexpectedly moved a business motion to suspend certain standing orders to enable all of its remaining stages to be taken on that day.[32] The reason was that a general election had been called for 1 May. Parliament would be prorogued at the end of the week, by which time all unfinished legislation would have to be either completed or abandoned. Amongst the most contentious pieces of unfinished business was the Crime (Sentences) Bill. An agreement had been reached by the Government and Opposition business managers that it should be returned to the Commons later that day to enable consideration to be given to Lords' amendments.

The decision to truncate further scrutiny on the Bill led to immediate protests by the peers who had gathered to debate a long list of 148 amendments, including the Government amendments on parole. The motion was strongly opposed by the Leader of the Liberal Democrats, Lord Rodgers of Quarry Bank,[33] but was supported by the Leader of the Opposition, Lord Richard.[34] He confirmed that the Labour Party had co-operated with the Conservative Government in trying to arrange a 'sensible ending' to the legislative programme.

[32] *Parl. Debates*, HL, 579, col. 768.

[33] Ibid., cols. 768–71.

[34] Ivor Richard QC had been a Labour Member of Parliament, 1964–74, and Parliamentary Under-Secretary (Army), Ministry of Defence, 1969–70; UK Permanent Representative to the United Nations, 1974–9; Chairman, Rhodesia Conference in Geneva, 1976; Member of the Commission of the European Communities, 1981–4. Created a life peer in 1990. Leader of the Opposition in the House of Lords, 1992–7, and Leader of the House, 1997–8.

The agreement covered not only the Crime (Sentences) Bill, but other Bills as well. Candidly, if somewhat undiplomatically, Richard added that he did not think it possible to 'unravel the package that has been agreed'.[35]

The Liberal Democrat Chief Whip, Lord Harris of Greenwich,[36] said that he had been consulted, but had made it clear that his party would not be able to agree to the curtailment. He reminded the House that a previous general election had been announced at a time when a Criminal Justice Bill was before the House in 1987. The Government and Opposition had then agreed that those parts of the Bill which were generally acceptable and had some urgency attached to them, such as the establishment of the Serious Fraud Office, should be enacted, while the more controversial matters should be re-introduced in the next Parliament. The Home Secretary of the day, Douglas Hurd, had handled the matter in a most sensitive fashion. Unhappily, said Harris, that had not happened on this occasion.[37]

Others who spoke in protest against the motion included Lord Barnett from the Labour benches, Lords Carr of Hadley, Carlisle of Bucklow, and Campbell of Alloway on the Conservative benches, and Baroness Williams of Crosby on the Liberal Democrat benches. Ackner, Bridge of Harwich, and Bingham of Cornhill added their voices from the cross-benches. Bingham expressed his dismay about the course it was proposed the House should adopt. The Bill had not been put forward as a short-term measure, a quick overnight panacea, an instant fix. It had been put forward as a measure intended to have profound and long-term effects on the lives of our fellow citizens and on the penal arrangements for those in custody. It was a measure which required mature deliberation. He continued:

> The need for such deliberation is greater because the bill's provisions do not represent the considered conclusions of a Royal Commission or a wide ranging committee of inquiry. They are not founded upon any independent research. They are not supported by most of those with responsibility for operating the system, and they have been widely condemned by most academic commentators. It is difficult to imagine measures more obviously

[35] *Parl. Debates*, HL, 579, *op. cit.*, col. 779.

[36] John Harris was personal assistant to Hugh Gaitskell when Leader of the Opposition, 1959–62, and Director of Publicity for the Labour Party, 1962–4. Life peer, 1974, and Minister of State, Home Office, 1974–9. Chairman of the Parole Board, 1979–82. Liberal Democrat Chief Whip, House of Lords, 1994–2001.

[37] *Parl. Debates*, HL, 579, *op. cit.*, col. 777. The passage of the Criminal Justice Acts of 1987 and 1988 is described in *Responses to Crime*, Vol. 2, pp. 195–201.

calling for searching and thoughtful scrutiny in this House. I have a deep fear that if we legislate in haste, we shall repent at leisure.[38]

After further interventions, the House divided on an amendment to exclude the Crime (Sentences) Bill from the business motion. One hundred and thirty-seven peers voted for the amendment and 185 against.[39] The unusual sight of the Leader and Chief Whip of both main parties in the same lobby must have encouraged many of their less questioning supporters to accompany them.

Although McIntosh had claimed that when the Bill went back to the Commons the Shadow Home Secretary and Labour MPs would vigorously support the Lords' amendment on minimum mandatory sentences, giving an assurance that every attempt to overturn it would be resisted,[40] there was a suspicion that Jack Straw anticipated it would be voted down in the Commons, and was willing to acquiesce in that outcome. In a situation of this sort a minority party comes into its own. The Liberal Democrats could call on sufficient peers to keep the Report stage going all night and into the next day. They put a whip on from 10.30 pm to ensure a strong attendance and, if necessary, to vote against the Bill on its Third Reading.

At 8.00 pm the Government threw in the towel. The Chief Whip, Lord Strathclyde, returned to the despatch box to make a further statement. By then the House had been sitting for three hours on the Bill. In that time only five of the forty-six groups of amendments had been discussed, leaving a further forty-one outstanding. It had become clear to him that a determination existed in certain quarters to prevent the Bill leaving the House before Prorogation. He had therefore discussed the situation with the Home Secretary. Howard had now renegotiated an agreement with the other parties that if the Bill was returned to the Commons in its present state, including the Opposition amendments to Part I, together with the Government's New Clause on parole in Part II and all of the remaining government amendments proposed to be made later in the evening, then the Government would not ask its supporters in the Commons to overturn the defeat it had suffered on the exceptions to mandatory sentencing.[41]

It was power politics at its most naked, but the climbdown by the Home Secretary ensured that the amended Bill was returned to the

[38] Parl. Debates, HL 579, col. 775.
[39] Ibid., cols. 783–5.
[40] Ibid., col. 773.
[41] Ibid., col. 838.

Commons, with amendments, shortly before midnight. The following evening, 19 March 1997, the Commons agreed to the Lords' amendment requiring a sentencing court to have regard to the circumstances relating to the offences or to the offender before passing either a mandatory life sentence or a minimum custodial sentence, with the further provision that a minimum custodial sentence should not be imposed if to do so would be unjust in all the circumstances. Howard complained that the Lords had driven 'a coach and horses' through the parts of the Bill dealing with burglars and drug dealers.[42] The amendments had been accepted only to get the rest of the Bill onto the statute book, and he undertook that they would be reversed as soon as possible after the forthcoming election.[43] MPs on both sides of the House knew that he was unlikely to be called upon to honour his assurance.

V

The general election held on 1 May 1997 returned 418 Labour Members of Parliament to Westminster and 165 Conservatives. The Liberal Democrat strength increased from twenty to forty-six. Jack Straw,[44] who for three years had overseen the transition in Labour policies towards crime, was appointed as Home Secretary in Tony Blair's first list of Cabinet members. Among the most immediate tasks awaiting him at the Home Office was to decide what to do about the Crime (Sentences) Act, passed into law only weeks before, but without fixed dates for the commencement of its most controversial provisions. Straw, having successfully evaded the label of 'soft on crime' while in Opposition, declined to give the Conservatives an early opportunity to return to the charge from their unaccustomed position on the Opposition benches in the House of Commons. Delayed implementation, so crucial to maintaining the credibility of Howard's policies, once again came to the rescue.

Three months later, immediately before the start of the Summer recess, the Home Secretary made a comprehensive statement in the

[42] *Parl. Debates*, HC, 292, col. 982, 19 Mar. 1997.

[43] Ibid., col. 983.

[44] President, National Union of Students, 1969–71; Deputy Leader, Inner London Education Authority, 1973–4; MP for Blackburn, 1979–; Principal Opposition Spokesman on Education, 1987–92; on the Environment (local government), 1992–4; and Home Affairs, 1994–7; Home Secretary, 1997–.

Commons about the new Government's plans for improving the process of criminal justice. After recapitulating the various manifesto commitments which would be brought before Parliament later in the year, he turned to the more sensitive matter of providing an effective sentencing system to ensure greater consistency and stricter punishment for serious repeat offences.[45] The automatic life sentence for repeat serious sexual and violent offenders would be implemented before the year end. The Government's planned legislation on crime and disorder would provide for extended supervision of other sexual and violent offenders after their release from prison. Straw claimed that the provisions of the Crime (Sentences) Act which prescribed minimum determinate sentences for persistent burglars and drug dealers had been significantly improved by Labour amendments, leaving the judges with sufficient discretion to avoid injustice. In the light of that he intended to implement the mandatory seven-year sentence for third-time drug traffickers later in the year.[46] The provision which would have far greater impact on the prison population, the three-year minimum sentence for third-time domestic burglars, would be held over.[47] Consideration would be given to implementing it in the light of resources and Prison Service capacity.

The Home Secretary went on to say that the aims behind the 'honesty in sentencing' objective would be met by requiring the court to explain what the sentence would mean in practice. Such guidance should include the time to be spent in prison, the period of supervision after release, and the period during which the offender might be recalled to prison. These requirements were superior to the complex provisions on early release in the Act, which would not be implemented.[48] In this way parole was saved. The judges were not resistant to the merits of spelling out the practical implications of a custodial sentence at the time of passing it, but preferred that the Government's commitment should be met by way of practice direction rather than legislative provision. The wording of the Direction subsequently issued by the Lord Chief Justice is printed as an Appendix to this Chapter.

[45] *Parl. Debates*, HC, 299, col. 342, 30 July 1997.

[46] Section 2 (mandatory life sentence on conviction for the second time of a serious sexual or violent offence) and Section 3 (minimum sentence of seven years for a third class A drug trafficking conviction) were both brought into effect on 1 Oct. 1997.

[47] Section 4 of the Crime (Sentences) Act 1997, providing a minimum sentence of three years' imprisonment for those convicted for the third time of an offence of domestic burglary, was not brought into effect until 1 Dec. 1999.

[48] *Parl. Debates*, HC, 299, *op. cit.*, col. 342.

In summary, two new mandatory sentences of imprisonment were brought into effect in October 1997, the first since the mandatory sentence for murder had replaced the death penalty thirty years before.[49] The 1997 Act also prescribed minimum prison sentences for persistent domestic burglars, the source of an undoubted menace and cause of fear to many householders, although implementation was postponed until an unspecified date in the future. Within months of the histrionic finale to the Act's passage through Parliament, the previous system of early release for prisoners serving short-term sentences, and selective parole for longer-term prisoners, which had been reorganized so radically by the Criminal Justice Act 1991,[50] was restored to what it had been before Howard's conversion to the seductive populist appeal of 'honesty in sentencing'. Section 107 of the new Government's Crime and Disorder Act 1998 repealed Section 8 and Sections 10–27 of the Crime (Sentences) Act 1997, and made some consequential changes to Section 9 of that Act. The repeals deleted fourteen pages from the statute book.

The practical effects of the two new mandatory sentences were not expected to be great.[51] Far more significant was the remaining unimplemented provision; and most significant of all was the lurking danger that once a precedent had been set a future government might find it difficult to resist pressure to introduce mandatory sentences in other contexts.

VI

In a detailed analysis of the application by the courts of the 'exceptional circumstances' saving clause as it would affect the automatic life sentence, Dr David Thomas, a leading authority on sentencing, argued that the meaning of the phrase should be interpreted by referring to the object of the legislation.[52] By enacting the relevant section

[49] Compulsory disqualification from driving imposed by law in the case of certain road traffic offences was not congruent with a sentence of imprisonment, potentially for a long period, on conviction for a serious criminal offence.

[50] See *Responses to Crime*, Vol. 2, pp. 182, 242, 452–4.

[51] See D. A. Thomas, 'The Crime (Sentences) Act 1997', [1998] Crim. L.R. 83. Dr Thomas is Reader in Criminal Justice at the University of Cambridge and a Fellow of Trinity Hall. He has been a consultant on sentencing to the Judicial Studies Board, and edits the reports on sentencing cases for the *Criminal Law Review*.

[52] Ibid., at p. 87. See also two articles by R. Henham in the *Modern Law Review*: 'Back to the Future on Sentencing: The 1996 White Paper', (1996) 59 *MLR* 861, and 'Making Sense of the Crime (Sentences) Act 1997', (1998) 61 *MLR* 223.

in the words used, Parliament had shown its concern about the dangerousness presented by an offender who for the second time had been convicted of one or more of an enumerated list of serious offences. If the court was satisfied that it would be safe to release the offender at the end of a commensurate determinate sentence, then the trial judge would be entitled to find that there were exceptional circumstances relating either to the offences or to the offender which justified the court in deciding that it would not be appropriate to impose a life sentence.[53]

Alternatively, if there was doubt as to the degree of risk of re-offending, the court might decide to pass the prescribed life sentence, but set a tariff in line with the parole eligibility date on a commensurate determinate sentence. This would enable a decision on release on licence to be made by a discretionary life sentence panel of the Parole Board which was experienced in assessing dangerousness.

The mandatory determinate sentence of at least seven years' imprisonment for a person aged eighteen or over on conviction for the third time of a class A drug trafficking offence had been aimed at professional drug dealers. Where there was information and sufficient evidence to enable the police to arrest and charge persons trading in the most harmful drugs for money, leading to convictions in the courts, they could already anticipate receiving a lengthy sentence of seven years or more, especially if they had been convicted twice before of similar offences on separate occasions. But inside and outside Parliament the concern had been not with the fate of professional drug dealers under the new regime, but with the much larger number of mainly young people selling small quantities of hard drugs to one another in order to finance their addiction. Their vulnerability was increased by the fact that it was not necessary for the two qualifying convictions to have been incurred after the Act

[53] This argument failed to persuade the Court of Appeal, Criminal Division, when it considered the interpretation of the expression 'exceptional circumstances'. In *R.* v. *Kelly*, heard in conjunction with *Attorney General's Reference No. 53 of 1998* (*R.* v. *Sandford*) [2000] 1 QB 198, Lord Bingham, CJ said that 'exceptional' had to be construed as an ordinary, familiar English adjective, and not as a term of art. It described a circumstance which was such as to form an exception which was out of the ordinary course, or unusual, or uncommon. To be exceptional a circumstance need not be unique, or unprecedented, or very rare; but it could not be one that was regularly or routinely or normally encountered. For the purpose of Section 2(2) of the Act, circumstances had not only to be exceptional, but also such as, in the court's opinion, justified it in not imposing a life sentence.

had come into force, nor for the offenders to have reached the age of eighteen at the time they were committed.

Anxieties of this kind led to the amendment in the Lords which had been carried against determined opposition by the Government on 13 February 1997, and which Howard had failed to reverse. As enacted, however, the court was empowered not to impose a custodial sentence of at least seven years' duration on third conviction if there were specific circumstances which would make the prescribed sentence unjust in all the circumstances. Where a judge decided not to impose the mandatory or prescribed sentence, he would be obliged to state in open court what the specific circumstances were. As it develops, case-law will determine the nature of the circumstances which will justify this exception. In the meantime, we can note Dr Thomas's succinct opinion that:

> A sentence will be unjust in all the circumstances if it would be considered manifestly excessive by reference to the conventional levels of sentence for that type of offence—that is to say, if it would be significantly longer than the court would have passed in the exercise of its unrestricted discretion.[54]

VII

Within the Home Office, as so often in the past, the main concern was with the prisons. Strenuous efforts had been made throughout the 1990s to reduce overcrowding: to end housing two or three inmates in a cell designed for one and the demeaning practice of 'slopping out'; to eliminate the use of police cells for remand prisoners; to strengthen security; and improve regimes. These aims were all at risk if the prison estate was again to be overwhelmed by numbers. The continuation of early release and parole ensured that the most potentially detrimental of Howard's proposals in terms of an increased prison population had been averted. Nor did there seem to be any immediate prospect of the three-year minimum sentence for persistent burglars being brought into force. The total number of extra prison places which would be needed as a result of the mandatory sentencing provisions of Sections 2 and 3 of the 1997 Act (an automatic life sentence on second conviction for a serious violent or sexual offence, and a minimum sentence of seven years'

[54] Crim. L.R., *op cit.*, at pp. 89–90.

imprisonment on conviction for a third class A drug trafficking offence) was uncertain, but was not expected to exceed 150 places by the end of the financial year 1999–2000.[55]

Throughout the period between Howard's Blackpool speech in the Autumn of 1995 and the enactment of primary legislation eighteen months later the prison population rose sharply. The monthly total of 51,100 for June 1995 had increased to 61,500 by June 1997.[56] In the Spring of 1997 the psychological barrier of 60,000 was surmounted for the first time in the twentieth century. By November 1997 the population in custody had reached 63,700,[57] a total well in excess of the maximum capacity of the prisons, including some new establishments recently brought into use. An audit of the resources available to the Prison Service and current and projected demands established that the prison population had risen by 17,000 or nearly 40 per cent in the four years to June 1997, and increased by 2,440 in the three months since the general election. A report by the Director General of the Prison Service, who had carried out the audit at the request of the new Government, commented that the most recent rise far exceeded any projection published before 1 May. The increase in that period alone was equivalent to the total capacity of four average-sized prisons.[58]

According to the Prison Reform Trust overcrowding, and all the evils with which it was associated, was once again a routine feature of life in the local and remand prisons. Prisoners were being moved daily far from their homes in a desperate bid to find spaces to house them.[59] The audit confirmed that the number of prisoners 'doubled', that is held two in a cell designed for one, had risen to 10,926 at the end of June 1997, and on current plans would have to increase still further to around 16,000 by early 1999. The level of purposeful activity for prisoners had dropped over the previous two years, thus

[55] Home Office, *Statistical Bulletin*, 2/98, pp. 7–8.

[56] Home Office, *Statistical Bulletin*, 18/97 and 5/98, Table 2: 'Population in custody by type of prisoner, Actuals'. Figures rounded up to the nearest 100.

[57] Ibid.

[58] The findings of the audit were given in a Written Answer by the Home Secretary in the House of Commons. The Answer also referred to an announcement made the previous day that the Prison Service would be authorized to spend up to an extra £43 million during the current year and 1998 to accommodate the projected numbers safely. *Parl. Debates*, HC, 298, cols. WA 759–60, 25 July 1997.

[59] Prison Reform Trust, 'A New Programme for Prison Reform', June 1997, p. 1.

limiting the scope for reducing the prospects of their re-offending when released.[60]

Dire as the situation was, none of the legislative measures in the Crime (Sentences) Act had caused this outcome directly. Nor could it be attributed to an increase in the number of offenders coming before the courts, or to a consistent upward trend in the volume of recorded crime. On the contrary, the statistics on recorded crime had fallen over four consecutive years in 1993–6, although the usual caveat must be entered that the number of crimes reported to the police, and recorded by them, is not to be taken as an accurate measure of the actual number of offences that have occurred. Between 1993 and 1995, for example, the *British Crime Survey*, a large-scale sample survey commissioned and published periodically by the Home Office, indicated that the total number of offences, whether reported or not, had increased by 2 per cent at a time when notifiable offences recorded by the police fell by 8 per cent.[61] Crimes go unreported mainly because victims feel that they are not serious enough, or that the police would be unable to do much about them, or would not be interested. Some victims feel that what has occurred is not a matter for the police, and would be better dealt with by themselves.[62]

An explanation must be sought elsewhere. The most convincing is that sentencers were making greater use of custody, and for longer periods of time, not because they had been directed to do so, but because they were responding to a climate of opinion.[63] Magistrates and most of the judges in the Crown Court are part of the communities

[60] For a well informed assessment of the implications of the audit's findings, see I. Dunbar and A. Langdon, *Tough Justice: Sentencing and Penal Policies in the 1990s*, Blackstone Press, London, 1998, pp. 150–1. Both authors had held senior posts on the Prisons Board. Ian Dunbar had been a Grade 1 Prison Governor, including at HMP Wakefield and Wormwood Scrubs, before becoming Regional Director for the South West and later Director of Inmate Administration in the Prison Service, 1990–4. Anthony Langdon had been Director of Operational Policy in the Prison Department in the 1980s; then moved to the Cabinet Office as an Under-Secretary in 1985, and returned to the Home Office as a Deputy Under-Secretary of State, 1989–95.

[61] 'The 1996 British Crime Survey, England and Wales', Home Office, *Statistical Bulletin*, Issue 19/96, p. 18. Under half of the BCS offences were reported to the police in 1995. Ibid., p. 4.

[62] Ibid., p. 23.

[63] See A. Ashworth and M. Hough, 'Sentencing and the Climate of Opinion', [1996] Crim. L.R. 776. Andrew Ashworth is Vinerian Professor of English Law at Oxford, and Michael Hough is Professor of Social Policy, South Bank University. Ashworth was Editor of the *Criminal Law Review*, 1975–98.

in which they work. They do not inhabit ivory towers. They are conscious of fluctuations in the state of opinion on criminal offending and attitudes towards punishment. The 1996 sweep of the *British Crime Survey* covered the latter aspect in particular detail and a revealing analysis of the findings was published in 1998.[64]

The public in England and Wales was shown by the survey as taking a jaundiced view of sentencers and sentencing. Eighty-two per cent of the sample thought that judges were out of touch with the public. The figure for magistrates was somewhat lower at 63 per cent. Four-fifths of people questioned thought that sentences were too lenient, half saying that they were much too lenient. The survey findings demonstrated equally clearly that such widespread public dissatisfaction was grounded, at least in part, in ignorance of current practice and of current crime trends. Those who were most dissatisfied were most likely to overestimate the growth in crime, and to underestimate the courts' use of imprisonment. Those most likely to underestimate the courts' use of imprisonment had lower educational attainment than others, were likely to be above average age, and were more likely to read tabloid newspapers.[65]

There can be no more vivid portrayal of the constituency at which Howard had aimed his overtly punitive policies, or of the ignorance and prejudices to which he appealed. It was the sentencers who had to bear the brunt of the consequences, and it is not surprising that they should resort to greater severity. As to the financial cost of containing a record number of prisoners, finding sites, designing, building, and staffing new prisons, while struggling to maintain the constructive work so vital for rehabilitation and crime reduction in the future, these problems were to be the inheritance of a new Government.

VIII

The advent of the Labour administration was marked by a noticeable, and intentional, shift in emphasis. The policies were those set out in the election Manifesto, and were rooted in the detailed preparatory work carried out during the final years in Opposition. The main priorities were: reducing delays in the system of criminal

[64] M. Hough and J. Roberts, 'Attitudes to punishment: findings from the British Crime Survey', Home Office Research Study No. 179, 1998.

[65] Ibid., p. viii.

justice by expediting the progress of cases from the point of charge to disposal by the court, especially those involving persistent young offenders; a new approach to offending in local communities, including anti-social neighbourhood disruption, racial harassment, and stalking; and extensive reforms in the system of youth justice. Taken overall, the strategy represented a move away from increasing penalties and towards changing attitudes. The phraseology employed, however, was less that of traditional penal reformers than of stern disciplinarians determined not to let miscreants escape retribution for their criminal, harmful, or offensive deeds or behaviour.

Very little was said by ministers or other government spokesmen about mandatory sentencing. Straw's lengthy statement in the Commons on 30 July 1997 had concentrated on improvements in the criminal justice system. The announcement of his intention to implement automatic life sentences for second-time serious sexual or violent offenders, and mandatory minimum seven-year sentences for traffickers in class A drugs on third conviction, had been included, but in a low key. The inference was that they had been policies left behind by the previous Government, and the cupboard was now being tidied up. It was too risky to throw them out completely, but there was no need to display them conspicuously.

The expectation in the Prison Service was that the three-year mandatory sentence for repeat burglars, a very numerous category, would continue to be postponed, perhaps even indefinitely. Yet the political antecedents of the Crime (Sentences) Act meant that factors other than logistics were always likely to come into play. From its inception at Blackpool in 1995, the legislation on mandatory sentences had been designed to win support for the party in power at the time. It had been strongly criticized by the higher judiciary, and owed nothing to the work of dispassionate Whitehall interdepartmental committees, pressure from special interest groups, or advice from any independent body such as the active Law Commission or the inactive Criminal Law Revision Committee.

Such high-minded considerations were unlikely to have been uppermost in the minds of the Home Office ministers and their political advisers when called upon over the New Year 1998–9 to make a contribution to a wider political initiative. This was aimed at demonstrating vigorous and effective 'joined-up government' at a time when its standing with the general public was thought to be in need of a boost. Mandatory sentencing fitted the bill. Lord Hurd of

Westwell, a former Home Secretary who did not agree with Straw's surprise decision to implement the outstanding mandatory sentence, put it succinctly: 'I think this is strength through unity week. He has been told to find something tough.'[66]

Politics and news management apart, two functional contexts bore on Straw's decision to activate the mandatory three-year sentence for repeat burglars. The first was the prevalence of the offence and the widespread harm done. In 1997 police recorded more than one million burglaries, over half of them involving breaking into private homes. Burglary as a whole accounted for more than one-fifth of all recorded crime in England and Wales. Taken together, England and Wales had the highest burglary rates of the eleven industrialized countries (including the United States and Canada, as well as some other European countries) which were featured in the International Crime Victimisation Survey.[67] Speaking at the Labour Party Annual Conference on 1 October 1998, the Home Secretary had committed the Government to spending an extra £50 million over the next three years targeting two million homes to beat the burglar. Straw claimed it to be the biggest co-ordinated initiative on burglary for many years.[68] As such, it formed an important element in the Government's wider crime reduction programme.

The second context was one never far from the mind of any Home Secretary. This was the size of the prison population in relation to the number of places available for the confinement of accused persons remanded in custody pending trial or sentence, as well as convicted and sentenced prisoners. After a period of rapid expansion, the prison population showed signs of stabilizing. In December 1998 the population was 64,100, a reduction on the September total of 65,900, and well below the high point of 66,516 reached in July of that year.[69]

[66] *The Times*, 13 Jan. 1999. Although serving for five and a half years as Foreign Secretary after his time at the Home Office, Hurd had retained an interest in the penal system. Since 1997 he had been an active Chairman of the Prison Reform Trust. He retired from the chairmanship in the Spring of 2001.

[67] Notes for Jack Straw's speech at the Labour Party Annual Conference, Blackpool, *News from Labour*, 1 Oct. 1998, p. 1.

[68] Ibid.

[69] *Prison Population Brief, England and Wales*, Research Development Statistics, Home Office, June 1999, pp. 1–2. Overcrowding continued to be a major problem in the local prisons. On 31 Jan. 1999 male local prisons, which had 19,691 places, were holding a total of 23,614 prisoners. On average they were 20 per cent overcrowded. Penal Affairs Consortium, *The Prison System: Regime and Population Trends*, August 1999, p. 1.

A home detention curfew monitored by electronic tagging, which was due to be introduced in January 1999, offered the prospect of some further relief. Although it was estimated that three-year mandatory sentences would add a further 4,000 or so to the prison population, it would take some time to build up to that figure since the two qualifying convictions would need to be committed after Section 4 of the Crime (Sentences) Act had been brought into force. Influenced by these considerations, Straw had asked Home Office officials to do some preparatory work before Christmas, although the Prison Service was not consulted on the implications at that stage.

By early January, therefore, the prison statistics offered a window of opportunity which might not remain open for long. Some close observers believed that, left to himself, Straw would have preferred to take no action. There was no sense of ownership, mandatory sentencing being part of an unwanted and controversial policy inherited from the previous Government. If implemented it would certainly be costly, and lead to a significant addition to the prison population, whereas its effectiveness as an instrument of crime reduction was unproven. But if the Home Secretary entertained doubts, he kept them to himself. Parliament was informed of his intention to implement by way of a reply to a Question for Written Answer from a Government supporter in the first week back after the Christmas Recess.[70]

IX

The next resort to mandatory sentencing owed nothing to earlier legislation, being in the mainstream of the Labour Government's own policies for far-reaching reforms in the procedures for handling young people below the age of eighteen who commit criminal offences. Many, although not all, of the youth justice provisions of the Crime and Disorder Act 1998, and the Youth Justice and Criminal Evidence Act which followed the next year, had gained a generally favourable reception inside and outside Parliament. There was a spirit of cautious optimism that carefully thought-out policies, which had been the subject of consultation and discussion with the

[70] *Parl. Debates*, HC, 323, col. WA 159, 12 Jan. 1999.

people and organizations responsible for delivering youth services in their localities, would result in real progress being made at the crucial age when so many habits of deviance are formed.

Yet the risk is that enthusiasts, however admirable the cause, may become zealots. In the pursuit of their objectives, visions can narrow and fundamental principles be jeopardized. Thus in the opening clause of the Youth Justice and Criminal Evidence Bill, which began its progress through Parliament in the House of Lords in December 1998, a clear mandatory sentencing requirement could be detected. This bound a sentencing court, when faced with a young first offender less than eighteen years of age, who accepted his or her guilt for an offence which did not deserve a custodial sentence,[71] to refer the young person to a youth offender panel. The intention was that the referral order should be widely used and become the main means of disposal for young people not previously convicted of a criminal offence.

The primary aim of the new sentence was to prevent re-offending. Associated with this was a more far-reaching social objective: to bring closer together the process of criminal justice and the interests of the victims and the wider community which had become undesirably marginalized. The youth offender panels would comprise representatives of the main locally based agencies: police, education, social services, probation, as well as the parents (or parent) of the young offender, or a representative of the local authority if in its care. A 'contract' between the offender and the panel would be drawn up in the shape of an agreed programme of behaviour for the young person to follow. Failure to comply could result in returning to court for resentencing. This would also be the outcome if there was a failure to agree. Victims might attend if they wished.

The design of the panels, and the procedures they would follow, were based on the principles of restorative justice.[72] Although it was

[71] In addition, the power would not be available for use where the offence was one for which the sentence was fixed by law, or where a hospital order or absolute discharge would be more appropriate. Youth Justice and Criminal Evidence Act 1999, Section 1(1).

[72] The principles underlying the concept of restorative justice were described in a White Paper published in November 1997 as restoration: young offenders apologizing to their victims and making amends for the harm they have done; reintegration: young offenders paying their debt to society, putting their crime behind them, and rejoining the law-abiding community; and responsibility: young offenders—and their parents—facing the consequences of their offending behaviour and taking responsibility for preventing further offending. *No More Excuses: A New Approach to Tackling Youth Crime in England and Wales*, Cm. 3809, The Stationery Office, 1997, p. 32.

not a new idea for an offender to be expected to make amends to the victim and/or the community at large, indeed it had been a central feature of the original concept of the community service orders imposed by the criminal courts since 1973, restorative justice was still in its infancy. Trial projects existed in some areas, notably a well publicized police-led initiative in the Thames Valley.[73] But the time for experiment was over. In the heady days after so lengthy a period in Opposition, Labour ministers were impatient to act. Much thought had been given to the development of new policies, on youth justice among many other topics, and now the moment had come to put them into practice. There were to be no ifs and buts. The necessary legislation would be introduced as soon as possible. Once enacted, the new provisions would be piloted in selected areas of the country.

In the event, the youth justice proposals were not included in the Crime and Disorder Act passed into law in the first session of the new Parliament. Instead they were joined with some unrelated Home Office legislation on special measures to protect vulnerable or intimidated witnesses giving evidence in criminal proceedings. The resulting composite Bill on Youth Justice and Criminal Evidence was introduced in the House of Lords, rather than in the Commons.

The merits of the policy of diverting young people from entry into the penal system at the start of what might otherwise develop into criminal careers were accepted virtually without question. But on Third Reading on 23 March 1999 a full-scale debate took place in the Lords concentrating on the mandatory nature of the referral order in the first clause of the Bill. A simple amendment, moved by the author, proposed the words: '[the] court may order the offender to be referred to a youth offender panel' in place of the drafting in Clause 1, which read: 'the court shall sentence the offender for the offence by ordering him to be referred to a youth offender panel'. In the debate which followed sixteen peers spoke from all parts of the House. Ten supported the amendment and six were opposed.

Two speeches from the cross-benches were listened to with particular attention. The first was by Lord Lane, a former Lord Chief Justice. Never a man to equivocate, he declared bluntly: 'the sad fact is that the mandatory sentence or mandatory disposal order will

[73] See C. Hoyle, 'Restorative Justice in the Thames Valley', 133 *Prison Service Journal*, 2001, pp. 37–40. Dr Carolyn Hoyle is a University Lecturer in Criminology and Fellow of Green College, Oxford.

inevitably be a potential miscarriage of justice.'[74] Later in the debate, Viscount Runciman of Doxford, who chaired the Royal Commission on Criminal Justice 1991–3, argued that precisely because of the enormous variation in the circumstances of cases coming before the courts it was not only dangerous in principle, but counter-productive in practice, to attempt to fetter the discretion of judges or magistrates by statute.[75] From the government benches Lord Warner, Chair of the Youth Justice Board, spoke in support of the Bill as drafted. It was concerned with the effectiveness of the sentence, as well as the elements of justice and fairness. It represented a break with the past to refer those who met the referral conditions to youth offender panels. He suggested it would be 'heroically optimistic about human nature' not to believe that some magistrates would be tempted to hang onto cases rather than make referrals.[76] After the Minister of State, Lord Williams of Mostyn,[77] had wound up for the Government, the amendment was put to a vote. The result was close: 149 voted Content and 144 Not Content, a majority of five.

The debate on the 'shall' to 'may' amendment continued in the House of Commons and covered much the same ground. It was the subject of a half-day sitting of the Standing Committee, and later occupied some two hours on the floor of the House at Report stage.[78] On each occasion, ministers declined to make any concession to meet the objections of principle that had persuaded a majority in the Lords, and the amendment was reversed by a division on party lines in Standing Committee.[79] The furthest the Home Secretary was willing to go on Report was to point out that if what he described as 'unanticipated inflexibilities' should arise, the Secretary of State would have power to make such amendments by regulation as he considered necessary to vary the descriptions of the offenders to whom the compulsory or discretionary referral conditions should apply.[80]

[74] *Parl. Debates*, HL, 598, col. 1159, 23 Mar. 1999.

[75] Ibid., col. 1163.

[76] Ibid., cols. 1161–2.

[77] QC, 1978. Leader, Wales and Chester Circuit, 1987–9; member of the Bar Council, 1986–92; Chairman, 1992. Life peer, 1992. Opposition spokesman in the House of Lords on Northern Ireland, Home and Legal Affairs, 1992–7. Parliamentary Under-Secretary of State, 1997–8, Minister of State, Home Office, 1998–9; Attorney General, 1999–2001; Leader of the House of Lords, 2001–.

[78] *Parl. Debates*, HC, 334, cols. 1204–34, 8 July 1999.

[79] *Parl. Debates*, HC, Youth Justice and Criminal Evidence Bill (Lords), Standing Committee E, col. 38, 8 June 1999.

[80] *Parl. Debates*, HC, 334, *op. cit.*, col. 1229.

But varying conditions did not go to the heart of the dispute. Whatever criteria were adopted to describe the categories eligible to be referred to youth offender panels, and however carefully constructed the contract drawn up by the panel for each young person, the reality remained that the court must, not may, make a referral order when sentencing any offender to whom the Act applies. That was the central feature of the objections which had been exhaustively rehearsed in both Houses.

Shortly before the Summer Recess at the end of July 1999 the Bill returned to the Lords for consideration of the amendments made by the Commons. This afforded an opportunity to debate the Commons' reasons for rejecting the alternative of discretionary, rather than mandatory, referrals. The arguments were repeated once again, without concession on either side, before the decision of the elected House was reluctantly accepted. In this way, a fourth mandatory sentence was added to the statute book. The fact that a referral order differed from a sentence in a conventional sense did not alter its nature as a compulsory disposal by the sentencing court.

The episode illustrated a perceptible tendency by the Government, some leading members of which had worked so single-mindedly in Opposition to develop original policies on criminal justice, to insist that every provision should be carried out in one particular way. Such a desire for total control is not necessary, indeed it is potentially dangerous. It introduces undesirable rigidity into the administration of justice. It diminishes the responsibility of sentencers, and sooner or later it is inevitable, as Lane had pointed out, that miscarriages of justice will result.

APPENDIX A

The practice direction printed below was given by Lord Bingham CJ at a sitting of the Court of Appeal, Criminal Division, with Garland and Rix JJ on 22 January 1998. It is reproduced with permission.

PRACTICE DIRECTION: CUSTODIAL SENTENCES

The practical effect of custodial sentences imposed by the courts is almost entirely governed by statutory provisions. Those statutory provisions, changed by Parliament from time to time, are not widely understood by the general public. It is desirable that when sentence is passed the practical effect of the sentence should be understood by the defendant, any victim and any member of the public who is present in court or reads a full report of the proceedings.

In future, whenever a custodial sentence is imposed on an offender, the court should explain the practical effect of the sentence in addition to complying with existing statutory requirements. This will be no more than an explanation; the sentence will be that pronounced by the court.

Sentencers should give the explanation in terms of their own choosing, taking care to ensure that the explanation is clear and accurate.

No form of words is prescribed. Annexed to this Practice Direction are short statements which may, adapted as necessary, be of value as models. These statements are based on the statutory provisions in force on 1 January 1998 and will of course require modification if those provisions are materially amended.

Sentencers will continue to give such explanation as they judge necessary of ancillary orders relating to matters such as disqualification, compensation, confiscation, costs and so on.

(sgd.) Bingham, CJ

ANNEX

Forms of words

Forms of words are provided for use where the offender

(1) will be a short term prisoner not subject to licence;
(2) will be a short term prisoner subject to licence;
(3) will be a long term prisoner;
(4) will be subject to a discretionary sentence of life imprisonment.

Sentencers will bear in mind that where an offender is sentenced to terms which are consecutive, or wholly or partly concurrent, they are to be treated as a single term: Criminal Justice Act 1991, s. 51(2).

(1) Total term less than 12 months:

The sentence is [ ] months.

You will serve half that sentence in prison/a young offender institution. After that time the rest of your sentence will be suspended and you will be released. Your release will not bring this sentence to an end. If after your release and before the end of the period covered by the sentence you commit any further offence, you may be ordered to return to custody to serve the balance of the original sentence outstanding at the date of the further offence, as well as being punished for that new offence.

Any time you have spent on remand in custody in connection with the offence(s) for which you are now being sentenced will count as part of the sentence to be served, unless it has already been counted.

(2) Total term of 12 months and less than 4 years:

The sentence is [ ] [months/years].

You will serve half that sentence in a prison/a young offender institution. After that time the rest of your sentence will be suspended and you will be released.

Your release will not bring this sentence to an end. If after your release and before the end of the period covered by the sentence you commit any further offence you may be ordered to return to custody to serve the balance of the original sentence outstanding at the date of the further offence, as well as being punished for that new offence.

Any time you have spent on remand in custody in connection with the offence[s] for which you are now being sentenced will count as part of the sentence to be served, unless it has already been counted.

After your release you will also be subject to supervision on licence until the end of three-quarters of the total sentence. [If an order has been made under section 44 of the Criminal Justice Act 1991: After your release you will also be subject to supervision on licence for the remainder of the sentence.]

If you fail to comply with any of the requirements of your licence then again you may be brought before a court which will have power to suspend your licence and order your return to custody.

(3) Total term of 4 years or more:

The sentence is [ ] [years/months].

Your case will not be considered by the Parole Board until you have served at least half that period in custody. Unless the Parole Board recommends earlier release, you will not be released until you have served two-thirds of that sentence. Your release will not bring the sentence to an end. Instead, the remainder will be suspended. If after your release and before the end of the period covered by the sentence you commit any further offence you may be ordered to return to custody to serve the balance of the original sentence outstanding at the date of the new offence as well as being punished for that new offence.

Any time you have spent in custody on remand in connection with the offence[s] for which you are now being sentenced will count as part of the sentence to be served, unless it has already been counted.

After your release you will also be subject to supervision on licence until the end of three-quarters of the total sentence. [If an order has been made under section 44 of the Criminal Justice Act 1991: After your release you will also be subject to supervision on licence for the remainder of the sentence.]

You will be liable to be recalled to prison if your licence is revoked, either on the recommendation of the Parole Board, or, if it is thought expedient in the public interest, by the Secretary of State.

(4) Discretionary life sentence:

The sentence of the court is life imprisonment/custody for life/detention for life under section 53(2)(3) of the Children and Young Persons Act 1933. For the purposes of section 28 of the Crime (Sentences) Act 1997 the court specifies a period of [x] years. That means that your case will not be considered by the Parole Board until you have served at least [x] years in custody. After that time the Parole Board will be entitled to consider your release. When it is satisfied that you need no longer be confined in custody for the protection of the public it will be able to direct your release. Until it is so satisfied you will remain in custody.

If you are released, it will be on terms that you are subject to a licence for the rest of your life and liable to be recalled to prison at any time if your licence is revoked, either on the recommendation of the Parole Board, or, if it is thought expedient in the public interest, by the Secretary of State.

3

Changing Course: Politics and Policy-Making, 1997–8

I

An integral part of the refashioning of the Labour Party during the latter stages of its long years in the political wilderness from 1979 to 1997 was a radical change in approach to criminal policy. Antipathy towards the police and a tendency to explain away offending behaviour in terms of social, economic, or environmental disadvantage were seen by the modernisers as being increasingly out of step with the public demand for greater protection from the consequences of criminal acts.

Throughout the Thatcher era the Conservatives had been successful in exploiting law and order as election issues, whereas Labour appeared to be generally defensive and reactive. Two considerations in particular had inhibited the mounting of a more effective political challenge. One was libertarian: a zealous attachment to civil rights not excluding civil disobedience when it seemed justifiable. The other, apparently inextricably linked with the conflict over industrial relations, was the right of trade unionists to take strike action, with secondary picketing at times leading to clashes with the police. With full television exposure, unruly scenes of violence and intimidation on the picket lines of the kind witnessed during the long drawn-out strike in the coal industry in 1984–5 could be seen as threatening by the general public.[1] The way in which John Smith, and after his unexpected death in May 1994, Tony Blair, steered their party away from supporting the confrontational tactics of the

[1] A high point was reached during a bitter dispute in the newspaper industry when several thousand demonstrators clashed with 1,744 police officers in violent scenes outside the printing plant of News International at Wapping on 3 May 1986. 175 officers were injured, 43 of whom required hospital treatment. In addition, 29 members of the public received injuries requiring hospital treatment. *Parl. Debates*, HC, 97 (6th ser.), col. 260 WA, 9 May, 1986.

militants falls outside the scope of this volume.[2] But it was the essential precursor to fresh approaches to crime and disorder.

In the new politics the keynote was to be the community and the neighbourhood. A national network was envisaged of local partnerships between police, local authority, and other agencies, working together to counter crime more effectively in the places where a majority of the people lived. The aim was to create safer communities, with a reduction in the frequency of offending by young people as the first priority. Although the involvement of local communities and the setting up of inter-agency partnerships to follow through crime control initiatives was not a novel idea,[3] nor one that was distinctively Labour in orientation, its adoption by the Shadow Cabinet propelled the concept to the forefront of national policy formation.

When the time came to introduce his legislative proposals to the House of Commons in 1998, Jack Straw described their roots. He admitted candidly that in the early 1980s the Labour Party had lost its way, not least by failing to listen to those whom it claimed to represent. In transforming the Party from one of opposition to one of government, he said Blair had ensured that policy-making would be inspired above all by the needs of its constituents. Among other things, that commitment had led to a serious examination of how to reverse the apparently inexorable rise in anti-social behaviour and teenage crime.[4]

As Opposition Home Affairs spokesman, Straw had drawn on the experience of some pioneering local authorities in different parts of the country. On a personal note he explained:

> I was struck by the degree to which the problems and experiences of my constituents had changed since I was first elected in 1979. Then, the great bulk of my constituency case work concerned housing complaints and social security, but that changed from the early 1990s. More and more people came to me complaining of intolerable anti-social behaviour, of harassment and of intimidation. Much of the trouble was caused by children and young people who were out of control. The criminal justice system appeared to be

[2] See Chapter 3, 'The Road to New Labour', in D. Butler and D. Kavanagh, *The British General Election of 1997*, Macmillan Press, Basingstoke and London, 1997, pp. 46–67, and P. Gould, *The Unfinished Revolution*, Little, Brown, London, 1998.

[3] See A. Crawford, *The Local Governance of Crime: Appeals to Community and Partnerships*, Clarendon Press, Oxford, 1997. This well researched analysis of the movement towards community-based crime control strategies raises some timely questions about democratic legitimacy and political accountability.

[4] *Parl. Debates*, HC, 310, col. 370, 8 Apr. 1998.

incapable of enforcing decent standards of public behaviour on children and adults alike . . .

In opposition, the views of colleagues in the House brought home to me the failures of the youth justice system. Three years ago, I wrote to every Labour Member of Parliament seeking their opinions on the youth justice system in their areas. I was stunned by the response. Every Member representing an English or a Welsh constituency who replied expressed dissatisfaction with that system of youth justice.

The bill is therefore born out of the experience of our constituents, and out of their sense of frustration with the current criminal justice system. That frustration is shared by the police and by other dedicated and skilled professionals who are expected to solve the problems, but who have been hampered by a slow, inconsistent and ineffective system.[5]

The sporadic empiricism that characterizes British policy-making, irrespective of party, meant that other sources besides the diligent concern of Labour MPs for the welfare of their constituents had contributed to the progressive development of the new policies. During the tenure of previous Conservative Governments the potential for a partnership approach towards crime prevention had been recognized, being tried out in a number of relatively small-scale projects such as the Safer Cities programme, and promoted in booklets and circulars issued by the Home Office. Non-governmental organizations, in particular the National Association for the Care and Resettlement of Offenders (NACRO) in a published report as early as 1986,[6] had also emphasized the pivotal role which local authorities should be encouraged to assume in efforts to prevent crime.

The same theme was taken up by an independent working group established by the Home Office Standing Conference on Crime Prevention which reported in August 1991.[7] Chaired by James Morgan, a management consultant and business efficiency adviser, and with Nigel Whiskin, Chief Executive of Crime Concern as special adviser,[8] the working group had to reconcile conflicting interests in recommending where the responsibility for taking the lead in crime prevention should lie. The police saw themselves as the natural

[5] Ibid., col. 371.

[6] *Crime Prevention and Community Safety: A New Role for Local Authorities*, NACRO, London, 1986.

[7] *Safer Communities: The local delivery of crime prevention through the partnership approach*, Home Office, Aug. 1991.

[8] For the origins of Crime Concern and its purposes, see *Responses to Crime*, Vol. 2, pp. 214, 218–20.

lead organization. But since much of what was needed to prevent crime in the community would involve local authority agencies and spending, it was not surprising that the local authorities felt they should be in the lead. The Morgan group promoted the idea of partnership between the two, and made a series of visits to find out what was happening on the ground. The results of their inquiries were not encouraging. Many partnerships were long on rhetoric and short on action. In some areas the partnership seemed to be an end in itself. There was no real consensus about what was meant by the terms 'crime prevention' and 'community safety'.[9]

In its report the working group found that crime prevention measures did interrelate at many points with the work of local government, as well as the diverse elements of the criminal justice system. The expression 'community safety' was preferred to 'crime prevention', since the latter was too often regarded as being solely the responsibility of the police. One of the most thought-provoking findings was that while crime prevention measures were a peripheral concern of all the agencies involved, it was a truly core activity for none. While the case for the partnership approach was virtually unchallenged, it was hardly tested.[10]

Moving on from its main findings to proposals for action, the Morgan report recommended that in the longer term local authorities, working closely with the police, should have:

> a clear statutory responsibility for the development and stimulation of community safety and crime prevention programmes, and for progressing at a local level a multi-agency approach to community safety.[11]

The priority of the new multi-agency local partnerships in preparing their action plans for community safety activities should be young people and their involvement with crime. Various initiatives were set out in what was described as a 'portfolio of community safety activities'.

The recommendations fell on stony ground. Both Kenneth Baker and his successor as Home Secretary, Kenneth Clarke, lacked confidence in local authorities as then constituted, tending to adopt generally dismissive attitudes towards them. Thus when the Government's response was published more than a year later it was no surprise that it should reject the proposal that local authorities, working with the

[9] Letter to the author from Nigel Whiskin, 10 Feb. 1999.

[10] *Safer Communities*, *op. cit.*, p. 3.

[11] Ibid., para. 6.9, p. 29.

police, should take the lead. 'The Government did not wish', it stated plainly:

> to burden local authorities with new statutory duties in this area, especially when . . . a good deal had been achieved at local level in developing crime prevention programmes within the existing statutory framework.[12]

For the members of the working group, the blow was softened when the Minister of State, Michael Jack, commissioned Crime Concern to write a handbook for local partnerships on crime prevention which was well received both in Britain and wider afield.

The seeds of the Morgan report, in particular that local authorities should have a statutory duty to develop and stimulate community safety and crime prevention programmes in their area, germinated on more fertile soil elsewhere. The general approach coincided with a central strand of what was emerging as the Labour Party's new policy. This went further than Morgan, or any other advisory group, had recommended. In future, exhortation and incentives were to be buttressed by direction. Having defined their objectives, local authorities, the police, and other agencies would be required by statute to work together to develop and implement strategies for reducing crime and disorder in the districts for which they shared responsibility.

II

Labour's plans to reform the system of youth justice were set out in a pre-Manifesto consultation paper published in May 1996.[13] The named authors were the Shadow Home Secretary, Jack Straw, and Alun Michael, Shadow Home Affairs Minister.[14] The document ran to nineteen pages and represented the outcome of a detailed study by a former Director of Social Services, Norman Warner,[15] working

[12] Home Office, *Response to the Report 'Safer Communities: The local delivery of crime prevention through the partnership approach'*, December 1992, p. 1.

[13] *Tackling Youth Crime: Reforming Youth Justice*, The Labour Party, 1996.

[14] Member, Cardiff City Council, 1973–89; JP, Cardiff, 1972; Chairman, Juvenile Bench, 1986–7. Opposition Spokesman on Home Affairs, 1992–7; Minister of State, Home Office, 1997–8; Secretary of State for Wales, 1998–9; First Secretary for Wales, National Assembly for Wales, 1999–2000.

[15] Civil servant (Ministry of Health, Social Services, and DHSS) 1959–85, latterly Under-Secretary, Supplementary Benefits Division, DHSS. Director of Social Services for Kent, 1985–91. Chairman, National Inquiry into Selection, Development and Management of Staff in Children's Homes, 1991–2; Senior Policy Adviser to Home Secretary, 1997–8; Chair, Youth Justice Board, 1998–. Life Peer, 1998.

with Straw, Michael, and a research assistant. Both before and after the General Election, when he accompanied Straw to the Home Office as his Senior Policy Adviser, Warner was amongst the most creative and influential people engaged in the intricate process of translating political ideas into practical policies. Alun Michael too, with many years' experience of working in the community on youth and crime issues in South Wales, had a key role in fostering links with the police and local authorities.

A parallel investigation of the harm attributable to youth offending, and its cost, was carried out by the Audit Commission.[16] This was begun early in 1995, and first published in November 1996, six months before the change in Government the following year.[17] As part of its wide remit, going beyond supervising the external audit of local authorities, police forces, probation services, and National Health Service agencies in England and Wales, the Commission was required by its terms of reference to undertake studies to enable it to make recommendations for improving 'the economy, efficiency and effectiveness' of these public services. It also had the freedom, unusual for a public body, to comment upon the impact of statutory provisions or guidance by central Government on their performance, assessed in terms of economy, efficiency, and effectiveness.[18] The study of young people and crime complemented previous reviews of other services for youth in the fields of education, health, social services, police, and probation.

In contrast with the annual criminal statistics, which showed that the total of notifiable offences recorded by the police had fallen for four consecutive years in 1993–6, the first such occurrence in the twentieth century,[19] the Audit Commission relied on the 1996 British Crime Survey of households. This indicated that crimes against individuals,

[16] The Audit Commission was established in 1983 to appoint and regulate the external auditors of local authorities in England and Wales. In 1990 its responsibilities were extended to include the National Health Service. Its wings have spread, and the National Audit Office (NAO) now audits the accounts of all government departments and agencies, as well as a wide range of other public bodies, including the Metropolitan Police. In interpreting its function of reporting to Parliament on the economy, efficiency, and effectiveness with which government bodies have used public money, the NAO audits outputs as well as financial operations, especially value for money audits.

[17] *Misspent Youth: Young People and Crime*, the Audit Commission, London, 1996.

[18] Ibid., p. 3.

[19] Home Office, *Criminal Statistics, England and Wales, 1996* (Cm. 3764), The Stationery Office, London, 1997, p. 16, para. 1.2.

such as theft, burglary, and assault, had increased by 73 per cent between 1981 and 1995, reaching an annual total of 19 million by 1995 for England and Wales. When losses to the retail trade and manufacturers were included, the overall cost to public services and victims was estimated to exceed £16 billion in that year.[20] A disproportionate amount of total crime was committed by young people, especially young males. In 1994 two out of every five known offenders were under the age of twenty-one, and a quarter were under eighteen.[21]

Despite the best efforts of the Home Office statisticians to explain that the annual figures for recorded crime did not tell the whole story, the discrepancies between the two systems of measurement afforded critics and supporters of the Government alike ample ammunition for political campaigning. The cautionary statement, included in the *Criminal Statistics for 1996*, that the British Crime Survey suggested less than half of all offences were reported to the police, and that only a quarter were recorded by them,[22] was disregarded by both sides shaping up for the coming general election.

For the Conservative Government the decline in recorded crime across the board was evidence of a positive response to the consciously punitive policies symbolized in Howard's triumphalist battle cry, 'Prison Works'. As recounted in the previous Chapter, the accent was on heavier punishment, both to incapacitate persistent offenders and those sentenced for more serious offences by longer periods of imprisonment, and to deter others. One of the more apparent weaknesses in this argument was that while the incidence of recorded property crime, and some other offences, had been falling, the same method of measurement showed that violent crime was steadily rising. Over the year 1996, inconveniently close to the election the following Spring, violent crime rose by 11 per cent. This was the largest increase in recorded violent crime since 1989. Within that total, offences of violence against the person rose by 12 per cent, robberies rose by 9 per cent, and sexual offences by 4 per cent.[23] In every year since 1980 recorded violent crime had shown an increase on the previous year.[24]

[20] *Misspent Youth*, *op. cit.*, p. 5.

[21] Ibid. There was nothing new about this finding. In the 1970s Home Office officials used as a rule of thumb that half of known offenders were under twenty-one, and a quarter under seventeen.

[22] *Criminal Statistics, England and Wales, 1996*, *op. cit.*, p. 16, para. 1.5.

[23] Ibid., p. 33.

[24] Ibid., p. 44, Table 2.1. The total violent crime classification was added to Table 2.1 for the first time in the *Criminal Statistics* for 1990. Comparative figures were

The Labour Party was not slow to exploit these trends. Selected statistics were deployed in the cross-fire on the floor of the House of Commons, in thc media, and at political meetings. It was the old politics at its most combative. But behind the foreground barrage new policies were taking shape. At the local level information was gathered on community-based crime prevention, and experiments in mediation and reparation. Those with first-hand experience were canvassed, and the available field research studied. Particularly convincing was the analysis contained in the impressive report of the Audit Commission, *Misspent Youth.* Following an exhaustive inquiry the study team, guided by an expert advisory panel, concluded that the existing system of dealing with youth crime was inefficient and expensive, while little was being done to deal effectively with juvenile nuisance. The current arrangements were failing the young people, who were not being guided away from offending towards constructive activities. They were also failing victims, who suffered from some young people's inconsiderate behaviour, and from vandalism, arson, and loss of property from thefts and burglaries. There was evidence of waste in a variety of forms: lost time, as public servants processed the same young offenders through the courts time and again; lost rents, as people refused to live in high crime areas; and lost business, as customers steered clear of the troubled areas. Not to be ignored was the waste of young people's positive potential.[25]

The Audit Commission report argued that resources needed to be shifted away from processing young offenders and towards dealing with their behaviour. At the same time, efforts to prevent offending and other forms of anti-social behaviour by young people needed to be co-ordinated between the different agencies involved. They should be targeted on deprived areas with high crime rates, and piloted and evaluated.[26] Inter-agency co-operation was a prevailing

shown back to 1980. In every year between 1980–90, with the trend continuing between 1990–7, there was an increase in the total number of recorded offences of violent crime compared with the previous year. A downturn occurred in 1998 after changes in the counting rules which came into effect in April of that year. The real underlying fall was thought to be smaller. Home Office, *Criminal Statistics for England and Wales 1998*, Cm. 4649, The Stationery Office, 2000, p. 29. The British Crime Survey and hospital accident and emergency admissions suggest that the actual incidence of criminal acts of violence is substantially in excess of the total number of offences recorded by the police.

[25] *Misspent Youth*, *op. cit.*, p. 96.

[26] Ibid.

theme of this and other research studies at the time. Some voices, although not many, warned that independent agencies could be seduced into co-ordinated systems of multi-agency action which might result in the stronger agencies, usually the police, shaping the agenda and enlisting the resources of other organizations.[27] Yet there could be little question that the thrust of most informed opinion, to which the Labour Party had by now become well attuned, was in the direction of joint action against crime by community residents and those with a responsibility to deliver properly functioning public services to them.

In March 1996 Straw had outlined his policies in writing for the Home Affairs Committee of the Parliamentary Labour Party. In the introduction to his paper[28] he said that in the previous eighteen months the word 'crisis' had often been used to describe the state of the criminal justice system. It was not too strong a word. Recorded crime had doubled, whilst the total number of people convicted or cautioned for those offences had fallen by 6 per cent since 1980.[29] There was much more crime and many more people were getting away with it. Home Office research showed that overall just one crime in fifty resulted in a conviction. For almost all crimes the proportion of offences resulting in a conviction had plummeted. For rape, it had fallen from 37 per cent in 1980 to 9 per cent in 1994. For domestic burglary, it had fallen from 9 per cent to 3 per cent over the same period. There was public alarm about the practice of cautioning by the police, and the Crown Prosecution Service did not command the public's confidence. Then came three crucial paragraphs:

> 12. Neighbourhoods have been seriously disrupted by the criminal anti-social behaviour of residents who often harass and intimidate law abiding people in their area so that their unlawful activities can continue unhindered. English criminal law is profoundly inefficient at dealing with chronic, allegedly lower level crime (including stalking) where it is the continuance of the bad behaviour which is so oppressive, and where the total impact of the crime is far greater than the sum of the parts.

[27] See a review by D. Garland of *The Local Governance of Crime*, *op. cit.* in 38 *Brit. J. Criminol.*, 1998, pp. 516–19. David Garland is Professor of Law and Sociology at New York University School of Law.

[28] Paper entitled *Honesty, Consistency and Progression in Sentencing*.

[29] The significance of using 1980 as the base date for the statistics was that it was the first full year after the Conservative Government came into power in 1979.

13. Persistent young offenders know that they can be arrested scores of times for offences like theft, burglary, taking and driving away, and may receive no worthwhile punishment or treatment.
14. On top of all this, there has been little action to tackle the underlying social and economic factors which help create environments in which crime may breed.[30]

It was to tackle this crisis that Labour had developed a strategy which was designed to be equally resolute in getting to grips with criminal offending and its causes. Labour wanted a society in which everyone had a stake, which gave everyone a realistic opportunity of sharing in its prosperity, and where there was a proper balance between rights and responsibilities. An effective criminal justice system which protected people and their communities[31] against crime was one part of that strategy. A high priority would be given to the partnership approach to crime reduction and prevention, and to better detection leading to a greater likelihood that criminals would be convicted. Five specific proposals were made, three of them relating to community safety and measures aimed at countering offending or anti-social behaviour by young people. They were:

- a new, pro-active approach to persistent criminal behaviour, like anti-social neighbourhood disruption, and stalking, with new preventative orders which build on the best of the civil and criminal law, and avoid the worst;
- an overhaul of the Crown Prosecution Service, with Crown Prosecutors for each police force area;
- major reforms to the youth justice service;
- effective regulation of the private security industry so that it works always in support of the police, and stops being a haven for serious criminals;

[30] *Honesty, Consistency and Progression in Sentencing*, *op. cit.*, p. 2.

[31] Although intended to imply a spirit of mutual co-operation and a sense of obligation towards the weak or vulnerable, communities can be defined also in terms of exclusivity. Easily recognizable communities which are based on culture, religion, occupation, or geographical location may implicitly exclude those who do not qualify for membership or conform to their requirements. For this reason, David Faulkner prefers the term citizenship. See his chapter on 'Public Services, Citizenship, and the State: the British Experience, 1967–97', in M. Freedland and S. Sciarra, *Public Services and Citizenship in European Law*, Clarendon Press, Oxford, 1998, p. 41. Before his retirement from the Civil Service, Faulkner had been the senior Home Office official responsible for the preparation of the Criminal Justice Act 1991. See *Responses to Crime*, Vol. 2, Chs. 5, 6, and 9. His book, entitled *Crime, State and Citizen*, was published by Waterside Press, Winchester, in June 2001.

- new duties on local authorities, in conjunction with the police, to develop community safety and crime prevention programmes and to take account of crime in all the decisions they make.[32]

Under the rubric 'We will be tough on crime and tough on the causes of crime' each of these proposals, save for the commitment to regulate the private security industry, was included in the draft Manifesto entitled *The Road to the Manifesto*, which was approved by the National Executive Committee (NEC) of the Labour Party on 2 July 1996. The document was then submitted to a vote by the party membership as a whole following the annual party conference in the Autumn, despite initial objections by the NEC that such a ballot would undermine the authority of conference. But Blair saw it as a way of binding to the party's policies those who might be discontented with the direction and pace of modernisation.[33] He did not want too detailed or comprehensive a programme, both to avoid giving hostages to fortune, and because of his conviction that 'promises should be concrete, costed and deliverable'.[34]

Well before the general election was called on 18 March 1997 Labour was fully prepared and impatient for the campaign to begin. The section on crime took up no more than two pages of the Manifesto. The headings were plain and direct: Youth Crime, Conviction and Sentencing, Disorder, Drugs, Victims, Prevention, and Gun Control.[35] Although the phrases designed to catch the eye at the head of the page were inevitably populist in tone, referring to police 'on the beat and not pushing paper', and a 'crackdown' on petty crimes and neighbourhood disorder, the substantive proposals for legislative change were more soberly worded, reflecting the work that had been done so thoroughly and for so long.

[32] *Honesty, Consistency and Progression in Sentencing*, *op. cit.*, p. 3.

[33] 'Modernise' and 'modernisation' are key words in the vocabulary of New Labour. As such, the ending with an 's' rather than a 'z' has been used consistently in Government documents since 1997 and is followed in this book.

[34] Butler and Kavanagh, *The British General Election of 1997*, *op. cit.*, pp. 53 and 62.

[35] In March 1996 sixteen children aged five and six, and one of their teachers, were shot and killed at a school at Dunblane in Scotland. Ten other pupils and three teachers were wounded. Thomas Hamilton, a man without any criminal record, fired 105 rounds with a self-loading pistol over the space of three or four minutes before shooting and killing himself. See Lord Cullen, *The Public Inquiry into the Shootings at Dunblane Primary School on 13 March 1996* (Cm. 3386), the Scottish Office, Edinburgh, 1996, p. 1. The scale of this outrage led to renewed demands for stricter controls on the possession of firearms.

The most specific commitment illustrated the influence of Labour's marketing advisers rather than their policy-makers. It was at their insistence, but with Blair's consent, that five pledges were added at the end of the election Manifesto. These had originated from intensive testing of focus groups, composed of traditional Conservative voters who were considering switching to Labour, in order to discover the issues of most direct concern to them and on which they wanted to see government action.[36] The wording of the single pledge on crime, reproduced for the campaign on a pocket-sized card in the form of a contract between Blair and the electorate, was 'Fast-track punishment for persistent young offenders by halving the time from arrest to sentencing'.[37]

According to Philip Gould, a political strategist who contributed to Labour's recovery after its long period of decline, and ultimately to victory in the general election of 1997, the credit for repositioning Labour as a party that would be tough both on crime and its causes belongs to Tony Blair. In a speech shortly after the abduction and beating to death in 1993 of a two-year-old child, James Bulger, by two boys aged ten, Blair had for the first time publicly attacked the liberal individualist consensus that had developed over crime, using the language of punishment and right and wrong:

> I believe that the breakdown in order is intimately linked to the break up of community. The importance of the notion of community is that it defines the relationship not only between us as individuals but between people and the society in which they live, one that is based on responsibilities as well as rights, on obligations as well as entitlements.
>
> . . . The historic problem of old socialism was the tendency to subsume the individual, rights, duties and all, within ideas of the 'public good', that at its worst came simply to mean the state. The failure of the present right is to believe that the absence of community means the presence of freedom. The task is to retrieve the notion of community from a narrow view of the state and put it to work again for the benefit of us all. A new community with a modern concept of citizenship is well overdue.[38]

[36] Philip Gould brings out the differences of opinion over the pledges between the communicators and the politicians in the Labour campaign in *The Unfinished Revolution*, *op. cit.*, pp. 267–72.

[37] *New Labour: Because Britain Deserves Better*, 1997, p. 40.

[38] Campaigns and Communications Directorate, the Labour Party, *News Release* of a speech by Tony Blair MP to Wellingborough Constituency Labour Party, 19 Feb. 1993.

'Perhaps more than anything', Gould wrote five years later, 'this change in perspective towards crime reconnected Labour with its electoral base.'[39] Most people, he continued, believe in punishment. They believe in right and wrong, and discipline and order:

> That for so long Labour denied this, that they sought to excuse the inexcusable on grounds of education, class or other disadvantages, was unacceptable to large numbers of the electorate who suffered the consequences of crime on a daily basis. Now, what Blair said seems common sense; then, it seemed, in the annals of many on the left, iconoclastic.[40]

III

Following the general election in May 1997 the Labour Party returned to power after an interval of eighteen years. Unlike either Margaret Thatcher or John Major, the new Prime Minister had a keen interest in, and knowledge of, criminal policy. More than that, as a strategist above all else, he saw how policies designed to combat crime and allay the fears of so many people was part of his wider appeal to the electorate. With an overall majority of 179 seats in the House of Commons, Tony Blair came to office with a considered set of policies, worked out over a lengthy period, which had gained support from much of informed opinion, as well as being able to rely on a Parliamentary majority so substantial that it was unlikely he would encounter any insuperable difficulties in implementing them.

The new Home Secretary had shadowed Michael Howard for three years. Although he had sometimes been worsted in adversarial exchanges across the floor, Jack Straw had earned the respect of both the House of Commons and a wider public as a man of substance and integrity. Far from being discordant with the values of New Labour, his disciplinarian and communitarian instincts ran with the tide. He was in favour of consultation with interested parties before governmental proposals were in their final shape, followed by firm action to see them through.

To ease the way for the onerous legislative programme necessary to implement the policies formulated in Opposition, Straw set up a task force on youth justice on 17 June 1997. The aim was two-fold: to maintain the momentum in reconciling pre-election policies with

[39] *The Unfinished Revolution, op. cit.*, p. 188.

[40] Ibid., p. 189.

the practicalities of government and the availability of resources, and to preserve and extend the contacts that had been forged with the police, the probation service, the magistracy, the statutory social services, and non-governmental organizations. Each of these, together with the Home Office, the Department of Health, and the Lord Chancellor's Department, was represented on the task force, with Norman Warner as chairman. The secretary, a civil servant on secondment to the Home Office from the Treasury, had acquired a fund of special knowledge as one of the authors of the Audit Commission report, *Misspent Youth*.[41]

Other action in the first weeks or months of the new Parliament included an announcement by the Prime Minister on 22 May at his first question and answer session with the public after the General Election that preventing witness intimidation and helping victims of crime was a Government priority, and confirming that an additional £1 million would be granted to Victim Support to expand its work and set up a national helpline.[42] On 24 July, as part of a wider review of Government spending, the Home Secretary announced a major investigation of the efficiency and effectiveness of the criminal justice system, including a review of his Department's £11.6 billion budget.[43]

On 1 September two short statutes inherited from the previous Government were brought into effect. The Sex Offenders Act 1997 required persons who had been convicted of certain sexual offences to notify to the police their name and home address, together with any subsequent changes of residence or name. There was no public access to information about the identity or the whereabouts of sex offenders. The second was the Knives Act 1997. This made it an offence to market[44] a knife in a way that indicated or suggested it was suitable for combat, or to stimulate or encourage violent behaviour. The Bill had been introduced by two back-benchers in the aftermath of the publicity following the killing of a popular schoolmaster, Philip Lawrence, who had been knifed to death outside his school.

[41] *Op. cit.* Mark Perfect, Secretary of the task force, was subsequently appointed as the first Secretary of the Youth Justice Board established by Section 41 of the Crime and Disorder Act 1998.

[42] The Victim Supportline was launched by the Home Secretary, Jack Straw, on 25 Feb. 1998.

[43] Home Office, *News Release*, 179/97, 24 July 1997.

[44] For the purposes of the Knives Act 1997 a person markets a knife if he sells or hires it, or offers or exposes it for sale or hire, or has it in his possession for the purpose of sale or hire.

Although a private member's Bill, it had been drafted with the assistance of government draftsmen and had the backing of business managers in the House of Commons.

The Knives Act, which came into force on 1 September 1997, was a prime example of reactive legislation, inspired by public indignation but resulting in very few prosecutions or convictions. During the two and a quarter years following its enactment there were no more than ten prosecutions under the Act in England and Wales, resulting in only three convictions.[45] More controversial than the Knives Act or the notification of the whereabouts of sex offenders was the issue of firearms regulation. With the tragedy of Dunblane still fresh in the public mind, many of the newly elected Members of Parliament wanted to go further than the partial ban on the possession of handguns which had been enacted in the dying days of the previous Parliament. By free votes in both Houses the category of prohibited weapons was extended to include small-calibre pistols.[46]

Another inheritance from the Conservative administration provided a precedent for what was to become one of the most strongly criticized provisions of the Crime and Disorder Bill when it was published in December 1997. The Protection from Harassment Act 1997 had created a novel mix of civil and criminal remedies for a 'course of conduct' which a reasonable person knows or ought to know amounted to harassment of another.[47] If proved, such conduct would be subject either to an injunction or to a civil action for damages. Breach of an injunction would be a criminal offence punishable on conviction by a term of imprisonment or a fine, or both. The criminal sections of the 1997 Act were not due to come into effect until 1 September 1998 and so there was no experience of the operation of the Act to draw upon. Nevertheless the objections of principle to the recourse to penal sanctions to enforce civil orders designed to counter anti-social behaviour were the same: the standard of proof would be lower than in a criminal trial; the behaviour

[45] *Parl. Debates*, HL, 608 (5th ser.), cols. WA 209, 27 Jan. 2000.

[46] The House of Lords further amended the Firearms (Amendment) Bill by exempting disabled persons from the ban on small-calibre weapons, and also those taking part in international shooting competitions. These amendments were rejected by the Commons and defeated by large majorities when sent back to the Lords. *Parl. Debates*, HL, 583, cols. 106–7 and 112–13, 11 Nov. 1997. The statute was enacted as the Firearms (Amendment) (No. 2) Act 1997.

[47] For a commentary on the Act, see T. Lawson-Cruttenden and N. Addison, *Blackstone's Guide to the Protection from Harassment Act 1997*, Blackstone Press, London, 1997.

complained of might fall short of criminal conduct; and the penalties were disproportionate.[48]

In the early stages of consultation the anti-social behaviour order was described as the community safety order. This reflected its origins in the pre-election process of policy-making when it had been conceived as a much needed protection for many people whose lives were made a misery by neighbourhood disorder. Not only did the policy fit well with the approach of New Labour, but it was close to the heart of the new Home Secretary. As a fourteen-year-old boy in a one-parent family living on a housing estate, Jack Straw had witnessed a dispute with some unruly neighbours which culminated in a physical assault on his mother. Later on, as an MP, he disclosed that he had always empathized with constituents experiencing the effects of neighbourhood disorder and understood how they felt.[49]

Even before Straw had become Shadow Home Secretary, while John Smith was Leader of the Opposition, as Environment spokesman he had been working with Blair, then the Home Affairs spokesman, on a joint paper on policies designed to counter the problems caused by disorder in reducing the quality of life. Although John Smith's early death and Tony Blair's succession as Party Leader meant that the paper was never completed, it left Straw with an ambition to legislate on improving the quality of life by initiating action against disorder. When the new ministerial team arrived at the Home Office, officials were surprised to find out how much detail had been worked out in advance.[50]

The change in the title of the proposed order, and the complex problems of defining the offending behaviour and remedies, came about after a consultation paper titled *Community Safety Order* had been published and the replies considered. There were 185 in all, five of which expressed concern about the appropriateness of the title. Four suggested it should be changed to 'anti-social behaviour (or conduct) order'. Responsive though the Government wished to appear (within

[48] Under both the Protection from Harassment Act 1997 and the Crime and Disorder Act 1998 the penalties were the same. If without reasonable excuse a person does anything he is prohibited from doing by an order of the court he shall be liable on summary conviction to imprisonment for a term not exceeding six months, or a fine not exceeding the statutory maximum, or both. On indictment a person found guilty of an offence is liable to imprisonment for a term not exceeding five years, or a fine, or both. Section 5(6) of the Protection from Harassment Act 1997 and Section 1(10) of the Crime and Disorder Act 1998.

[49] BBC Radio 4, *Desert Island Discs*, 12 July 1998.

[50] Author's interview with Jack Straw, 5 Jan. 1998.

limits) to the views of those consulted, this hardly seemed sufficient to make a change. More weighty were the views of the departmental officials at the Home Office and the draftsman of the legislation, now close to its final stages of preparation. They concluded that the title 'community safety order' was confusing, especially since they were at that time describing what later became the 'sex offender order' as the 'community protection order'. The title 'anti-social behaviour order' was preferred on the grounds that it retained the element of community relevance in the use of the term 'social', but pinpointed more accurately what the order was actually about.[51]

Consultation in advance of the introduction of legislation on crime and disorder in the first session of Parliament was on a scale unrivalled since the preliminaries to the Criminal Justice Act 1991. No less than nine consultation documents were issued by the Home Office between 9 September and 5 November 1997 (see Table 3) and summaries of the replies were placed in the Libraries of both Houses of Parliament.[52]

Table 3. *Crime and Disorder Bill: Consultation Documents, 1997*

Title	Publication date
Community Safety Order	9 September 1997
Drug Treatment and Testing Order*	Mid-September 1997
Getting to Grips with Crime: A New Framework for Local Action	17 September 1997
Tackling Youth Crime	25 September 1997
Racial Violence and Harassment	2 October 1997
New National and Local Focus on Youth Crime	9 October 1997
Tackling Delays in the Youth Justice System	15 October 1997
Reducing Remand Delays*	23 October 1997
Community Protection Order	5 November 1997

* Informal consultation documents

[51] Letter to the author from Norman Warner, 9 Feb. 1998.

[52] In addition to the anti-social behaviour order, three other consultation papers on the reform of the youth justice system attracted a substantial response. By 8 Dec.1997 a total of 297 responses had been received to the consultation paper *Tackling*

Useful though the consultative process was as a means of disseminating practical information to many of those who would have a responsibility for implementing the new policies, some sceptics regarded it as not being genuinely consultative since it did not allow for objections of principle directed towards the purpose or method of the new orders. An example was the lack of any scope for comments on the consistency or otherwise of the prohibitory anti-social behaviour order (as it became) with the provisions of the European Convention on Human Rights. Although once in Government the Lord Chancellor, Lord Irvine of Lairg,[53] became publicly identified with the incorporation of the Convention into domestic law, Whitehall boundaries determined that the legislation fell within the purview of the Home Office. Since the same boundaries were reflected in Labour's Shadow ministerial teams, it was Warner who had drafted the original consultation paper on this topic for Straw before the election. In doing so he drew on discussions with others at some 'preparation for government' seminars held at Templeton College, Oxford. When the time came the Home Office bid for the Bill in the first Queen's Speech, and it was the Home Office that prepared the White Paper, drafted the instructions for Parliamentary Counsel, and serviced the Bill during its passage through Parliament.

Since so much of the preliminary consultation, on the human rights issue as well as the changes in criminal policy, had taken place before the election, it is probably more accurate to describe the pre-legislative process as informative rather than consultative, at least in terms of those policy intentions which had been the subject of such long drawn-out preparation. There the Government's mind was made up.

The next stage was the publication on 27 November of a White Paper, sternly entitled *No More Excuses—A New Approach to Tackling Youth Crime in England and Wales*.[54] In a statement to the House of Commons, the Home Secretary reiterated that there could be no more excuses for youth crime. Members would have seen the problems in their own constituencies. There were children whose

Youth Crime, 250 responses to the consultation paper *New National and Local Focus on Youth Crime*, and 177 responses to the consultation paper *Tackling Delays in the Youth Justice System*. *Parl. Debates*, HC, 303, col. 7 WA, 15 Dec. 1997.

[53] QC, 1978; Recorder of the Crown Court, 1985–8; Deputy High Court Judge, 1987–97. Created a life peer 1987; Opposition spokesman in the House of Lords on legal affairs and Shadow Lord Chancellor, 1992–7. Lord Chancellor since 1997.

[54] Cm. 3809, 1997.

misbehaviour went unchecked and escalated into crime, and children who offended repeatedly, with no meaningful intervention, and came to court only for their cases to be adjourned time after time. When finally sentenced, many received no more than a conditional discharge. There was no punishment, no chance for them to make amends, and no action to tackle the cause of their offending. One of the fundamental deficiencies of the youth justice system, Straw said, was that different agencies worked to different, even conflicting, objectives. The Crime and Disorder Bill, shortly to be introduced, would make it clear for the first time that the principal aim of the youth justice system was to prevent offending by young people. All youth justice practitioners would be under a duty to take account of that aim.[55] For them too, the unspoken message was, there would be no more excuses.

IV

If the full range of Manifesto commitments was to be implemented as early as possible in the new Parliament, the Government's business managers were faced with a heavy legislative programme. To spread the load it was decided to start the Bills on criminal justice and law reform in the House of Lords. They contained proposals on crime and disorder, far-reaching changes in the system of youth justice, additional protection for vulnerable and intimidated witnesses, the reform of legal aid, and the incorporation into domestic law of the European Convention on Human Rights. Bills to enable referendums to be held before any devolution of powers to Scotland and Wales, and for a referendum on setting up a Greater London Authority, as well as legislation on education and social security, would start in the elected House.

Co-ordinating a timetable for the despatch of business by two such dissimilar assemblies as the Lords and Commons in each Parliamentary session depends on unwritten conventions and a degree of tolerance by the leaders and whips of the main parties in each House. The Commons recognized that the legal expertise of the Lords, as well as a strong interest in criminal justice issues, qualified it to make the initial scrutiny of Labour's pre-election policies once they

55 *Parl. Debates*, HC, 301, col. 1089, 27 Nov. 1997.

had been translated into legislative form. Few, if any, of the main features were likely to provoke controversy to the point of rejection. Moreover, there was a strong front-bench team composed of Lords Irvine of Lairg, Williams of Mostyn, and Falconer of Thoroton.[56] All three quickly earned the respect of their ministerial colleagues, while both Irvine and Falconer had the additional advantage of having been close personal friends and professional colleagues of the Prime Minister during his years in Opposition and earlier career at the Bar. As Lord Chancellor, Irvine had been deeply involved in consultations and negotiations with the higher judiciary, the Bar Council, the Law Society, and other professional associations over the preliminaries to the Human Rights and Access to Justice Bills, while Williams and Falconer had shown themselves sensitive in their handling of representations by penal reform groups[57] and organized special interests.

The Crime and Disorder Bill received its Second Reading on 16 December 1997 in the House of Lords. It was a long Bill of ninety-six clauses on introduction, which had grown to 121 sections and ten schedules by the time of its enactment seven months later. In addition to the anti-social behaviour orders, designed to control persons acting in a way likely to cause harassment, alarm, or distress, there were sex offender, child safety, and parenting orders. The *doli incapax* rule[58] was to be abolished, and local authorities would have power to declare child curfews. Repeated police cautions for children and young persons would be replaced by a single reprimand and final warning. A new structure for the system of youth justice, both national and local, was set out, with additional time-limits applicable to persons aged under eighteen. Detention and training orders were to be introduced for young offenders, and drug treatment and testing orders for offenders aged sixteen or over. A novel form of extended sentence, part custodial and part to be served on licence in the community after release, augmented the sentencing powers of the

[56] QC, 1991. Created a life peer in 1997. Solicitor General, 1997–8; Minister of State, Cabinet Office, 1998–.

[57] The main penal reform groups which seek to influence criminal justice legislation are JUSTICE, NACRO (the National Association for the Care and Resettlement of Offenders), the Howard League for Penal Reform, the Prison Reform Trust, and Liberty (the National Council for Civil Liberties). Each of these organizations is a member of the Penal Affairs Consortium, numbering thirty-four organizations in February 1998. By June 2000 the total had increased to thirty-nine.

[58] *Doli incapax* means inability to commit evil. Under this rule children aged between ten and fourteen were presumed to be incapable of committing a criminal offence unless the presumption could be rebutted by the prosecution.

courts, and a number of new offences of racially aggravated violence and harassment were created. The Court of Appeal would have an obligation to produce sentencing guidelines, and would be assisted by a sentencing panel acting as an advisory body.[59] The death penalty was to be abolished for treason and piracy.[60]

An unusual feature of statute law was the duty imposed on local authorities and the police to exercise their various functions 'with due regard' to their likely effect, and the need to do all they reasonably could to prevent crime and disorder in their areas.[61] While avoiding the word 'duty', earlier clauses had placed local authorities and the police under an obligation to co-operate in the formulation and implementation of crime reduction strategies. The only previous precedent was to be found in Section 71 of the Race Relations Act 1976 which required both local and police authorities to ensure that their various functions were carried out 'with due regard' to the need to eliminate unlawful racial discrimination and to promote equality of opportunity and good relations between persons of different racial groups.

At the start of the decade, during the preparation of the Criminal Justice Act 1991, there had been much discussion within the Home Office whether the duty imposed by Section 71 of the Race Relations Act 1976 should be extended to the criminal justice system as a whole. In the upshot, it was considered inappropriate for the courts to have to interpret a general duty of this kind. The result was a curious oddity tacked onto the end of the Criminal Justice Act 1991. Section 95 required the Secretary of State to publish each year such information as he considered expedient for the purpose of enabling persons engaged in the administration of criminal justice to become

[59] The items listed in the text are only a selection of the provisions of the Crime and Disorder Bill as introduced in December 1997. For a comprehensive and informative description of the contents of the legislation, see R. Leng, R. D. Taylor, and M. Wasik, *Blackstone's Guide to the Crime and Disorder Act 1998*, Blackstone Press, London, 1998.

[60] These obsolete provisions dated from the Treason Act of 1814 and the Piracy Act of 1837. Abolition of the last remaining civilian offences carrying the death penalty enabled the United Kingdom to ratify the Sixth Protocol to the European Convention on Human Rights 1982, Article 1 of which provided for the abolition of the death penalty in peacetime. See R. G. Hood, *The Death Penalty*, second revised and updated edition, Clarendon Press, Oxford, 1996, pp. 10–15, 227–8. The Protocol was signed by the Home Secretary on 27 Jan. 1999, and subsequently ratified by both Houses of Parliament.

[61] This formulation was enacted unchanged in Section 17(1) of the Crime and Disorder Act 1998.

aware of the financial implications of their decisions, or facilitating the performance by such persons of their duty to avoid discriminating against any person on the grounds of race or sex, or any other improper ground.[62]

For understandable reasons, draftsmen have always disliked duties such as those contained in Section 71 of the Race Relations Act 1976. The objections are that there is no obvious mechanism for the effective enforcement of duties expressed in such general terms, and that for all practical purposes such provisions are little more than declaratory.[63] Similar objections could have been applied to the statutory principal aim of the youth justice system in Section 37(1) of the Crime and Disorder Act 1998: 'It shall be the principal aim of the youth justice system to prevent offending by children and young persons', for which it was hard to find any real precedent. The aim overlaid, but did not supersede, existing statutory provisions governing welfare considerations, notably in the Children and Young Persons Act 1933 and the Children Act 1989, and the justice considerations of the Criminal Justice Act 1991. There was no pre-existing statutory provision setting out the principal aim or purpose for the youth justice system.

To the new Government and its advisers such pedantic reservations were less compelling than the unequivocal message conveyed to all those who would have the responsibility for making the Act work. If statutory exhortations were instrumental in developing a positive spirit of commitment and co-operation by the services to which they applied, then that would be justification enough. If the notion of local authority audits and action plans, including targets for reducing crime, could not guarantee compliance with statutory duties in a legal sense, at least they could ensure that an awareness of such duties was not divorced from the practical function of service delivery. Viewed in

[62] Nearly a decade later, replying to a Parliamentary Question on how the obligation placed on the Secretary of State by Section 95 of the Criminal Justice Act 1991 had been interpreted in the intervening years, the Government replied that it regularly produced statistics and research reports on the criminal justice system which included information on race, gender, and costs as required under Section 95. A number of relevant publications were cited. *Parl. Debates*, HL, 617, col. WA 9, 9 Oct. 2000.

[63] The only available form of enforcement would be by an application to the High Court for judicial review. If it could be shown that a person making a decision had disregarded an objective to which it was his statutory duty to have regard, then the decision could be upset. See Lord Lloyd of Berwick, *Parl. Debates*, HL, 597, col. 335, 11 Feb. 1999.

that light, the creation of statutory duties was part of a wider perspective.[64]

Sections 5 and 6 of the Crime and Disorder Act 1998 required each of the responsible local authorities to co-operate with the police, probation committee, health authority, and any person or body prescribed by order of the Secretary of State, in formulating and implementing a strategy for the reduction of crime and disorder in their areas. Before formulating its strategy the responsible authority would be obliged to carry out a review of the levels and patterns of crime and disorder in the area; to prepare an analysis of the review; to publish a report of the analysis; and to obtain views on the report of persons or bodies in the area, whether by holding public meetings or otherwise. That was not the end of it. Section 6(4) required that the strategy should include the objectives to be pursued both by the responsible authorities and co-operating persons or bodies, or other persons acting under agreements with the responsible authorities. Long-term and short-term performance targets were required for measuring the extent to which the objectives were reached. After formulating a strategy, Section 6(5) required the publication of a document including details of co-operating persons or bodies, as well as the review, the report, and the strategy, and in particular stating objectives and performance targets.

Remarkable as it is to find what was essentially a code of good practice incorporated into primary legislation in such prescriptive detail, it was a characteristic example of a significant new trend in public policy-making. It stemmed from the same pre-election determination to communicate effectively a detailed strategy that had been carefully thought out, without allowing scope for deviations which would diffuse its impact. Once in office, a stream of administrative instructions was issued, with a directive force which would have been regarded as bordering on the constitutionally improper in the days of the Wilson and Callaghan Governments. Yet the Prime

[64] In September 1998 the Home Office published a protocol or framework document to support the statutory aim in Section 37(1) of the Crime and Disorder Act 1998. It had been proposed by the Home Secretary's Youth Justice Task Force and included in the White Paper, *No More Excuses*. The document was prepared by six Government departments in close consultation with a wide range of bodies and individuals involved in the Youth Justice system. It set out how the relevant agencies should work together to meet the principal statutory aim of preventing offending by children and young persons, and the associated non-statutory objectives. *Crime and Disorder Act 1995, Youth Justice: The statutory principal aim of preventing offending by children and young people*, The Home Office, Communication Directorate, 1998.

Minister and leadership of the Labour Party were hardly alone in regarding the purpose of politics as winning power through elections. What distinguished New Labour from its predecessors was the way in which it carried through the techniques forged in Opposition into Government, with the stated intention of remaining there for longer than one Parliament.

V

The anticipated challenge to the anti-social behaviour order, although it could not fail to attract notice since it was conspicuously placed in the first clause of the Crime and Disorder Bill, never materialized in either House. A powerful critique of the proposal had been published by six eminent academic lawyers and criminologists,[65] and supported by others.[66] The order was denounced as being neither sensible nor carefully targeted. It took sweepingly defined conduct within its ambit, granted local agencies virtually unlimited discretion to seek highly restrictive orders, jettisoned fundamental legal protections for the grant of such orders, and authorized potentially draconian and wholly disproportionate penalties for violations of them. While the Government claimed that the measure was aimed at those who terrorize their neighbours, its actual reach was much broader and covered a wide spectrum of conduct deemed 'anti-social', whether criminal or not. The authors regretted that one of the Government's first major proposals on criminal justice policy was of such a character.[67]

It might have been anticipated that even such forthright objections would cut little ice in the Commons, where a large majority of MPs had so recently been elected with a Manifesto commitment to

[65] A. Ashworth (Vinerian Professor of English Law, Oxford), J. Gardner (Reader in Legal Philosophy, King's College, London), R. Morgan (Professor of Criminal Justice, Bristol), A. T. H. Smith (Professor of Criminal and Public Laws, Cambridge), A. von Hirsch (Hon. Professor of Penal Theory and Penal Law, Cambridge), and M. Wasik (Professor of Law, Manchester), 'Neighbouring on the Oppressive: The Government's "Anti-Social Behaviour Order" Proposals', 16 *Criminal Justice*, Feb. 1998, pp. 7–14. The article had been widely circulated before publication.

[66] See A. Rutherford, 'A Bill to be tough on crime', 148 *New Law Journal*, 9 Jan. 1998, pp. 13–14. Andrew Rutherford is Professor of Law and Criminal Policy at the University of Southampton and was Chairman of the Howard League for Penal Reform, 1983–99.

[67] A. Ashworth and others, *op. cit.*, pp. 7–8.

introduce legislation to tackle the unacceptable level of anti-social behaviour.[68] Nor were the Conservative survivors from the previous Parliament likely to be any better disposed since the right of an aggrieved person to seek a civil order from the courts, with criminal sanctions for breach, closely resembled the Protection from Harassment Act which had been passed into law the previous year while their own party was still in office. More surprisingly, the rift between the professors and the politicians extended also to the Lords. Although all of the front-bench spokesmen when a series of amendments to the clause were debated in Committee on 3 February 1997 were lawyers (four QCs and one non-practising barrister),[69] with two retired law lords taking part, none of the amendments were pressed to a division.

When asked by the veteran Labour solicitor, Lord Mishcon,[70] if he was aware of the anxiety within the legal profession to see more precise definitions of what was involved, Lord Williams of Mostyn replied that he was aware of the anxiety, but believed it to be misconceived. The anti-social behaviour order was 'merely a prohibition . . . analogous to an injunction'.[71] The prohibited activity was limited only in so far as it was necessary to protect people in the area concerned from harassment, alarm, or distress. The wording of Clause 1, he claimed, was precise and had been very carefully considered. In summary, the Minister's argument was that a complainant would not have direct access to a Magistrates' court acting in a civil capacity, but would need to convince the local authority or the police to apply for an order after consultation with each other because, in the wording of the Bill, the person whose behaviour was complained of had acted:

> in an anti-social manner, that is to say, in a manner that caused or was likely to cause harassment, alarm or distress to one or more persons not of the same household as himself,[72]

[68] *New Labour: Because Britain Deserves Better*, 1997, p. 23.

[69] Lords Williams of Mostyn (Lab.), Falconer of Thoroton (Lab.), Goodhart (Lib. Dem.), and Thomas of Gresford (Lib. Dem.) were QCs, and Lord Henley (Con.) a member of the Bar.

[70] Senior Partner, Messrs Mishcon de Reya. Life peer, 1978; Opposition spokesman in the House of Lords on home affairs, 1983–90, and on legal affairs, 1983–92. Previously member and chairman of committees of London County Council, 1946–65, and Greater London Council (1964–7).

[71] *Parl. Debates*, HL, 585, col. 513, 3 Feb. 1998.

[72] Crime and Disorder Act 1998, Section 1(1)(a).

and that such an order was necessary to protect persons in the area from further anti-social acts. It would be a defence to an application that the behaviour was reasonable in the circumstances.

The most impressive speech in a long evening spent debating a clutch of amendments to Clause 1, which occupied four and a half hours, came from Lord Goodhart, a former Chairman of the Executive Committee of JUSTICE (1988–94), speaking from the Liberal Democrat front bench. Even he welcomed the anti-social behaviour order in principle as being 'capable of meeting a perceived need'.[73] His objections to the detailed terms were four, which to an extent endorsed the concerns of the academic lawyers. First, the threshold of the orders was too low; secondly, the power to make the order was not adequately defined or clarified; thirdly, the penalties for breach were excessive; and fourthly, the discretion of the courts was unreasonably restricted. Despite identifying these flaws, Liberal Democrats did not go as far as the academics, who had concluded that even with improvements the scheme was beyond redemption and should be abandoned altogether.[74] Total rejection, however, fell outside the boundaries of practical politics, and Government spokesmen in both Houses were eloquent in defending the Bill's provisions by emphasizing the plight of the people it was intended to benefit.

The prevailing Parliamentary sentiment, originating with Labour but broadly accepted by the other main parties, was that people living in poorer localities where crime and offensive behaviour were rampant, some of them vulnerable and lonely, others members of ethnic minorities, were entitled to a greater degree of protection than they were receiving. The press might be strident, the lawyers might argue, and test cases might come before the domestic courts or the Court of Human Rights in Strasbourg. But in Parliament at least it was a sign that a political consensus had begun to re-emerge after the long years when such an outcome had become increasingly rare. In this instance it could hardly be described as a liberal consensus, but that did not detract from its significance.[75]

[73] *Parl. Debates*, HL, 585, *op. cit.*, p. 14.

[74] 16 *Criminal Justice 1998*, *op. cit.*, p. 14.

[75] That the symbolism may have been more important than the reality was suggested by the sparing use made of anti-social behaviour orders by the courts initially. Between April 1999, when the relevant provisions of the Act came into force, and July 2000, only about ninety orders had been made in England and Wales. *Parl. Debates*, HL, 615, col. WA 86, 18 July 2000.

VI

Two other topics, neither of them to be found in the original Bill, interrupted its otherwise uneventful progress towards the statute book. The first was very familiar to regular participants in Lords' debates on criminal justice policies. It was the desire to resurrect an independent advisory council on the penal system, broadly comparable to the body which had been abolished in the early years of the Thatcher Government.[76] The second had even less connection with the content of the Bill, and appealed to a far wider constituency. In its final stages in the Commons, the Bill had become a vehicle for campaigners to reduce the age of consent for homosexual activity between males from eighteen to sixteen. The contrast between the two extra coaches hitched onto the legislative train as it neared the terminus could not have been more striking. One was a quintessential insider's issue, strongly felt and tenaciously argued by its protagonists, but with little or no public resonance. The other was special interest politics at its most intense, with the way of life of very many people directly affected by the outcome, and deep emotions aroused.

The proposal to establish a standing advisory council on criminal justice and the penal system attracted strong support from the judicial members of the House of Lords. The purpose of the clause, in the elegant phrasing of the Lord Chief Justice, Lord Bingham, when it was first debated in Committee, was:

> to provide the Home Secretary and the Government with a reservoir of wise, informed, objective and non-partisan advice on the important and intractable problems which confront him, them, and us.[77]

The prime mover in carrying an amendment against the Government on Third Reading was the retired law lord, Lord Ackner. He argued that a standing council could help to provide a wider understanding of the limited contribution that imprisonment can make to an effective law and order policy. The public should be made aware of the

[76] See *Responses to Crime*, Vol. 2, pp. 148–51, for an account of the reasons for the abolition of the Advisory Council on the Penal System in 1980. This was cited by Lord Hurd of Westwell, a former Home Secretary, in the House of Lords debate in Committee on 3 Mar. 1998 on an amendment to the Crime and Disorder Bill to re-establish a standing advisory council on criminal justice and the penal system. *Parl. Debates*, HL, 586, col. 1135, 3 Mar. 1998.

[77] Ibid., col. 1132.

very limited extent to which rehabilitation can be achieved when serious overcrowding was on the increase. Research was needed into the penal systems of other European countries to discover why their prison populations were significantly lower and how they had managed to persuade their publics to accept punishment within the community.[78] In the division lobby Ackner won the support of an impressive array of judicial and political elder statesmen.

Among those voting for the amendment were the previous Lord Chancellor, Lord Mackay of Clashfern; Lord Lane,[79] one of Bingham's predecessors as Lord Chief Justice; the former Lord Chief Justice of Northern Ireland;[80] two ex-Home Secretaries;[81] and three other Home Office ministers from an earlier era. Only the current Home Office minister, Lord Williams of Mostyn, and the Opposition spokesman, Lord Henley, argued against the proposal. Although the latter attempted to walk a tightrope, declaring that his party would be supporting neither the amendment nor the Government,[82] a significant number of Conservatives voted for the amendment, as did a majority of the Liberal Democrats, and a handful of Labour peers. But the real strength showed in the attraction of the idea of an independent advisory body to the cross-benchers. With the division coming at a convenient hour, just before half-past four on a Tuesday afternoon, the conditions for a successful challenge to the Government were at an optimum. The result was close, with the House voting by 114 to 105 in favour of the amendment.[83]

The Home Secretary had not been passive before the vote in the Lords. During the Report stage he had gone to some lengths to explain to a number of influential peers, including Hurd, the reasons why he was reluctant to accept the amendment. Bingham had been a primary target. On 16 March the Lord Chief Justice had called on Straw at the Home Office to discuss his concerns about several of the functions and powers of the youth courts, especially when exercisable by a single justice or by justices' clerks. The Home Secretary was

[78] *Parl. Debates*, HL, 588, col. 157, 31 Mar. 1998.

[79] Judge of the High Court of Justice, Queen's Bench Division, 1966–74; Lord Justice of Appeal, 1974–9; Lord of Appeal in Ordinary, 1979–80; Lord Chief Justice of England, 1980–92. Created a life peer on becoming a Law Lord in 1979. Member of the Parole Board, 1970–2 (Vice-Chairman, 1972).

[80] Lord Lowry. Judge of the High Court of Justice (N. I.), 1964–71; Lord Chief Justice of Northern Ireland, 1971–88; Lord of Appeal in Ordinary, 1988–94. Chairman, N. Ireland Constitutional Convention, 1975.

[81] Lord Jenkins of Hillhead and Lord Hurd of Westwell.

[82] *Parl. Debates*, HL, 588, *op. cit.*, col. 163.

[83] Ibid., cols. 170–2.

conciliatory, and offered some amendments to be tabled at Third Reading to meet Bingham's concerns, which also had been the subject of representations by the Magistrates' Association and the Justices' Clerks' Society. But by far the larger part of a lengthy letter which Straw sent to his visitor later the same day was devoted to a rehearsal of his objections to the proposal for an advisory council. Straw's personal imprint (rarely so evident in ministerial correspondence on detailed policy issues) justifies putting the relevant passages on record verbatim:

> We also discussed the proposal to establish an advisory council on criminal justice and the penal system. As I explained, I am not attracted to this idea. A standing advisory council of this sort seems to me to reflect past rather than present or future needs. The old Advisory Council on the Penal System may well have fulfilled a valuable role—although it certainly had its failings as well—but I believe that it had, in fact, come to the end of its useful life by the early 1980s. Other, more focused, sources of advice were already developing and have developed since then. These mean that Government has available to it a range of objective and informed advice which can be provided in a more flexible and responsive way than would have been the case with the old Advisory Council—or, indeed, than would be the case with any new standing body with a wide ranging remit.
>
> We have, for example, the Criminal Justice Consultative Council, . . . which as you know has on it representatives from across the whole range of the criminal justice system and which is underpinned by local, practitioner-level groups thus ensuring that it has a well informed understanding of the practicalities, as well as being able to take a broader and more strategic view when appropriate.
>
> Then there is the Trial Issues Group, also supported by sub-groups, which has a wealth of experience in practical and procedural issues, and Her Majesty's Chief Inspectors of Prisons and Probation, both of whom produce thematic reports on issues of concern in the penal field, for example. Added to these we have the Law Commission which advises on the adequacy and effectiveness of the criminal law, and the National Audit Office and the Audit Commission, both of which have a role to play in advising on efficiency and effectiveness in this area. As preparation for the reforms to youth justice, I established a very representative Youth Justice Task Force.
>
> When the Crime and Disorder Bill has completed its passage we will have two further bodies—the Youth Justice Board, which will provide advice on the operation of the youth justice system, and the Sentencing Advisory Panel which will need to have regard to the range of disposals available, their effectiveness and their appropriateness for different types of offence and offender when drawing up proposals for the Court of Appeal. It will, of

course, itself have the benefit of advice from a wide range of organisations, and will publish its advice.

Reading the debate on Lord Ackner's amendment I am struck that the prime concern of many is about sentencing policy, including numbers in prison. The gap here in advice really will be met I believe by the Sentencing Advisory Panel.

Taken together this is a formidable array of bodies which seems to me to cover the area of criminal justice/penal policy very effectively, as you will see from the annex to this letter, which attempts to set this out in tabular form. On top of them there is the House of Commons Select Committee on Home Affairs, whose terms of reference enable it to cover the whole area of criminal justice and penal policy and which consults widely, producing authoritative and well researched reports on a range of issues.

Ultimately it is the responsibility of Government, when bringing forward criminal justice and penal policy proposals, to consult all those concerned (and a separate Council could not substitute for the Government in that respect); to take decisions; and to submit its proposals to Parliamentary scrutiny: indeed, this is really at the heart of the debate. While I understand the desire for an 'apolitical' debate, issues relating to the criminal justice system and penal policy are so central to good order and government that I cannot see them ever being wholly free from political content, the more so when the effectiveness of measures to reduce crime is high in public concern.

This is not, of course, to say that as a Government we will not want to seek advice on new policy proposals when that would be helpful. As you know, we have already issued a series of consultation documents on a whole range of issues and I certainly do not rule out the possibility of drawing together groups of experts in particular fields to offer advice when that would be helpful, just as we have done, for example, with the Youth Justice Task Force.

You mentioned three particular issues on which you thought advice would be, or would have been, helpful—the whole question of juries in fraud trials; abolition of the right to jury trial for either-way cases, and Part II of the Crime (Sentences) Act. So far as the first two are concerned, they have, of course, already been the subject of considered, independent advice. The Roskill Committee examined the question of fraud trials and made specific proposals. As for the right to jury trial in either-way cases, this was dealt with by the Royal Commission on Criminal Justice before being considered further in the Narey Report. The issues and the evidence have been made widely available through both of these Committees—the question now is whether the Government considers further action is needed on either issue and on that we are consulting on the first and are proposing to consult on the second. The proposals in the Crime (Sentences) Act were clearly different and did not result from reports of this sort, although they were the subject of consultation in the previous Government's White Paper 'Protecting the Public'. Looking to the future these are all issues on which one or more of the bodies to which I have already referred would be available to offer advice.

In conclusion, therefore, I really do not believe that a standing advisory council of the sort proposed would bring added value to the process of policy development in this field. The area where we believe there may have been a gap in the information available to the courts has, with your help and support, been filled by the Sentencing Advisory Panel.

As a Government we remain, however, committed to openness and consultation and I can assure you that we will continue to consult widely and to listen to the views expressed not only by the established bodies in the field but also by other informed commentators.[84]

Annexed to the letter was a schedule showing the potential sources of advice available to the Home Secretary on the treatment of juveniles and adults by the criminal justice and penal system. It is reproduced as Table 4.

The reasoned arguments were not repeated by the Home Secretary when the Bill was debated by the Commons on Second Reading. Straw simply said that he had considered the proposal very carefully, and in the light of that consideration had decided to seek its deletion in Committee. The Bill already provided for a new sentencing advisory panel and a national Youth Justice Board. The Government had concluded that:

another unfocused body would cause unnecessary duplication and significant delay in dealing with the many problems of the criminal justice system.[85]

Only the Liberal Democrats supported the retention of the proposal, and the amendment was duly removed without any difficulties arising in the Commons. When the Bill returned to the Lords for consideration of Commons' amendments shortly before the Summer Recess, Ackner divided the House again on a motion to disagree with the Commons. By now much of his support had ebbed away and he attracted no more than sixty-six votes, with 127 peers against sending it back for further consideration.[86]

[84] Letter from the Home Secretary, Rt. Hon. Jack Straw, to the Rt. Hon. The Lord Bingham of Cornhill, Lord Chief Justice, 16 Mar. 1998.

[85] *Parl. Debates*, HC, 310, col. 378, 8 Apr. 1998.

[86] *Parl. Debates*, HL, 592, cols. 928–9, 22 July 1998.

Table 4. *Potential Sources of Advice on Criminal Justice and the Penal System, 1998*

	The law	Procedure	Sentencing/Treatment of offenders	Delivery
Juveniles	• Topic-specific Advisory Councils (e.g. on Juvenile Drinking) • Youth Justice Board	• Probable Crime and Disorder Act Inter-Agency Group(s) on Reparation Orders, Action Plan Orders, etc. • Youth Justice Board	• Youth Justice Board	• Social Services Inspectorate (DoH) • Youth Justice Board
Adults and Juveniles	• Law Commission • Topic-specific Advisory Councils (e.g. on the Misuse of Drugs) • House of Commons Select Committee on Home Affairs	• Trials Issues Group • Criminal Justice Consultative Council • Project-specific Inter-Agency Groups (e.g. Crime (Sentences) Act Pilot Steering Group) • House of Commons Select Committee on Home Affairs	• Sentencing Advisory Panel • Law Commission (e.g. Offences Against the Person) • HM Chief Inspector of Prisons • HM Chief Inspector of Probation • UK Anti-Drugs Co-Ordinator • House of Commons Select Committee on Home Affairs	• HM Chief Inspector of Prisons • HM Chief Inspector of Probation • Criminal Justice Consultative Council (Special Conferences) • Trials Issues Group • NAO • Audit Commission

Source: The Home Office, 1998.

VII

The origins of the second issue to enliven the closing stages of the Crime and Disorder Bill were even more remote from its content and purpose. In 1994 a young gay man, Euan Sutherland, supported by the campaigning organization Stonewall, had submitted an application to the European Commission of Human Rights in Strasbourg alleging a violation of Article 8 taken in conjunction with Article 14 of the Convention.[87] The basis of his complaint was that although the minimum age for lawful homosexual acts had been reduced from twenty-one to eighteen there was still discrimination against homosexuals in that the age of consent for heterosexual activity was sixteen. Two years later, after an oral hearing on 21 May 1996, the Commission found that Sutherland's application raised complex issues of law and fact which required determination on the merits. Consequently, by a majority of fourteen to four, it was declared admissible and referred to the Court.[88]

Before the preliminary finding was issued, and acting on legal advice, the Government decided not to contest it and instead to negotiate with Sutherland, Stonewall, and one other applicant from the United Kingdom. Agreement was reached that the parties would stay their proceedings in the European Court of Human Rights on the basis of undertakings to be provided by the Government. These undertakings were then incorporated in a formal document lodged with the Court on 21 October 1997 inviting it to extend the time for receiving memorials or written observations pending completion of Parliamentary consideration. The first undertaking was that 'at the earliest appropriate opportunity' the Government would arrange for a free vote in the House of Commons on whether the age of consent for homosexual acts should be reduced from eighteen to sixteen. The second was that if a majority of MPs voted in favour of a reduction

[87] Application 25186/94. Euan Sutherland was aged sixteen at the time of the application. Article 8 of the Convention recognizes the right to respect for private and family life, home, and correspondence, and Article 14 protects freedom from discrimination.

[88] *Sutherland* v. *United Kingdom* (1997) 24 EHRR CD 22. For a description of the two-tier process at Strasbourg, see *Responses to Crime*, Vol. 2, ch. 8, 'Human Rights: Enforcing the Convention', pp. 347–403. The judgment of the European Court of Human Rights in the case of *Thynne, Wilson, and Gunnell* v. *United Kingdom* (1991) 13 EHRR 666 led to the judicialization of the procedures attached to discretionary life sentences. From 1 Nov. 1998 the procedure was reformed so that hearings were held only by an enlarged court sitting permanently, without a preliminary hearing on admissibility.

in the age of consent for homosexual acts to sixteen, then the Government would 'bring forward legislation to implement the will of Parliament' in time to be completed by the end of the next Parliamentary session at the latest.[89]

The next step came when the Crime and Disorder Bill, having completed its passage through the House of Lords, was in Committee in the Commons. Although the Government had earlier declined to include a provision lowering the age of consent in the Bill, this had not prevented a cluster of amendments being tabled by back-benchers for debate on the floor of the House at Report stage on 22 June 1998. The main one, a new clause tabled by Ann Keen, recently elected as a Labour MP and a campaigner for homosexual rights, aimed to eliminate what she said was regarded by many people as the discrimination inherent in a differential age of consent for certain sexual acts between males, or between a male and a female. Although equalizing the age of consent at sixteen was the predominant theme of the debate, a secondary issue was the concern of some MPs to increase the protection of sixteen- and seventeen-year-olds from any abuse of positions of authority, influence, or trust by persons who owed them a duty of care. Another amendment aimed to delete the requirement that no more than two males should be present when lawful homosexual acts took place in private.

There were no whips on, and the votes on the first two new clauses were cross-party. What was referred to as the privacy amendment was not put to a vote. In the first division, the proposal to equalize the age of consent at sixteen was carried by a majority of over two hundred, 336 voting for the new clause and 129 against.[90] Thirteen Labour members, including the Government Deputy Chief Whip, voted against, and seventeen Conservative members (including two shadow ministers) voted in favour. The Prime Minister, the Home Secretary, and eight other Cabinet ministers voted for the new clause. Neither the Leader of the Opposition nor the Leader of the Liberal Democrats were present for the vote. Ann Taylor and David Blunkett, both of whom had voted against a reduction to sixteen in 1994, and eight other members of the Cabinet did not vote.[91] In the

[89] Document lodged with the European Court of Human Rights, 21 Oct. 1997 in the cases of *Euan Sutherland* v. *United Kingdom*, and *Christopher Morris* v. *United Kingdom*. Copy placed in the Library of the House of Commons.

[90] *Parl. Debates*, HC, 314, cols. 805–8, 22 June 1998.

[91] House of Commons Library, *Research Paper 99/4*, pp. 24–5.

second division, an amendment by a Labour MP, Joe Ashton, setting the age of consent for both parties at eighteen where one party was in a position of authority, influence, or trust in relation to the other, was defeated by 234 votes to 194.[92]

The composition of the House of Lords enabled clergy as well as politicians to join the debate when the Bill was returned containing the new clause equalizing the age of consent. The Bishop of Winchester, intervening early in the debate on a motion moved by Baroness Young to disagree with the Commons amendment, said that his speech would represent the statements of the House of Bishops of the Church of England as published on 21 June. The Archbishop of Canterbury was prevented from attending because of the Lambeth Conference, but had explained in an article in *The Times* published that morning why he could not support a reduction in the age of consent to sixteen. There was a widespread assumption, the Bishop observed, that homosexual activity in general was as appropriate and desirable as heterosexual activity, with the choice between them presented as equal options, as it were on a supermarket shelf. Such an assumption was not consistent with the Christian teaching that sex was a gift of God for the enriching of lives within the context of marriage. It ought not to be treated casually and outside a strong framework of moral values. It was his belief that:

> Parliament should be very wary indeed about deserting the wisdom in these matters not only of the Christian faith but of the other major faiths too.[93]

Although he was supported later in the debate by the former Archbishop of York, Lord Habgood, the Bishop's Bench showed that it too had room for more than one view when the Bishop of Bath and Wells, currently Chairman of the Children's Society, spoke and voted in favour of the Commons amendment.[94]

More extreme than any of the Anglicans was the retired Chief Rabbi, Lord Jakobovits, who denounced the Sexual Offences Act 1956, which he described as having legitimized homosexual and other unnatural acts among consenting adults as a violation of the laws of God and nature that could not endure in the long run.[95]

[92] *Parl. Debates*, HC, 314, *op. cit.*, cols. 808–11.
[93] *Parl. Debates*, HL, 592, col. 943, 22 July 1998.
[94] He was joined in the Division Lobby by the Bishops of Lincoln and Oxford.
[95] Ibid., col. 950.

These speeches by religious leaders could not have been made either in the Commons or in a reformed Upper House based solely on election, and were an authoritative expression of opinion not otherwise available in a Parliamentary forum.

Lord Lester of Herne Hill, greatly experienced in the law and institutions of the European Convention on Human Rights, reminded the peers that the United Kingdom was bound by the Convention, and that by rejecting the Commons amendment, which he regarded as entirely plain, simple, and workable, restoring equality and nothing more, the Government would render itself unable to comply with its international treaty obligations.[96] To Lord Williams of Mostyn, replying from the Government front bench, the moral imperative was equality before the law. It was a matter of indifference whether it was equality for children of sixteen, for women, or for a black man trying to get work, for a Jew, or for a Moslem.[97] Despite his debating skill, it was evident that Baroness Young had the support of a clear majority while winding up. When the vote was taken, 290 peers voted against the new clause which had been added in the Commons, and 122 for it. As in the other House, there was some cross-party voting, with three former Conservative Cabinet Ministers supporting reduction to sixteen.

The disagreement between the two Houses left the Government in a quandary. The Commons vote had been a back-bench initiative, and carried the risk of delaying the enactment of the Crime and Disorder Bill until the late Autumn. If the Commons insisted on its amendment and sent it back to the Lords there was a distinct possibility that it would be rejected again, with the result that the Bill would not receive the Royal Assent before the Summer Recess as planned. On 28 July the Home Secretary persuaded a reluctant House of Commons not to insist on its amendment to equalize the age of consent for homosexual and heterosexual activity at the age of sixteen. He explained that the Crime and Disorder Bill was a major measure on law and order, giving effect to twelve Manifesto commitments that would have a significant impact on the safety and well-being of Members' constituents. Its provisions had been widely and enthusiastically welcomed by the public and the police, and received substantial support from both sides of the House.[98] Certain provisions were due to come into force on Royal Assent, which was

[96] *Parl. Debates*, HL, 592, col. 950. [97] Ibid., col. 968.

[98] *Parl. Debates*, HC, 317, cols. 176–211, 28 July 1998.

expected by the end of July, with the full implementation of a timetable containing about twenty-five separate items due to start on 30 September.

Straw gave an unequivocal commitment that the Government would honour the formal undertakings it had given in the document lodged with the European Court of Human Rights the previous year. This was to introduce separate legislation in the next session of Parliament so as 'to ensure a conclusive resolution of the issue on a free vote and remove the unjustified discrimination that has persisted for too long'.[99] With the front-bench spokesmen for the Conservatives and Liberal Democrats agreeing that the only course of action was for the Commons to accept the Lords' amendment, the outcome was never in doubt. That did not prevent Tony Benn from making an out-and-out attack on the House of Lords and its lack of accountability. When the Question was put he said that he would shout 'No' on principle. He did not expect any support, but at least he would have the satisfaction of making his voice heard in support of democracy.[100] After a lengthy debate, the Government motion was accepted without a vote.

The foresight of the Home Secretary in persuading his ministerial and party colleagues in the House of Commons to detach the intensely controversial issue of the age of consent from his Crime and Disorder Bill was borne out by subsequent events. Another two years were to pass before the legislative process eventually reached a conclusion. In accordance with Straw's undertaking, a Sexual Offences (Amendment) Bill was introduced early in the 1998–9 Parliamentary session. Its effect would be to make the age of consent for sexual activity the same for male homosexuals as for heterosexuals and lesbians: sixteen in England, Wales, and Scotland, and seventeen in Northern Ireland. At Second Reading in the Commons the Bill was agreed by 313 votes in favour to 130 against.[101] But when it reached the Lords, it was rejected on Second Reading by 222 to 146 votes,[102] and therefore fell in that session.

An identical Bill was introduced in the next session and again passed all stages in the Commons in February 2000. In the Lords it received a Second Reading on 11 April 2000, but faced further challenge at Committee stage on 13 November 2000. This time the Lords were aware that if the Bill was amended in a form unacceptable to the

[99] Ibid., col. 184. [100] Ibid., col. 197.
[101] *Parl. Debates*, HC, 324, cols. 110–13, 25 Jan. 1999.
[102] *Parl. Debates*, HL, 599, cols. 758–61, 13 Apr. 1999.

Commons, or defeated for a second time in successive sessions, the Government could then use its powers under the Parliament Act 1911, as amended in 1949, to pass the Bill into law without the consent of the Lords. Notwithstanding the likelihood of this outcome, a series of amendments were carried at Committee stage, again by a comfortable majority of 205 to 144.[103] Their effect was to accept, although without any real consensus, the principle of equalizing the age of consent for homosexual or heterosexual acts for both males and females at sixteen, but to make eighteen the minimum age for lawful anal intercourse, whether by consenting males or females.

The compromise was acceptable neither to the Government nor to the campaigners for homosexual equality, nor, perhaps more crucially, to several child welfare charities. The NSPCC, for example, was on record as supporting a uniform age of consent at sixteen for both homosexual and heterosexual relations.[104] It was already near the end of the Parliamentary session and time was running out. No Report or Third Reading stages were scheduled, with the result that the Bill had not been passed by the Lords by the time the session ended. As such it fell under the terms of the Parliament Acts[105] and was presented for Royal Assent at the end of the session without the agreement of the Lords.

[103] *Parl. Debates*, HL, 619, cols. 62–5, 13 Nov. 2000.

[104] National Society for the Prevention of Cruelty to Children, *Parliamentary Briefing*, Sexual Offences (Amendment) Bill, House of Lords, 13 Nov. 2000, p. 1.

[105] Under the terms of the Parliament Act 1911 the powers of the Lords to reject a Bill outright were replaced by a so-called suspensory veto. Any Commons public Bill (except a Bill to extend the life of a Parliament or a money Bill) which had passed the Commons in three successive sessions, whether or not a General Election were to intervene, could be presented for Royal Assent without the agreement of the Lords, provided that certain conditions were satisfied. These included a minimum period of two years between the Commons giving the Bill a Second Reading in the first session and a Third Reading in the third session, and a requirement that the Lords had received the Bill at least one month before the end of each of the three sessions. Under the Act, a Bill is deemed to be rejected by the Lords if it is not passed by the Lords without amendment, or with such amendments only as may be agreed with the Commons.

These provisions were further modified by the Parliament Act 1949 which reduced the three sessions to two, and the minimum period between the Second Reading in the first session and Third Reading in the second to one year. Since 1949 only three Bills have become law without the consent of the Lords: the War Crimes Act in 1991, the European Parliamentary Elections Act in 1999, and the Sexual Offences (Amendment) Act in 2000. This abstract is taken from a chapter on the House of Lords by Dr R. H. Walters, Clerk of Public Bills, House of Lords, for inclusion in *The British Constitution in the Twentieth Century*, edited by V. B. Bogdanor, due to be published by the Oxford University Press for the British Academy in 2002.

VIII

The Crime and Disorder Bill received the Royal Assent, as intended, shortly before the Summer Recess at the end of July 1998. The vicissitudes it encountered in its closing stages were an unexpected deviation, not affecting its significance as the most important enactment on criminal justice since the Criminal Justice Act 1991 at the start of the decade. Like the earlier Act, it embodied a clear sense of vision and purpose. The objectives of making radical changes in the complex and fragmented ways of dealing with young offenders, and the partnership approach to crime prevention, were the product of long years of detailed inquiry and consideration. Political support had been built up within the Labour Party, and a spirit of potential co-operation fostered with the instrumental agencies which would have the responsibility for carrying out the policies of a new Government when the day came. As some critics were not slow to point out, there was nothing distinctively socialist, nor conventionally liberal, about the policies that were developed. But nor had the 1991 Act been based on right-wing ideology. That came later with the overt punitiveness of the Crime (Sentences) Act 1997.

As measured in terms of the time spent and detailed amendment of the Crime and Disorder legislation, Parliament had been assiduous. Tables 5 to 8 show that, excluding the Second Reading debates in each House on the aims of the Bill, a combined total of more than one hundred hours was spent in scrutinizing its contents. Twenty-seven new clauses were added, and 557 amendments made. The overwhelming majority were tabled by the Government, often as a result of second thoughts or corrections to the drafting, but sometimes in response to arguments raised by Opposition spokesmen or back-bench MPs or peers. Nevertheless the dominance of the executive over the legislature was demonstrated once again.

Despite the magnitude of the Parliamentary effort, the reality is that legislation is no more than an intermediate stage in the progress from the original formulation of policies by the political parties in Government, or in Opposition preparing to be in Government, and their implementation. Successful implementation, in the sense of the accurate fulfilment of the intentions of ministers and civil servants, typically depends less on the wording of a statute than on the connected factors of motivation and money. If the policies were carefully

Table 5. *Crime and Disorder Bill 1997–8: House of Lords, hours of sitting*

Stage	Date	Duration (hours/minutes)
Committee Stage	3 February 1998	6.11
	10 February	8.55
	12 February	5.08
	24 February	6.20
	3 March	5.30
Report Stage	17 March	7.08
	19 March	6.05
Third Reading	31 March	6.09
Total time:	51 hours, 26 minutes	

Source: Public Bill Office, House of Lords.

thought out and effectively communicated, as these had been, and their objectives were accepted by most of those who would have the responsibility of making them work, as these were, then the first requirement would have been achieved. But initial commitment can soon be dissipated if the necessary financial resources are not forthcoming.

Examples of ambitious legislative initiatives which have foundered on this rock include the intention of the Children and Young Persons Act 1969 to terminate junior detention centres and facilitate the removal of all offenders under seventeen years old from Prison Department care. Instead, the numbers grew, a fourfold increase in young persons being sent to custody in the 1970s. The reasons were complex, but included insufficient local authority secure accommodation. Desirable as the objective was, it prompted the reaction: why commit local authority current and capital expenditure to save the central Government expense?

The financial resources necessary to give effect to the changes brought about by the Crime and Disorder Act were more abundant than for many of its recent predecessors. One year after a review of government spending had been initiated in July 1997, which had included a close investigation of the efficiency and effectiveness of the criminal justice system, the results of the overall comprehensive spending review, and its impact on the Home Office, were announced

Table 6. *Crime and Disorder Bill 1997–8: new clauses and amendments tabled in the House of Lords*

	(a) Number tabled		(b) Number made		Tabled by the Government		Tabled by the Opposition		Tabled by Other Members	
	New Clauses	Amend-ments	New Clauses	Amend-ments	New Clauses	Amend-ments	New Clauses	Amend-ments	New Clauses	Amend-ments
Committee	6	387	1	131	1	130	1	116	4	140
Report Stage	17	231	5	113	4	116	1	31	12	84
Third Reading	14	105	5	79	4	78	10	5	–	22
Totals	37	723	11	323	9	324	12	152	16	246

Source: Public Bill Office, House of Lords.

Table 7. *Crime and Disorder Bill 1997–8: House of Commons Standing Committee, hours of sitting*

	Morning (hours/minutes)	Evening (hours/minutes)
28 April 1998	2.30	–
30 April	2.30	2.27
5 May	2.30	2.29
7 May	2.30	2.26
12 May	2.11	2.29
14 May	2.30	2.18
19 May	2.30	2.23
21 May	2.30	2.39
2 June	2.30	1.45
4 June	2.30	2.24
9 June	2.30	2.10
11 June	2.08	–
Total time:	52 hours, 49 minutes	

Source: Public Bill Office, House of Commons.

by Straw. He said that resources would be targeted where they were most needed to deliver the Manifesto commitments. The Home Office would receive an additional £3 billion over the next three years. Of this total, £250 million over a similar period would be invested in a crime reduction strategy. The Home Secretary confidently asserted that it would be the first time that a centrally co-ordinated programme of such magnitude, drawing on the findings of research and with a built-in provision for evaluation, had been put in place anywhere in the world.[106] It was a large claim but one that, for a time at least, seemed to hold out the possibility of a move away from the concentration on imprisonment and other penal sanctions that had characterized the punitive populism of the previous Government.

Yet, at the same time, a less obvious change had taken place. The 'no more excuses' mentality had led to certain forms of non-criminal behaviour being classified as unacceptable, although not illegal. Anti-social behaviour, irresponsible parenting, and the more serious forms of drug abuse were made subject to civil orders. In the making

[106] *Parl. Debates*, HC, 316, col. 915, 21 July 1998.

Table 8. *Crime and Disorder Bill 1997–8: new clauses and amendments tabled in the House of Commons*

	(a) Number tabled		(b) Number made		of (b) Government		of (b) Opposition		of (b) Other Members	
	New Clauses	Amend-ments	New Clauses	Amend-ments	New Clauses	Amend-ments	New Clauses	Amend-ments	New Clauses	Amend-ments
Committee of whole House	–	–	–	–	–	–	–	–	–	–
Standing Committee	34	491	12	119	12	119	–	–	–	–
Report stage	12	165	4	115	4*	115	–	–	–	–

* One new clause relating to the age of consent for homosexual activity was tabled by Government back-benchers. Four consequential amendments were tabled by back-benchers, but were signed by a minister and thus technically became Government amendments.

Source: Public Bill Office, House of Commons.

of such orders a lower standard of proof would apply than the standard required for conviction in a criminal trial. Failure to comply with such an order would be a criminal offence attracting severe penalties. The purity of the concept of dispensing justice had been diluted, although not abandoned.

4

Reforms in the Criminal Process I: The Crown Prosecution Service

I

The practice of separating the functions of investigating and prosecuting criminal offences is not embedded in any legal principle or procedure. It belongs to a larger complex of law and political decision-making characterized by priorities shifting constantly between protecting the general public from the harmful consequences of criminal offending, and safeguarding the civil rights of persons suspected or accused of having committed criminal offences. There is no fixed relationship or coherent balance between the two: they are horses that need to be driven abreast. If one gets too far ahead of the other, the stability of any vehicle to which they are harnessed will be imperilled.[1]

Until the Prosecution of Offences Act 1985 the police were not only responsible for investigating most criminal offences, but in a large number of cases they also decided on whether to prosecute following their investigation, and conducted the process of prosecution when a decision to prosecute had been made. Many prosecutions for minor offences, including the majority of motoring offences, were conducted throughout by police officers who thus appeared as advocates in the Magistrates' courts.[2] More serious offences, typically those prosecuted in the Crown Court, were conducted by lawyers instructed by the police, solicitors or counsel either in private practice or employed by Prosecuting Solicitors' Departments established by County or Metropolitan County Councils.

[1] A noted Dutch authority makes the same point: 'Although on specific cases the interests of law enforcement and those of legal protection may contrast, they remain two sides of the same medal, two perspectives on the same matter'. See A. C't Hart, 'Criminal Law Enforcement and Legal Protection', paper published by the Howard League for Penal Reform, 1999, p. 12. The author, a former prosecutor, is Professor of Criminal Law and Criminal Procedure at Leiden University.

[2] Review of the Crown Prosecution Service, *Report*, Cm. 3960, The Stationery Office, 1998, p. 33.

By the mid-1980s, with one important exception, there were Prosecuting Solicitors' Departments in all but six counties in England and Wales. Some had only recently been established and may not have been very effective, but others, particularly in the major provincial conurbations, had been operating for a long time and provided a layer of independent judgment between the police and the process of prosecution. The exception was London, where the Metropolitan Police had its own Prosecuting Solicitors' Department. As its name implied, the Department was part of, and under the control of, the Metropolitan Police.

Major prosecutions at the Central Criminal Court in the City of London were usually handled by the Director of Public Prosecutions, who would brief prosecuting counsel to represent the Crown. Since 1879 the Director of Public Prosecutions has been empowered by statute to intervene in cases which appear to him:

> to be of importance or difficulty, or in which special circumstances seem to him to render his action necessary to secure the due prosecution of an offender.[3]

The Prosecution of Offences Act of that year was followed by legislation in 1884 and 1908, consolidated in the Prosecution of Offences Act 1979. The terms of the Consolidation Act enabled the Director to assume responsibility for the further conduct of any prosecution, including discontinuation at any stage if he thought fit.

Criminal prosecutions are also instituted by a cluster of non-police regulatory agencies. They include the Inland Revenue,[4] Customs and Excise,[5] the Post Office, and other public bodies with statutory

[3] The Office of the Director of Public Prosecutions originated from the Prosecution of Offences Act 1879 and was the result of pressures throughout middle years of the nineteenth century for a system of public prosecution. The Director was to be appointed by the Home Secretary, although his duties were to be exercised under the superintendence of the Attorney General. The Director's powers and duties were defined in very broad terms, the details being left to regulations made under the Act. See Royal Commission on Criminal Procedure, *The Investigation and Prosecution of Criminal Offences in England and Wales: The Law and Procedure*, Cmnd. 8092-1, HMSO, London, 1981, p. 55. In this volume, separate from the main report, the Royal Commission provided a useful historical survey of the processes that lead up to a criminal trial in England and Wales.

[4] The Queen's Bench Divisional Court, Lord Woolf, CJ presiding, decided that the Commissioners of Inland Revenue had power to prosecute on indictment before the Crown Court without the consent of the Attorney General. *R.* v. *Criminal Cases Review Commission, ex parte Hunt*, reported in *The Times*, 24 Nov. 2000.

[5] A review by John Gower QC (a Circuit Judge, 1972–96) and Sir Anthony Hammond (formerly Treasury Solicitor) concerning the conduct of Customs and

responsibilities in such areas as consumer protection, health and safety at work, and pollution control. Local authorities have certain powers to initiate prosecutions, for example by their environmental health officers. While most regulatory agencies have wide discretion in deciding whether to prosecute, they usually regard prosecution in the courts for all save the most serious cases as a last resort after warnings have been given and informal settlements sought. The degrees of commitment to a compliance strategy, as distinct from deterrent or sanctioning strategies, may differ.[6]

Of far longer standing is the right of an individual citizen to bring a private prosecution if the state declines to do so. Although still in use, the exercise of this ancient right is now subject to considerable restrictions. The law governing the right of private prosecution was explained in an earlier volume of *Responses to Crime*, with some examples.[7] The replacement of private prosecutions in England and Wales by police intervention dates from the nineteenth century. It was a consequence of evolutionary historical development rather than any deliberate decision to confer such a responsibility on the police. None of the statutes setting up police forces in England and Wales mentioned a prosecutorial role, nor did the police have any duty to prosecute other than that deriving from their general duty to enforce the law.[8]

The development in Scotland was markedly different. There a public official, known as the procurator-fiscal, is responsible for both investigating and prosecuting criminal offences. A procurator-fiscal, with assistants and deputes, is appointed for each Sheriff Court district. They are legally qualified civil servants, appointed by the Lord Advocate, and are normally debarred from private practice. The procurator-fiscal: makes the investigations on which criminal charges may be founded; takes the precognitions of potential witnesses; receives instructions from the Lord Advocate and Advocate Deputes in the Crown Office, who decide in which court and on what

Excise prosecutions was due to be completed by the end of October 2000. The Government stated that it would carefully consider the recommendations made by the review, and undertook to lay a summary of its proposals for the future handling of such prosecutions before Parliament. *Parl. Debates*, HL, 616 (5th ser.), col. WA 220, 4 Oct. 2000.

[6] See A. Ashworth, *The Criminal Process: An Evaluative Study*, 2nd edn., Oxford University Press, 1998, pp. 150–1.

[7] Windlesham, *Responses to Crime*, Vol. 2, Clarendon Press, Oxford, 1993, pp. 24–6.

[8] Cmnd. 8092-1, *op. cit.*, p. 49.

charges prosecutions should proceed; and conducts prosecutions in the Sheriff Court. The procurator-fiscal also has a responsibility for making inquiries into cases of sudden or suspicious deaths on behalf of the Lord Advocate.[9]

II

Unease about the propriety and effectiveness of the concentration in the hands of the police of powers both to investigate and to prosecute most crime in England and Wales became evident in the first half of the twentieth century. In 1929, and again in 1962, Royal Commissions recommended the separation of the investigative and prosecuting functions,[10] but no action was taken. By the 1970s, allegations about some particularly conspicuous incidents of police misconduct in the investigation of crime reignited the demand for a thorough and independent review of the whole criminal process from the start of the investigation to the point of trial.[11] As Prime Minister, James Callaghan announced the appointment of a Royal Commission in June 1977 which was formally appointed by Royal Warrant in February 1978, with Sir Cyril Philips as Chairman.

Three years later, after exhaustive inquiries, the Royal Commission recommended that there should be 'no further delay' in establishing a statutorily based prosecution service for every police force area in England and Wales. A dignified title of Crown prosecutor was suggested, with functions to be specified by statute. These should include: the conduct of all criminal cases once the decision to initiate proceedings had been taken by the police; the giving of legal advice to the police on prosecution matters; the provision of advocates in the Magistrates' court; and the briefing of counsel where appropriate.[12]

On the pivotal matter of the stage at which the prosecutorial functions of the police should end and those of the new service begin, the

[9] For further information, see *The Laws of Scotland*: Stair Memorial Encyclopaedia, Vol. 13, The Law Society of Scotland and Butterworths, Edinburgh, 1992. 'The Modern System of Criminal Prosecution in Scotland' is described at paras. 1430–5. The author is indebted to Lord Mackay of Drumadoon QC (Solicitor General for Scotland, 1995–6; Lord Advocate, 1996–7) for this description of the office of procurator-fiscal.

[10] Cmnd. 3960, *op. cit.*, p. 33.

[11] See *Responses to Crime*, Vol. 2, *op. cit.*, pp. 126–7.

[12] Royal Commission on Criminal Procedure, *Report*, Cmnd. 8092, HMSO, 1981, p. 186, para. 9.2.

Royal Commission recommended that the point of charge or the issue of a summons should mark the division of responsibilities between police and prosecutor. The police should no longer act as advocates in Magistrates' courts. As to whether the prosecution service should be local or national in character and accountability, the Commission equivocated, before coming down in favour of a service that should be 'locally based, but with certain national features'.[13]

A majority of the Commission recommended that the Crown Prosecutor should be accountable to a new police and prosecutions authority, seen as a development of the existing police authorities. It would be similarly constituted and cover the same territory. Ministerial accountability to Parliament would extend to those aspects of the prosecution system for which ministers were responsible, including the ethical and professional standards of local prosecutors and prosecuting policy in general. National guidelines should be promulgated. The Crown Prosecutor should not take over responsibility for prosecutions by official agencies. The right to bring a private prosecution should be retained.[14]

The right of the private citizen to bring a criminal prosecution, which the Commission had recommended should be retained, would have been restricted in practice since an application would have to be made in the first instance to a Crown Prosecutor. If the prosecutor declined to take up the case, the aggrieved individual would then be able to make an application to a Magistrates' court for leave to commence proceedings.[15] This proposal was rejected by the Government, mainly because it saw no sufficient justification for abolishing the right in its traditional form, but also because it feared an adverse reaction in Parliament. Public expenditure was a further factor, since the Commission had proposed that where the court gave leave for a private prosecution 'this should automatically carry with it a right for the prosecutor's reasonable costs to be paid out of public funds'.[16] In the outcome, the only change made in the subsequent legislation was an extension of the power of the High Court to restrain a vexatious litigant in criminal as well as civil proceedings.[17]

[13] Ibid., para. 9.4. [14] Ibid., p. 187, paras. 9.4–9.7. [15] Ibid., para. 9.7.

[16] Ibid., p. 162, para. 7.51. The Commission expressed the hope that such a provision would serve to remove the financial obstacle to private prosecution, while at the same time reminding the court that leave should be given only for prosecutions which it was proper to finance out of public funds.

[17] Prosecution of Offences Act 1985, Section 24.

The ambivalent organizational structure, 'locally based, but with certain national features', attracted more comment than the demarcation between police and prosecutorial functions. By the time the report was published in January 1981, the Conservatives had returned to power, with William Whitelaw as Home Secretary.[18] To one of the least partisan of all senior politicians the fact that the Commission had been set up by a Government of one party, and that its recommendations fell to be considered by the opposing party, was no reason why decisions on implementation should not be taken with an open mind. Yet amongst many of his Parliamentary and ministerial colleagues, the Prime Minister, Margaret Thatcher, foremost amongst them, there was an ingrained distrust of local government and its penumbra. For them, any idea of making a new and important national service, with such sensitive functions, locally accountable was unthinkable.

At the Home Office a more specific cause for concern was in the front of the minds of ministers and officials responsible for policing. It arose from the hostile attitude taken by some Labour-controlled police authorities towards the decisions of their Chief Constable on the deployment of police officers at the sometimes violent demonstrations which occurred during the industrial action in the coal industry referred to in an earlier Chapter. There was also a long-running dispute in Derbyshire between the Chief Constable and the police authority which was denying him the resources he believed to be necessary for the efficient operation of his force.

An amalgam of these considerations led Whitelaw to set up an interdepartmental working party of officials with broad terms of reference to reshape the Commission's proposals for the organization of the new service. As Chairman he turned to a sage and experienced Home Office Under-Secretary of State, W. J. Bohan. The working party was left free to form its own opinions, and there were no foregone conclusions. While taking account of the recent experience in the police service, the officials were also concerned by the possibilities of conflict that were seen as inherent in the Commission's proposal to place responsibility for prosecuting policy in general at national level, but responsibility for providing resources at local level.

[18] William Whitelaw was Home Secretary 1979–83. After being created a Viscount in 1983, he went to the House of Lords as Lord President of the Council and Leader of the House until his retirement on grounds of ill health in January 1988. Throughout most of this period he was in effect Deputy Prime Minister to Margaret Thatcher, although the title was not then used. He died in 1999.

Three options were identified: an integrated national system, a decentralized national system, and a local system. Of these the first was preferred, partly on grounds of cost-effectiveness, but principally because of the importance attached to consistency in reaching policy decisions and 'ensuring the fact and appearance of independence of the prosecutor from possible improper local influence and from the police service'.[19] In reaching this conclusion the working party acknowledged that while an integrated national structure would add significantly to the formal extent of the responsibilities of the Director of Public Prosecutions and the Law Officers for the prosecution of offences, the fundamental nature of their responsibilities would be unchanged.

Six months later this reasoning was endorsed by the Government in a White Paper which stated robustly that it did not believe it would be 'a proper or efficient arrangement to make the Crown prosecutor accountable in any respect to a local body'.[20] By then, the tone was that of a thrusting new Home Secretary, Leon Brittan,[21] who had succeeded Whitelaw after the General Election in June 1983.

The White Paper did not reveal that consideration had been given to a more radical approach. In a submission to ministers covering the working party's report, Home Office officials had canvassed the possibility of devising ways of keeping guilty pleas for less serious offences out of the Magistrates' courts altogether. In such cases in Scotland the procurator-fiscal had a power to make a conditional offer to an alleged offender regarding any offence triable in the district court, i.e. minor summary offences. The substance of the offer would be that if the offender paid a modest fixed financial penalty, or an instalment of it, to the district court within a specified time, proceedings would not be brought. Such 'fiscal fines' did not count as criminal convictions, although a record of them was kept locally by the procurator-fiscal.[22]

[19] *Report of the Working Party on Prosecution Arrangements*, published as an annex to Cmnd. 9074, below, p. 30.

[20] Home Office and Law Officers' Department, *An Independent Prosecution Service for England and Wales*, Cmnd. 9074, HMSO, 1983, p. 9.

[21] Minister of State, Home Office, 1979–81; Chief Secretary to the Treasury, 1981–3; Home Secretary, 1983–5. Secretary of State for Trade and Industry, 1985–6. A Vice-President of the European Commission, 1989–93 and 1995–9. Life peer, 2000.

[22] Royal Commission on Criminal Justice, *Report*, Cm. 2263, p. 83, HMSO, London, 1993.

Similar prosecutorial discretion was to be found in a number of other jurisdictions in Europe, including the Netherlands. Although a policy of diversion had clear advantages on grounds of greater efficiency and economy, easing the pressure both on the courts and the prosecution service, the Home Secretary, himself a practising barrister before his ministerial career, would not hear of it and the idea was taken no further.

The proposal did not die, however, being resurrected by a subsequent public inquiry, the Royal Commission on Criminal Justice, set up under the chairmanship of Viscount Runciman in 1991. Two years later, its report recommended that prosecution fines on the Scottish model, but with a range of fines instead of one level of fine, should be introduced in England and Wales for use instead of prosecution in appropriate cases.[23] As before, despite its practical advantages and savings in court time and cost, the recommendation failed to commend itself to ministers, and no action was taken.

Another idea, equally ambitious, was being contemplated by civil servants in the Criminal Department of the Home Office when the new prosecution service was in its formative stages. This stemmed from the search for ways of achieving more consistent sentencing. In the early 1980s mounting public concern about discrepancies in the sentences imposed for similar offences had led to a broadening of the scope of appellate review by the Criminal Division of the Court of Appeal. In a series of guideline judgments the then Lord Chief Justice, Lord Lane, went beyond the facts of the actual cases before the Court to enunciate some general principles of sentencing, sometimes accompanied by a graduated scale of penalties for similar offences which judges in the Crown Court would be expected to follow in the future.[24] The Judicial Studies Board, working closely with the Home Office as well as the higher judiciary, also took an active interest in encouraging consistency in sentencing.[25]

Was there scope to go further? With strong leadership from the Lord Chief Justice and the successive Appeal Court Justices who chaired the Judicial Studies Board, professional resistance to change had been diminished, if not entirely overcome. Was it unthinkable

[23] Royal Commission on Criminal Justice, *Report*, Cm. 2263, p. 198, HMSO, London, 1993. Recommendation No. 113.

[24] For an account of the development of guideline judgments by the Court of Appeal, Criminal Division, see *Responses to Crime*, Vol. 2, pp. 173–6.

[25] Ibid., pp. 176–81.

that prosecution counsel should be enabled to assist the court on the appropriateness of the sentence once the guilt of a defendant had been established? Again, this notion proved a bridge too far for successive Home Secretaries, and the project was put back onto the shelf of interesting ideas not proceeded with.

III

As Bohan's working party had recommended, the structure decided upon for the Crown Prosecution Service (CPS) was a national organization with local branch offices responsible for the conduct of all police-initiated prosecutions. It was to be headed by the Director of Public Prosecutions, subject to the 'superintendence of the Attorney General'.[26] Thus after the Prosecution of Offences Act 1985 came into force the then Director of Public Prosecutions, Sir Thomas Hetherington, was appointed to head the service, while retaining his existing responsibilities. On his retirement in 1987 he was succeeded as Director of Public Prosecutions and Head of the Crown Prosecution Service by the First Senior Prosecuting Counsel to the Crown at the Central Criminal Court, Allan Green QC.[27]

Interposed between the police and the courts, the CPS had to prise apart the existing institutions, creating space to take on, consolidate, and develop functions previously discharged by still extant and powerful agencies. The crucial relationship, and the most difficult in the early stages, was with the police. Some of the clashes may have arisen from the understandable motivation of CPS staff to demonstrate their independence. Yet a degree of friction was inherent in the process that had been devised. The rejection of the model of distinct separation of the investigative and prosecutorial functions, that could be found in many other jurisdictions, left with the police the preliminary decision to charge a suspect and, if so, what charge to bring. At that stage a preliminary view might be formed as to the suspect's guilt. But suspicion was not enough for the CPS. Its task was to review the particulars of the case, and decide whether the evidence

[26] Prosecution of Offences Act 1985, Section 3(1). The Royal Commission on Criminal Procedure had envisaged retaining the office of Director of Public Prosecutions. Cm. 8092, *op. cit.*, paras. 7.54–7.57 at pp. 162–3.

[27] Sir Allan Green resigned for personal reasons in 1991. He had been knighted the same year.

resulting from police investigations was sufficient to prove the charge to the standard of proof required in a criminal trial, and for there to be a realistic prospect of conviction.

Where the reviewer concluded that further evidence was needed, the police could be requested to obtain it. Unlike the procurator-fiscal in Scotland, there was no power to order a police officer to pursue further inquiries. If no additional evidence was forthcoming, and the reviewer was still not satisfied that the available evidence justified the charge, the CPS would then either substitute a lesser charge or discontinue the prosecution altogether. The issues of downgrading and discontinuance emerged early, and were to remain a principal cause of discord between CPS staff and the police at working level. Before long they also became magnets for critical political and media attention.

The inadequate staffing of the CPS, and the consequent impact of staff shortages on the operation of the courts, was the cause of persistent problems from the start. The original intention had been to launch the service simultaneously throughout England and Wales in October 1986. Ministers decided, however, to advance the timetable by six months to 1 April 1986 in six areas affected by the policy to abolish the metropolitan counties of Greater Manchester, Merseyside, South Yorkshire, West Yorkshire, West Midlands, and Durham/Northumbria.[28] In London, because of recruitment difficulties and a large backlog of inherited work from various agencies, a phased introduction took place. This began in May, but had not been completed by 1 October 1986.

The decision for an early start in some of the most populous parts of the country left even less time in those areas for the daunting sequence of appointing the Crown Prosecutors, agreeing staff complements and rates of pay, recruiting or transferring staff from existing agencies, establishing working practices with the police and other agencies, training the newly appointed staff, laying down guidelines, locating and fitting out office accommodation, and designing financial and administrative systems. A further reason why the legislative process had been initiated earlier than planned by officials was the desire of ministers to announce decisions on the setting up of the CPS to coincide with their proposals for handling complaints against the

[28] National Audit Office, *Review of the Crown Prosecution Service*, HC 345, HMSO, London, 1989, p. 7.

police and the rationalization of police powers contained in the Police and Criminal Evidence Bill.[29]

The service began with a maximum complement of 1,593 lawyers and 2,130 law clerks or administration staff. The DPP later informed the Home Affairs Committee of the House of Commons that many people considered these totals to fall far short of the numbers required. Although the initial complement had been increased, the greatest problem facing the CPS in its formative phase had been the recruitment and retention of staff, particularly of competent lawyers. By the end of the decade most areas in the country still had not been fully staffed for more than brief periods, and the great majority had always been understaffed. In some areas shortages amounted to nearly 30 per cent. A number of well qualified people recruited in the preliminary stages left immediately before the CPS became operational, and since then the service had lost experienced staff to the private sector.[30] At the beginning of April 1987 the service was 529 short of its total complement of lawyers, by then increased to 1,773, and twelve months later, at the end of March 1988, it was still 459 lawyers below complement.[31] The shortage was most acute in London, where the transition had only been achieved by the secondment of substantial numbers of lawyers from the metropolitan areas.

In retrospect it is easy to see that the requisite staff numbers were consistently underestimated. A report submitted to the House of Commons by the Comptroller and Auditor General in 1989 explained that estimating the manpower and financial resources required for the CPS had been difficult because of the lack of any uniform system for conducting police prosecutions and paying for them under the preceding regime. Whereas most county authorities had their own prosecuting solicitors' department, a few others still relied on police officers with varying degrees of support from private lawyers. Greater London was a special case, since the Prosecuting Solicitors' Department had been controlled by the Metropolitan Police. A further complication nationally was that prosecution work undertaken by the police was often not identified separately from other duties. Nor was there any clear or consistent

[29] Ibid.

[30] House of Commons paper 118-II, Session 1989–90, Home Affairs Committee, Fourth Report, *Crown Prosecution Service*, Vol. II, p. 5, paras. 2.1 and 2.2.

[31] Letter to the Attorney General from Allan Green, published as an introduction to the first *Annual Report* of the Crown Prosecution Service for the period April 1987 to March 1988, HMSO, 1988, p. 5.

method of recording prosecution costs, some of which were recovered from central Government funds, while others were borne by local or police authorities.[32]

The initial Home Office estimate suggested that the new service would require some 2,500 staff, and would release about 600 police officers from other duties. Because of the lack of any firm costings of the previous arrangements these estimates were heavily qualified, and no attempt was made to quantify the total costs. When the Prosecution of Offences Bill was debated on Second Reading in the House of Commons, the Home Secretary went no further than saying that the cost of the new service would 'depend very largely on the numbers of staff to be employed by it'. This could not be finally determined until the report from the consultants had been received. The cost of a national system, he added incautiously, was not expected to be significantly higher than a local one.[33]

It seems curious that the report from the consultants, Arthur Andersen, an associate of one of the largest and best known firms of chartered accountants, should have contained no estimates of cost, however guarded. Their report was a detailed and lengthy document in three volumes, but all of the calculations were based on projections of manpower and staffing. When submitted in April 1985 the consultants' report indicated that total staffing requirements would be 3,750, more than one-third higher than the original Home Office figure. On this basis the Treasury accepted a complement of 3,755 from the national start date of 1 October 1986. By then it was already evident that the total was inadequate and it was increased to 4,497 six months later, with effect from 1 April 1987.

The moment of truth came when the Lord Chancellor's Department and the Home Office attempted to compare the cost of the CPS with the cost of the previous arrangements. In broad terms, the previous arrangements would have cost £70 million for 1987–8, compared with an estimated expenditure of £110 million for the CPS in the same year. Even that estimate was qualified in that it might not take full account of accommodation costs and general administration. In the event, the outcome for 1987–8 was £134 million,[34] nearly double the pre-CPS total.

[32] HC 345, *op. cit.*, p. 7.

[33] *Parl. Debates*, HC, 77 (6th ser.), col. 152, 16 Apr. 1985.

[34] HC 345, *op. cit.*, pp. 7–8.

Not surprisingly, the extent of the excess of actual cost over the planning assumptions attracted the attention of the Comptroller and Auditor General.[35] His report identified four 'main contributory factors'. They were:

(a) the original Home Office estimates had been based on the responses to questionnaires sent to Chief Constables and Chief Prosecuting Solicitors, not on any time study at working level; this approach was preferred to a more intrusive and intensive time study, but it allowed considerable scope for error;
(b) the estimates had overlooked the impact on Service resources of the need to record and supply data by which their performance could be monitored and judged;
(c) under the previous system prosecuting solicitors acted as advisers to the police and operated on a solicitor/client basis; it would have been difficult for them to appreciate the manpower implications of having to account for their decisions under a national independent prosecution service;
(d) subsequent changes in the working environment, including increases in the Crown Court workload and procedural changes such as tape-recording of police interviews and the right of accused persons to seek advance disclosure of the case against them.[36]

The first and most significant of the identifiable contributory factors, tactfully described as allowing 'considerable scope for error', touched on potentially contentious ground. Some informed observers speculated privately on how vigorously the police had resisted the temptation to understate their costs, not in order to impoverish the new service, but with an awareness that the financial contribution made by central Government to their own votes would be reduced accordingly.

IV

In his written submission to the Commons' Home Affairs Committee in 1990 Allan Green conceded that the CPS had been 'the subject of considerable publicity, much of it adverse'.[37] Some criticism had been

[35] The Comptroller and Auditor General is head of the National Audit Office (NAO) employing some 900 staff in 1989. The Comptroller and NAO are independent of the Government and certify the accounts of all Government Departments and a range of other public sector bodies. See Chapter 3, n. 16, above.

[36] HC 345, *op. cit.*, p. 8.

[37] HC 118-II, *op. cit.*, para. 1.3.

justified, but much stemmed from a failure to appreciate fully the duties, responsibilities, and powers (or lack of them) of the service, and from a tendency to hold it responsible for the shortcomings of others over whom it had no control. He accepted that some mistakes were inevitable in the handling of nearly five million cases since the inception of the CPS, but argued that only a minute proportion of the cases dealt with had provoked adverse comment. Over the previous three years performance had substantially improved and the volume of criticism had declined.[38]

A continuing source of adverse comment, in the Crown Court especially, was the number of cases not ready for trial on the date set for the court hearing. Some judges became accustomed to giving expression to their frustration by rebuking the CPS in open court, even though the cause of the delay might have been beyond its control. Information requested from the police or Probation Service, or medical or forensic science reports, were often not available. A significant factor in the mid-1990s was a long backlog of work in preparing DNA analyses by the Forensic Science Service, an executive agency with which the police, rather than the CPS, normally maintained working contact.[39] None of these shortcomings, trying as they must have been, warranted the experiences in court described by some CPS lawyers as 'ritual humiliation'.[40]

Of equal importance to its role in the courts was the relationship between the CPS and the police. The early annual reports contained numerous references to the need to improve liaison with the police at all levels. Proper consultation on cases of discontinuance was essential, with CPS attendance being urged at police conferences to explain the work of the service and ventilate any difficulties or misunderstandings. Late delivery of police files, and inadequate details on which to base decisions on prosecution, led to comments such as 'several areas are disappointed that they have not always had the degree of co-operation from operational police ranks that they would like'.[41]

[38] HC 118-II, *op. cit.*, para. 1.3.

[39] Section 62 of the Police and Criminal Evidence Act 1984, enabling blood or semen samples to be taken was amended in 1995 to permit a greater range of samples to be taken without the consent of the suspected person. This led to a huge increase in the number of samples submitted to the Forensic Science Service. Review of the Crown Prosecution Service, *Report*, Cm. 3960, The Stationery Office, 1998, p. 100.

[40] Ibid., p. 96.

[41] Crown Prosecution Service, *Annual Report, 1987–8*, *op. cit.*, p. 35.

In the exercise of their duties Crown Prosecutors did not enjoy unrestricted discretion. They were bound to conform to a Code of Practice. As required by Section 10 of the Prosecution of Offences Act 1985, a Code was drawn up giving guidance on the general principles to be applied by Crown Prosecutors in determining whether proceedings should be instituted or, where proceedings had been instituted, whether they should be discontinued, and what charges should be preferred. The Code was open to periodic amendment by the Director, and published annually with a report to the Attorney General.[42] It was intended as a public statement of the principles upon which the Crown Prosecution Service exercised its statutory functions. The document was detailed in scope and aimed at providing practical guidance for those who would be taking decisions on prosecuting in the name of the service. Among the most important of its contents was an explanation of the two tests which had to be satisfied if a prosecution was to go forward.

The first test was that of evidential sufficiency. The Code stated that a prosecution should not be started or continued unless the Crown Prosecutor was satisfied that there was 'admissible, substantial, and reliable evidence that a criminal offence known to the law' had been committed by an identifiable person. A *prima facie* case against the suspect would no longer be sufficient; there needed to be enough evidence to support a realistic prospect of conviction. Once satisfied that the evidence could justify proceedings, the Crown Prosecutor had then to consider as a second test whether the public interest required a prosecution.[43] Factors leading to a decision not to prosecute would vary from case to case but, broadly speaking, the graver the offence, the less likelihood there would be that the public interest would allow of a disposal less than by prosecution, such as by way of a caution.

In its original version the Code set out some examples of where proceedings might not be required. Considerations included the likely penalty and cost of a prosecution, the staleness of the case, the youth, old age, infirmity, mental illness, or stress of the suspect, the complainant's attitude, and peripheral defendants. By the time of

[42] A new version of the original code was published in the *Annual Report, 1987–8*, ibid., at pp. 60–72.

[43] There has never been a rule that suspected criminal offences must automatically be the subject of prosecution. A classic statement in Parliament to this effect by Sir Hartley Shawcross when Attorney General, and subsequently endorsed by his successors, was repeated in the code. *Parl. Debates*, HC, 483 (5th ser.), col. 681, 29 Jan. 1951.

the third edition, although the Code still listed some common factors against prosecution, it preceded them with a longer list itemizing common public interest factors which favoured prosecution.[44]

While the advantages are self-evident in terms of saving court time and cost by prosecuting only the more serious cases where there is a realistic prospect of conviction, the arguments against are also persuasive. The chief objections are of remoteness, lack of accountability, and insufficient regard for the rights of victims. Since the CPS lawyer reviewing the case would probably have no prior knowledge of the circumstances, a decision on whether or not there was a realistic prospect of obtaining a conviction would be taken on the papers. In the absence of any direct contact with the accused or the victim, a subjective assessment would be made of how a jury or magistrate might react on the basis of a file prepared by the police.[45] Witness statements, for example, might not provide any indication of how a witness would perform in court, nor of the reluctance of some complainants to give evidence when the moment comes. Yet, in the generality of cases, the discretion of the reviewer is virtually unrestricted, provided that the guidelines contained in the Code and supporting manual are properly observed. The decision is taken in private, there is no appeal, and no apparent public accountability for what is a significant quasi-judicial act.[46]

It was not long, however, before the expanding scope of judicial review brought decisions not to prosecute within the reach of the courts. In December 1996, and again in February 1997, leave was granted for judicial review by the Divisional Court to applicants seeking to quash decisions taken by the CPS not to prosecute the police officers involved in two unrelated incidents of deaths in police custody. In both cases an inquest jury had returned a verdict of death by unlawful killing. Whereas this was an important factor to be taken into account, the current state of the law is that an inquest, being essentially a fact-finding procedure, is not to be equated with a

[44] Crown Prosecution Service, *Annual Report, 1997–8*, The Stationery Office, 1998, p. 31.

[45] For a strongly argued critique, see D. Rose, *In the Name of the Law*, Jonathan Cape, London, 1996, pp. 133–7.

[46] The Report of the Review Committee headed by Sir Iain Glidewell in 1998 commented that 'A decision to discontinue made by a Crown Prosecutor is probably the most important and at present the most independent decision he makes'. It recommended that in future there should be a formal requirement for the prosecutor to obtain a supporting opinion from a superior in any case in which a decision to discontinue is doubtful or difficult. Cm. 3960, *op. cit.*, p. 81.

verdict of guilt following a criminal trial.[47] Nevertheless, as a recently retired circuit judge, who had been appointed in July 1997 to conduct an inquiry into CPS decision-making in relation to deaths in custody and related matters, was to comment:

> It is a perception, and I believe it is one that is commonly held not only in ethnic minorities but more widely, that the close working relationship between the CPS and the police leads to favoured treatment of the police.[48]

From the cases he had examined in the course of his inquiry he did not believe it to be a justified perception, but it was an understandable one.

Following the judicial review proceedings, the Crown Prosecution Service carried out an internal review of the cases against the police officers involved in the deaths in custody of the two men. In the outcome, no prosecution was brought against any police officer involved in the death of one of the deceased. A prosecution for manslaughter was, however, brought against the police officers involved in the death of the other man. This prosecution concluded on 27 July 1999 with all the officers being acquitted by a jury.[49]

Apart from certain errors and inadequacies in the affidavits presented by the CPS to the Court, there were more profound considerations of individual responsibility and public accountability to

[47] In *R.* v. *South London Coroner, ex parte Thompson and Others*, reported in *The Times*, 9 July 1982, Lord Lane, CJ said: '. . . it should not be forgotten that an inquest is a fact-finding exercise and not a method of apportioning guilt . . . In an inquest it should never be forgotten that there are no parties, there is no indictment, there is no prosecution, there is no defence, there is no trial, simply an attempt to establish facts. It is an inquisitorial process, a process of investigation quite unlike a criminal trial where the prosecutor accuses and the accused defends, the judge holding the balance or the ring, whichever metaphor one chooses to use.' In more recent cases in the Queen's Bench Divisional Court, *R.* v. *DPP, ex parte Jennifer Jones* (6 June 1996, unreported) Auld, LJ said '. . . The jury's verdict is not determinative in this matter. In my view it is for the prosecutor to make up his own mind on the material before him.' In *R.* v. *DPP, ex parte Hitchens* (13 June 1997, unreported) Brooke, LJ said that the verdict was 'an important matter for the Crown Prosecution Service to take into account. But it could not be regarded as conclusive.'

[48] His Honour Gerald Butler QC, *Inquiry into Crown Prosecution Service Decision-Making in Relation to Deaths in Custody and Related Matters*, The Stationery Office, 1999, p. 50. The Inquiry was set up in July 1997 to look into the handling by the CPS of the separate cases of Mr O. Lapite and Mr R. J. O'Brien, both of whom had died while in police custody in 1994. The terms of reference were later expanded to consider the implications for the CPS of some related issues arising out of a judgment delivered in July 1997 by the Divisional Court in the case of *Treadaway* v. *Chief Constable of Police for the West Midlands*, reported in *The Times*, 25 Oct. 1994.

[49] *Parl. Debates*, HL, 609, col. WA 15, 1 Feb. 2000.

be addressed. In neither case had it been possible to identify exactly who had taken the crucial decision not to prosecute, having considered all of the available and relevant information about the circumstances of the deaths in custody. Although the external inquiry found no evidence of any unfair bias in the review process, the system of reporting upwards from the Central Casework Unit at headquarters in London, through several tiers of the CPS hierarchy to the DPP herself, was condemned as inefficient and fundamentally unsound. It recommended that the decision-maker should be clearly identified and of appropriate seniority.[50]

By 1994 the number of cases discontinued in that year had risen to some 160,000, representing about 11 per cent of the total. This marked a sharp increase of approximately 50 per cent since 1986.[51] The proportion then stabilized. Over the next three-year period, 1995–8, the annual totals of cases discontinued varied between 152,729 and 164,436, with an annual average over a five-year period close to 12 per cent. The statistics cases included terminated in other ways, such as where no evidence was offered by the prosecution in court, or where applications had been made to withdraw a prosecution. Although the year-on-year national totals showed little variation, there was 'a great disparity in discontinuance rates between CPS areas'. This satisfied the Review team set up after the General Election in May 1997 that no unofficial tariff was being applied by the CPS.[52] Nevertheless, 12 per cent represented a significant proportion of all cases considered, and was a feature that regularly attracted unfavourable, if not always well informed, publicity.

V

Decisions on individual cases apart, the principal reasons why the CPS found it so difficult to establish itself as a respected and effective independent element in the system of criminal justice were institutional, administrative, and financial. The initial tensions between CPS prosecutors and the police at operational level endured for longer than had been anticipated. The Glidewell Report observed

[50] *Inquiry into Crown Prosecution Service Decision-Making in Relation to Deaths in Custody and Related Matters*, *op. cit.*, p. 51.

[51] Rose, *In the Name of the Law*, *op. cit.*, p. 135.

[52] Cm. 3960, *Report*, *op. cit.*, p. 79.

that many police officers resented their loss of control over the conduct of prosecutions which they had launched. At the same time, the Review team found that in some areas staff of the newly established CPS were so keen to establish a role for themselves and to assert their independence that, 'no doubt unconsciously', they created a gulf in the relationship between the CPS and the police locally.[53] A similar comment had been made by Sir Allan Green in his evidence to the Public Accounts Committee in 1989:

> In many ways the very convenient relationship between the police and their County Prosecuting Solicitors disappeared. I think that suddenly a steel curtain came down between the two services and this went a bit too far. People in both services, both the police force and ourselves, felt that we must keep our distance, we must not talk to each other, we must not communicate, the CPS is independent of the police and must be seen to be so.[54]

Listing practices in the courts were another source of friction between the CPS, the police, and the courts.

The administrative structure evidently lacked the stability needed for the service to put down roots. When the CPS began to operate in 1986 the organizational design was of a national headquarters in London and thirty-one areas, each headed by a Chief Crown Prosecutor, and with a comparable workload. The following year, to ease the administrative burden on the centre, four Regional Directors were appointed. They survived for only two years after the first of many reviews found them to have added an unnecessary layer of management. So began a continuous cycle of internal and external structural reviews on a scale which it is hard to believe can have been endured by any other public body in modern times. Buried in the appendices of the Glidewell Report was a painstakingly compiled list identifying no less than fifty-one 'major internal or external reviews concerning the Crown Prosecution Service between 1989–98'.[55]

As a response to shortages of manpower and other resources the number of areas was reduced to thirteen in 1993. The area offices would be responsible for the performance and management of a group of local branch offices, making up a network of ninety-three branches over England and Wales as a whole. It was to these branches, each led by a Branch Crown Prosecutor, that the bulk of the casework was devolved. Some managerial functions and powers were devolved from headquarters to the areas, but before long it

[53] Ibid., p. 37. [54] Quoted at ibid. [55] Ibid., Appendix C, pp. 235–6.

appeared that the reorganization had resulted in a greater degree of control and authority being concentrated in the national headquarters than had been the case previously. Fewer areas also entailed greater remoteness from the police and made good working relationships with CPS managers harder to achieve. While the Glidewell review acknowledged that the 1993 changes did have the effect of welding the CPS into a national organization, its Report concluded that the price paid in terms of over-centralization of management was too great. The verdict was that, however good its intentions, on balance the reorganization had been a mistake.[56]

The professional criticisms of the performance of the CPS, and the discontent of many of its employees, spilled over into the political and Parliamentary arena, but never became a dominant topic either in terms of media coverage or widespread public concern. The Director of Public Prosecutions since 1992, Barbara Mills,[57] had earned a public profile as an energetic and articulate head of the service who did not shy away from defending it vigorously when the need to do so arose. She would probably have survived the periodic sniping by the tabloid press provided that she retained the support of the Law Officers. If the Conservatives had continued in office, a gradual improvement in the quality of the service might have been anticipated, with the administrative problems and uneasy relations with the police and the judiciary being resolved over time without recourse to further governmental intervention. But all the signs were that Conservative electoral support was in decline, coinciding with the emergence of the new and more interventionist approach to criminal policy by the Labour Party, described in the previous Chapter.

The publication of Labour's detailed proposals for the reform of the CPS was delayed until 18 April 1997, less than two weeks before polling day in the General Election on 1 May 1997, when the campaign was already in full swing. The delay was caused by some unreconciled differences of opinion between Lord Irvine of Lairg, the Shadow Lord Chancellor, and the more traditionalist John Morris,

[56] Cm. 3960, *Report*, *op. cit.*, p. 2.

[57] Barbara Mills QC was Junior Treasury Counsel at the Central Criminal Court, 1981–6, and Director of the Serious Fraud Office, 1990–2. Director of Public Prosecutions and Head of the Crown Prosecution Service, 1992–8. DBE, 1997. In April 1999 she was appointed Adjudicator for the Inland Revenue (including the former Contributions Agency), HM Customs and Excise, and the Valuation Office.

the Shadow Attorney General.[58] The timing meant that when the document finally appeared it attracted minimal attention. The election Manifesto included a brief but incisive paragraph:

> The job of the Crown Prosecution Service is to prosecute criminals effectively. There is strong evidence that the CPS is over-centralised, bureaucratic and inefficient, with cases too often dropped, delayed, or downgraded to lesser offences. Labour will decentralise the CPS, with local Crown Prosecutors co-operating more effectively with local police forces.[59]

A nineteen-page policy paper, entitled *The Case for the Prosecution: Labour's plans for the reform of the CPS*, opened with a compelling statement, the accuracy of which was later challenged:

> At the heart of the criminal justice system lies a paradox—whilst the number of recorded crimes has soared over the last decade and a half, the number of people convicted or cautioned for those crimes has dropped.
>
> As a result, only 1 crime in 50 now results in a conviction.
>
> This growing gap between the number of crimes committed and convicted offenders is one of the most worrying aspects of the current operation of the criminal justice system.

Once in office after the election victory, the new Government lost no time in acting on its Manifesto commitment. On 21 May 1997 the Attorney General, John Morris, declared an intention to reorganize the CPS from thirteen areas to forty-two. Each new area would correspond to that of a police force outside London, with an additional area covering both the Metropolitan Police and City of London Police areas. At the same time he announced that an independent review of the service would be established 'under the auspices of a person of the calibre of a High Court Judge, to examine more closely the internal structures of the CPS, together with its policies and procedures . . .'.[60] The following month, a former Lord Justice of Appeal, Sir Iain Glidewell,[61] was appointed to conduct the review.

[58] QC, 1973. Parliamentary Secretary, Ministry of Power, 1964–6; Joint Parliamentary Secretary, Ministry of Transport, 1966–8; Minister of Defence (Equipment), 1968–70; Secretary of State for Wales, 1974–9. When appointed as Attorney General in 1997, John Morris was the only Minister in Tony Blair's Administration who had previously served in Cabinet.

[59] *New Labour: Because Britain Deserves Better*, 1997, p. 23.

[60] *Parl. Debates*, HC, 294, col. 73W, 21 May 1997.

[61] Judge of the High Court of Justice, Queen's Bench Division, 1980–5; Presiding Judge, NE Circuit, 1982–5; Lord Justice of Appeal, 1985–95. Chairman, Judicial Studies Board, 1989–92; Member, Senate of Inns of Court and the Bar, 1976–9; conducted inquiry into Heathrow Airport Fourth Terminal, 1978.

He would be assisted by Sir Geoffrey Dear, a recently retired senior police officer,[62] and a person with management and organizational experience.[63] Shortly afterwards, Robert McFarland, formerly a Chief Executive in the BOC Group, was appointed in that capacity.

The remit of the review team was to examine the organization and structure of the CPS, within the prescribed framework of a national headquarters and Chief Crown Prosecutors based in all police force areas, together with the policies and procedures of the service, and to consider whether, and if so what, changes were necessary to provide for the more effective and efficient prosecution of crime through local public prosecutors.[64] The clear intention was that links with the police should be strengthened. In the interim the CPS continued to operate as before in the thirteen geographical areas, each headed by a Chief Crown Prosecutor, fulfilling its prosecutorial responsibilities via the existing network of ninety-three local branch offices.

In 1997–8 an internal Inspectorate became fully operational, carrying out visits and publishing reports on the work of local branches.[65] Two years later the Crown Prosecution Service Inspectorate Act 2000 put the Inspectorate onto a statutory basis, and provided for a Chief Inspector to be appointed by the Attorney General. The change was intended to strengthen the influence of the Inspectorate as recommended by Glidewell.[66] Whereas previously the Chief Inspector and his staff had been either permanent members of the CPS staff or on loan, in future the Inspectorate would be external to the CPS and separately funded. The Chief Inspector would be answerable to the Attorney General, and submit an annual report which would be laid before Parliament.

VI

The Glidewell review turned out to be a far-reaching and penetrating investigation, taking longer than the six months envisaged originally. In spite of the thoroughness of its preparation, a comprehensive

[62] Assistant Commissioner, Metropolitan Police, 1981–5; Chief Constable, West Midlands Police, 1985–90; HM Inspector of Constabulary, 1990–7. Knighted, 1997.

[63] *Parl. Debates*, HC, 295, col. 533W, 12 June 1997.

[64] Cm. 3960, *op. cit.*, p. 219.

[65] Crown Prosecution Service, *Annual Report 1997–8*, The Stationery Office, 1998, pp. 20–1.

[66] Cm. 3960, Recommendations 68–72, p. 25.

report of 263 printed pages, containing seventy-five recommendations, was completed and delivered to the Attorney General only a month after the Government's first year in office.[67] One of the recommendations was acted on as a matter of urgency before the publication of the full report in June 1998. This was the appointment of a Chief Executive to be in charge of the 'management of the system and the administration of the organization', who would 'probably not be a lawyer'.[68] The Chief Executive would be second in rank to the DPP, thus enabling the Director to concentrate on the considerable legal responsibilities and public answerability which went with the position. Mark Addison, a senior civil servant, whose current appointment was Director of the Better Regulation Unit at the Cabinet Office, with previous experience at 10 Downing Street as a private secretary to the Prime Minister in the Thatcher years, was selected and appointed as Chief Executive on 5 June 1998. In November, one highly qualified prosecutor followed another when David Calvert-Smith[69] succeeded Dame Barbara Mills as Director of Public Prosecutions and Head of the CPS.

The outgoing Director had become in some respects a scapegoat for the woes of the CPS. Responsibility for the 1993 reorganization, singled out for criticism in the Glidewell Report, was laid at her door, and there was no doubt that morale throughout the service was low. Though both Morris and Mills were determined to maintain cordial professional relations, and her contract still had a year to run, she agreed to resign as soon as a suitable replacement could be found. The search was not easy since, in spite of the transfer of administrative responsibilities onto other shoulders, the appointment of Director of Public Prosecutions had come to be regarded as something of a poisoned chalice. In the outcome, the Attorney General and the Government as a whole were mightily relieved when a practising criminal lawyer of the stature of Calvert-Smith, at the time Chairman of the Criminal Bar Association, agreed to take on the job.

The service reviewed by Glidewell had an overall staff totalling 5,699, of whom 1,983 were lawyers, and 45 legal trainees. The balance was made up of caseworkers and administrators. Over a period

[67] For a penetrating critique of the Report of the Glidewell Review, see the editorial article, 'Review of the Crown Prosecution Service' [1998] Crim. L.R. 517–20.

[68] Recommendation 49, *op. cit.*, p. 22.

[69] QC, 1997. A Recorder of the Crown Court, 1986–98; Junior Treasury Counsel, 1986–91; Senior Treasury Counsel, 1991–5; First Senior Treasury Counsel, 1995–8.

when staff numbers had been reduced from a peak of 6,407 in 1995, costs had risen year on year to £300 million in 1997–8.[70] The contrast with the cost in the same year of legal aid for defendants in criminal cases, which at £682 million was more than double the cost of the prosecution service, was described by the review team as stark.[71]

In the opening section of their Report the authors gave their overall assessment. They wrote that the CPS had:

> the potential to become a lively, successful and esteemed part of the criminal justice system, but that, sadly, none of these adjectives applies to the Service as a whole at present. If the Service—by which we mean all the members of its staff—is to achieve its potential, it faces three challenges. Firstly, there must be a change in the priority given to the various levels of casework; the 'centre of gravity' must move from the bulk of relatively minor cases in the Magistrates' Court in order to concentrate on more serious crime, particularly the gravest types, in the Crown Court. Secondly, the overall organisation, the structure and the style of management of the CPS will have to change. Government has started this process by deciding that the CPS should in future be divided into 42 Areas, each headed by a Chief Crown Prosecutor. Each of these CCPs should be given as much freedom as possible to run his Area in his own way, and he should support his staff to enable them to get on with the core job of prosecuting. Thirdly, the CPS must establish more clearly its position as an integral part of the criminal justice process.[72]

The Report commented that the role of the CPS within the criminal justice system had not been spelt out, or put into the context of key objectives and related performance indicators. Nor had the crucial relationships with the police and courts been properly defined. As to one of the key functions, the preparation of case files, neither the police nor the CPS had overall responsibility. Glidewell recommended that in future the CPS should take responsibility for the prosecution process immediately following a charge, and for arranging the initial hearing in the Magistrates' court. The CPS should also

[70] Cm. 3960, *op. cit.*, pp. 42–3. The total planned expenditure for the CPS of £282 million in 1998–9 (the figure used in the Glidewell Report) was revised to £300 million in the reconciliation of cash plans and outturn. The Law Officers' Departments, *Departmental Report*, Cm. 4207, 1999, p. 11.

[71] Cm. 3960, *op. cit.*, p. 43. The comparison fails to take account of the fact that much of the cost of the early stages of a prosecution is borne by the police. Defence costs are typically incurred from an earlier stage in the process than CPS costs. See Chapter 5, Table 9 and its interpretation.

[72] Ibid., pp. 6–7.

be responsible for ensuring the availability of witnesses and warning them when their presence would be required.

No change was recommended in the responsibility of the police for the investigation of criminal offences, nor for the charging of suspects. The preliminary preparation of case papers would often depend on information in the hands of the police. There should in future be a single integrated unit to assemble and manage case files combining information from both police and CPS sources.[73] Other recommendations included: timeliness targets; the presence of a CPS lawyer in overall charge of all CPS staff in every major Crown Court centre; involvement in the arrangements for listing cases in the Crown Court; the re-establishment of small groups of special casework lawyers and support staff to work alongside the National Crime Squad in countering organized criminal activity; greater priority to be given to the more serious cases; and the appointment in each area of a business manager accountable to the Chief Crown Prosecutor for planning, budgeting, financial controls, and the efficiency of the prosecution process.

In a ringing final paragraph the review team forthrightly stated that once the new structure and procedures were in place the CPS should be given the opportunity to settle down and make the new systems work. There should be no further major changes to, nor review of, the CPS or any major part of it for a considerable period of time.[74]

VII

The transparently independent character of the Glidewell review was illustrated by the summary rejection of one of the central planks on which Labour's plans for reform of the CPS had rested. This was a widely publicized, and too readily accepted, assertion that only one crime in fifty resulted in a conviction. The inference was that the fault lay with the CPS for insufficient zeal in prosecuting cases where the police had identified suspects. The assertion featured prominently in the introduction to Labour's pre-election policy paper, *The Case for the Prosecution*, but did not survive closer scrutiny. After a detailed examination of the relevant statistics, and distinguishing between the

[73] Ibid., p. 7. [74] Ibid., p. 216.

British Crime Survey data and offences reported to the police, the review team concluded in blunt language that the fifty to one criticisms were 'ill-founded' and could not be sustained.[75]

In the House of Commons the Attorney General paid tribute to Dame Barbara Mills for her generosity in agreeing to stand aside before the end of her contractual period so that a successor could be appointed to drive forward the necessary changes. He said that over a period of some nine years' public service, first as Director of the Serious Fraud Office and then as DPP, she had provided strong leadership, and that her contribution would long be valued.[76] The seventy-five recommendations of the report covered a wide range of proposals. The Government accepted the thrust of the proposals for reordering CPS priorities to focus more on the core business of prosecuting, greater separation of management and legal work, greater autonomy for the areas, and better prospects for the staff.

The recommendation of the appointment of a Chief Executive, the Attorney General said, had been accepted and implemented without delay. Mark Addison was to take up his appointment within a matter of days and would consider the recommendations on the detailed internal management of the CPS as one of his first tasks. A number of proposals related to the responsibilities of other ministers, notably the Home Secretary and Lord Chancellor. Decisions would be taken in consultation with them. Interested organizations, practitioners, or any others who might be affected were invited to put forward their views. The Government intended to publish a formal response in due course covering each recommendation, whether it would be implemented, and if so how.[77]

The sole cautionary note raised by interested organizations when the Glidewell Report was published was whether closer identification with the police could have the effect of undermining the independence of the CPS. Although an important point calling for continuous vigilance, it was in a sense yesterday's message and was mentioned in no more than two of the reported comments. One was the response of the civil rights organization, Liberty, and the other the First Division Association representing the senior lawyers and administrators employed by the CPS. All the other reported reactions were favourable, including those of the Bar Council and the Law Society.

[75] Cm. 3960, *op. cit.*, p. 73.

[76] *Parl. Debates*, HC, 313, col. 44, 1 June 1998.

[77] Ibid.

Six months later the Attorney General informed Parliament that of the recommendations internal to the CPS the Government proposed that thirty-nine should be accepted, in whole or in part, with thirteen others under consideration, considered, or noted. Of the twenty-three inter-agency recommendations, seven had been accepted, wholly or in part, with sixteen remaining under consideration or considered.[78] In June of the following year, shortly before his resignation as Attorney General,[79] John Morris announced that the total number of recommendations accepted, accepted in part or in principle, or implemented, had reached sixty-four. Two recommendations, on transferring the responsibility for warning witnesses from the police to the CPS, and on the installation of a new costing system, had been rejected, although the concerns which had prompted them were being addressed in other ways. The remainder had been noted or considered.

Morris ended a lengthy Written Answer to a Question put down by a government supporter on a prudently optimistic note. The cultural, structural, and organizational changes needed to be carefully managed. It was a lesson from the past that to rush change was a recipe for error. Good will and a determination to work together to make a better system had enabled 'brisk progress' to be made. He paid tribute to all members of the CPS staff who had faced a period of uncertainty with 'professional resolve'. The reforms would, he believed, enhance their individual roles, increase their job satisfaction, and lead to improved morale. Morris concluded by saying that the Glidewell reforms laid a 'sure foundation' for a better Crown Prosecution Service and a better criminal justice system working for the benefit of the community. The CPS had embarked on its new start, with the potential to fulfil what Glidewell had described as 'a lively, successful, and esteemed part of the criminal justice system'.[80] Standing further away, many informed observers of the scene believed that the most significant change was to separate court work from administration, not simply at national level but in the areas as well.

Written Parliamentary statements replying to Questions seeking factual information, on which a minister cannot be challenged

[78] *Parl. Debates*, HC, 321, cols. 68–69W, 30 Nov. 1998.

[79] John Morris resigned as Attorney General at the age of sixty-seven on 29 July 1999, being succeeded by Lord Williams of Mostyn QC. He was knighted in the same year.

[80] *Parl. Debates*, HC, 334, col. 15W, 28 June 1999.

immediately on the floor of either House, are a specialized form of political communication. They are drafted by civil servants and are designed to satisfy, or at least to avoid alienating, diverse interests. As in the Attorney General's statement on 28 June 1999 there may be people to be thanked for public services honourably performed, detailed information to be put on record, and government employees encouraged. A comprehensive chart, running to fourteen pages, summarized the Government's detailed response to the numerous recommendations contained in the Glidewell review. It would have been the product of several weeks or even months of close inter-departmental consultation, and with many of the directly connected interests.

The language of any minister announcing the results of such an exhaustive process will inevitably tend towards the portentous. Simpler, and more down to earth in the hopes expressed for the future, was the wording of a letter from the Attorney General sent to the author two days afterwards:

Attorney General

9 Buckingham Gate
London SW1E 6JP

30 June 1999

Dear Lord Windlesham

The Lord Chancellor has, on my behalf, replied to your Parliamentary question concerning Sir Iain Glidewell's Report into the CPS. I thought I would take this opportunity to write to you to provide further details.

On Monday, I responded to a written Parliamentary question concerning the Glidewell Report. In my answer I was able to provide the Government's final response to the Report. That is not to say there is no more work to be done! We have though, I believe, turned something of a corner with the Crown Prosecution Service, and set upon a fresh start to what I think we all intend to be a brighter future.

I enclose a copy extract from Hansard for Monday 28 June 1999 along with a copy of the chart referred to in the text.

Yours sincerely

John Morris

5

Reforms in the Criminal Process II: The Defendants

I

Before the Access to Justice Act 1999 the defence of persons suspected or accused of criminal offences rested upon a haphazard amalgam of procedural rules, privately paid legal advice and representation, and the public financing of lawyers in private practice. The procedural rules had been developed piecemeal, primarily to ensure fair trials for defendants in court, being supplemented by various common law or statutory protections at pre-trial stages. The Judges' Rules, for instance, dating originally from 1906, were an early example of safeguards intended to protect persons being interviewed by police officers from self-incrimination or oppression.[1]

The roots of criminal legal aid extend back to the start of the twentieth century: the plight of needy and unrepresented defendants in jury trials leading to the passage of the Poor Prisoners' Defence Act 1903.[2] Strengthened by a later Act of the same name in 1930,[3] the focus remained on representation in court, with no advice or assistance being available on other criminal matters until 1959. In that

[1] The Judges' Rules were rules of practice drawn up by the High Court governing the questioning and charging of suspects by the police. These were superseded by primary and subordinate legislation, currently incorporated in the Police and Criminal Evidence Act 1984 and the Secretary of State's Code of Practice under Part VI of that Act, as amended in 1999.

[2] For an informative historical account of the development of criminal legal aid in England and Wales, see T. Goriely in *Access to Criminal Justice*, R. Young and D. Wall (eds.), Blackstone Press, London, 1996, pp. 26–54.

[3] After the 1930 Act legal aid was granted automatically in trials for murder, and in jury trials the requirement was removed that prisoners should disclose their defence at committal. In non-murder cases magistrates were given wide discretion to grant legal aid where the defendants' means were insufficient and it appeared to them 'to be desirable in the interests of justice'. Poor Prisoners' Defence Act 1930, Section 1(3)(b). The same Act provided limited help in summary trials, but only where the gravity of the charge or exceptional circumstances made it desirable in the interests of justice. Ibid., p. 40.

year the first legal advice scheme was set up which reimbursed private solicitors from public funds on a case-by-case basis.[4] An international obligation had been added in 1951 when the United Kingdom was the first signatory to ratify the European Convention on Human Rights.[5] Article 6(3)(c) of the Convention provided that a defendant had a right:

> to defend himself in person or through legal assistance of his own choosing or, if he has not sufficient means to pay for legal assistance, to be given it free when the interests of justice so require.

Over the years the interests of justice and the inability of a defendant or suspect to pay for legal assistance or representation at court have become recognized as the basic criteria for the grant of legal aid from public funds. Today the scope of eligibility for legal aid has broadened to include cases where loss of liberty or livelihood is likely, or a substantial question of law is involved, or the accused is unable to understand the proceedings, or there is a need to trace or interview witnesses, or where it is in the interests of another person that the accused is represented. Each of these factors will be taken into account in deciding whether or not the interests of justice require the grant of legal aid from public funds. A defendant will also qualify for non-contributory legal aid if he or she or their partner either receive one of a small number of means-tested benefits, or their weekly disposable income and capital are below stated limits. A contribution may be required if weekly disposable income and capital are above those limits. There are no upper limits in criminal legal aid.[6]

By the mid-1960s legal representation had become standard in virtually all jury trials. A departmental committee set up in 1964 found that it was rare for anyone to appear before a jury unrepresented. A

[4] *Access to Criminal Justice*, R. Young and D. Wall (eds.), Blackstone Press, London, 1996, p. 43.

[5] The right of individuals to petition the European Commission of Human Rights, and recognition of the compulsory jurisdiction of the European Court of Human Rights, followed in 1966. For a full account of the early history of British accession, and the growing significance of the European Human Rights Convention for British law and practice, see Chapter 8, 'Human Rights: Enforcing the Convention', *Responses to Crime*, Vol. 2, pp. 347–403. The Human Rights Act 1998 incorporated the Convention into domestic law.

[6] Lord Irvine of Lairg answering a Parliamentary Question from the author on what are the criteria for deciding which defendants involved in criminal proceedings are eligible to receive legal aid from public funds. *Parl. Debates*, HL, 600 (5th ser.), cols. WA 11–12, 26 April 1999.

survey indicated that 95.7 per cent of defendants pleading not guilty were legally represented, as were 80.6 per cent of those pleading guilty.[7] In the majority of cases the funding came from defence certificates for legal aid granted by committing justices or the superior court. The costs were paid by the clerk of the court and reimbursed by the Home Office. The committee noted that the attitude of the courts towards the grant of legal aid had become progressively more liberal. The change had been particularly noticeable since 1960 and was attributed largely to the guidance given by the Lord Chief Justice which had been circulated to the courts by the Home Office. Legal aid, 'once a concession only to be granted in exceptional cases', was being granted 'fairly widely by the courts', and the charge on public funds had 'grown very considerably'.[8]

The pace of development in the Magistrates' courts was slower, but accelerated rapidly after 1960 when responsibility for meeting the costs of legal aid was transferred from local ratepayers to national taxation. By 1983 the net cost of legal aid in the Magistrates' courts had risen from £549,215 in 1966–7 to almost £54 million, a five-fold increase in real terms.[9] By that time the Lord Chancellor's Department had taken over the responsibility for funding criminal legal aid from the Home Office.

The steep upward trend in costs continued in the late 1980s and into the mid-1990s. A milestone was the Police and Criminal Evidence Act 1984 which created new rights for persons suspected of having committed a criminal offence. Under Section 58(1) a person arrested and held in custody at a police station or other premises was entitled, on request, to consult a solicitor privately at any time. Anyone making such a request must be permitted to consult a solicitor as soon as practicable, except in certain circumstances defined in the Act. Persons attending voluntarily for questioning by the police have a similar entitlement.[10] Advice and assistance may be provided by an individual's own solicitor, or by a solicitor selected from a list held at the police station, or more commonly by a duty solicitor on call at most police stations. Each year large numbers of suspects, or persons voluntarily helping the police with their

[7] *Report of the Departmental Committee on Legal Aid in Criminal Proceedings*, Cmnd. 2934, HMSO, London, 1966, Table 5, p. 11. The Committee was chaired by Widgery J, later to become Lord Widgery, Lord Chief Justice of England, 1971–80.

[8] Ibid., para. 50, p. 13.

[9] T. Goriely, *op. cit.*, p. 45.

[10] Police and Criminal Evidence Act 1984, Sections 29 and 59.

inquiries, are assisted under the duty solicitor scheme. The total in 1993–4 was 642,802.[11]

By 1997–8 the annual cost of providing criminal legal aid was rising at what the Government described as 'an alarming rate'.[12] Whereas in 1992–3 the cost of all forms of criminal legal aid had amounted to a total of £507 million, by 1997–8 it had risen to £733 million. This represented an increase of 44 per cent, compared to general inflation of 13 per cent over that five-year period. Over the same period the number of legal aid orders for representation at court also rose, but at a lower rate of 10 per cent (from 563,788 in 1992–3 to 618,621 in 1997–8). In the most expensive part of the system, the higher criminal courts, i.e. the Crown Court and above, spending had risen from £221 million in 1992–3 to £349 million in 1997–8, an increase of 58 per cent, while the number of cases had remained constant at 124,000.[13]

Recognition of the need, on public expenditure grounds, to curb the cumulative cost of legal aid, for civil disputes as well as in criminal proceedings, was not peculiar to the Labour Government which took office in May 1997. Even before Lord Mackay of Clashfern had been appointed as Lord Chancellor ten years earlier, his Department had made recommendations as part of a Legal Efficiency Survey in the previous year. These included proposals for the more effective collection of financial contributions from defendants in criminal trials according to their needs. The Royal Commission on Criminal Justice endorsed this proposal in its Report in 1993.[14] By then a number of other money-saving ideas were current in Whitehall, including ways of reducing eligibility to receive free legal aid for advice and assistance pre-trial, or free representation at court, and requiring more defendants to pay contributions, possibly over an extended period.

Although the terms of reference for the Royal Commission in 1991 specifically included consideration of 'the arrangements for the

[11] Lord Chancellor's Department, *Legal Aid—Targeting Need*, Cm. 2854, HMSO, London, 1995, p. 105.

[12] Lord Chancellor's Department, *Modernising Justice: The Government's plans for reforming legal services and the courts*, Cm. 4155, The Stationery Office, 1998, p. 60.

[13] Ibid.

[14] Royal Commission on Criminal Justice, *Report*, Cm. 2263, HMSO, 1993, p. 117. The Commission commented that the scheme recommended by the Lord Chancellor's Department in 1986 had much to commend it. Its advantages and disadvantages should be further explored with a view to its introduction if that proved justified.

defence of accused persons, access to legal advice, and access to expert evidence', its Report had little to say about the organization or funding of criminal legal aid. Indeed, it coolly remarked that, while not questioning the need to control public expenditure as in other fields, legal aid accounted for only 5 per cent of the overall expenditure on the criminal justice system.[15] The Commission declined to be drawn into the controversy about whether or not standard fees (as opposed to fees directly related to the cost of the actual work done on a case) should be extended from the Crown Court, where they were already a feature of legal aid, to the Magistrates' courts. The furthest its Report went was a cautious recommendation that legal aid fees be kept under review to ensure their adequacy in attracting sufficient numbers of competent solicitors, properly trained to present cases in the Magistrates' courts. Standards of performance should be kept under review.[16]

II

If the need to find ways of containing the upward surge in the annual cost of criminal legal aid was the principal factor generating momentum for reform, it was not the only one. From the point of view of the Treasury the system of paying for legal aid was objectionable *per se*, not simply because of its total cost, but because of the open-ended nature of the expenditure. Whereas the courts had some control in making decisions on who was eligible for legal aid when granting certificates, they were not financially accountable. The other forms of legally aided advice and assistance that had developed to supplement representation in court were even less susceptible to controlling, or even forecasting, the costs before they had been incurred.

By the time the varied provisions for legal aid, civil as well as criminal, came under review in the 1990s there were four distinct categories of publicly funded schemes available for those suspected or accused of a criminal offence. They were: the police station duty solicitor scheme; the 'green form' scheme which could be used for giving initial advice to potential defendants not in police custody; criminal legal aid to cover the cost of preparing the defence and presenting it

[15] Ibid., p. 117.

[16] Recommendation 175, ibid., p. 204.

in court; and a court-based duty solicitor scheme to assist defendants who arrived in court unrepresented and agreed to plead guilty. Save in exceptional circumstances, a court-based duty solicitor could not offer advice or representation in connection with a non-imprisonable offence. Nor might a duty solicitor provide representation in committal proceedings, or on a not guilty plea. No means test applied to the first and last of these schemes. The second was subject to a simple means test; and the third and largest category, involving preparing the case and representing the defendant in court, was subject to both a means test and a merits test.[17]

The first major step towards reform came in May 1995 with the publication of a consultation paper issued by the Lord Chancellor's Department.[18] It was a lengthy document of 116 pages covering civil as well as criminal legal aid. While recognizing the substantial differences between the two systems, notably that persons charged with a criminal offence have no choice about defending themselves, whereas participants in civil cases have more freedom of action both as to the way a case proceeds and its outcome,[19] the remedy proposed was the same.

This was the mechanism of block-funded contracts between an agent, probably the area office of the Legal Aid Board, and a supplier of legal services to clients for a specified period and at an agreed cost. The contract would cover the type of services to be provided, as well as the quality, volume, and price. It would guarantee income to the supplier, provided that the contractual conditions were met.[20] The suppliers would be franchised firms of solicitors specializing in legal aid work in such areas as family law and personal injury, as well as criminal work in the Magistrates' courts. Non-solicitor agency organizations, for instance the Citizens Advice Bureaux and Housing Aid Centres, would also be eligible to receive contracts as suppliers if they showed themselves capable of delivering advice and assistance in areas of social welfare law to the

[17] R. Young and D. Wall, 'Criminal Justice, Legal Aid, and the Defence of Liberty', in *Access to Criminal Justice*, *op. cit.*, pp. 2–3. A defendant without sufficient means to pay for legal representation must also show that the grant of legal aid is desirable 'in the interests of justice'.

[18] Cm. 2854, *op. cit.* The Green Paper was circulated for comment with a warning that it did not represent the final views of the Government. Indeed the name of the Lord Chancellor, Lord Mackay of Clashfern, appeared nowhere in it, not even in an Introduction to the document.

[19] Ibid., p. xi.

[20] Ibid., p. 22.

same standard as solicitors. This would be a way of extending the supplier base for services in social welfare law which were under-provided by current suppliers.[21]

Most ambitious of all was the then Government's belief that block contracts should be contained within an overall predetermined budget for legal services. A prospective budget was claimed to be a practical means of controlling the growth in expenditure on legal aid. That was something, in the sharp comment of the Green Paper, that had 'plainly been absent under the present scheme'.[22] The justification for such a radical, and in criminal legal aid possibly unattainable, goal was explained in a passage of the purest Treasury orthodoxy:

> The Government believes that it is right to make judgments about what the country can afford to spend in any one year on publicly funded legal services. It makes similar decisions across a whole range of other programmes such as the Courts, the Police, Prisons, the Health Service, and Education. In deciding what it can afford to spend on publicly funded legal services the Government would need to take into account a number of factors including the likely level of demand, the state of the economy and the efficiency of the service.[23]

Such arguments failed to convince majority opinion in the legal profession, including the solicitors' representative body, the Law Society, which was closely involved with the administration of legal aid. Faced with a degree of hostility seldom encountered by the holders of his high office, the Lord Chancellor took his case to a wider public. In a series of articles and interviews, Mackay, an advocate of the front rank while in practice, showed that he had not lost the ability to adjust his arguments to selected audiences. Readers of *The Daily Mail* may have been expected to share his suspicion that legal aid had 'fallen victim to the unhealthy compensation culture that [was] gripping the country'. No other public service was 'provided in such an uncontrolled, extravagant way'. He intended to put a stop to such abuses.[24] More measured was his explanation in *The Times* that progress in reforming legal aid would be made 'in careful stages, piloting the changes and consulting widely to make sure that we get the details right'. The reforms had four main objectives: to control the total cost of legal aid; to increase value for money; to target

[21] Ibid., p. 23. [22] Ibid., p. 28. [23] Ibid., para. 4.28, p. 28.
[24] *The Daily Mail*, 20 Dec. 1996.

appropriate services on the most deserving cases; and to ensure fair treatment for everyone involved.[25]

Fiscal prudence rather than party politics was also evident in the approach of the Shadow Lord Chancellor, Lord Irvine of Lairg. In the previous year he had made it clear that under Labour there would be 'no new money to throw at the problems of legal aid'.[26] The solution called for structural change. His ambition was to restore legal aid to the status of a highly regarded social service, but the ability of any Lord Chancellor to 'fight his corner' with the Treasury was dependent on the courts and legal profession 'putting their house in order'. He did not see legal aid as a distinct issue 'hermetically sealed from reform'. The best way to save money was not to exclude people from access to justice, but to cut the unacceptable cost of litigation and its delays.[27]

It was no surprise therefore that the Labour Manifesto for the general election in May 1997 should include an undertaking to make 'a wide-ranging review both of the reform of the civil justice system and Legal Aid'. A community legal service would:

> develop local, regional and national plans for the development of Legal Aid according to the needs and priorities of regions and areas.

The key to success would be 'to promote a partnership between the voluntary sector, the legal profession and the Legal Aid Board'.[28] No distinction was made in the Manifesto between civil and criminal legal aid.

The proposal to set up a review of civil justice was overtaken by two substantial reports by Lord Woolf published in 1995 and 1996 under the rubric 'Access to Justice'.[29] In making his analysis, Woolf identified what he regarded as the fundamental weaknesses of civil justice. The main causes were excessive delay; excessive cost; undue complexity; uncertainty over the amount of time and money likely to be involved in bringing a case; and unfairness where a financially stronger party could exploit the failings of the system to defeat an opponent. The system of civil justice as a whole was too fragmented in the way it was organized, and too adversarial as cases were run by

[25] *The Times*, 22 Oct. 1996.

[26] *The Daily Telegraph*, 20 June 1995.

[27] Ibid.

[28] *New Labour—Because Britain Deserves Better*, The Labour Party, 1997, p. 35.

[29] *Access to Justice: Interim Report to the Lord Chancellor on the civil justice system in England and Wales*, HMSO, London, 1995; and *Access to Justice: Final Report to the Lord Chancellor on the civil justice system in England and Wales*, HMSO, London, 1996.

the parties and not by the courts.[30] The Woolf proposals were well received, by both the judiciary and the Government, and rendered any further review of civil justice otiose. In brief, the object was to drive down cost and delay in court proceedings through firm judicial management, and to promote more settlements.[31]

The reform of criminal legal aid, already seen as an urgent practical necessity, thus became subsumed into a wider and grander design: the modernisation of the justice system as a whole. In the words of Lord Irvine of Lairg, by now Lord Chancellor:

> Together these changes will create a justice system that is no longer so daunting, so uncertain and so expensive that ordinary people have no real access to justice. People will be able to find out what their rights are, and if necessary protect and enforce them, at a predictable and reasonable cost in a system that serves everyone.[32]

Earlier, Irvine had colourfully described legal aid as 'a leviathan with a ferocious appetite'.[33] Although the occupant of the Woolsack had changed, the determination of the Treasury to restrain public expenditure had not.

In the context of legal aid, the objectives of 'predictable and reasonable cost' were to be pursued by adapting the previous Government's approach of block-funded contracts with selected firms of solicitors for the provision of legal services. Pilot schemes were already underway. In November 1996 the Legal Aid Board had begun to pilot contracts with solicitors' firms to provide advice and assistance in civil matters. A pilot of contracts to provide mediation in family cases under the legal aid scheme followed in May 1997. In June 1998 a further pilot scheme was authorized covering advice and assistance in criminal cases, which in February 1999 was extended to cover representation in youth courts.[34]

[30] *Access to Justice: Final Report*, ibid., p. 2.

[31] Lord Irvine of Lairg, *Parl. Debates*, HL, 606, col. 167, 26 Oct. 1999.

[32] Lord Chancellor's Department, *Modernising Justice: The Government's plans for reforming legal services and the courts*, Cm. 4155, The Stationery Office, 1998, p. 3. The appropriateness of the title was questioned by Lord Mackay of Clashfern on the grounds that as the principles of justice are timeless it cannot be possible to modernise justice. *Parl. Debates*, HL, 595, col. 1116, 14 Dec. 1998.

[33] On 18 Oct. 1997 the Lord Chancellor had unveiled his plans for reforming the civil justice and legal aid systems in a keynote address to the Solicitor's Annual Conference in Cardiff; transcript, p. 1.

[34] Access to Justice Act 1999, *Explanatory Notes*, The Stationery Office, 1999, para. 39, p. 9. Post-enactment explanatory notes were prepared by the Lord Chancellor's Department to assist readers in understanding the Act. They did not form part of the Act and had not been endorsed by Parliament.

A relic of the earlier attempts to bring the cost of criminal legal aid under control was the requirement of contributions from those with sufficient means to pay for their own defence. The necessary means testing had proved in practice to be a complex and costly process. Fewer than 1 per cent of applicants were refused criminal legal aid because they could afford to pay for their defence. Another 5 per cent were required to pay a contribution. Experience had shown, however, that the total value of contributions collected was barely enough to meet the cost of administering the means-testing process. In 1997–8 contributions paid amounted to £6.2 million, with the direct cost of assessing and collection estimated at approximately £5 million.

There were also hidden costs. For example, where the documentary evidence needed for a means test was incomplete the case would be adjourned, causing delay and inconvenience to other criminal justice agencies, as well as witnesses and victims.[35] Instead, to avoid the accusation that the taxpayer was having to meet the cost of defending rich criminals, a judge in the Crown Court would be enabled to order a convicted defendant to pay part or all of the defence costs at the conclusion of the trial. Orders for costs would also be able to take account of assets which had been frozen, or which had only come to light during the case.

III

A new structure for legally aided services was set out in the first part of the Access to Justice Bill introduced in the House of Lords in December 1998. The existing system of legal aid, and the Legal Aid Board, would be replaced by a smaller Legal Services Commission, with between seven and twelve members appointed by the Lord Chancellor. The Commission would manage different schemes for funding services in civil and criminal matters. These would be known as the Community Legal Service and the Criminal Defence Service. If, in the longer term, it proved more effective to administer the two schemes separately because of their different objectives, the Bill contained a power to split the Legal Services Commission into two free-standing bodies. It was not considered practicable to set up two new

[35] Cm. 4155, *op. cit.*, para. 6.26, p. 65.

bodies from the outset, as the existing infrastructure and expertise of the Legal Aid Board was needed to manage the transition.[36]

The establishment of a new defence service, with powers to represent a defendant from arrest to trial, came as a surprise. In a letter to *The Times* on 5 December 1998, the Chairman of the Bar Council, Heather Hallett QC, said that the first the Bar knew of it was when the White Paper, *Modernising Justice*, had been published on 2 December. That was the same day as the Bill's introduction. Animosity over the lack of prior consultation with the professional bodies which would be directly affected by the provisions of the Bill was aggravated by the Government's intention that, in addition to contracting for the services of lawyers in private practice, the Criminal Defence Service would be enabled to employ lawyers directly as salaried defenders. At the Second Reading on 14 December, the Lord Chancellor had to endure a vituperative tirade from one who in his day had been among the most eloquent of all defence counsel. Lord Hutchinson of Lullington[37] declared:

> As the independence of the prosecutor is swept away, there emerges—ten days ago—predictably undiscussed, without warning to the public or the profession, what I would call the sinister figure of the state salaried defender, paid, selected and controlled by the state. That fine warrior is to be sent out to do battle on the field of liberty and human rights, with his opposite number, his local colleague at arms, the salaried state prosecutor—an all-state contest. As many others have long predicted, introduce a state prosecutor and the state defender follows as night follows day—the dark night of dependence and control, the other side of the coin.
>
> What next? Instead of the interests of justice being paramount, the culture of negotiated justice will prevail . . . Plea bargaining already exists, but not behind closed doors. However, there will be plea bargaining behind closed doors, pressures to abort trials, cosy relationships between prosecution and defence to maintain the conviction count and the volume of cases and to minimize the cost. That cosiness will soon extend to the court itself, which will be anxious to rid itself of the stubborn and determined advocate who wastes the judge's time.[38]

In an assembly containing as many distinguished lawyers as the House of Lords it was inevitable that the rights of audience in the higher courts, for solicitors as well as employed lawyers, would be a

[36] Access to Justice Act 1999, *Explanatory Notes*, *op. cit.*, p. 13.
[37] QC, 1961. Recorder of Bath, 1962–72, of the Crown Court, 1972–6.
[38] *Parl. Debates*, HL, 595, col. 1149, 14 Dec. 1998.

contentious issue. The ingrained belief of many peers experienced in advocacy was that in the higher courts, where a defendant's liberty and reputation might be at stake, only a lawyer in private practice would have the necessary independence to ensure that justice was done. Another cause for anxiety was that standards of advocacy and representation in courts and tribunals would deteriorate. Both of these concerns or 'apprehensions' were shared by a majority of the High Court judges who had been consulted by the designated judges, the Lord Chief Justice and the Master of the Rolls.[39] In the course of the Parliamentary debates, however, it emerged that neither Bingham nor Woolf themselves fully shared them.[40]

The Lord Chancellor was blunt and outspoken. To him, and hence to the Government, the issue was one of restrictive practices. The Bill was:

> designed to abolish, once and for all, the disgraceful restrictive practices which have prevented Crown Prosecutors and other employed lawyers from appearing in the higher courts, regardless of their qualifications.[41]

In future, all barristers and solicitors would have rights of audience, to be exercised in accordance with the qualification regulations and rules of the appropriate authorized bodies. It would be for the Bar Council and the Law Society to regulate the rights of audience of their members, but in doing so they would not be able 'to discriminate against employed barristers and solicitors, as they currently do'.[42]

Despite Irvine's belligerent stance, or perhaps because of it, amendments were twice carried in the Lords deleting the powers of the Legal Services Commission to employ salaried defenders directly. Twice the Commons restored the powers. On 26 July 1999, with the start of the Summer Recess looming later in the same week, the Bill returned to the Lords once again. This time the Lord Chancellor was more conciliatory, complimenting the House on the effective exercise of its role as a revising chamber.

The Bill, he said, was now 'replete with improvements made either in your Lordships' House, or in the other place following suggestions first made here'.[43] The purposes and objectives clauses for

[39] *Parl. Debates*, HL, 595, col. 1125.
[40] *Parl. Debates*, HL, 595, cols. 1125–6, and col. 1153.
[41] *Parl. Debates*, HL, 596, col. 1140, 28 Jan. 1999. [42] Ibid., col. 1141.
[43] *Parl. Debates*, HL, 604, col. 1300, 26 July 1999.

the community legal service and the criminal defence service 'drew heavily' on a principles clause proposed by Lord Lloyd of Berwick, a Law Lord.[44] A critical report from the Lords Select Committee on Delegated Powers and Deregulation[45] had led to 'a substantial package' of government amendments limiting the powers of the Lord Chancellor to give directions to the Legal Services Commission. A new clause on litigation funding agreements owed its existence to the persistence of Lord Goodhart, a front-bench spokesman for the Liberal Democrats. As for Lord Ackner, his greatest critic, and the mover of the amendments carried against the Government preventing the Legal Services Commission from employing salaried lawyers as part of the Criminal Defence Service, he had inspired the addition of a code for salaried defenders.

On the Opposition front bench the Shadow Lord Chancellor, Lord Kingsland,[46] was unpersuaded, remaining fearful of the idea of a state-employed representative defending the accused in a criminal case. He found it repugnant in principle. It was even more repugnant if both prosecutor and defender were employed by the state. While not seeking to question the integrity or professionalism of criminal lawyers employed by the state, he believed the duty to one's employer and the duty to the court to be irreconcilable.[47] After some further exchanges, the Lords accepted the greater legitimacy of the elected chamber. It did not attempt to reverse the twice-expressed will of the Commons, nor to delay by several months the enactment of such far-reaching reforms in the administration of legal aid.

IV

Initially at least, the two services established by the Access to Justice Act 1999, the Community Legal Service (CLS) and the Criminal Defence Service (CDS), lacked a separate corporate identity of their

[44] QC, 1967. Judge of the High Court of Justice, Queen's Bench Division, 1978–84; Lord Justice of Appeal, 1984–93; Lord of Appeal in Ordinary, 1993–9. Vice-Chairman, Parole Board, 1984–5 (member, 1983–5). Chairman, Security Commission, 1992–9; Vice-Chairman, 1985–92.

[45] House of Lords, Session 1998–9 Select Committee on Delegated Powers and Deregulation, *5th Report*, HL Paper 17, 13 Jan. 1999.

[46] Formerly Sir Christopher Prout QC. Created a life peer as Lord Kingsland, 1994. Member of the European Parliament, 1979–94; Chairman and Leader, European Democratic Group, 1987–92.

[47] *Parl. Debates*, HL, 604, *op. cit.*, cols. 1303–4.

own. Each service would comprise the sum of the activities funded by the Legal Services Commission, in either the civil or the criminal field. Although both Services would be managed by the Commission when it succeeded the Legal Aid Board in April 2000, a crucial difference was that while the CLS would be required to operate within a fixed annual budget, the CDS would not.[48]

In the first phase the priorities for the CDS were concentrated on three main areas. These were the development of contracts between the Legal Services Commission and firms of solicitors for advice and assistance, including the duty solicitor schemes and representation in the Magistrates' courts; individual case contracts for very high-cost cases; and contracts for representation in the Crown Court.[49] In addition to these main areas there would be groundwork common to all elements, such as the development of quality standards, accreditation, monitoring, and auditing.

The priority accorded to very high-cost criminal cases reflected a concern expressed several times during the Parliamentary debates, and shared by the Legal Aid Board. It was that a small number of highly expensive cases were taking an increasingly disproportionate share of the total expenditure on criminal legal aid. In 1996–7, 42 per cent of legal aid spending in the Crown Court, amounting to almost £116 million, went on just 1 per cent of the total number of cases. This worked out at an average of £115,627 per case.[50]

Research commissioned by the Lord Chancellor's Department examined a list of cases in which individual payments of more than £25,000 were made to solicitors' firms in 1995–6. There were 355 such payments and 274 cases. Fraud, and fraud-related offences, accounted for 172 of the payments. Murders accounted for sixty-three, drugs cases for sixty, robberies for ten, and sexual offences for eight. The remaining forty-two payments related to a mixture of offences. When analysed by value rather than number, the concentration on fraud became even more apparent. Fraud, or fraud-related, payments consumed 70 per cent of the expenditure, with murder at 12 per cent, drugs cases at 8 per cent, and all others together amounting to 10 per cent. Even within these high-cost cases, there was a concentration of expenditure at the top end. Only eleven

[48] Legal Aid Board, *Introducing Contracts for Criminal Defence Services with Lawyers in Private Practice, Criminal Defence Services: A Consultation Paper*, Aug. 1999, p. 14.

[49] Ibid., p. 5.

[50] *Modernising Justice*, Cm. 4155, *op. cit.*, p. 61.

cases involved solicitor payments of over £500,000, but between them they accounted for some £13 million, or 40 per cent of solicitor expenditure on high-cost cases. All save one of the cases were fraud or fraud-related. The remaining case was a murder.[51]

Large-scale fraud cases attracted intense public and media interest because of the notoriety of some of the defendants, as well as the magnitude of the sums of money involved. By mid-1999 the most costly case to date had been the prosecution by the Serious Fraud Office of Robert Maxwell's two sons after their father's sudden death and the collapse of his business empire. At the conclusion of the legal proceedings the total amount spent on legal aid added up to £15.9 million. Defence lawyers in the Guinness case received £2.4 million from legal aid;[52] those in the BCCI case received £4.3 million; and those in the Brent-Walker case £2.3 million.[53]

The level of fees charged by leading counsel and their juniors in legally aided criminal appeals before the House of Lords sitting in its judicial capacity also attracted critical attention. In October 1998 a Report was published revealing the high fees submitted by a number of well known QCs. The Appeal Committee of the House of Lords, to which the matter had been referred,[54] declined to rule on whether the fees which had been charged by counsel in a number of cases were proper, or at what level they should be fixed. The Law Lords accepted that there was public concern about the cost of legal aid, and in particular about the rate at which counsel were being remunerated out of public funds. Their report offered some cautiously expressed guidance which they hoped might 'go some way to alleviate concern about the payment of fees which appear to be out of line with the norm'.[55]

[51] Summary taken from Legal Aid Board, *Ensuring Quality and Controlling Cost in Very High Cost Criminal Cases, Criminal Defence Services: A Consultation Paper*, Aug. 1999, p. 3.

[52] The trial of the first group of defendants lasted for 113 days. A second trial of two additional defendants was terminated after 54 days on compassionate grounds, owing to the failing health of one of the defendants.

[53] *The Independent*, 3 Aug. 1999.

[54] House of Lords, Appeal Committee, *Report on the Clerk of the Parliaments' Reference Regarding Criminal Legal Aid Taxation*, HL 145, 14 Oct. 1998. The Clerk of the Parliaments, having received a report from the Taxing Officer, considered that the size of the fees involved in a number of cases raised certain matters of principle which ought to be considered by the Lords of Appeal. Accordingly, he referred the matter to the Appeal Committee.

[55] Ibid., paras. 47–8, p. 14.

The *ex post facto* method for settling the fees of counsel of the necessary standing, having regard to the weight, seriousness, and public importance of major trials for fraud and other serious criminal offences, had already been condemned in a review commissioned by the Lord Chancellor shortly after the formation of the Labour Government in 1997. It was the considered opinion of Sir Peter Middleton, a former Permanent Secretary at HM Treasury (1983–91), that:

> payment calculated after the event on the basis of an hourly rate for all work done offers the greatest rewards to the least efficient providers.[56]

Fraud trials exacerbated the problem because of their complexity and length, but were not the only category of cases which would fall outside the standard CDS block-contract arrangements.

In the White Paper, *Modernising Justice*, the Government had accepted that different mechanisms would be needed where a trial was expected to last for more than twenty-five days. The Legal Aid Board went further in its consultation paper on controlling cost and ensuring quality in very high-cost criminal cases, pointing out that the top 1 per cent of cases, in cost terms, were not necessarily 'wholly coterminous' with cases where the trial was expected to last for more than twenty-five days.[57] Both factors would need to be taken into account in devising individual case contract arrangements. The criteria for the special category would be twofold:

> where the characteristics of the cases are such that they cannot be included within the standard contract arrangements which will cover the great majority of Crown Court cases

and:

> where the cost of the cases is so high, and therefore the potential impact on the overall budget for criminal defence services is so great, that specific, tailored arrangements need to be made for them, and higher levels of direct CDS management attention need to be paid to them.[58]

[56] Cited in Legal Aid Board, *Ensuring Quality and Controlling Cost in Very High Cost Criminal Cases*, *op. cit.*, p. 23.

[57] Ibid., p. 5.

[58] Ibid., pp. 5–6.

V

Although understandable in management terms, given the determination of the Government and the Legal Aid Board/Legal Services Commission to control costs, the reference to 'the overall budget for criminal defence services' was potentially misleading. In effect the total annual expenditure on criminal defence, unlike the predetermined budget for civil and family assistance, would not be cash-limited. Such an apparently generous policy decision was motivated not by any governmental magnanimity, but by a legal obligation coinciding with changes in the methods of controlling public expenditure. The entitlement under the European Convention on Human Rights of a person charged with a criminal offence to free legal assistance if without sufficient means to pay for it, and when the interests of justice so required, was noted earlier in this Chapter. British practice was generally in line with Article 6 of the Convention, but since the incorporation of the Convention in the Human Rights Act 1998 it had been converted into an enforceable Convention right in the British courts with effect from the date on which the substantive provisions of the Act came into force, 2 October 2000.

It was essentially for these reasons that, unlike the CLS,[59] all CDS expenditure would be determined by demand. Efforts would be made to forecast expenditure more accurately than hitherto, and as far as possible to ensure that out-turns matched the predicted profiles.[60] Under the existing system, as Irvine frankly admitted, the reality was that the funds available for civil legal aid were those left over after the prior demands of the criminal defence budget had been met. So he saw it as crucial for the costs to be contained.[61] The problem facing any reformer was that only the very rich and the relatively poor could afford to go to law, while criminal legal aid was eating up the bulk of the money that could be afforded. By virtue of Section 18 of the Access to Justice Act 1999, the Lord Chancellor is under a statutory obligation to pay to the Legal Services Commission:

[59] Civil and family assistance provided by the CLS is subject to a controlled (predetermined) budget, while representation in court on civil and family matters continues to be demand-led, albeit subject to a tougher merits test under a new Funding Code.

[60] Cited in Legal Aid Board, *Introducing Contracts for Criminal Defence Services with Lawyers in Private Practice*, *op. cit.*, p. 14.

[61] *Parl. Debates*, HL, 595, col. 1116, 14 Dec. 1998.

such sums as are required to meet the costs of any advice, assistance and representation funded by the Commission as part of the Criminal Defence Service.

The Act also stated that in funding services as part of the CDS 'the Commission shall aim to obtain the best possible value for money'.[62]

In this way the ideal of free legal advice and assistance, distinct from and additional to representation in courts, which had first featured in the visionary Legal Aid and Advice Act of 1949,[63] was finally translated into a legal right enforceable in the courts. The total cost was already high, and will no doubt continue to be so, although value for money and other nostrums will be brought to bear to ensure that public funds are not profligately expended. The outcome of demand-led growth of criminal legal aid in the 1990s, including the cost of legal advice and assistance for suspects and those helping the police with their inquiries, has far exceeded the annual costs incurred by the Crown Prosecution Service and the Serious Fraud Office in prosecuting criminal defendants. Some comparative statistics for expenditure on the prosecution and defence over the five-year period from 1994–5 to 1998–9 are shown in Table 9.

Nevertheless it would be misleading to take at face value the conclusion that by the end of the twentieth century the net annual cost of criminal legal aid in the Magistrates' courts and the Crown Court in England and Wales, supplemented by the cost of providing advice and assistance on criminal matters pre-trial, had reached levels that were more than double the gross annual cost of prosecution brought by the two principal prosecution agencies. The missing factor is police costs. In England and Wales much of the cost of prosecution is incurred by the police. For example, the police start virtually all prosecutions, and take all No Further Action (NFA) and cautioning decisions. Defence costs will often be incurred in these cases, but CPS costs very rarely. In cases to be prosecuted, the police prepare for the Crown Prosecution Service a file of evidence and other documents, such as a summary of the case. The CPS may

[62] Access to Justice Act 1999, Section 18(3).

[63] Owing to an economic crisis, leading to the devaluation of sterling by the Labour Government in September 1949, implementation of the Legal Aid and Advice Act was postponed. The Conservatives came to power in 1951 and when the first legal advice scheme was eventually set up in 1959 it was limited to paying private solicitors on a case-by-case basis. T. Goriely, *op. cit.*, p. 43.

Table 9. *Prosecution of defendants, criminal legal aid, and advice and assistance in criminal matters: annual expenditure 1994–9*

	1994–5	1995–6	1996–7	1997–8	1998–9
Prosecution of defendants by the Crown Prosecution Service and Serious Fraud Office[a] (gross expenditure, £ million)	328.821	332.409	336.403	336.756	344.332
Criminal legal aid in the Magistrates' and Crown Courts[b] (net expenditure, £ million)	464.38	498.03	538.69	590.76	627.16
Advice and assistance in criminal matters (net expenditure, £ million)	104.16	118.20	129.49	143.57	148.55

[a] Not including private prosecutions or prosecutions brought by other agencies.
[b] Legal aid expenditure includes the cost of defending actions brought by all prosecuting agencies and by private individuals.

Source: Lord Chancellor's Department, Oct. 1999; 1998–9 totals corrected Jan. 2001.

also ask the police to carry out further inquiries, or to obtain further evidence.[64]

Defence solicitors do not receive an equivalent amount of help from any outside source, and have to bear the total cost of defending a case. Moreover, the published statistics only count prosecutions brought by the CPS and the Serious Fraud Office for more serious offences, whereas criminal legal aid applies to all cases, whether prosecuted in the Crown Court or in the Magistrates' courts. Although HM Customs and Excise and the Inland Revenue prosecute relatively few cases compared with the CPS, drug trafficking and revenue offences are relatively expensive to prosecute. These points are made, not to deny that defence costs have risen more sharply than those of the CPS, but to put a gloss on some of the more exaggerated claims put forward to justify the need for reform on the basis of cost comparisons.

[64] Dr Richard Young, Assistant Director of the Centre for Criminological Research and Probation Studies Unit at the University of Oxford, recommended this qualification to the published statistics. Letter of 16 Mar. 2000.

VI

At a meeting with the author after the enactment of the Access to Justice legislation, the Lord Chancellor undertook to provide further information for the record under three headings. They were: the evolution of the Criminal Defence Service; a structure for the CDS/Leadership issues; and what action would be taken if the money ran out. The resulting letter was a document of unusual authority and candour, and is therefore reprinted verbatim as an Appendix to this Chapter. A commentary is added to assist readers unfamiliar with the complex system of financial controls operated by central Government.[65]

The essential controls on expenditure are, for the immediate year, the Parliamentary system of votes and supplementary votes, and, for the years ahead, the public expenditure allocations decided through comprehensive spending reviews. As in most structures of financial allocation, Treasury rules oblige those who administer funds to try to keep within their allocations by economy, efficiency, or where practicable by delaying projects or expenditures and cutting out items that are discretionary or of relatively low priority. Equally, the rules leave scope for a Department to argue for additional money, either in the immediate year or, exceptionally, for future years, without waiting for the outcome of the next comprehensive spending review.

Although the Legal Services Commission will administer both the Community Legal Service and the Criminal Defence Service, these will be funded by separate vote subheads. The Commission will have no discretion to move money from the one to the other. Spending above vote provision would require a request to the Lord Chancellor's Department.[66] Officials would consider the strength of the case and advise the Minister accordingly. They would examine closely whether any compensating reduction could

[65] Both the commentary in the Appendix and the description of the system for controlling public expenditure in Part VI draw on information supplied by a retired senior civil servant on the basis of his experience of public expenditure processes, and impressions of the changes made since 1997. The author records his gratitude to Sydney Norris, Home Office Principal Finance Officer and Director of Planning and Finance, 1990–6; and Finance Director, HM Prison Service, 1996–7.

[66] Although the Legal Services Commission does not have discretion to move money between the CLS and the CDS, the Lord Chancellor can at any time redetermine the CLS Fund. This would not be done lightly since any redetermination must be laid before Parliament.

be made elsewhere in the Lord Chancellor's expenditures, both to fulfil their Department's obligations to try to stay within provision, and because any request to the Treasury to support a Supplementary Estimate would be strengthened if it would not result in an overall increase in expenditure. If they approached the Treasury without any proposals for compensating reductions (i.e. asking for a net increase in expenditure rather than for permission to vire from one part of the vote to another, or from one vote to another) they could expect intense scrutiny as Treasury officials sought to show where they considered that savings could be made. In this respect, legal aid expenditure is no different from any other government expenditure.

Cash limits on particular segments of voted expenditure have less prominence in the Treasury's control of public expenditure than in the past. Greater emphasis is now placed on each Department's responsibility to stay within the total allocation that it has received in the most recent spending review, assisted by greater discretion to transfer funds from one type of expenditure to another within the total. But it is likely that any Department seeking an increase in its allocation would have just as much of a struggle with the Treasury as it would have done when seeking an increased cash limit in earlier years.

On the assumption that the best possible prediction of expenditure requirements for the delivery of legal aid has been made in conformity with government policy, and having made their case fully in the comprehensive spending review, officials in the Lord Chancellor's Department anticipated that the money allocated to them would be sufficient. But they recognized that their calculations could be thrown out of kilter by unforeseen developments. If that happened and the Department was unable to find off-setting savings within departmental votes, it would have to ask the Treasury for an increase from the Reserve.

The further ahead they extend, the more uncertain predictions become. The risk of additional demand through unforeseen circumstances is consequently higher in the second and third years of the period covered by a spending review. Equally, the further ahead the prudent financial controller looks, the more time there is to influence events in such a way as to reduce demand. Policy options to secure the desired level of legal services in the future, without exceeding spending limits, could be expected to include: limiting the costs of process, including the level of fees paid to lawyers; changing legal aid eligibility; and promoting methods of access to the courts that do not involve public expenditure, as exemplified by the introduction of a no win, no fee system for personal injury cases.

Other precautionary steps were taken to ensure that expenditure on legal aid should not be dominated by demand. Contracting with franchised firms of solicitors for the provision of specified standards of service was seen as a way of ensuring good quality service at affordable cost. The anticipated consequence was that resources would be directed towards certain priorities, such as social welfare, the protection of children, and incidents of domestic violence. The application of a more stringent merits test under the Funding Code meant that weak and non-cost effective cases would no longer be financed at the public expense. The Lord Chancellor's Department argued that none of these measures were primarily aimed at cost-cutting, pointing to the increased overall expenditure on the CLS. As a result of the spending review for 2000 the CLS received an extra £260 million over the next three years. CLS partnerships were also being developed to meet hitherto unmet local priority needs.[67]

VII

If bringing expenditure under control was at the heart of the reform of the system of legal aid, civil as well as criminal, this long-sought policy objective had become assimilated into the Labour Government's modernising mission. The retention of lawyers in private practice, but subject to specific franchise requirements prescribing the quality of the service provided as well as its cost, would be supplemented on the criminal side by the employment of a limited number of full-time salaried defenders. The resulting scheme was a compromise, but essentially an evolutionary one, replacing the old structures which had grown up piecemeal and had developed such evident flaws.

In the interval between the passage of the Access to Justice Act and the inauguration of the Criminal Defence Service in April 2001, the immediate priority was the development of contractual processes with lawyers in private practice. A Criminal Contracting Pilot scheme had been set up by the Legal Aid Board in June 1998 covering seventy franchised firms of solicitors in six geographical

[67] Letter from D. A. Hill, Head of Public Legal Services Division, Lord Chancellor's Department, 24 Jan. 2001.

locations.[68] Each undertook to supply advice and assistance in criminal cases under the existing system of legal aid, the purpose being to provide information on the design and implementation of future contracts for the new criminal defence services. The pilot scheme was researched by a team led by Professor Lee Bridges,[69] and resulted in two reports: one addressing the quality of service, and the other work structures and pricing.[70] The pilot project was confined to testing the provision of pre-trial legal advice and assistance on the basis of negotiated contract prices for a specified number of hours of authorized work. It did not extend to representation in court, whether by duty solicitors or salaried defenders.

From April 2001, when the Criminal Defence Service was due to come into being, there will be provision for the preliminary stages of a mixed system consisting of contracted private practice lawyers and salaried lawyers employed directly by the Legal Services Commission. By these means the Government claimed it would meet its obligations to ensure that individuals who are the subject of criminal investigations or criminal proceedings have access to legal assistance where the interests of justice requires it, and where they cannot afford it themselves.[71]

By the Autumn of 2000 it was apparent that, without reneging on the commitment to a mixed system, the salaried defender initiative would be slow-moving and on a small scale. The initial period of operation would be a start-up phase, coinciding with a research programme extending over a period of four years. The original aim was to commence the provision of salaried services at three locations in April 2001. This meant that the first locations might be selected before the research team was appointed. It was expected

[68] Manchester, London, Portsmouth, Reading, Blackburn, and Shrewsbury/Telford. Legal Services Commission, *Criminal Defence Service: Duty Solicitor Arrangements, 2001*, draft for consultation, August 2000.

[69] Director of the Legal Research Institute at the University of Warwick.

[70] *An Evaluation of The Legal Services Commission's Pilot Project on Contracting Criminal Legal Advice and Assistance, Executive Summary*. The two research reports were titled 'Work Patterns and Costs under Criminal Contracting', by L. Bridges and A. Abubaker, and 'Quality in Criminal Defence Services', by L. Bridges, E. Cape, A. Abubaker, and C. Bennett; Legal Services Commission, August 2000.

[71] Lord Chancellor's Department, *Criminal Defence Service: Establishing a Salaried Defence Service and Draft Code of Conduct for Salaried Defenders Employed by the Legal Services Commission*, CP 9/00, June 2000, p. 1. Four, rather than three, public defender offices, in Birmingham, Liverpool, Middlesbrough, and Swansea, were announced by the Lord Chancellor's Department on 14 Mar. 2001. They were expected to open in May, with two more offices being set up when the initial four had been assessed.

that the researchers should be in place in time to contribute to the decisions on the location of a further three offices, making a total of six during the initial four-year period. The Commission, together with the heads of the salaried offices and the Lord Chancellor's Department, would consider the development of the initial six offices, and whether any additional offices should be opened during that period.[72]

Overall responsibility for the management of salaried defenders' work would lie initially with the Commission's Head of Criminal Services. Once the Service was fully developed salaried defenders would report to a senior lawyer charged with protecting and promoting their professional integrity. In the formative stages the research programme was seen as an integral part of the project, enabling comparisons to be made between the salaried service and the performance of contracted lawyers in private practice. Performance would be tested against the most commonly voiced criticisms: independence, choice of representative, underfunding, case overload, and restriction of access. Individuals seeking criminal defence services would not be required by the Legal Services Commission to choose a salaried defender rather than a lawyer in private practice.[73] During, and at the end of, the four-year period the Government was expected to review the Service and make decisions on its future development.[74]

Until then, legal advice and representation for the large majority of eligible defendants, as well as for suspects and other individuals involved in criminal investigations or proceedings, would be provided by firms of solicitors franchised by the Legal Services Commission. The services provided would be in accordance with the requirements of a General Criminal Contract. In draft form, this document had been the subject of intensive consultation between the Commission and the Law Society, the Criminal Law Solicitors' Association, and the London Criminal Courts Solicitors' Association. More than 140 written responses were also received and considered. When published in December 2000 the Contract document ran to 217 printed pages, setting out in detail the structure of the contracted scheme, the terms of the contracts, the different types

[72] Legal Services Commission, *Specification for research of salaried defenders for the Legal Services Commission*, Sep. 2000, paras. 4.4 and 4.5, p. 9.

[73] CP 9/00, *op. cit.*, p. 6.

[74] Ibid., p. 4.

of contract work, and the arrangements for payment.[75] Since in criminal defence work the competence of individual lawyers is a prerequisite of effective representation, the General Criminal Contract also included sections on quality and performance standards. Each standard included a target against which performance would be measured.

VIII

An unexpected last-minute hitch occurred before the legislation came into effect. The sections of the Access to Justice Act 1999 replacing the existing legal aid scheme with the Criminal Defence Service were due to be implemented on 2 April 2001. Late in the previous year, however, when the detailed secondary legislation necessary to support their implementation was being drafted, the Lord Chancellor was advised that on the most likely construction the Act omitted a power to provide advice and assistance in all of the circumstances in which it was currently available. Since it was the Government's intention to maintain the broad range of help available, this was a significant omission. Under the current legislation individuals involved in criminal investigations or criminal proceedings were entitled to legal advice and assistance, including limited representation in certain circumstances at a court or other hearing. This was known as Assistance by Way of Representation, or more commonly as ABWOR, and it formed the basis of the widely used duty solicitor scheme. There were also a number of other situations where, although full legal aid might not be justified, the Human Rights Act required that representation was available at a hearing.[76]

[75] Legal Services Commission, *General Criminal Contract*, Dec. 2000. Shortly after the publication of the General Criminal Contract the Council of the Law Society advised practitioners not to sign it at that stage. The advice was repeated on 14 Feb. and 1 Mar. 2001 when practitioners, having assessed the impact of the contract package, concluded that its introduction would lead to their income from criminal work being significantly reduced. On 8 Mar. 2001, after last-ditch negotiations with the Legal Services Commission had resulted in improvements being made to the original proposals, the Law Society advised practitioners to sign the contracts in order to continue practising after 2 Apr. 2001. Out of a total of 2,962 firms invited to contract the Legal Services Commission received 2,838 signed contracts by 29 Mar. 2001.

[76] Letter from Lord Bach, Parliamentary Secretary, Lord Chancellor's Department, 8 Dec. 2000.

Ministers explained it had always been the Government's policy to preserve this form of assistance, but that the interaction of amendments made during the passage of the legislation through Parliament had resulted in the unintended consequence that the continued provision of this form of limited representation would probably not be possible.[77] To remedy the defect a short and uncontroversial Bill was introduced in the Lords, which was the subject of a brief debate on Second Reading on the last day before the Christmas Recess.[78] The subsequent stages followed in the New Year. In the course of the debate, the Parliamentary Secretary at the Lord Chancellor's Department, Lord Bach, made use of the opportunity to refer to what he described as 'any confusion that might have arisen between the terms criminal defence service and salaried defence service'. The first was the name given to the service which would provide all forms of publicly funded legal help for individuals facing a criminal investigation or prosecution. The vast majority of expenditure on the criminal defence service, in the region of £430 million per year, would be needed to pay independent solicitors and barristers representing those accused of criminal offences. The salaried defence service would be 'a tiny part of the criminal defence service'. It was expected to be very small in the foreseeable future, with only six offices planned, compared with the 3,000 or more solicitors' firms which would have a contract with the Legal Services Commission for the provision of criminal defence services. Thus in 'the vast majority of cases' for which the Bill provided a form of representation to be known as 'advocacy assistance', the service would be provided by private practitioners.[79]

Such sensitivity to hostile opinion reflected the uphill nature of the task of reforming just one aspect of entrenched professional practice. Step-by-step progress there might be, but there was no sign of inspirational leadership from ministers or any other potential patrons. Perhaps cautious incremental change was the British way. Perhaps the comprehensive research programme would yield results that could not have been anticipated and might generate more zest. Perhaps the Treasury had been reluctant to fund a larger-scale, but more costly, approach. One casualty of the slow-moving bureaucratic and research-based approach was likely to be the scope for idealism

[77] Letter from Lord Bach, Parliamentary Secretary, Lord Chancellor's Department, 8 Dec. 2000.

[78] *Parl. Debates*, HL, 620, cols. 845–50, 21 Dec. 2000.

[79] Ibid., col. 846.

which had been a driving force in the very different evolution of legal services for indigent persons accused of criminal offending in the United States. That is the topic of the next Chapter.

APPENDIX B

FROM THE RIGHT HONOURABLE THE LORD IRVINE OF LAIRG

HOUSE OF LORDS,
LONDON SW1A OPW

10 January 2000

Dear David,

CRIMINAL DEFENCE SERVICE

When we met on 23 September 1999 to discuss the Criminal Defence Service (CDS), I agreed to provide you with further information on various aspects of the CDS. I do apologise for the delay in replying.

Evolution of the Criminal Defence Service

After the Election, a cross-departmental review of the criminal justice system was initiated, as was a comprehensive spending review. I commissioned Sir Peter Middleton to conduct a review of civil justice and legal aid. On 18th October 1997, in my keynote speech to the Law Society's annual conference, I said that I proposed to extend contracting to criminal legal aid, but that '. . . we need to work hard to decide how the interests of justice in criminal cases—particularly the rights of defendants and the need to avoid delay—can be dovetailed with a contracting system managed by the Legal Aid Board'.

The Department initiated an internal review of criminal defence services in November 1997. The review was initiated in the context of the cross-departmental review of the criminal justice system and the Department's comprehensive spending review. The recommendations made by the internal review were the basis of the reform of criminal defence services set out in the White Paper 'Modernising Justice', which proposed the establishment of a Criminal Defence Service to replace the current criminal legal aid system. As I had been granted an early slot for a Bill in the session starting in November 1998, there was no time for formal consultation. However, you should look at my comments in Parliament in Committee stage of the Access to Justice Bill on 26 January 1999, when I said that:

> . . . I can only assume that those who feel taken by surprise have not been reading the newspapers and the legal journals, much less listening to the speeches that I and my Minister of State have been making over the past year or so.

For example, in July 1997, Frances Gibb interviewed Geoff Hoon, then my Parliamentary Secretary, for *The Times*. What followed was an article headlined 'Ministers study plan for public defenders', which reported that the Government was considering the use of salaried lawyers to defend in criminal cases. The article stated that this was one of several options being studied in a wide-ranging review of the legal aid system.

Also in July 1997, Mr Hoon said in response to an oral Parliamentary Question about public defenders:

> . . . We have not ruled out the possibility of engaging employed solicitors, or indeed solicitors under specially designed contracts for particular kinds of work, if those would be the most suitable arrangements in all the circumstances . . . We have not ruled out the possibility of having employed lawyers; indeed, there is likely to be a pilot scheme in Scotland in due course which will allow us to test precisely the quality of the service that is made available.

Michael Grieve's report of an interview with Mr Hoon in the December 1997 edition of *Counsel* magazine stated:

> . . . He does not expect that a 'Public Defender' approach, (in the sense of lawyers being employed by a public body), is the right way to deliver the general run of these services but will deploy the best approach in particular circumstances.

A Structure for the CDS/Leadership issues

The Access to Justice Act gives powers to create a Criminal Defence Service which will, as I said in Parliament on second reading of the Access to Justice Bill on the 14 December 1998:

> . . . ensure that those who appear before our courts and risk imprisonment receive high quality legal defence services.

The major changes from the existing system of criminal legal aid are that, in future, only those lawyers who have contracts with the Criminal Defence Service and fulfil quality criteria will be able to represent assisted clients. The other change is that the CDS will be able to employ lawyers directly.

For the foreseeable future the Legal Services Commission will run the CDS, and the Community Legal Service (CLS). There may be advantages in the longer term in establishing two completely separate and clearly-focused bodies to administer the schemes, but for the present it would be wrong to talk in terms of there being a distinct structure to the CDS. I anticipate, however, that there would be a department within the Commission responsible for the running of the CDS.

When considering salaried defenders specifically, as I said in debate in Parliament on 26 July 1999, there are two options for funding and administering salaried services within a mixed system. They are:

> . . . direct employment by the Commission and employment by separate not-for-profit bodies established and maintained by the Commission for the purposes of providing criminal defence services.

Any salaried defenders employed by the Commission will be operationally independent from the rest of the Commission. They will be organised in a separate unit or units, and will not have responsibilities for any other of the Commission's functions. They will report to a senior lawyer responsible for managing them in a way that respects and protects their professional integrity. As I said at our meeting, I feel it is very important that the people we attract to be salaried defenders should be lawyers of high quality with enthusiasm and commitment. It would be equally important that those managing the service, whether at the LSC or at local offices, should recognise the need to encourage these qualities and to lead by example.

Under section 16 of the Access to Justice Act 1999 there is statutory provision for the Legal Services Commission to prepare a code of conduct to be observed by employees of the Commission, and employees of any body established and maintained by the Commission. The code includes duties to:

- avoid discrimination
- protect the interests of the individuals for whom services are provided
- the court
- avoid conflicts of interest, and
- confidentiality

and duties on employees who are members of a professional body to comply with the rules of the body.

Furthermore, section 42 of the Act imposes on advocates and litigators a statutory duty to the court to act with independence in the interests of justice; and a duty to comply with their professional bodies' rules of conduct. Those duties override any other civil law obligation which a person may be under, including the duty to the client or a contractual obligation to an employer or to anyone else.

We shall, in any event, be consulting early this year on the code of conduct and on detailed proposals for salaried defenders before establishing small pilots in 2001 to test and evaluate different models for providing services through salaried defenders.

What action would be taken if the money ran out?

There is not an overall 'legal aid' budget or cash limit. Both the CLS and the CDS will form part of my departmental spending limit, in common with spending on the Court Service, magistrates' courts, my Headquarters, the Legal Service Commission's administrative budget and various offices.

There is no question of money simply running out because we are moving away from paying bills out of an annual budget to purchasing services in advance. In non-criminal matters, contracts for providing services, once the new scheme is up and running, will be let for up to three years and will be structured so that the providers supply a steady stream of services to meet the needs and priorities identified nationally and locally. If demand rises ahead of supply, it would be open to me to seek additional resources either from within my own budget or by asking my colleagues to make more money available from the Exchequer.

I should emphasise that under the new scheme we will be assessing need in advance and publishing plans for meeting it on a prioritised basis. With good data it will generally be possible to see pressures well in advance and therefore we will have time to decide how to deal with them. However if there are sudden surges in demand in a particular area, we will have powers to react flexibly and to move resources about.

There is, I realise, a particular concern about the relationship between the money available for civil and family matters, the CLS and for criminal cases under the CDS. Our international obligations require that legal representation is available to all those charged with a criminal offence. This means that the CDS will have a prior claim on the available funding. However, this does not mean that funding will automatically be transferred from the CLS if expenditure on criminal advice, assistance and representation is greater than expected.

Yours ever

Derry

COMMENTARY ON THE FINAL PART OF APPENDIX B

'WHAT ACTION WOULD BE TAKEN IF THE MONEY RAN OUT?'

There is not an overall 'legal aid' budget or cash limit

Earlier in this Chapter an apparent distinction was noted between the firm limit on Community Legal Service funding for civil legal aid, and an open-ended provision for Criminal Defence Service financing of criminal legal aid. The past tendency for the demands of criminal legal aid to limit the funds that could be made available for civil legal aid was noted. Under the new arrangements, however, it would be misleading to think of the Legal Services Commission as having an overall fixed budget for legal aid within which the costs of criminal legal aid would have to be met at the expense of civil legal aid. There will be two types of money voted by Parliament for two types of activity. If either proves insufficient, the Commission will need to approach the Lord Chancellor's Department. It will not be a case of robbing Peter to pay Paul.

Both the CLS and the CDS will form part of my departmental spending limit . . .

Like other departmental ministers, the Lord Chancellor is expected to manage his Department within the resources allocated to it.

. . . purchasing services in advance . . . contracts . . . will be let for up to three years and will be structured so that providers supply a steady stream of services . . .

This system is intended to produce predictability and an additional element of control as the contractors will be seeking to manage the provision of a service within the contractual terms. If they want to vary the contract because of unforeseen demand, or because they are increasing their available resources, they will need to negotiate with the Department. They cannot simply increase the level of services and get paid for it.

If demand rises ahead of supply, it would be open to me to seek additional resources either from within my own budget or by asking my colleagues to make more money available from the Exchequer.

Here the Lord Chancellor describes the process of internal management, subject to Treasury approval and Parliamentary sanction if moving between vote subheads, and the process of making a claim on the Reserve for that year, or arguing for extra money in future years in the Spending Review. The next paragraph explains why he expects demand to be more predictable in the future, and why he expects to be able to plan flexibly to meet demand. The final paragraph acknowledges that failure to provide legal representation in criminal cases could lead to a challenge under the provisions of the European Convention on Human Rights.

This means that the CDS will have a prior claim on the available funding

Quite apart from any domestic policy considerations, the provision of legal aid is bound to have a high priority in public expenditure planning because of the UK's international obligations.

However, this does not mean that funding will automatically be transferred from the CLS if expenditure on criminal advice, assistance and representation is greater than expected.

As explained above, the Legal Services Commission does not have the right or the obligation to move money from the one to the other. Any risk of overspending will be for the Lord Chancellor to cope with. He does not necessarily need to find the savings from civil legal aid, rather than savings on Crown Court or other heads of expenditure.

6
Public Defenders: American Style

I

The fact that publicly funded legal defence costs should outweigh those of the prosecution[1] is a feature of the British system that legislators, judges, and criminal justice practitioners in the United States find incomprehensible. In America, ever since a historic ruling of the Supreme Court in 1963, all defendants charged with a felony offence are entitled to representation by counsel at a fair trial, irrespective of wealth or poverty.[2] The issues are no longer the recognition of a right rooted in the Sixth Amendment to the Constitution,[3] but lie in difficulties of finding the money and resources for it to be honoured effectively.

What follows is an excursus into comparative study, for only the second time in the four volumes of *Responses to Crime*.[4] It is offered

[1] See Table 9 above. Police costs are not included in the official prosecution statistics.

[2] *Gideon* v. *Wainwright*, 372 U.S. 335 (1963). Earlier in *Powell* v. *Alabama*, 287 U.S. 45 (1932), the Supreme Court held that due process required states to accord the right to counsel to defendants charged with capital crimes and, if indigent, in some circumstances to have counsel appointed for them. In that case the Court set aside for the first time a state criminal conviction because the procedure used to obtain it was unfair.

[3] The Sixth Amendment to the Constitution of the United States formed part of the Bill of Rights ratified in 1791. The wording of the amendment in full is as follows: 'In all criminal prosecutions the accused shall enjoy the right to a speedy and public trial, by an impartial jury of the State and district wherein the crime shall have been committed; which district shall have been previously ascertained by law, and to be informed of the nature and cause of the accusation; to be confronted with the witnesses against him; to have compulsory process for obtaining witnesses in his favor, and to have the assistance of counsel for his defence'. Seven of the original thirteen states adopted constitutions shortly after independence which included provisions for a right to counsel. But for a long period due process remained a vague concept, and the right to an attorney was largely ignored in practice. See S. Walker, *Popular Justice: A History of American Criminal Justice*, 2nd edition, Oxford University Press, New York, 1998, p. 38.

[4] Volume 3 of *Responses to Crime* (1996) contains a descriptive and analytical account of the legislative objectives and passage of the federal Violent Crime Control and Law Enforcement Act of 1994, Pub. L. 103–322; 108 Stat. 1796. In revised and expanded form that study was included in the author's later book, *Politics, Punishment, and Populism*, published by Oxford University Press in New York in 1998.

in the hope that it may help British readers to comprehend a topical feature of American law and practice, and to identify any comparisons relevant to the reorganized Criminal Defence Service. American readers may note with wonderment how it is that two cultures, which share so much in their common law origins and procedures, should have diverged so widely in the practical application of broadly similar principles of justice.

Unlike many other far-reaching changes in the law, which are the culmination of persistent campaigns promoted by organized interests, the decision in *Gideon* v. *Wainwright* was a tribute to the tenacity of a single defendant who had been denied legal representation at his trial. Partly because of the uplifting way in which an obscure prisoner's petition, addressed to the Supreme Court of the United States, set off a sequence of events which lived up to the highest ideals of American democracy, but also because of Anthony Lewis's classic account in his book, *Gideon's Trumpet*,[5] the case quickly became, and has remained, one of the best known in modern American legal history.

Over the previous three decades the Supreme Court had been developing, case by case, a series of constitutional restraints on almost every aspect of law enforcement by states, from arrest through trial and sentence to appeal.[6] Although the process had predated the appointment of Chief Justice Warren in 1953,[7] and continued after he retired, the influence of the Warren court was in many ways the high point in the enlargement of civil rights. Consequently, while *Gideon*'s case marked a decisive shift in the law on the right to counsel at trial, it should be seen in the context of a wider trend. According to Lewis's stylish appraisal, during the 1960s the Supreme Court was developing a whole panoply of new freedoms for the individual, so enlarging the dimensions of liberty.[8]

[5] *Gideon's Trumpet* was first published by Random House, New York, in 1964. A British edition by Bodley Head, London, followed in 1966. The most recent paperback edition was published by Vintage Books, a division of Random House, New York, in 1989.

[6] Ibid., Vintage Books edition, 1989, p. 219.

[7] Earl Warren, a former Republican Governor of California, was appointed Chief Justice by President Eisenhower in 1953 and served until his retirement in 1969. Following the assassination of President Kennedy in November 1963, Warren was appointed to head a commission of inquiry into the circumstances of the killing. He died in 1974.

[8] *Gideon's Trumpet*, *op. cit.*, p. 220.

The constitutional requirement that every defendant in a capital or non-capital felony case standing trial in a state court, as well as a federal court, should be provided with a qualified lawyer regardless of the defendant's ability to pay, was further extended in 1972. In *Argersinger* v. *Hamlin*[9] the Supreme Court held that the right of an indigent defendant to the assistance of counsel in a criminal trial was not governed by the classification of the offence, nor by whether a jury trial was required. Accused persons should not be deprived of their liberty as a result of criminal prosecution, whether for a felony or a misdemeanour, if they had been denied the assistance of counsel. In delivering the opinion of the Court, Justice Douglas stated that in the absence of 'a knowing and intelligent waiver, no person may be imprisoned for any offence, whether classified as petty, misdemeanor or felony', unless represented by counsel at trial.[10]

The limitation of the right to counsel in misdemeanour and petty offence cases to situations where imprisonment was imposed led to considerable debate on how the Court's ruling in *Argersinger* should be implemented. A literal interpretation appeared to restrict the right to counsel to defendants who were actually imprisoned. But that outcome would not be known until the conclusion of the trial, after sentence had been passed following a finding of guilt. Of necessity, counsel would need to be appointed before trial or a guilty plea. In the interests of greater clarity many states subsequently enacted statutes requiring, at a minimum, that counsel be afforded wherever there was a possibility of imprisonment.[11]

The right to legal representation was also broadened to include various types of pre-trial proceedings. These covered preliminary hearings,[12] line-up identifications,[13] and custodial interrogations.[14] In contrast with the unmistakably libertarian motivation for these changes, a gulf opened up between the enunciation of legal rights by the courts and their fulfilment. The right to effective representation by counsel had been granted to specified categories of person, either

[9] 407 U.S. 25 (1972).

[10] Ibid. at 37.

[11] American Bar Association, *ABA Standards for Criminal Justice: Providing Defense Services*, 3rd edition, Washington, D.C., 1992, p. 63. This formulation is consistent with ABA Standard 5-5.1 which states that counsel should be provided in all proceedings for offences punishable by death or incarceration, regardless of their denomination as felonies, misdemeanours, or otherwise.

[12] *Coleman* v. *Alabama*, 399 U.S. 1 (1970).

[13] *United States* v. *Wade*, 388 U.S. 218 (1967).

[14] *Miranda* v. *Arizona*, 384 U.S. 436 (1966).

accused or suspected of having committed a criminal offence. But there was no accompanying duty to fund the practical consequences. What the Constitution had given, lack of resources had taken away.[15]

Since there were only an insignificant number of criminal prosecutions in the federal district courts in the mid and late 1960s, this being before the tidal wave of persons charged with offences under federal drugs legislation, the financial burden fell on the states. Willingly or otherwise, states had to accept that in order to comply with federal constitutional law they were now required to ensure that legal representation was provided in state courts for large numbers of indigent defendants at the public expense.[16] In some states such a right already existed, especially in capital cases, but in others it did not. Court structures meant that in about half of the states the responsibility for providing indigent defence was passed on to the counties.

County jurisdictions vary greatly in size, from those with very small populations to Cook County in Illinois, containing the City of Chicago,[17] and Los Angeles County in California, containing the City of Los Angeles. Unlike state legislatures, which have wide powers to tax citizens to pay for services, counties normally have limited powers to raise taxes, the main sources of locally generated revenue being property and sales taxes. Even where counties did have a substantial tax base, there were periodic budget deficits. When savings had to be made there were few, if any, services less popular with electors, and hence with some of their representatives, than providing money for the defence of persons charged with criminal offences, many of whom would be convicted and receive custodial sentences. Thus, from the very start, the system of indigent defence was based on precarious financial foundations.

[15] For this aphorism the author is indebted to Philip Heymann, James Barr Ames Professor of Law at Harvard Law School. Heymann's resignation as Deputy Attorney General of the United States in 1994 is discussed in Vol. 3 of *Responses to Crime* at pp. 260–1.

[16] There are few reliable statistics on the number of indigent defendants. The Bureau of Justice Statistics of the U.S. Department of Justice estimated that in 1992 about 80 per cent of defendants charged with felonies in the seventy-five largest counties nationally were indigent. Approximately three-quarters of all inmates in state prisons had been represented by public defenders or some other public-provided attorney. Bureau of Justice Statistics, *Indigent Defense*, 1, 1995. Cited in D. Cole, *No Equal Justice: Race and Class in the American Criminal Justice System*, New Press, New York; I. B. Tauris, London, 1999, p. 66.

[17] The Chicago Metropolitan Area is larger, extending to suburbs covered by five other counties as well as Cook.

II

With some exceptions, throughout the process of criminal justice in America quality goes with money. Idealism and professional standards certainly count, and indeed played a critically important part in setting up many of the original public defender agencies. But in the early days, especially with counsel assigned by trial court judges, the picture could be very different. Not only might counsel be poorly paid, professionally inept, or politically aligned with the judge, but they might have been appointed only because they happened to be present in the court-room when a defendant was brought in. A task force set up by the Criminal Justice Standards Committee of the American Bar Association stated:

> This method of assignment obviously is unlikely to achieve an equitable distribution of assignments among the qualified members of the bar, and in some jurisdictions the practice has given rise to a cadre of mediocre lawyers who wait in the courtroom in hopes of receiving an appointment.[18]

Most fair-minded observers believe that both the general standard of competence and the independence of counsel assigned by the courts have improved significantly since *Gideon* and the early stages of indigent defence entitlements. Yet the record undoubtedly contains blemishes. There are still places in America, and not only in the South, where there is a marked shortage of well qualified assigned counsel. The combination of low fees and sometimes intolerably heavy work-loads has led to situations where the standard of representation for the accused by court-appointed attorneys has been plainly inferior to that of the prosecution. When that happens, the constitutionally protected rights of the defendant are negated by the inability of the state to ensure genuine equality before the law for poor people on trial for criminal offences carrying severe penalties. In the words of a trenchant critic writing on this topic in 1999, 'a constitutional right is only as good as the lawyer one has to assert it'.[19]

Since 1984 a required standard of performance by counsel has been set by the US Supreme Court. It can be succinctly stated as the provision of reasonably effective assistance to the accused. In *Strickland* v. *Washington* the Court held that:

[18] *ABA Standards for Criminal Justice*, 3rd edition, *op. cit.*, p. 31.
[19] D. Cole, *No Equal Justice*, *op. cit.*, p. 95.

The benchmark for judging any claim of ineffectiveness must be whether counsel's conduct so undermined the proper functioning of the adversarial process that the trial cannot be relied on as having produced a just result.[20]

The test was a demanding one, and intentionally so to avoid a proliferation of ineffectiveness challenges. Giving the opinion of the Court, Justice O'Connor warned that:

Criminal trials resolved unfavorably to the defendant would increasingly come to be followed by a second trial, this one of counsel's unsuccessful defense. Counsel's performance and even willingness to serve could be adversely affected. Intensive scrutiny of counsel and rigid requirements for acceptable assistance could dampen the ardor and impair the independence of defense counsel, discourage the acceptance of assigned cases, and undermine the trust between attorney and client.[21]

It is hard to compare the effectiveness of the different types of counsel representing indigent defendants. Until the mid-1990s there were two main categories: assigned counsel, that is private attorneys appointed by the court and paid on a case-by-case basis, often on a low scale of fees, and salaried counsel usually employed full-time by public defender agencies. Although funded by counties or the state, these agencies characteristically displayed a high degree of independence. More recently, contracted services for specified blocks of work between courts or local government and attorneys or law firms have added a third way of delivering indigent defence services.

There has been little systematic research on the effectiveness of different types of counsel, although much anecdotal opinion circulates. Such research as has been undertaken, with the results published, indicates that the type of defence counsel, whether an assigned private attorney or a public defender, is not an important determinant in case outcome.[22] But case outcomes are not the same as the maintenance of professional standards or client satisfaction. In the early days of indigent defence there was an indication that a majority of defendants preferred assigned counsel to public defenders. The best explanation was the simplest: that clients prefer attorneys who spend time with them to those who do not.[23] High work-loads and restricted resources may limit the amount of time

[20] 466 U.S. 668 (1984), at 686.

[21] Ibid. at 690.

[22] F. Feeny and P. Jackson, 'Public Defenders, Assigned Counsel, and Retained Counsel: Does the type of Criminal Defense Counsel Matter?', *22 Rutgers Law Journal*, 361 (1991) at pp. 407–9.

[23] Ibid., p. 408.

available for public defenders to spend with defendants, although it is likely that other factors may also be at play. Perhaps the most significant feature of the emergent systems was that they offered diversity and, to some extent, choice to defendants.

III

So far this commentary has been at the level of generality, identifying legal rights and outlining the means that have been developed to give effect to them. Now it is time to discuss in more detail how services for indigents operate in two contrasting court jurisdictions and political entities. Although not capable of a comprehensive formal definition, the term 'indigent defendants' is usually taken to include individuals who are unable to post a bail bond and are routinely detained for up to forty-five days prior to arraignment, without access to counsel.[24] The first case history is the State of Indiana, comprising ninety-two counties, the largest of which, Marion County, contains the City of Indianapolis with a population of about one million. The second is the five counties of New York City which fall within the jurisdiction of the First and Second Judicial Departments of the Supreme Court of New York State. Neither example can be regarded as typical, for there is no single model to which a majority of states or counties have conformed. But while developments elsewhere will have differed from the systems developed in Indiana and New York City, there is no reason to believe that between them they do not span a range which reflects and illuminates recent American experience.

More than a century before *Gideon* v. *Wainwright* the Indiana Supreme Court in *Webb* v. *Baird*[25] held that indigent criminal defendants had a right to an attorney at public expense. The decision was grounded neither in constitution nor statute, but in what the Court saw as the duties of civilized communities and self-respecting courts:[26]

[24] See *Improving State and Local Criminal Justice Systems*, Office of Justice Programs, U.S. Department of Justice, Washington, D.C., 1998, p. 1.

[25] 6 Ind. 13 (1854).

[26] Comment of Frank Sullivan Jr, Associate Justice of the Supreme Court of Indiana. The author acknowledges his gratitude to Justice Sullivan for his encouragement and assistance in providing information. This account of the development of indigent defence in Indiana reproduces in part his remarks at a national symposium convened at the U.S. Department of Justice in Washington, D.C. on 25–6 Feb.

> It is not to be thought of, in a civilized community, for a moment, that any citizen put in jeopardy of life or liberty, should be debarred of counsel because he was too poor to employ such aid. No Court could be respected, or respect itself, to sit and hear such a trial. The defense of the poor, in such cases, is a duty . . . which will be at once conceded as essential to the accused, to the Court, and to the public.[27]

The Supreme Court of the state went on to affirm the trial court's mandate that the county should compensate Baird for his representation of an indigent criminal defendant. From this decision onwards, Indiana trial court judges, elected on a county-by-county basis, appointed indigent defence counsel and mandated their compensation from their respective county treasuries.

That system was still in place in 1989 when the Indiana General Assembly passed, and the Governor signed into law, an Act creating a new state-wide Public Defender Commission. It was not a comprehensive reform measure, being targeted in particular at the problem of indigent defence counsel in capital cases. County court judges would still appoint defence counsel in death penalty cases, who would be paid from county funds. But the new Commission was charged with developing standards for such defence services and, in a change of fundamental financial and administrative significance, it was authorized to approve reimbursement of up to 50 per cent of death penalty defence costs to be paid from state funds to counties which complied with the standards. Thus a system was created which contained a powerful incentive to raise and maintain standards broadly in line with those promulgated by the American Bar Association.

Standards were developed by the Indiana Public Defender Commission and adopted in 1991 which in capital cases required the appointment of two defence lawyers, each meeting certain specified experience and training criteria. The appointed lawyer's work-load was limited to a specified number of cases and no new cases could be

1999 by the Office of Justice Programs and the Bureau of Justice Assistance. Professor Norman Lefstein, Dean of the Indiana University School of Law, Indianapolis, and Chairman of the Indiana Public Defender Commission since its inception, was overall moderator at the symposium, with the Attorney General, Janet Reno, as the keynote speaker. He too has been an invaluable source of information and guidance. Neither Justice Sullivan nor Dean Lefstein has any responsibility for the opinions stated by the author in this review. A second national symposium on indigent defence, also moderated by Lefstein, was held in Washington, D.C. on 29–30 June 2000.

[27] *Op. cit.*, 6 Ind. 18 (1854).

assigned within thirty days of the trial date. The lawyers were to be paid at a prescribed hourly rate, and provided with adequate funds for investigative, expert, and other services necessary to prepare and present an adequate defence. Compliance with these standards was then mandated by the State Supreme Court in all capital cases with an indigent defendant.[28]

The next step came in 1993 when the state legislature passed, and the Governor approved, an amendment to the Public Defender Commission Act extending the offer of state reimbursement of the cost of indigent defence to non-capital cases, again contingent upon a county's compliance with Commission-established standards. The reimbursement level was initially set at 25 per cent of local costs, amended by the legislature in 1997 to 40 per cent, except for misdemeanours.

The standards for non-capital cases required participating counties to establish public defender boards to plan and administer indigent defence services in their own counties. The local board would need to make provision for the appointment of counsel at public expense for all persons financially unable to obtain adequate representation without substantial hardship to themselves or their families.[29] Counsel so appointed must meet specified experience requirements which vary depending on the seriousness of the charge. Once appointed, the work-load of counsel is limited to specified case-loads. Payment of salaried, or contractual, public defenders must be at rates substantially comparable to similar positions in the county prosecutor's office. Minimum hourly rates of payment were prescribed for counsel employed on a case-by-case basis, and provision would need to be made to meet the cost of investigative, expert, and other services, and for office expenses.

Unlike the capital defence programme, the non-capital programme is optional. By December 1999 rather more than one-third, i.e. thirty-five of the ninety-two counties, were eligible to receive reimbursement, including Marion County. The estimated annual cost to the state for both capital and non-capital programmes was

[28] Indiana Criminal Rule 24.

[29] The substantial hardship test for determining indigency was adopted by the Indiana Supreme Court in *Moore* v. *State* (1980), Ind., 401 N.E. 2d 676, at 678–9, and has been cited with approval in subsequent appellate opinions. It is that the defendant does not have to be totally without means to be entitled to counsel. If he legitimately lacks financial resources to employ an attorney without imposing substantial hardship on himself or his family, the court must appoint counsel to defend him.

expected to increase from an estimated $3.8 million for fiscal year 1999[30] to $5.6 million for fiscal year 2000. Reimbursement to all counties for capital cases was additional to these amounts.

By these means, standards of representation in Indiana are directly connected to substantial incentive payments. Oversight is in the hands of the state-appointed Public Defender Commission. Under its initial enabling legislation, the Commission had seven members. Three were appointed by the Governor, three by the Chief Justice of the Supreme Court of Indiana, and one by the Board of Trustees of the Indiana Criminal Justice Institute. In 1993 the political link was strengthened when the General Assembly added four legislators to the Commission. Two were appointed by the Speaker of the House, and two by the Senate President *pro tempore*. The political context is of continuing importance because Indiana is not a state with much tolerance towards crime or offenders. It is a death penalty state; lengthy prison sentences are authorized, usually with statutorily prescribed minimum terms; and sentences are frequently enhanced on the basis of habitual-offender status. Appropriations for prisons is one of the fastest growing segments of the state budget.[31]

While accepting the constitutional imperative of providing effective assistance of counsel, hostile public opinion can be aroused by allegations of mismanagement, or abuse of public funds, or of agenda-setting for wider reforms in criminal justice that go beyond the legal representation of persons accused of criminal offences which, if proved, may lead to loss of liberty. Above all else is the adverse publicity attracted by the very high costs that can be incurred in capital cases. Emotive headlines and media reporting of the most notorious murder trials and convictions can generate an unsympathetic environment, to say the least, towards the rights of the defendants in such cases. A front-page newspaper story in 1999 provides a prime example:

> Indiana taxpayers spent more than half a million dollars to defend triple murderer John M. Stephenson on his way to Death Row. For child killer Stephen K. Sherwood, the defense price tag was $352,890 . . . Price tags like these have prompted prosecutors to ask the Indiana Supreme Court to limit

[30] The fiscal year begins on 1 July and ends on 30 June annually.

[31] Extracted from the remarks of Justice Sullivan at the Department of Justice Symposium referred to at n. 26, above.

the amount of money that can be paid to attorneys appointed to represent poor defendants in death penalty cases.[32]

Populist sentiments of this kind are not peculiar to Indiana. They would be echoed in many other places. But the report from one newspaper in one city is illustrative of the turbulent currents of opinion which swirl around indigent defence systems. If their viability is to be maintained, and their weaknesses remedied, the support of legislators, as well as judges and the executive branch of government, is indispensable.

IV

The Indiana model, making the provision of state funds to county-based defender organizations conditional on compliance with standards set by a state-wide Public Defender Commission, had an advantage noticeably absent in New York City.[33] Although in both systems compliance is non-mandatory, there is a stronger incentive to comply where a mechanism is in place directly linking the supply of funds to the maintenance of standards. In New York City it is the opposite. While a high proportion of the funding for the various organizations providing defence services for indigent defendants comes from the City Council, restrictions on both the overall amount and the method of allocation have led to failures to comply with standards.

Unlike Indiana, where oversight is exercised by a state-appointed commission, in New York City the authority and responsibility for monitoring the performance of organizations providing indigent defence services derives from the courts. It is of comparatively recent origin going back to events in 1994. In that year, reacting to a four-day strike by the Legal Aid Society's criminal defence staff, the City of New York resolved to contract with alternative organizations to provide legal representation to indigent defendants in criminal cases. By distributing part of the public defence work to a number of smaller providers, the Mayor hoped to limit the potential for future

[32] *The Indianapolis Star*, 14 Feb. 1999.

[33] New York City comprises the counties of Bronx, Kings (Brooklyn), New York (Manhattan), Queens, and Richmond (Staten Island). Although the designation may be different, the counties in the City of New York are the geographical equivalents of the five boroughs. In 1997 the total population was 7,342,636.

disruption.[34] Concerned that the City would concentrate on cost rather than quality in the selection of potential contractors, the New York County Lawyers' Association, joined by the Association of the Bar of the City of New York and the Bronx Bar Association, first approached the City with a proposal to establish an oversight mechanism.[35]

When the City declined, the bar associations approached the Appellate Division of the First Department of the New York Supreme Court,[36] which had traditionally been concerned with the quality of services provided by counsel in the trial courts within its jurisdiction. With the agreement, and on the recommendation, of both the City and the three bar associations, rules were enacted by the Court in Autumn 1995 to enable an Indigent Defense Organization Oversight Committee to be established.[37] A Committee consisting of eight volunteer lawyers was then appointed, and standards and guidelines drawn up against which performance would be measured. Once these had been promulgated by the Appellate Division on 1 July 1996, the Committee began its monitoring work.

Each organization providing defence services in Manhattan and the Bronx was asked to submit written documentation of compliance with the general requirements, and to respond to a questionnaire requesting specific information. After receiving this information, members of the Committee, accompanied by additional lawyers from the three participating bar associations, visited the offices of the organizations. Staff were interviewed, but the Committee decided against observing defence lawyers in the courts. Unless carried out on a more consistent and substantial basis than the resources of the Committee allowed, it was feared that the results would be merely anecdotal and fail to provide a meaningful basis for assessment.

Since its establishment the Committee submitted annual reports for each of the four years 1996–9, monitoring and reporting on the performance and professional conduct of any organization representing

[34] *The New York Times*, 19 May 1997.

[35] This description of the origins of the Indigent Defense Organization Oversight Committee draws on Appendix C of the Committee's Third Report to the Appellate Division First Department for the year 1998.

[36] The courts of New York State are divided into four judicial departments and twelve judicial districts. The First Department consists of counties within the First and Twelfth Districts, and includes Manhattan and the Bronx. Brooklyn, Queens, and Staten Island fall within the Second Judicial Department.

[37] 22 NYCCR, Part 613, the 'Rules'.

indigent parties in criminal proceedings in the First Department, and the lawyers in their employ. On 31 December 1996, in its first report, the Oversight Committee concluded that as of Autumn 1996 each of the three organizations then providing criminal defence services to indigent defendants provided quality representation generally meeting the standards formulated by the Committee. The three organizations were the Legal Aid Society, the Neighborhood Defender Service of Harlem, and the Office of the Appellate Defender (First Department Assigned Counsel Corporation).

The origins of the first two of these service providers demonstrate the different ways in which indigent defence has developed. The Legal Aid Society is the nation's oldest legal services organization. Founded late in the nineteenth century, it dated from an era of private charities and philanthropic ventures that proliferated as the wealth of the City and the size of its population expanded, but bringing poverty, court disputes, and offending in train. By 1996 the Legal Aid Society (LAS) was a large-scale operation, well known and respected in the civic life of New York. Its funding came mainly from the City Council, although substantial amounts were donated each year in grants and gifts from the private sector, in particular the prosperous community of lawyers in private practice.

The bulk of LAS criminal work in the First Department was concentrated at three locations: a New York County Office in Manhattan, a Bronx County Office, and a Criminal Appeals Bureau. Over two hundred lawyers or full-time equivalents were employed in this work, although the total qualified legal staff, in civil as well as criminal practice, amounted to more than double that number. Additional city-wide services provided by LAS included a juvenile rights division, civil support and representation, a special litigation unit, services for indigent immigrants and parolees, a small but newsworthy federal defender unit,[38] and a paralegal programme. Since capital punishment had been reinstituted in the State of New York in 1995, the LAS Capital Defense Unit had worked under a contract

[38] Throughout 1998 the Federal Defender Division was experiencing the impact of increased federal prosecution of cases facing the death penalty if convicted. Although the numbers were small, no more than six cases being assigned in that year, each of them was demanding of resources, and some were the subject of intense public interest. In August 1998, for example, LAS was appointed by the court to represent one of the men charged under federal law with the bombing of the United States Embassy in Nairobi, Kenya. In that incident twelve Americans and 250 Kenyans had been killed, and many more injured.

with the State Capital Defender Office to provide representation to persons within the City of New York.[39] In all, some 200,000 indigent defendants at the criminal and supreme courts in the City were represented by the Society's services in 1997. This total included cases in the boroughs of Brooklyn, Queens, and Staten Island which were outside the jurisdiction of the First Department of the Appellate Division.

The Neighborhood Defender Service (NDS) of Harlem was much smaller, newer, and more precisely focused. It had been inaugurated by the Vera Institute of Justice[40] in the Spring of 1990. The aim was an ambitious one: to advance the development of new techniques in the public provision of legal representation to indigent criminal defendants. The chosen method was to demonstrate that by restructuring the manner in which legal representation is delivered, public defender organizations can provide better services to their clients, in ways that both improve the quality of justice generally, and reduce the costs of unnecessary incarceration and delay.[41]

The project stemmed from the enthusiasm and inspirational leadership of a Yale Law School graduate, Christopher Stone, who had first gained experience working in a well established legal assistance outreach programme in New Haven, Connecticut. Later he had served with the Public Defender Office at Washington, D.C., and on the staff of Vera in New York. The proposal struck a responsive chord with another, more veteran, idealist, Mario Cuomo, then Governor of the State of New York. In his State of the State message in January 1990 Cuomo said:

> For the public defense sector this year, I propose the establishment of a pilot program to determine the efficacy of providing services in the form of team representation. Under this proposed model, a client's needs would be served by a defense team that includes defense attorneys, paralegals and other professionals. This would allow case preparation to begin earlier, leading to faster dispositions and reduced pretrial detention time.[42]

[39] In 1998 the Capital Defense Unit represented thirteen clients potentially facing the death penalty under State law.

[40] The Vera Institute of Justice is a New York based private non-profit organization dedicated to making government policies and practices fairer, more humane, and more efficient. Working in collaboration with government officials, Vera designs and implements innovative policies intended to expand the provision of justice and improve the quality of urban life. It also conducts original research, and has an active publishing programme.

[41] The Neighborhood Defense Service of Harlem, *1991 Annual Report*, p. 1.

[42] Ibid., p. 2.

In May 1990 a five-year contract with Vera was approved by the New York City Board of Estimates. This enabled offices to be opened in Harlem, a pilot scheme launched, and a staff of about sixty recruited and trained. Full operations began in December 1990. The central feature of the new neighbourhood defender service was to provide access to lawyers for poor residents in a defined locality as soon as an arrest had been made, or even before, rather than waiting for a court to assign counsel at a later stage in the criminal process. The NDS lawyer would be retained as counsel by the suspect in the same way that other clients retain a lawyer in private practice to represent them, but without a fee or any other contribution to costs. Unlike most court-based public defenders, who typically meet clients only a few minutes before their appearance in court, with little or no opportunity to make the prior investigations necessary to place the case in its proper context, NDS lawyers were not acting alone. Their distinctive characteristic was that they formed part of a multidisciplinary and locally based team comprising other lawyers, clerical staff, and community workers.

This system enabled NDS to provide continuity of advocacy in court should the lawyer be unable to stay with the case throughout what might be a lengthy period, and to offer clients help with personal and family problems that may have led them into trouble. Although most of the work was criminal, NDS was committed from the start to helping clients with civil matters arising from their criminal cases. These might include eviction from housing, loss of parental rights because of arrest for child neglect or abuse, deportation orders for immigrants in trouble with the law, and seizures of cash, cars, or other property in the course of drug arrests.[43] The financing for a specialized civil team ended with the rest of the NDS contract-funding in June 1996, but there were plans to revive it if and when financial resources allowed.

In its first full year of operation, NDS handled 1,685 cases for 1,164 clients in 1991. The clients were a representative cross-section, except that 86 per cent were male. Their age range was from thirteen to sixty-one. The average age was twenty-eight, the same as the average of all persons charged with offences in the Manhattan criminal courts. About three-quarters, 73 per cent, were African-American

[43] 'The Civil Fallout', *Public Defenders in the Neighborhood: A Harlem Law Office Stresses Teamwork, Early Investigation*, National Institute of Justice, Washington, D.C., 1999, p. 5.

and 24 per cent Hispanic, although only 5 per cent identified Spanish as their primary language. White and other ethnic groups accounted for 1 per cent and 2 per cent respectively. Most had never been convicted of a felony previously (73 per cent) and had family ties in the neighbourhood. Twenty-seven per cent had a previous felony conviction when they first came to NDS. The only qualifying requirements were that NDS clients live within the Harlem service area and be unable to afford private counsel.[44]

By the time the initial contract with the City for the five-year demonstration project came to an end, NDS had represented more than five thousand clients in more than six thousand criminal cases, and had established itself as a positive presence in the courts and in the community. Both the New York City Council and the State of New York acknowledged this in agreeing to keep the basic service in operation until the end of the current year.[45] As with other experimental projects funded for a limited initial period, during which the value of the work had become accepted, a period of acute uncertainty followed, leading to a near shutdown in 1996. In May of that year, however, an extraordinary event in the short history of neighbourhood-based public defence occurred in New York City. It was graphically described by Stone:

> A large crowd of residents from Harlem—men, women, and children—appeared at City Hall to demonstrate their support for a local service that was threatened with elimination by the Mayor's proposed budget. At stake was not a library, a child care facility, a health clinic, or a senior citizens' center. The City Council was holding hearings that day on the city's budget for indigent defense, and the service that these citizens wanted to preserve was the Neighborhood Defender Service of Harlem (NDS)—their local public defender. The effect on the City Council members was electrifying; no one had ever seen ordinary citizens turn out in such numbers for budget hearings on this subject before. Within a few weeks, the City Council and the Mayor had agreed to restore funding to NDS.[46]

From then on NDS was funded by the City Council on a year-by-year basis. Although the funding arrangements did not sit easily with the policy of contracts for fixed terms following a competitive

[44] Neighborhood Defense Service of Harlem, *1991 Annual Report*, *op. cit.*, pp. 5–6.
[45] *Public Offenders in the Neighborhood*, *op. cit.*, p. 4.
[46] 'The Lessons of Neighborhood-Focused Public Defense', *Crime and Place: Plenary Papers of the 1997 Conference on Criminal Justice Research and Evaluation*, National Institute of Justice, Washington, D.C., July 1998, p. 93.

solicitation process,[47] the outcome was tolerated by Mayor Giuliani as a political compromise.

The reports of the Oversight Committee for 1996 and 1997 were both favourable, commenting that although operating on a reduced scale NDS had experienced no trouble in recruiting staff, despite its financial uncertainties. It had attracted a diverse group of staff lawyers (over 50 per cent African-American or Latino, and 50 per cent female), with a demonstrated commitment to public service. The standards for legal qualifications, training, supervision and evaluation, work-loads, support services, and case management were all met. The team approach, whereby if the primary lawyer was unavailable another member of the team already familiar with the case could appear for the client, was especially commended. The Oversight Committee commented: 'This approach seems to be ideal in many ways and might be a model for other Defense Organizations'.[48] It should be noted, however, that in terms of the totality of prosecutions in the criminal courts throughout the five boroughs of New York City, the number of cases handled by NDS was small, and the cost per case to public funds markedly higher than other providers. If once again quality went with money, in this instance the diversity of funding was reinforced by vision and originality.

V

The verdict of the Oversight Committee on the performance of the far larger Legal Aid Society in 1997 was more critical. There was no question, their report said, that LAS was handling too many cases with too few staff and too little support. The high work-load was having an adverse impact on all aspects of representation.[49] Lawyers were giving less attention to clients, finding it more difficult to make personal appearances at their cases, and had less time to investigate

[47] In November 1996 the Office of the Co-ordinator of Criminal Justice for the City of New York issued a Request for Proposals (RFP) soliciting proposals for the provision of indigent defence services on the trial level in New York, Bronx, and Richmond Counties, and on the appellate level in the First Department of the Appellate Division of the Supreme Court of the State of New York to provide representation on cases that would otherwise have been assigned to the Legal Aid Society.

[48] First Department Indigent Defense Organization Oversight Committee, *Report for 1997*, p. 36.

[49] Ibid., p. 5.

or draft motions, or to prepare for trial. The effects of budget cuts and increased work-loads for staff were especially evident at the New York County Office in Manhattan, which was 'struggling to meet the needs of clients and the Courts, and where any task that is not an emergency is postponed'.[50] The courts were unhappy, and clients were not receiving the services they deserved.

Under almost every heading of the performance standards the LAS, and its New York County Office in particular, was found wanting. Ongoing training for senior staff was 'spotty'; the supervision of less experienced lawyers was inadequate; no formal process was in place to evaluate work; there were not enough investigators, with the result that lawyers were left to conduct their own investigations, but without sufficient time to do so. Most important of all were the excessive work-loads of the trial lawyers.

During the fiscal year ending 30 June 1997 the New York County Office was assigned a total of 76,132 new cases, of which 42,849 survived arraignment. These cases were handled by a staff of about 117 (full-time equivalent) lawyers. On these figures the average full-time lawyer would be assigned 650 cases. Even basing case-load numbers only upon cases surviving arraignment, each LAS lawyer would be required to handle an average of 366 cases during the year. Although few lawyers handled more than 150 new felony assignments, most who handled over 100 felony assignments also handled over 150 misdemeanour assignments. The Oversight Committee found that some lawyers were handling as many as 250 or 500 misdemeanour assignments in addition to 100 new felonies. As at 30 June 1997 LAS lawyers at the New York County Office carried an average of thirty-seven open felony cases, although some of them carried more than sixty.[51]

The direct cause of this sorry state of affairs was attributed to the reorganization of the indigent defence services funded by the City of New York, effected in 1997 following a solicitation process in the previous year. In the interests of competition with the primary provider, and of controlling costs, three more organizations had been added to the existing three. The revised contractual arrangements were significantly different from LAS or NDS. Each of the new contract organizations undertook to provide defence services

[50] First Department Indigent Defense Organization Oversight Committee, *Report for 1997*, p. 5.

[51] Ibid., p. 17.

for a predetermined number of cases in return for a fixed sum of money. There was no obligation to take on more cases than the number specified in their contracts. New York County Defender Services contracted to handle 12,500 cases annually; Bronx Defenders contracted for 10,000; and the Center for Appellate Litigation for 200 appeals each year. In the optimistic, but erroneous, belief that the work-loads of the existing organizations would be reduced proportionately, their budgets were reduced by the amounts necessary for the City to fund the new contracted organizations.

Having been so forthright in their strictures of its performance, the members of the Oversight Committee had no hesitation in attributing the root cause of LAS shortcomings to the City's decision to contract with the new defence organizations. In a telling example, the Report cited the decision of Bronx Defenders in the Spring of 1998 to reduce its intake flow by 20 per cent simply by eliminating one arraignment shift a month when it realized that it was picking up cases at a faster rate than necessary to meet its contractual commitment.

By this action, Bronx Defenders was able to maintain the 'comfortable work-load' for which it had planned, while Legal Aid Services, as the primary provider, was obligated to pick up the additional clients, and the extra shift in the Bronx, but without additional funding.[52] The new organizations were also able to offer better salary packages and working conditions which attracted many experienced and talented LAS lawyers. Another pertinent cost saving was that since they were required by the terms of their contracts to hire only experienced staff they did not incur the expense of new attorney training and supervision that LAS had to provide for most of its staff replacements.

Replying to the criticisms contained in the 1997 Report of the Oversight Committee, the Criminal Justice Co-ordinator for the Mayor's administration insisted that the system of financing indigent defence was working. The problem, he claimed, was a lack of efficiency and a need for better management at Legal Aid. 'We think the system is functioning very well,' he was reported as saying. 'Competition is a good thing. It will make the Legal Aid Society into a better organization.'[53] The Co-ordinator added that the administration's aim was to

[52] Ibid., p. 6. For a profile of Bronx Defenders shortly after the renewal of its contract for a second two-year term, see D. E. Rovella, *National Law Journal*, 31 Jan. 2000, pp. A1 and A9. The contracted total was raised from 10,000 to 12,500 cases annually.

[53] *The New York Times*, 26 Aug. 1998.

strengthen both the system and Legal Aid. Competitive bidding was already making it a more dynamic organization, and he praised the Society for the management changes that had been made. But it needed to do more.[54]

In the previous year the value of independent critical oversight had been recognized at the City Hall. On 20 May 1997 the then Criminal Justice Co-ordinator had written to the Presiding Justice of the Appellate Division, Second Judicial Department, regarding the newly contracted defence providers in that Department. Two of these, Queens Law Associates (QLA) and Brooklyn Defender Services (BDS), had been operating in their respective boroughs since the Summer of 1996. Each had contracts to represent 10,000 indigent criminal defendants annually. A third provider, Appellate Advocates (AA), had a contract to handle 200 criminal appeals. As far as the Co-ordinator knew, no problems or complaints had arisen with respect to any of these entities.[55] But as the first anniversary approached it would be useful to have a review of performance and staffing, as well as the quality of work, from the point of view of the court system. Any recommendations for improvements would be welcome. As a result of this approach an Oversight Committee was appointed for the Criminal Defense Organizations in the Second Judicial Department.

In February 1998 the Committee submitted its Report. After careful review and evaluation it concluded that each of the three defender groups had met its contracted commitments to the apparent satisfaction of the judiciary and members of the bar:

> These young law firms function well and are respected by their peers and members of the judiciary before whom the attorneys practice . . . The evaluations by their peers and members of the judiciary were in the range of good to excellent. It would appear that each contract provider is more than capable of fulfilling its obligations at the current caseload.[56]

The overall conclusion was that the three defence organizations were providing quality representation of indigent defendants and complying with their contractual obligations to the City of New York.[57]

[54] *The New York Times*, 26 Aug. 1998.

[55] Letter from Katherine Lapp to Hon. Guy Mangano, 20 May 1997.

[56] *Report of the Oversight Committee for Criminal Defense Organizations, Appellate Division: Second Department*, p. 16.

[57] Ibid.

VI

Earlier in the decade, in 1992, the American Bar Association (ABA) had included in the third edition of its published standards a new part on contract defence services.[58] The commentary noted the emergence and growing use of this type of delivery service over the previous two decades. In 1973 a national survey made no mention of contracts for defence services. Since then, there had been a rapid growth in their use. The most recent data available at the time the standards were under revision showed that contracts for services accounted for about 11 per cent of all defender services in the country. In several states, however, it was the most common form of representation in serious criminal matters. Some of the original contract programmes had grown out of a legitimate public concern to contain the costs incurred when public defender offices were forced to declare conflicts of interest and reject potential clients, sometimes in large percentages. Other programmes, 'unfortunately', had adopted the use of flat-fee contracts with competitive bidding by potential providers of services, based solely on a concern for the cheapest possible system.[59]

The ABA drafting committee did not mince its words. Experience over the previous decade, it wrote, showed that such programmes had conspicuously failed to provide quality representation to the accused, and in many cases resulted in even higher costs to the jurisdiction than if another model had been chosen. In a resolution of 1985, the ABA condemned the use of contracts awarded only on the basis of cost. Its Criminal Justice Standards Committee in 1992 reiterated that the ABA did not endorse the use of contracts for services as a viable, separate, 'stand-alone' component for the delivery of defence services. In every jurisdiction the primary component should be a public defender office, where conditions permitted, with an administered assigned counsel panel as a secondary component. Contracted services might form part of a larger, mixed system.[60] This was the pattern that had been followed in New York City.

[58] Contract services were defined as the provision of defence services over a period of time to a determined population of individuals or in a determined jurisdiction at a contractual rate offered and controlled by a government or representative thereof. *ABA Standards for Criminal Justice*, 3rd edition, *op. cit.*, p. 44.

[59] Ibid., p. 6.

[60] Ibid., pp. 6–7.

For public officials at City Hall, answering to elected representatives for such large expenditures, contracting held out promise as an effective instrument of financial control. Assuming a full take-up of the agreed number of cases, the cost per case could be calculated in advance, leaving little or no scope for overspending. Good quality representation could be achieved, so the reasoning went, by the requirement that only experienced attorneys should be employed. Yet by 1997 no more than four of the new contractors for defendants facing criminal charges were operational, either in the First or Second Judicial Departments. The total number of cases was fixed by contract and would not be exceeded. The same applied to two smaller organizations contracted to represent appellants. In effect the provider of last resort, LAS was left with an open-ended commitment to represent all indigent persons arrested in the City, unless they were represented by one of the contracted organizations, or by NDS, or by assigned counsel. The outcome was that in 1997 the Criminal Defense Division of LAS represented over 200,000 defendants in the City as a whole, a total that was maintained in the following year.

Of its nature, the actual demand, and the scale of overloading, could be ascertained with accuracy only after the year-end when the financial liability had already been incurred. The cancellation of the previous contract with LAS and the negotiation of a new one generated uncertainty throughout the organization. Originally the City had envisioned alternative providers in each of the boroughs. The withdrawal of $11 million to pay for the new contracted organizations necessitated lay-offs across the Society, resulting in disaffection between the City and the Society, both among those who could no longer be employed and those who remained. It also led to lawsuits.[61]

The adverse impact of reduced funding on this scale would have been even greater but for the generous response to a special appeal to New York law firms. More than a hundred responded, with several of the most famous names at the top of the list of donors. Together they contributed $4.75 million. Foundation support was also strong, coming in with $895,000, supplemented by the proceeds of fund-raising events reaching out beyond the legal community, and by private gifts.[62]

[61] Legal Aid Society, *Annual Report, 1997*, Report from the President, p. 1.
[62] Ibid.

The 1998 Report of the First Department Oversight Committee brought no comfort for LAS. Whereas Bronx Defenders, New York County Defender Services, and the Bronx County Office of LAS were all in 'substantial compliance with the Standards' and were 'generally providing quality representation to their clients',[63] the standard of representation by LAS at its New York County Office covering Manhattan had not significantly improved. Indeed some judges had expressed the view that it had continued to deteriorate.[64] The underlying causes were unchanged. The departure reported in the previous year of significant numbers of experienced LAS trial lawyers and supervisors to the contracted services in Manhattan and the Bronx had been supplemented by a further outflow to the new organizations awarded City contracts in the Second Judicial Department covering the boroughs of Brooklyn and Queens.

The central issue was that for more than thirty years LAS had been the default defence organization responsible for all cases city-wide. That responsibility continued, even though its public funding had been reduced from $79.3 million in the fiscal year 1994 to $52 million in the fiscal year 1999. As a response to the gravity of the situation the City Council had allocated an extra $10 million to the LAS budget for 1999, but Mayor Giuliani had refused to release the funds.

To make matters worse, a new factor had become apparent in 1998. Giuliani's crackdown on petty offending and anti-social behaviour had led to large numbers of street arrests. In Manhattan especially, 'quality of life' offences like jumping subway turnstiles were swamping the arraignment process. Lawyers found that they were spending many hours in criminal court representing numerous clients charged with a variety of minor misdemeanours. The sheer volume of cases put an additional strain on the already overstretched resources of LAS, leading to some criminal court judges in New York County expressing their dissatisfaction with the ability of LAS to handle its responsibilities. By the year-end the Oversight Committee reported that the New York County trial office of LAS had responded to 'the onslaught of arrests for minor offences' by instituting an arraignment unit with the objective of enabling less serious cases to be disposed of more expeditiously, so freeing lawyers to concentrate on felonies and triable cases.[65] While any relief was

[63] First Department Indigent Defense Organization Oversight Committee, *Report for 1998*, p. 5.

[64] Ibid., p. 6.

[65] Ibid., p. 7.

welcome, the heart of the problem, financing the defence of an infinite number of indigent cases from a finite sum of money, remained unresolved.[66]

VII

The travails of the Legal Aid Society concentrated attention on the necessity for an adequate supply of assigned counsel when no agency was available to represent a defendant. Yet in one of the more prosperous states in the nation there was a mounting crisis caused by a sharp decline in the number of counsel willing to accept assignment by the court so as to enable the state to comply with its constitutional and statutory mandate to provide counsel to individuals financially unable to hire their own attorney. By January 2000 the situation had become so serious that the Chief Administrative Judge of the Unified Court System of the State of New York, Jonathan Lippman, and the Deputy Chief Administrative Judge for Justice Initiatives, Juanita Bing Newton, issued a report describing the 'dramatic impact that the exodus of attorneys from the assigned counsel panels has had on the justice system'.[67]

Whereas in 1989 there had been 1,030 lawyers on the assigned counsel panel for criminal cases who were actively taking assignments in the First Department, ten years later the panel had barely 400 attorneys actively taking assignments, a decrease of over 60 per cent. The decline in the criminal case panel for the Second Department had been even more sharp. In 1989 that panel had 940 attorneys. By 1999 it had declined to about 300 attorneys taking assignments: a reduction of nearly 70 per cent.[68] Over the same period, the demand for their work increased. Total arrest case filings in New York City, for example, were 15.2 per cent higher in 1998 than in 1989.[69]

[66] The Report of the Oversight Committee for 1999 was not received until this book was in the press. No site visits were conducted in that year, and the Committee had little new to say about the contract defense offices, repeating some observations made in previous years. The focus was on the Legal Aid Society since, as default provider, it had experienced the most trouble in complying with the guidelines. Letter of 8 Feb. 2001 from Adele Bernhard, Chair, Indigent Defense Organization Oversight Committee, First Judicial Department, New York Supreme Court, Appellate Division.

[67] *Assigned Counsel Compensation in New York: A Growing Crisis*, State of New York, Unified Court System, Jan. 2000, p. 1.

[68] Ibid., p. 9.

[69] Ibid., p. 10.

At least part of the problem was caused by a low scale of fees which had not been increased since 1986. $40 per hour was payable for in-court work, and $25 per hour for out-of-court work.[70] The report concluded that the failure to increase the rates of hourly compensation over a period of fourteen years so that they no longer even covered average overhead expenses had drastically reduced the number of attorneys willing to accept assignment. Major disruption and delay in the adjudication of cases had resulted. Without immediate, and meaningful, fee increases the crisis would become irreversible, with an entire generation of young lawyers having no interest in acquiring the critically important skills and experience needed to perform assigned counsel work.[71]

The solution proposed was to increase the rates to $75 per hour for felony and Family Court cases,[72] and to $60 per hour for non-felony cases. Existing differentials for in-court and out-of-court work should be eliminated. In order to facilitate future rate increases a bipartisan commission should be established to review the adequacy of rates and to make non-binding recommendations. Since the cost of assigned counsel fell on counties, the state government should share the additional burden. The mandatory surcharges, payable by every individual in New York convicted of an offence under state law, were an appropriate source of revenue to finance the proposed increases. Prior to 1996 all mandatory surcharge revenue had been remitted to the State's Criminal Justice Improvement Account. But subsequently the greater part, amounting to an estimated $70.4 million out of a total of $84 million in the fiscal year 1999, had simply gone into the State General Fund. If this amount was dedicated to funding assigned counsel fees, it would pay for essentially the entire cost of raising the fees to the recommended level.[73] Although local governments would continue to pay assigned counsel costs up to the current rates, they would be spared the cost of the additional funding. Moreover, all of the mandatory surcharge revenue would be

[70] These rates were the lowest payable by any but one other state. Only New Jersey paid less, and there the system was different, with an extensive state-wide public defender office, and assigned counsel handling no more than 10 per cent of indigent criminal cases. States with considerably lower *per capita* income than New York, such as Alabama, Arkansas, and Louisiana, paid assigned counsel at higher rates. Ibid., p. 6.

[71] Ibid., p. 26.

[72] This rate was comparable to the federal district courts for the Southern and Eastern Districts of New York which compensated attorneys in criminal cases at a rate of $75 per hour. Ibid., pp. 19–20.

[73] Ibid., p. 23.

channelled back into the criminal justice system for which it had originally been intended.

In her State of the Judiciary Address 2000 Judith S. Kaye, Chief Judge of the State of New York, threw her weight behind the proposal, adding a further suggestion. Each year, she pointed out, millions of dollars in court fines and mandatory surcharges went unpaid. Not all of the money was collectible, but some of it was. Experience had shown that governmental institutions were not equipped to function as collection agencies, and were not particularly successful at the task. In the months to come the court system in New York would be contracting on a pilot basis with private firms to collect fines and surcharges in six designated localities where it was estimated that millions of dollars were outstanding. With the help of the legislature that programme could and should be expanded statewide, with the proceeds being dedicated to increased fees for assigned counsel.[74]

The immediate reaction by the State Governor, George Pataki, was discouraging. At a press conference on the day after the Chief Judge's annual address, Pataki brusquely acknowledged that he had different priorities. Increasing fees paid to lawyers representing indigent clients was not one of them. He had no intention of diverting court-generated fees to fund the initiative, and was unlikely to support any increase in assigned counsel rates, no matter what the source of funding.[75] One consequence of his negative response was to reduce still further the availability of assigned counsel. While emphasizing that the action of a group of Brooklyn lawyers in refusing assignments was 'not any form of strike', their spokesman described it as an adjustment to the economic reality imposed by a fee structure that had remained static since 1986.[76] In Manhattan too an ad-hoc group of assigned counsel indicated that they would not take on any new cases in 2001.

Remarking that persistence and optimism were the hallmarks of a Chief Judge, Judith Kaye returned to the subject of the inadequacy of assigned counsel rates in her State of the Judiciary Address in January 2001. The situation had worsened. Assigned counsel fees of $40 an hour for in-court work and $25 an hour for out-of-court work

[74] *The State of the Judiciary*, New York Courts, 10 Jan. 2000, pp. 16–18.

[75] 223 *The New York Law Journal* (*NYLJ*), No. 8, col. 4, 12 Jan. 2000.

[76] 224 *NYLJ*, No. 116, col. 3, 18 Dec. 2000.

were barely adequate fifteen years before when they had been set by the legislation. 'Today', she continued:

> they have decimated assigned counsel panels. And the consequences are severe. Criminal matters are repeatedly adjourned, delaying justice for victim and accused alike . . . It is the responsibility of all of us in government to address this deepening crisis now. We simply cannot let another year pass without resolving this problem.[77]

Later the same month negotiations on the State Judiciary Budget indicated a change in attitude on the part of the Governor. Although no line item to increase assigned counsel fees was included, there was a strong possibility that before the legislative session was over the crisis would be addressed. The Governor and the legislative leaders in the State Senate and Assembly undertook to work together to increase the rates, and expressed unusual optimism that a solution could be negotiated.[78] The Chief Administrative Judge, Jonathan Lippman, saw the development as 'a strong, positive signal for an assigned counsel increase this year'.[79]

VIII

If funding bodies feel compelled to adopt cost per case as a yardstick for measuring the effectiveness of indigent defence services, as has been the experience in New York City, assessing the true quality of a service calls for a more rounded approach. Two non-financial values are client satisfaction and lawyerly standards. Client satisfaction was mentioned above, and is important if accused persons and their families are to feel that they have been treated respectfully, soundly advised of their legal rights, and effectively represented at a fair trial.

Lawyerly standards are harder to pin down. Some of the attorneys working in not-for-profit defender agencies are youngish and ideologically driven. Others are more seasoned lawyers. Of the first category, many will be recent graduates from law schools, including some of the best known, who are embarking on a rite of passage to a lifetime in the professional practice of law. While their rates of pay and working conditions do not compare with those enjoyed by many

[77] *The State of the Judiciary 2001*, pp. 18–19.
[78] 225 *NYLJ*, No. 11, col. 3, 17 Jan. 2001.
[79] Personal message from Judge Lippman, 5 Feb. 2001.

of their contemporaries in private practice, thus postponing their ability to repay student loans,[80] they may have personal qualities and motivation which particularly suit them for working with indigents. Judges are well placed to ensure that proper standards of advocacy are maintained, while professional competence may be assessed regularly by external oversight committees or supervisory commissions.

Sustaining the motivation of public defenders' commitment to their clients is a constant problem,[81] aggravated by overwork, time pressures, and sometimes clients who are difficult to represent. Another, less obvious characteristic is the progressive erosion of personal confidence that can result from defending people, some of whose criminal acts have been the source of so much harm and grief to their victims.[82] As vocations fade many public defenders move on to other forms of work. Such career moves should not be regarded as the consequences of individual or institutional failure. The key point is that replenishments in the shape of similarly motivated successor generations should continue to come forward.

How is success to be measured in such a setting? Acquittal or conviction is hardly an appropriate criterion, as it might be for prosecutors, since so many clients will be pleading guilty. If questioned as to how they interpret their mission, public defenders are accustomed to refer to the zealous representation of their clients' interests. If pressed further on what constitutes a successful zealous defence, the answer may be a reduction in the sentence that might have been expected in the absence of effective representation. To those familiar with the workings of criminal justice it is not a bad reply. But to many of the general public, defence attorneys are frequently caricatured as being on the wrong side of a line separating people working for law

[80] When interviewed early in 2000 Daniel Greenberg, President and Attorney-in-Chief of the Legal Aid Society, did not see any decline in recruitment from law schools as a result of the high cost of legal education, pointing out that some universities had put in place 'loan forgiveness' programmes to subsidize graduates going into public service careers. However, LAS may not be typical of less prominent public defender agencies. Greenberg was Director of Clinical Programs at Harvard Law School, 1987–95. He bears no responsibility for any of the comments on LAS in the text of this Chapter.

[81] See C. J. Ogletree, Jr., 'Beyond Justifications: Seeking Motivations to Sustain Public Defenders', 106 *Harvard Law Review* (1993), 1239–94. Charles Ogletree is Director of the Criminal Justice Institute at Harvard Law School, and a former Deputy Director of the District of Columbia Public Defender Service.

[82] Ibid., p. 1267.

enforcement from people who are motivated to work for suspects, defendants, and prisoners. The impromptu remark attributed to an Attorney General in the Reagan administration, describing the American Civil Liberties Union (ACLU) as part of 'the criminal's lobby', may have been incautious and unfair, but it was by no means a lone voice.

As Attorney General throughout the Clinton administration, Janet Reno[83] had a very different outlook. Before her appointment, while a State Attorney in Florida, she had served as a member of an ABA commission on developing standards for juvenile justice. Although in the 1990s there was little federal money available to support state or local public defender programmes, she maintained a sympathetic interest which heightened towards the end of her long tenure at the Justice Department.

The first stirrings of more active federal interest in indigent defence since the 1980s came early in 1998 when the Attorney General convened a meeting on 27 January between senior Department of Justice officials and eight representatives of criminal defence organizations. The purpose was to explore ways of improving the quality of defence services for indigent defendants. A preliminary step was to identify successful programmes across the country in which public defenders, prosecutors, and other key figures were collaborating to create a more effective and efficient criminal justice system.[84]

Three priorities were established. The first was to discover if any of the existing sources of federal funding to state projects might be tapped for public defender programmes. Those offering the greatest promise were seen as the Edward Byrne Memorial State and Law Enforcement Assistance Administration (LEAA) grants, and access to Violence Against Women Act (VAWA) funds. There were also some other funded programmes which could be available to the component parts of the criminal justice system. Apart from funding, two further priorities identified at the meeting were managing increasing case-loads for public defenders, and providing them with the same advanced technology as was currently available to prosecutors.

[83] State Attorney, 11th Judicial Circuit, Florida, 1978–93; Assistant State Attorney, 1973–6. Attorney General of the United States, 1993–2001.

[84] Bureau of Justice Assistance Monograph, *Improving State and Local Criminal Justice Systems*, U.S. Department of Justice, Oct. 1998, NCJ 173391, p. 1. The Director of the Bureau, Nancy Gist, was the motivator of much of the heightened interest taken in indigent defence both at the Department of Justice and elsewhere.

At the conclusion of the January meeting the Attorney General requested the American Bar Association, Bar Information Program, to prepare a brief report on current collaborations between public defenders, prosecutors, and other criminal justice agencies.[85] The resulting report, issued by the Bureau of Justice Assistance in October of the same year, identified seven basic models of collaboration employed by jurisdictions across the country, and described some noteworthy initiatives under each heading.

One initiative which caught the eye because of its imagery emanated from the Attorney General's home state of Florida. There, during the 1995 legislative session, the state courts system, the Florida State Attorneys Association, the Florida Public Defenders Association, and the office of the state Attorney General, joined together to form a coalition called 'Fill the Gap'. The purpose was to illustrate to the state legislature that additional funding would be needed to remedy the imbalance that was apparent between the three components of the criminal justice system. These were described as the front end (law enforcement), the back end (corrections), and the middle (courts, prosecution, and criminal defence). It was not only in Florida that the front and back ends were traditionally much better funded than the middle, or the 'gap'.

At the time the coalition was formed, the state of Florida was poised to receive substantial federal funds for the front and back ends, but none for the middle component through which all cases had to flow. The proposition developed by the coalition partners, speaking with one voice, was that failure by the state to fill the gap would compromise their efforts to bring crime under control. Although flat funding between the financial years 1995 and 1996 had been anticipated, the legislature responded to the pressure by allocating an increase roughly double that of the previous year.[86] Elsewhere coalitions modelled on that in Florida adopted similar tactics to 'fill the gap'.

For public defenders to be accepted as participants in such coalitions it is first necessary for them to establish a claim to equal status with prosecutors and law enforcement officers. Let us return briefly to Indiana. When a former prosecutor took over as Marion County's

[85] The report was prepared by the Spangenberg Group for the American Bar Association, Bar Information Program, and published by the Bureau of Justice Assistance (BJA), Office of Justice Programs.

[86] *Improving State and Local Criminal Justice Systems*, *op. cit.*, p. 6.

Chief Public Defender one year after the Indianapolis-based agency had opened its doors he found it in dire financial straits.[87] Worse still were public accusations of fiscal irresponsibility and mismanagement of local funds. Inquiries revealed that the allegations were not well founded. After a series of individual meetings with members of the City-County Council, explaining the legitimate reasons for a shortfall, an additional $500,000 was negotiated to keep the agency running through the rest of the year. The increase was authorized unanimously by the appropriation committee.

The Chief Public Defender, David Cook, had the advantage of being already well known and respected in the local community. Furthermore, as a long-serving senior prosecutor he could open doors that others could not. But he admitted that his background was something of an obstacle in his own office where he had to overcome initial suspicions. By the time he had doubled the budget, strengthened the quality of representation, and won more trials than ever before, such doubts were eradicated. Yet in conservative Marion County, Cook noted, 'there are many people who still struggle with the concept of why we have to do all this to begin with'.[88] Working at improving the public image of indigent defence, persuading the funding bodies and their constituencies that money is not being spent recklessly, and that there are principles which it is important to protect, are the keys to recognition of the equal status of public defenders with both prosecutors and law enforcement.

IX

In the Spring of 1998, for the first time in more than ten years, the Department of Justice began to document the state of indigent defence services nationally.[89] Some examples were cited earlier in this

[87] National Defender Leadership Project, *Ultimate Advocacy: A Defender's Guide to Strategic Management*, Vera Institute of Justice, New York, 1999, p. 26.

[88] Ibid., p. 28.

[89] Data collection for a national survey of indigent defence systems commenced in late Summer 1998, and a published report followed in Nov. 2000. With funding from the Bureau of Justice Assistance, the Bureau of Justice Statistics worked closely with the American Bar Association, the National Association of Criminal Defense Lawyers, the National Legal Aid and Defenders Association, and other indigent defence providers in preparing the report. It showed that an estimated total of $1.2 billion was spent on indigent criminal defence in the nation's 100 most populous counties during 1999. About 73 per cent was spent on public defender programmes, 21 per

Chapter. Janet Reno admitted that, despite the investment of considerable resources, the promise of *Gideon* was not completely fulfilled.[90] Indigent defendants did not invariably receive effective assistance from counsel. Sometimes the failure was caused by lack of resources. Sometimes it stemmed from the absence of a structure in the state to provide adequately for the indigent. Whatever the cause, such failings inevitably eroded 'the community's sense of justice and the aspiration of our system to equal justice under the law'.[91] As Attorney General she had opened up a dialogue with judges, prosecutors, and defence attorneys, and urged every state to take the occasion to review its indigent legal defence services and recommit itself to the promise of *Gideon*.

Her appeal was a strong one, resonating notions of justice that are deeply embedded in American political culture. The resurgence in the 1990s of interest in improving the extent and effectiveness of indigent defence services originated from a collective desire to right the scales of justice to give more equal weight to the defence. In America, more than in Britain, some see an inherent contradiction in the practice of publicly funding offenders who have rejected the authority of the State. Even so, the imperative need to provide for public protection has to be matched by judicial procedures to ensure that suspects and accused persons receive fair treatment. The capacity of the adversarial system to deliver a just outcome, particularly in jury trials, depends to a large extent on the ability of the prosecution and the defence to perform their duties with equal effectiveness.

The constitutional right to a fair trial led to legal representation being granted to poor people three decades ago by the Supreme Court. Since then, public defender systems have proliferated. Some have ensured representation for their clients at a high professional level. Others, many others, have been neither sufficiently funded nor

cent on assigned counsel programmes, and about 6 per cent on awarded contracts. County governments provided 60 per cent, and state governments 25 per cent of the total funding. Out of 4.2 million cases legally represented at public expense in the hundred most populous counties, public defenders handled about 82 per cent, assigned counsel attorneys 15 per cent, and contract attorneys about 3 per cent. Indigent criminal defence expenditures accounted for 3 per cent of all local criminal justice expenditures, and 16 per cent of judicial expenditures, in these counties. The hundred most populous counties comprised approximately 42 per cent of the 1999 U.S. population. Bureau of Justice Statistics, *Bulletin*, 'Indigent Defense Services in Large Counties, 1999', by C. De Frances and M. Litras, U.S. Department of Justice, Nov. 2000, NCJ 184932, pp. 1–3.

[90] *USA Today*, 18 Mar. 1998.

[91] Ibid.

adequately staffed to meet the demand. Often the result has been insufficient time for case preparation, restricted access to experts needed to assist the defence, and far too heavy case-loads. For the reasons explored in this Chapter, human and financial resources have been inadequate to bring the scales of justice into balance. Although much has been achieved, the unavoidable conclusion must be that there is still a long way to go before that objective is fully realized.

7

Reforms in the Criminal Process III: Mode of Trial

I

An authoritative account of the methods used by the Labour leadership to refashion the Party and win the 1997 General Election with such an overwhelming majority was noted in an earlier Chapter. The title chosen by its author, Philip Gould, was 'The Unfinished Revolution'.[1] The book argued that the process of modernisation must not stop with the election victory. The links so laboriously built up connecting the leadership with its electoral supporters should not be allowed to fall into disuse. To the surprise of many veteran politicians and commentators, who had heard this sort of thing before seeing governments, weighed down by the compelling pressures of public business, becoming more and more remote, Tony Blair in office not only kept a watchful eye on fluctuations in public opinion towards the Labour administration, but continued to woo the electorate with the same zeal as he had shown in Opposition.

Each week the Prime Minister's regular meeting to discuss government business with the Cabinet Secretary, Sir Richard Wilson,[2] was preceded by an hour-long session with his closest political advisers.[3] The 9 a.m. 'office meeting' on Monday mornings became something of an institution.[4] The two most senior special advisers, Jonathan

[1] See Chapter 3 above, pp. 61–3, 71–3, and notes 2, 36–40.

[2] Deputy Secretary, Cabinet Office, 1987–90; Deputy Secretary, HM Treasury, 1990–2; Permanent Secretary, Department of the Environment, 1992–4; Permanent Under-Secretary of State, Home Office, 1994–7. Secretary of the Cabinet and Head of the Home Civil Service, 1998–.

[3] The Sixth Report of the Committee on Standards in Public Life noted that the number of special advisers employed at 10 Downing Street had risen from eight in 1997 to 25 in December 1999. *Reinforcing Standards: Review of the First Report of the Committee on Standards in Public Life*, Vol. 1, Report, Jan. 2000, p. 69.

[4] D. Kavanagh and A. Seldon, *The Powers Behind The Prime Minister*, HarperCollins, London, 1999, pp. 271–2, and private information.

Powell, Chief of Staff, and Alastair Campbell, the Press Secretary at Number Ten, had executive powers to give directions to career civil servants,[5] whereas Gould, the key adviser on strategy and polling, was a consultant with private clients. As a practising politician and proven tactician Peter Mandelson[6] had a standing invitation to attend during the earlier years of the 1997–2001 Government.

Once devolution to Scotland and Wales were out of the way the domestic agenda concentrated on the objective of bringing about perceptible improvements in selected policy areas: health, education, crime, jobs, and the economy. Primary legislation was necessary to effect some of the changes, including some controversial measures designed to counter criminal offending which would affect the rights and liberties of individuals.

In the Autumn of 1999, close to the half-way point of a five-year Parliament, polling data indicated not only that crime was a major issue of concern, but that doubts were growing as to the ability of the Government to counter it.[7] Many neighbourhoods were considered to be unsafe; street crime, actual or perceived, was seen as threatening; drugs were feared; and values of citizenship eroded. At the centre of Government the reduction of crime and the need for improved protection of the public were recognized as a priority.

The orientation of the policy response was predetermined. 'Tough' was already well established as a New Labour keyword. When endorsed by focus group research its appeal had become part of Blair's political identity.[8] Before the election the tag had been attached to Labour's approach to criminal offending: 'tough on crime; tough on the causes of crime', and the Prime Minister had shown no signs of abandoning it in office. Once priorities had been

[5] Authorized by Order in Council. For an informative description of the increase in numbers, functions, and powers of special advisers to Ministers, see *Reinforcing Standards*, *op. cit.*, pp. 68–83.

[6] Director of Campaigns and Communications, the Labour Party, 1985–90. MP for Hartlepool, 1992; Minister without Portfolio, Cabinet Office, 1997–8; Secretary of State for Trade and Industry, 1998; resigned Dec. 1998. Rejoined Cabinet in Oct. 1999 as Secretary of State for Northern Ireland, and resigned a second time from ministerial office in Jan. 2001.

[7] A MORI poll conducted in Dec. 1999 showed that 61 per cent of respondents thought that the Government had not improved law and order since it was elected in May 1997. The percentage had risen from 59 per cent in Jan. 1999. *British Public Opinion*, MORI, Jan.–Feb. 2000, p. 8.

[8] See N. Fairclough, *New Labour, New Language*?, Routledge, London and New York, 2000, pp. 106–7. Norman Fairclough is Professor of Language in Social Life at Lancaster University.

determined at Number Ten, and action requested, it was for departmental ministers to come forward with proposals which would further the strategic objectives.

At this point one of the most sophisticated of all skills required by the British system of government comes into play. Which of the range of policy changes already worked up within government departments are most likely to contribute towards the realization of centrally determined objectives? What new ideas are in circulation? Who will do the work, and what will be the impact of new policies on related activities or services? Never far from the front of the minds of departmental ministers and officials will be the questions: what will be the cost, and where will the money come from?

Not all the measures coming under the rubric of protecting the public emanated from the Home Office. Out of a total of six distinct crime or punishment-related items included in a 'tough on crime' section of the Queen's Speech at the start of the third session of the Parliament elected in May 1997, four were Home Office measures. There were powers for mandatory drug testing of defined categories of person including those arrested on suspicion of having committed a criminal offence; the reform of the Probation Services in England and Wales; preventing unsuitable persons from working with children; and a potentially controversial proposal to end the right of defendants to elect to be tried by jury when charged with middle-range offences triable either summarily in the Magistrates' courts or on indictment in the Crown Court. The latter was the subject of a self-contained single-subject Bill, thus averting the risk of other measures requiring primary legislation being jeopardized if brought forward in the same Bill as the trial by jury issue.

The Queen's Speech also forecast provisions in a Child Support, Pensions, and Social Security Bill enabling penalties to be imposed on absent parents who refused to support their children. In certain circumstances the court would be enabled to order a non-resident parent to be disqualified from holding or obtaining a driving licence. A second, and even more contentious, legislative change was that a large number of offenders, originally estimated to be of the order of 30,000 each year, who failed to comply with the terms of community orders would have their social security benefits either withdrawn or reduced. In commenting on the latter proposal the Prime Minister was reported as saying that community service orders should be 'real penalties. If offenders did not carry them out it seems strange that we should end up subsidising them from the state.'[9]

Insofar as there was a common thread connecting these measures it was coercive practicality, even where the penalty had no connection with the offending behaviour, e.g. driving licences and eligibility for social security benefit. The tests by which practicality was judged would be the managerial hallmarks of modernisation: performance indicators, more effective delivery of public services, and value for money.

II

The most contentious of the crime-related proposals, the limitation of the right to jury trial, was not a new one. In 1993 the Royal Commission on Criminal Justice had recommended that in contested cases involving either-way offences the defendant should no longer have the right to insist on trial by a jury.[10] Where the Crown Prosecution Service and the defendant had agreed that the case was suitable for summary trial, it should proceed to trial in a Magistrates' court. The case would go on to the Crown Court for trial if both the prosecution and defence agreed that it should be tried on indictment. Where the defence did not agree with the prosecution proposal on which court should try the case, the matter should be referred to the Magistrates for decision. Any enabling legislation should refer to various matters, including potential loss of reputation, which the Magistrates would be expected to take into account in determining the mode of trial.[11]

The Conservative Government's final response was not given until nearly three years later. In June 1996 ministers accepted the importance of preventing business going unnecessarily to the Crown Court, and noted that in recent years there had been a large increase in the proportion of cases triable either way which had been committed to the Crown Court for trial. But the conclusion was that:

[9] *The Times*, 15 Nov. 1999, reporting an interview with Tony Blair on Sky Television. The partially successful Parliamentary challenge to the loss of benefit sanctions in the Child Support, Pensions and Social Security Act 2000 is described in Chapter 8 below.

[10] Royal Commission on Criminal Justice, *Report* (Cm. 2263), HMSO, London, 1993, Recommendation 114, p. 198.

[11] Ibid., Recommendation 115.

such a fundamental change in the right to jury trial as that proposed by the Royal Commission should not be undertaken unless it is clear that it would be the only possible way of achieving the objective.[12]

Following a period of consultation in the previous year the Government had concluded that a better way of achieving the objective, without stepping out on the thin ice of restricting trial by jury, was to oblige defendants to indicate their plea before the mode of trial was decided.[13] A clause to that effect was inserted into the Criminal Procedure and Investigations Act 1996, amending the Magistrates' Courts Act 1980.[14] A third option was to reclassify some either-way offences so that they would be dealt with summarily in the Magistrates' courts without the option of a Crown Court trial.[15] This was the course followed in making drink/driving offences not resulting in death under Sections 4 and 5 of the Road Traffic Act 1988 triable summarily only, by Section 9 of the Road Traffic Offenders Act 1988. Prior to the change such offences had been triable either way under legislation enacted in 1972.[16]

Each of these stratagems to reduce the number of cases going to the Crown Court was considered again in a managerially inspired review of the causes of delay in the criminal justice system. It was carried out briskly between October 1996 and February 1997 by a single reviewer, Martin Narey, at the time a rising Home Office official.[17] In his report he argued that the 'plea before venue' initiative

[12] Lord Chancellor's Department, Home Office, and Law Officer's Department, *Royal Commission on Criminal Justice: Final Government Response*; June 1996, p. 26.

[13] Ibid.

[14] Section 49 of the Criminal Procedure and Investigations Act 1996 relates to an accused person's intention as to plea when brought before the Magistrates' court on information charging an offence triable either way.

[15] A consultation document titled 'Mode of Trial' (Cm. 2908, HMSO, London, 1995), published the previous July, discussed at paras. 7–14 the alternative of retaining more business in the lower courts by reclassifying certain offences as summary-only. The document noted that driving while disqualified, taking a motor vehicle without authority, common assault and battery, and criminal damage over £400 but less than £2,000 (subsequently raised to £5,000 by Section 46 of the Criminal Justice and Public Order Act 1994) had been reclassified as summary-only offences by the Criminal Justice Act 1988.

[16] Road Traffic Act 1972, Sections 5 and 6 and Schedule 4, Part I. This Act was repealed by the Road Traffic Consequential Provisions Act 1988.

[17] Martin Narey joined HM Prison Service in 1982. After serving in prison establishments he held a variety of posts, both at Prison Service Headquarters and the Home Office. He joined the Board of the Prison Service as Director of Regimes in January 1998, becoming Director General in December of that year at the unusually early age of forty-three.

was complementary to removing the right of the defendant to elect a jury trial, and not an alternative to it. However successful the plea before venue was, Narey did not believe it would reduce defendant elections.[18] Limiting the volume of cases going to the Crown Court by reclassifying some either-way offences, although it might divert a significant total away from the Crown Court, was rejected as an unsatisfactory solution.

The main argument put forward against reclassification was that if thefts of small monetary value became triable summarily only, rather than either way, it would mean there would be no circumstances in which such cases could go to the Crown Court even if the Magistrates considered that a jury trial was appropriate.[19] The same reasoning could have been applied to the 1988 reclassification, but it had not led to insuperable difficulties. In the outcome, the reclassification as summary of offences of common assault, unauthorized taking of a motor vehicle,[20] and criminal damage below a certain value (set at £2,000, later increased to £5,000), as well as certain road traffic offences by separate legislation, resulted in a decline of 5 per cent (approximately 5,500 cases) in the number of accused persons tried at the Crown Court between 1988–9. No other offences have been reclassified as summary-only since 1988.[21]

The statistics cited by Narey indicated that as many as one-quarter of the total Crown Court case-load in the year ended September 1996 was made up of defendants in the either-way category who had elected trial at the Crown Court. A large majority of these defendants, estimated at about two-thirds, subsequently pleaded guilty.[22] The Reviewer was forthright in his conclusion. In his view, a substantial proportion of elections were:

> little more than an expensive manipulation of the criminal justice system and are not concerned with any wish to establish innocence in front of a jury. Those defendants who have a valid reason for electing, such as the potential damage to their reputation, should be able to make their case to magistrates who should be free to commit the case to the Crown Court. But

[18] Home Office, *Review of Delay in the Criminal Justice System, A Report*, Feb. 1997, p. 34.

[19] Ibid., p. 33.

[20] For a comment on the subsequent introduction of a new offence of aggravated vehicle taking, see the Home Secretary's letter to the author dated 23 Feb. 2000, reproduced later in this Chapter.

[21] *Parl. Debates*, HL, 608 (5th ser.), col. WA 39, 15 Dec. 1999.

[22] *A Report*, *op. cit.*, p. 32.

the automatic veto on the magistrates' decision on mode of trial . . . should be removed.[23]

The vocabulary of politics can be revealing. The transformation of what had hitherto been regarded as an established right of accused persons to have either-way charges heard by a jury, into an automatic veto on the exercise of discretion by Magistrates, was symptomatic of a changing tide of opinion. When the recommendation was considered in the dying days of the Conservative Government in February 1997 the Home Secretary, Michael Howard, had been cautious. He said he recognized that the proposal to leave with the Magistrates the decision as to which either-way cases should be tried summarily, and which in the Crown Court, was 'extremely sensitive'.[24] Any proposal to limit the availability of jury trial was bound to arouse strong feelings. It was a central feature of the system of justice and one to which the Government was entirely committed. He would not wish to restrict it without 'very careful thought'. On the other hand, the recommendation in the Narey Report would offer substantial practical advantages. It would divert from the Crown Court contested cases, often of a petty nature, which did not need to be there. Moreover, it might facilitate another of the Review's recommendations, similarly favoured by the Royal Commission, that the most serious cases triable only in the Crown Court should start there from the outset, rather than spending about half of their life in the Magistrates' courts awaiting committal.[25]

Howard referred also to the possibility of a right of appeal against a Magistrates' decision not to allow a case to go to the Crown Court for trial.[26] This comment was not taken up at the time by the Shadow Home Secretary, Jack Straw, although later he was to cite it as a reason for his conversion to acceptance of the same policy when in Government. While still in Opposition in February 1997 he roundly rejected cutting down the right to jury trial as making the system less fair. It was, he declared, 'not only wrong, but short-sighted, and likely to prove ineffective'.[27] He urged the Home Secretary not to accept the proposal. Loss of reputation, which was to become a matter of dispute in the later legislation, evidently counted for much in Straw's mind:

[23] *A Report*, *op. cit.*, p. 2.

[24] *Parl. Debates*, HC, 291 (6th ser.), col. 431, 27 Feb. 1997.

[25] Ibid., col. 432. [26] Ibid. [27] Ibid., col. 433.

If a police officer or an MP or even the Secretary of State was charged with an offence of dishonesty, would they not insist on being tried by a jury? If that is the case, why should others be denied this right of election?[28]

III

The next step was the publication of another consultation paper in July 1998.[29] The document showed that there had been a steady decrease over the previous ten years in the proportion of either-way cases committed to the Crown Court for trial which arrived there by way of election. In 1987 elected cases had accounted for 53 per cent of committals for trial. In the decade since then Table 10 shows that the proportion had fallen to 28 per cent of either-way cases commited on the election of the defendant. The actual number of elected cases which proceeded to trial was much lower, since more often than not the defendant subsequently pleaded guilty.

Table 10. *Committals for trial in the Crown Court, either-way offences, 1987–97*

Year	Either-way offences committed for trial	Year on year % change	% of either-way cases committed on election of defendant
1987	95,854	–	53
1988	105,505	+10	45
1989	98,542	−7	42
1990	94,149	−4	38
1991	97,622	+4	36
1992	91,829	−6	37
1993	75,867	−17	35
1994	71,436	−6	35
1995	79,324	+11	33
1996	71,654	−10	32
1997	77,804	+9	28

Source: Attorney General's Department. Statistics relate only to prosecutions by the Crown Prosecution Service.

[28] *The Independent*, 27 Mar. 1997.

[29] Home Office, *Determining Mode of Trial in Either-Way Cases: A Consultation Paper*, July 1998.

For a time it seemed that the hesitation which had marked the approach of the previous Government might continue under Labour. The options were rehearsed once again with the arguments for and against removing the right of election being fairly set out. One hundred and thirty-three responses were received, circumspectly described by the Home Office as covering 'a range of views'.[30] Yet even those with an ear close to the ground had picked up no signals that a dramatic conversion was about to be announced.

Ministers were later to argue that ending the unqualified right to jury trial for certain categories of defendant was not motivated primarily by financial considerations but was to 'improve the system'.[31] Of the ways of improving the system the most credible was the reduction of delays in court proceedings. This objective had been a central strand of Labour policy since before the 1997 general election. Although the electoral promise had been confined to halving the time between arrest and sentencing for persistent young offenders,[32] reducing delays across the criminal process as a whole had been a clear priority for Home Office ministers throughout. Yet, according to their Department's own research, delay was only the eighth out of eleven reasons given by defendants as to why they chose trial in the Crown Court. In practice, delays in listing Magistrates' court trials, and further delays caused by trials being adjourned part-heard, were such that Crown Court trials were likely to be concluded just as soon, if not sooner.[33]

A further factor was a constant for all Home Secretaries, irrespective of party. In December 1998 Martin Narey, the author of the review of the causes of delays in the criminal justice system, had beewas appointed Director General of the Prison Service following the unexpectedly early retirement of Richard Tilt. Narey believed that the recommendations contained in his Report, if implemented in full, would have the effect of reducing the pressures on the prison population. If some 12,000 defendants annually were tried in the Magistrates' courts instead of the Crown Court,[34] there would be fewer prisoners

[30] *Parl. Debates*, HC, 333, col. WA 54, 14 June 1999.

[31] *Parl. Debates*, HC, 339, col. 749, 25 Nov. 1999.

[32] Before the Labour Government took office the national average time for bringing young offenders to trial was 142 days. The target was to reduce it to 71 days.

[33] The Law Society, *Parliamentary Brief* for Criminal Justice (Mode of Trial) (No. 2) Bill, Second Reading: House of Commons, 7 Mar. 2000.

[34] Estimated savings in remand time, the shorter sentences likely to be passed in the Magistrates' courts than in the Crown Court, and the lower cost of trying cases

held on remand awaiting trial, and in all probability more prisoners serving shorter terms of imprisonment because of the limitations on the Magistrates' sentencing powers.[35] The most valuable benefit of all would be that the relief would come in the local prisons where over-crowding was a far more acute problem than in the training prisons.

Another influence on Straw's change of mind was more subtle, and may have been decisive. He, and his predecessors, had to face the full weight of public censure by the higher judiciary over mandatory sentencing. Resolute as the Lord Chief Justice, Lord Bingham, had been on that issue, and on others where he believed the independence of the judiciary might be endangered, he had indicated that with one important proviso he was not opposed to changes being made in the mode of trial. The proviso was that there should be a right of appeal for a defendant denied trial by jury in any either-way case. Since both the Lord Chancellor and the Attorney General were of the same mind, Straw needed little persuading to ensure that a provision for appeal to the Crown Court following a Magistrates' court decision on the mode of trial was included on the face of the Bill. Thus by the time of the Second Reading debate in the House of Lords in December 1999 the Attorney General, Lord Williams of Mostyn, was able to inform the House that, although it was not possible for Bingham to be present, he had been authorized to say the Lord Chief Justice was in support of the curtailment of the automatic right to trial by jury which the Bill would bring about.[36] Bingham's personal contribution was reserved for the next stage of the debate.

Once the Home Secretary's mind was made up, and the Departmental consultations in Whitehall completed, it had to be decided how, where, and by whom the Government's adoption of a policy that Straw had earlier rejected so robustly should be made public. At such moments special advisers come to the fore. The chosen platform indicated the audience to which the policy was judged most likely to appeal: the Home Secretary's traditional speech at the annual conference of the Police Federation at Blackpool. The setting was hardly the most auspicious for a significant shift in policy bearing on free choice

summarily, were forecast using a flows and costs model developed by the Home Office in collaboration with the Lord Chancellor's Department and the Crown Prosecution Service. *Parl. Debates*, HL, 607, col. WA 103, 9 Dec. 1999.

[35] Magistrates' sentencing powers are limited to a maximum of six months' imprisonment in respect of one offence, or a total of twelve months' imprisonment for two or more offences.

[36] *Parl. Debates*, HL, 607, col. 920, 2 Dec. 1999.

and individual liberty, such values taking second place to what was described evocatively as abuse of the system. It had long been a source of irritation to police officers and others, Straw declared, that defendants in many cases were working the system by demanding Crown Court trial for no good reason other than to delay proceedings.[37]

The content of the speech had been reported earlier the same day on the front page of *The Daily Mail*, although the editorial was critical.[38] Straw himself then confirmed the forthcoming announcement, discussing the proposal in an interview on the *Today* programme on BBC Radio 4. Although a pre-arranged Question had been put down for Written Answer in the House of Commons that afternoon, 19 May 1999, the Opposition tabled a debatable Private Notice Question which left Mike O'Brien, the unfortunate Parliamentary Under-Secretary of State for the Home Department, facing a querulous House for half an hour defending the Home Secretary's decision to inform the Police Federation and the media of his intentions before making them known in the House of Commons.

The Speaker was drawn into the exchanges, confirming, as she had made very clear on previous occasions, that she deprecated statements made in the media before the House. She would continue to use her best endeavours, she said, to ensure that leaks or information given to the media should cease.[39]

IV

The Government's intentions had been so widely forecast that there was ample time for opposition to gather strength inside and outside Parliament. On the day of the Queen's Speech, 17 November 1999, each MP, irrespective of party, and some selected peers, received a personal letter from the Chairman of the Bar Council, Daniel Brennan QC.[40] It was a foretaste of what was to come, and in an early intervention the Bar Council skilfully marked out the reasons that were to become the principal elements in the controversy. First,

[37] Home Office, *Press Release*, 155/99, 19 May 1999.

[38] The editorial concluded that it was difficult to view the Home Secretary's plans with anything but deep misgiving.

[39] Betty Boothroyd MP; *Parl. Debates*, HC, 331, cols. 1074–5, 19 May 1999.

[40] Daniel Brennan was created a life peer in March 2000. He followed another former Bar Council Chairman, Peter Goldsmith QC, onto the Government benches in the Lords. Goldsmith was appointed Attorney General in June 2001.

and most fundamental, was the reality that the proposal would give Magistrates the power to decide whether a defendant should be tried in the Crown Court for any offence in the intermediate category. Brennan's letter explained:

> This decision, the Government has suggested, will be based on whether the JP thinks the defendant before him has a reputation to defend. This is highly objectionable from a judicial and social perspective. It will create a two-tier system of justice, with middle-class defendants given privileged access to the Crown Courts if Magistrates decide they have a 'good reputation'. These figures are very disturbing . . .
>
> It will hit Black Britons worst—the evidence is they get a raw deal in the lower courts, and trust a representative jury much more than the predominantly white magistracy. Government research at Leicester Magistrates' Court showed that 13% of black defendants were sentenced to immediate custody for theft offences compared with 5% of whites. White defendants are granted unconditional bail at a rate of 60% compared with 44% for black defendants.
>
> We do not regard the Home Secretary's proposal for limited appeals against the Magistrates' decisions as an adequate safeguard. It will create extra cost and delay in the court system, with endless appeals and challenges to JPs' decisions. In summary, the move is a disturbing threat to our ancient liberties, which date back to Magna Carta, and before. This is not a lawyer-led issue; it is a matter of our basic constitutional rights. . . .[41]

While the Government's main justification was being undermined by the downward trend in the number of persons charged with either-way offences who elected to go to the Crown Court for trial, and with the likelihood of the rate of decline continuing as the full impact of the plea before venue procedure became more widely felt, the principal supporting line of argument was also crumbling. The flaw in the contention that once the option had been exercised in the Magistrates' court a high proportion of defendants subsequently changed their plea to guilty, with the result that no jury trial actually took place in the Crown Court, was that in many cases the original charge had been reduced. This trait was of particular significance where the accused belonged to one of the ethnic minorities. Both Home Office and independent research showed that black and Asian defendants not only had higher rates of acquittal, but also that the charges against them were dropped or reduced more often than white defendants. Professor Lee Bridges, a leading

[41] Reproduced with permission.

authority,[42] argued that these findings were consistent with a pattern of police discrimination in overcharging ethnic minority suspects. When such defendants elected jury trial a more thorough review of the evidence would be made by the Crown Prosecution Service which frequently resulted in the charges being altered.[43]

By the time of the Second Reading of the Criminal Justice (Mode of Trial) Bill the tide of informed opinion, in Parliament, in the broadsheet press, and in most if not all quarters of the legal profession, was running against the Government. Liberal Democrats and Conservatives alike had been forthright in their criticism in both Houses during the Debates on the Address, with few signs of enthusiasm on the Government back-benches. Thus the stage was set for confrontation when the Bill was introduced in the Lords and debated on Second Reading on 2 December 1999. Out of a total of twenty-two speakers, eighteen were opposed. Only three Labour back-benchers gave unequivocal support to the Attorney General who moved the Second Reading, and also replied to the debate. The most effective was Lord Warner, who was by then Chairman of the Youth Justice Board, but when the decisions had been taken was Senior Policy Adviser to the Home Secretary. He was challenged by an outspoken Labour critic, Baroness Kennedy of The Shaws,[44] to say whether he had advised in favour of making the change, but had declined to answer.[45] No cross-benchers, Liberal Democrats, or Conservatives spoke in support; indeed they vied in their condemnation of the aims of the Bill.

Modern technology was harnessed to the cause of political lobbying. A website was set up by a group of lawyers providing ready access to a detailed summary of government plans, an exposition of what was wrong with them, and suggested wording for standard letters of protest or emails to MPs. More significant than any lobbying was a sea change which had occurred in the legislative relationship between the two Houses of Parliament as a result of the passing of

[42] Lee Bridges had been an active member of the Lord Chancellor's Advisory Committee on Legal Education and Conduct (ACLEC) until its abolition on 1 Jan. 2000 under Section 35(1) of the Access to Justice Act 1999. The eighth and final Annual Report of the Advisory Committee was published on 15 Dec. 1999. ACLEC was replaced by the Legal Services Advisory Panel.

[43] Letter from Professor Bridges to the Editor, *The Times*, 25 Nov. 1999.

[44] Helena Kennedy QC was created a life peer in 1997, and was appointed Chair of the British Council in the following year.

[45] *Parl. Debates*, HL, 607, col. 984, 2 Dec. 1999.

the House of Lords Act at the conclusion of the previous session three months earlier. With the departure of most of the hereditary peers, the transitional House, as it was described pending further reform,[46] sensed that it had acquired a new legitimacy. The old conventions of self-restraint no longer applied, or not to the same extent. The time had come to assert the rights and duties of the reconstituted Upper House of Parliament. What issue could be better suited to test the boundaries of a still fluid relationship than a policy, previously rejected by Labour when in Opposition, which to many of its traditional supporters was seen as authoritarian and illiberal? The Home Secretary's dismissive references to his critics as woolly minded Hampstead liberals,[47] or lawyers only interested in preserving their own earnings, alienated still further many of those inside and outside Parliament who had doubts about the wisdom of the course he was intent on pursuing.

Party politics inevitably played a part. For the Conservatives it was a heaven-sent opportunity to embarrass the Government on a front where it was vulnerable. Although the proposal to limit the right to jury trial had been considered by the Conservatives when in power, Michael Howard was circumspect and had been careful to avoid any commitment to implement this recommendation of the Narey Report. It was Straw who had to explain his change of heart. For the Liberal Democrats it was an issue of principle which enabled the Party to distinguish itself from the authoritarian tendencies of New Labour.

The climax came early in the New Year of 2000. At Committee stage on 20 January a cross-party amendment was tabled to restore the right of a person accused of an offence triable either way to choose trial by jury in the Crown Court. The four sponsors had been carefully chosen to span each of the main groupings in the House: the Government benches, the Conservative and Liberal Democrat Opposition benches, and the independent cross-benchers.[48] The wording of the amendment was straightforward. It simply added to the opening clause of the Bill, which prescribed that the court should

[46] *Modernising Parliament: Reforming the House of Lords*, Cm. 4183, The Stationery Office, Jan. 1999, pp. 31–4.

[47] Reported comments on a speech to the Institute for Public Policy Research on 14 Jan. 2000.

[48] The four sponsors, in the order shown on the amendment as printed, were Lord Cope of Berkeley (Con.), Lord Thomas of Gresford (Lib. Dem.), Lord Ackner (Ind.), and Baroness Kennedy of the Shaws (Lab.).

consider whether the accused ought to be tried summarily or on indictment, the words 'and on the application of the accused, shall order that he be tried on indictment'.[49]

The amendment was moved by Lord Cope of Berkeley, an experienced former MP and Minister in the Commons,[50] and currently the Opposition front-bench spokesman on Home Affairs in the Lords. In the course of a workmanlike and trenchant speech he revealed that, of the estimated net saving of £105 million, the Government anticipated that only about one-third (£39 million) would come in the courts, with £66 million being the expected saving in the costs of the Prison Service.[51] This was an important corrective to the assumption that savings over £100 million would be achieved in the court system.

The speech that followed was one of the highlights of the debate. Lord Jenkins of Hillhead, twice Home Secretary in Labour Governments and a founder of the Social Democratic Party,[52] spoke from the Liberal Democrat benches. He had been moved to intervene, he said, only because Straw in his much publicized 'woolly liberal' speech had called in aid his own action in introducing majority verdicts in criminal trials in the Criminal Justice Act 1967. 'I suppose I should be flattered by the attempt of the Home Secretary to enlist me', he observed,

> because I thought that previously he had regarded me as the epitome of a woolly Hampstead liberal, even though I have never inhabited those salubrious heights and have never been particularly addicted to woolly clothing. However, I am proud to be a liberal, both with a small 'l' and a capital 'L'.[53]

Jenkins went on to point out that the introduction of majority verdicts of eleven to one, or at least ten to two, had not removed anyone's right to trial by jury. It had been designed to meet a specific evil of the intimidation of one, or occasionally two, of the most vulnerable or

[49] *Parl. Debates*, HL, 608, col. 1246, 20 Jan. 2000. The Bill substituted new wording for Sections 19–22 of the Magistrates' Courts Act 1980 (offences triable either way: determination of mode of trial).

[50] A Government Whip (1979–87), and Deputy Chief Whip, 1983–7. Minister of State: Department of Employment, 1987–9; Northern Ireland Office, 1989–90. Deputy Chairman and Joint Treasurer, Conservative Party, 1990–2; HM Paymaster-General, 1992–4. Created a life peer in 1997.

[51] *Parl. Debates*, HL, 608, *op. cit.*, col. 1247.

[52] Minister of Aviation, 1964–5; Home Secretary, 1965–7 and 1974–6; Chancellor of the Exchequer, 1967–70. President of the European Commission, 1977–81. First Leader, Social and Democratic Party, 1982–3 (Joint Leadership, 1981–2).

[53] *Parl. Debates*, HL, 608, *op. cit.*, col. 1251.

amenable jurors. Although convincing evidence had been accumulating, the change was proposed only after he had consulted some of those possessing both 'keen liberal consciences and a closer knowledge of the functioning of the courts' than he had himself.[54] He utterly rejected the view that the current proposal was in any way the equivalent of the introduction of majority verdicts. His peroration was a classic of sophisticated invective:

> The Home Secretary called in aid, in a way that I think was intended to be friendly, my willingness to risk for majority verdicts a mounting liberal reputation, as it was put, as Home Secretary. I must say to the Home Secretary, I hope with equal friendliness, that I do not think he is in equal danger. He has not as yet much of a liberal reputation to lose. But there must always be hope for the future. If he will accept the defeat of this measure—if that is the wish of your Lordships—with a good grace, if he will be less grudging on freedom of information, and if he will take less of a knee-jerk *Daily Mail* attitude to the whole complex question of crime and punishment, then maybe, by the end of this Parliament, his reputation for humane sagacity might begin to gleam a little more brightly.[55]

V

Although lacking Jenkins' elegance, the speech of Lord Bingham was the most closely argued of the debate, which lasted for three and a quarter hours. Speaking with the authority of his high office as Lord Chief Justice of England, Bingham began with first principles, setting out an analysis of the requirements of criminal procedure. At all levels the process in the criminal courts should be such as would: promote the fair disposal of cases; minimize the risk of miscarriages of justice; achieve such expedition and efficiency as was consistent with fairness; and command public confidence in the administration of justice.[56] The present procedure, allowing a defendant to elect trial by judge and jury on an either-way offence, did not lead to unfairness or miscarriages of justice; nor did it undermine public confidence. There was therefore no imperative need to change the existing procedure on the ground that it failed those important tests. If it did, the rule would have been changed long ago.

[54] Lord Gardiner (Lord Chancellor 1964–70), Lord Hutchinson of Lullington QC, and Michael Foot MP.

[55] *Op. cit.*, col. 1252.

[56] Ibid.

He went on to argue that there were nevertheless weaknesses in the existing procedure. A broad band of offences were triable either way. Some were serious, others relatively trivial. Some were eminently suitable to trial by judge and jury; others were not. The inevitable result was that, at the election of the defendant, some cases ended up before a judge and jury in the Crown Court which did not merit that mode of trial. Delays resulted, exacerbated when defendants pleaded guilty only after reaching the Crown Court. Congestion, already a problem, was increased, sometimes causing persons charged with serious offences to be released because their trials could not be accommodated before their custody time limits expired.

It was clear to him, Bingham continued, that any new procedure introduced to remedy these weaknesses must satisfy the tests which he had already mentioned. He accepted that many Lords were apprehensive that the procedure set out in the Bill would not meet those criteria, but it was not an opinion which he shared.[57] The next step in his argument was to list some of the summary offences of considerable seriousness over which Magistrates currently had exclusive jurisdiction. The exercise of their powers to decide questions of guilt and sentence in such cases did not arouse anxiety because the public had confidence that Magistrates brought to their task the qualities of fairness, open-mindedness, human insight, and common sense which had commended them for appointment in the first place. There was no reason to fear that under the new proposals Magistrates would hang on to cases which more properly should be tried in the Crown Court. The only reservation in his speech came when he admitted that he was 'not enamoured' of the provisions in the part of the Bill which required Magistrates in reaching their decision on mode of trial to consider the effect of conviction or punishment on a defendant's livelihood or reputation. To rebut claims of good character, a defendant's previous convictions could be disclosed to the court. Bingham said that he would prefer to give the court a wide and almost undirected discretion.[58]

A corner of the veil which customarily hangs over any consultation between Government and the judiciary on legislative change was lifted later in Bingham's speech. Unlike his predecessor in office but one, Lord Lane, who was sitting nearby on the cross-benches, the present Chief Justice was open to discussion with ministers about

[57] *Parl. Debates*, HL, 608, *op. cit.*, col. 1253. [58] Ibid., col. 1254.

proposals which affected the courts while still in the formative stage.[59] He disclosed that on 22 October 1998 the question of mode of trial had been considered by a small group of senior judges concerned with criminal law and practice. Those attending included: Lord Justice Rose, Vice-President of the Court of Appeal, Criminal Division; the then senior presiding High Court Judge; his successor as senior presiding judge; and himself. Although another member of the group, Mr Justice Mitchell, whose knowledge of criminal law and practice was unrivalled, was absent, he had expressed full concurrence with the view taken. That view was that the proposed change could be supported if, but only if, the Magistrates' decision on jurisdiction was subject to an appeal to a circuit judge.

No such provision had been part of the Home Secretary's original proposal, although it was subsequently accepted by the Government. On the basis of that acceptance Bingham had commended the proposal both in a public speech at the Lord Mayor of London's annual dinner for the judges and at a subsequent meeting of the High Court bench, totalling almost a hundred judges, at which the issue had been ventilated. On both occasions there had been near unanimity of judicial opinion in favour of making the change.[60]

Despite a strong whip and a crowded chamber no more than two Government back-benchers, Lords Lipsey and Mackenzie of Framwellgate, spoke in support of the Bill. They were easily outnumbered by Labour sceptics (Lord Shore of Stepney, and a former front-bench spokesman on Home Affairs, Lord Mishcon) combining with the root-and-branch opponents (Baronesses Mallalieu and Kennedy of the Shaws). All the Liberal Democrat and Conservative speakers were opposed. The only relief for the Government came from the cross-benches where a well respected Magistrate, Lord Tenby, put forward the view of the Magistrates' Association. Like Bingham, he was critical of the provision relating to livelihood and reputation, but on 'the central plank of the Bill' he remained convinced that it was 'entirely proper and long overdue to remove the right of defendants to be able to choose the trial venue in so called each-way cases'.[61]

[59] For an account of Lord Lane's arm's-length relationship with the Home Secretary when changes in criminal policy were under consideration in the 1980s, see *Responses to Crime*, Vol. 2, pp. 181–4.

[60] *Parl. Debates*, HL, 608, *op. cit.*, col. 1255. It does not follow that the outcome would have been the same if the Circuit Judges or Recorders who try the bulk of criminal cases in the Crown Court had been included in the sample.

[61] Ibid., col. 1268.

Support for Bingham came also from his immediate predecessor as Master of the Rolls, Lord Donaldson of Lymington,[62] speaking from the cross-benches.

After concluding speeches by the Lord Advocate,[63] calling in aid the experience in Scotland, and the Attorney General once again deploying the full force of his eloquence to defend the Government's proposals, the amendment was put to the vote. The result was 222 voting content and 126 not content.[64] A margin of nearly a hundred in favour of the amendment could only be interpreted as a crushing defeat for the Government, the heaviest since the House of Lords Act had come into effect the previous November. While neither Bingham nor any other serving judge voted, six out of the seven peers present who had held high judicial office went into the lobby against making the change. Donaldson was not joined by any other retired judge in the not content lobby. His unpersuaded brethren were Ackner, Brightman, Lane, Oliver of Aylmerton, Simon of Glaisdale, and Wilberforce.

An analysis of the voting showed that out of a nominal total of 181 peers taking the Labour whip,[65] 109 voted not content. Eight Labour peers voted for the amendment, with an unknown number of abstentions. The abstainers included several authoritative voices on criminal policy, including the former leader, Lord Richard, as well as Lords Archer of Sandwell[66] and Mishcon. Although it would be wrong to assume that the difference between the effective voting strength of 151 (181 minus thirty) and 109 represented the number of Labour peers opposed to the policy of their own party,[67] nevertheless defeat on this scale was a highly publicized setback for the Government.

[62] See Chapter 2, n. 12 above.

[63] Lord Hardie QC, Lord Advocate, 1997–2000; Dean of the Faculty of Advocates (Scotland), 1994–7; Treasurer, 1989–94.

[64] *Parl. Debates*, HL, 608, *op. cit.*, cols. 1294–7.

[65] Government whips regarded some thirty Labour peers as being permanently absent owing to age, infirmity, or serious illness, so reducing the total voting strength to 151. The author is indebted to Lord Carter, Government Chief Whip (1997–) for the information on the number of peers taking the Labour whip.

[66] Chairman of the Society of Labour Lawyers, 1971–4 and Solicitor General, 1974–9. Created a life peer in 1992, and Chairman, Council on Tribunals, 1992–9.

[67] The potential turnout, even on a three-line whip, was reduced by peers who were unavoidably absent due to visits abroad, a severe epidemic of flu, or inescapable public engagements. Such factors did not solely affect peers on the Government benches, but applied similarly to other parts of the House.

The fact that the outcome was not unexpected was demonstrated by the Leader of the House, Baroness Jay. Immediately after the result of the division had been declared the Leader of the Opposition, Lord Strathclyde, asked what were the Government's intentions on the future of the Bill. In reply, Lady Jay accepted that the passing of the amendment effectively killed the Bill. As amended, it no longer represented Government policy. The Home Secretary would shortly make a statement, but she was in a position to tell the House that the Government would not proceed with the Bill. A No. 2 Bill would be introduced in the Commons in the current session.[68] Consequently she proposed that the Committee stage of the Bill should be suspended. After further exchanges between the front benches the House moved on to other business.

VI

Such an instant and dismissive response, with the implication that the Government intended to lose little time in introducing a substitute Bill in the Commons, and then use its large and well disciplined majority to force it through regardless of the views of the Lords and much informed opinion, failed to meet the strength of the objections raised, either inside or outside Parliament. A vital factor to which inadequate attention had been paid was the rooted belief of ethnic minorities that they would receive a fairer trial if their case was heard by a jury. Then there was the apparently unquestioning acceptance of the division of criminal offences into three categories of ascending seriousness for the purpose of determining the mode of trial.

For over a century, in an attempt to be fair to persons accused of criminal offences of intermediate seriousness or variable seriousness, defendants accused of an offence triable either way must either consent to summary trial in the Magistrates' court or elect to go for trial in the Crown Court. In the Crown Court all indictable offences to which the accused pleads not guilty are triable by a judge and jury; so too are the either-way offences, including several of the most common offences such as theft, handling stolen goods, obtaining by deception, and burglary, which are committed to the Crown Court

[68] *Parl. Debates*, HL, 608, *op. cit.*, col. 1297.

by the Magistrates' courts.[69] As already noted, a further refinement, added by statute in 1996, was the plea before venue procedure brought into force in October 1997. That provision required defendants to indicate to the Magistrates whether they intended to plead guilty or not guilty to the offences charged. On a guilty plea, the Magistrates would either assume jurisdiction themselves or, if the offence was of such seriousness that the appropriate sentence was likely to be outwith their powers, they would commit the case to the Crown Court for sentence.[70]

Whether or not these complex procedures constituted a specific right to jury trial has been questioned. Although the Royal Commission on Criminal Justice did not reject the use of the term 'right', as it did the right of silence,[71] it recommended that the procedure for determining the mode of trial should be changed 'in order to secure a more rational division of either-way cases between the Magistrates' courts and the Crown Court'.[72] The Commissioners did not believe that the decision should be left to the defendant, 'though he or she should have a voice in the matter'.[73] The managerial and slightly patronizing tone hardly did justice to the notion of civil rights.

While not of universal application, even within the British Isles since in Scotland it is the prosecutor and not the defendant who decides in which court an accused person is prosecuted,[74] an acknowledged right of defendants accused of certain offences in the criminal jurisdictions of England and Wales to choose to be tried before a jury has existed for more than a century. It has been widely exercised, and does not exist only in the abstract. It is the direct

[69] A. Ashworth, *The Criminal Process: An Evaluative Study*, 2nd edition, Oxford University Press, 1998, p. 243. Since 1997 Andrew Ashworth has been Vinerian Professor of English Law and a Fellow of All Souls College, Oxford. Editor, *Criminal Law Review*, 1975–99.

[70] Ibid.

[71] In the heading to Chapter Four of its Report, the Royal Commission printed the 'Right of Silence' in inverted commas, referring to it in the text as 'the so-called right of silence—that is, in this context, the prohibition against adverse comment at trial on a defendant's refusal to answer police questioning . . .'. The Royal Commission on Criminal Justice, *Report*, Cm. 2263, HMSO, London, 1993, p. 49.

[72] Ibid., p. 87.

[73] Ibid.

[74] For a full explanation of the current procedures in Scotland, see the speech of the Lord Advocate during the House of Lords Committee stage debate on the Criminal Justice (Mode of Trial) Bill. *Parl. Debates*, HL, 608, *op. cit.*, cols. 1286–7. Drawing on Scottish experience, Peter Duff has argued that the proposed removal of an English defendant's right to elect trial by jury is not as objectionable as its critics claimed. 'The Defendant's Right to Trial by Jury: A Neighbour's View' [2000] Crim. L.R. 85.

progeny of an Act of Parliament which has periodically been revised and updated. It is binding on the courts, with remedies for any breach. In short, it is an enforceable statutory entitlement which can neither be ignored nor altered by the executive or judiciary without the sanction of Parliament.

The contrast with the situation in the United States, the largest and most relevant common law comparator, is instructive. The importance of jury trial was recognized by the Constitution and the Bill of Rights from the start. In post-colonial America it was seen not only as an essential feature of a fair trial, embodied in Article III of the Constitution,[75] but also as a check on judicial power, much as the Congress was designed to check the power of the executive branch of Government.[76] The Fifth, Sixth, and Seventh Amendments all protected the safeguard of trial by jury in federal court proceedings in specific ways. The Fifth Amendment provided that no person should be 'held to answer for a capital, or otherwise infamous crime, unless on a presentment or indictment of a Grand Jury'. It was the function of a grand jury or panel to review complaints in criminal cases, hear the evidence of the prosecutor, and decide whether to issue an indictment that would bring the accused person to trial. A contemporary, and highly visible, application of this two-centuries-old procedure was when President Clinton was called to testify before a federal grand jury[77] in the sequence of events culminating in his impeachment by the House of Representatives, and his subsequent trial and acquittal by the Senate. The Sixth Amendment guarantees the right to a speedy and public trial before an impartial jury in federal criminal prosecutions; and the Seventh Amendment provides for jury trial in certain civil suits.

The Sixth Amendment right to jury trial in criminal cases has been refined, and its application extended to state criminal prosecutions,

[75] 'The Trial of all Crimes, except in Cases of Impeachment, shall be by Jury; and such Trial shall be held in the State where the said Crimes shall have been committed; but when not committed within any State, the Trial shall be at such Place or Places as the Congress may by Law have directed.' Article III, Section 2, of the Constitution of the United States.

[76] *West's Encyclopaedia of American Law*, Vol. 5, 1998, p. 302.

[77] Historically one of the functions of the grand jury has been to act as an investigative body for inquiring into the conduct of public officials. Although contemporary practice varies between states and the federal jurisdiction, a common purpose is to examine possible crimes and to develop evidence which may not currently be available to the prosecution. See *Black's Law Dictionary*, 7th edition, West Group, St. Paul, 1999, p. 706, and other sources.

as a result of decisions of the Supreme Court. In *Duncan* v. *Louisiana*[78] the Court held by a majority of seven to two that the right to trial by jury, already guaranteed to defendants in criminal cases tried in federal courts by Article III of the Constitution and the Sixth Amendment, was also applicable to defendants tried in state courts. Delivering the opinion of the Court, Justice White said that the right to jury trial in serious criminal cases was a fundamental right, and hence must be recognized by the states as part of their obligation to extend due process of law under the Fourteenth Amendment to all persons within their jurisdiction.[79] The Supreme Court has held that this guarantee does not extend to 'petty offences', which are defined as crimes punishable by a potential sentence of less than six months' imprisonment.[80] Despite the fact that most states now ensure jury trial in criminal cases going well beyond what the Supreme Court requires, the practice of 'bench trials' by a judge alone, the accused having renounced the right to jury trial, is widespread.[81]

Another analogy with the United States, although fortunately less widespread, is the sense of alienation on the part of many defendants of Afro-Caribbean or Asian origin from the entire process of criminal justice, from questioning and arrest to trial and penalty. At the height of the controversy over the mode of trial, the Howard League for Penal Reform published some statistics on ethnic minorities and the criminal justice system. An analysis showed that black people faced a higher prospect of being imprisoned than either white people or South Asians, notwithstanding the absence of evidence to suggest that people from ethnic minority groups commit more offences than white people. They were also six times more likely to be stopped and searched by the police and more likely to be arrested.[82] It is undeniably

[78] 88 S. Ct. 1444 (1968). [79] Ibid., 1450.

[80] *Baldwin* v. *New York*, 90 S. Ct. 1886 at 1888 (1970).

[81] In 1997 twenty states provided for a right to jury trial for virtually all criminal offences; and seven others for all offences punishable by any length of imprisonment. Only ten states did not provide a right to jury trial more extensive than that required by the Supreme Court. Colleen P. Murphy, 'The Narrowing of the Entitlement to Criminal Jury Trial', (1997) *Wisconsin Law Review* 133, 170–1. See also *Thomas* v. *City of Montgomery*, 690 So. 2d 546 (Ala. Cr. App. 1997) at 547. The decision whether to be tried before a judge alone, or before a judge and jury, is usually for the defendant, although in some jurisdictions the consent of the prosecutor is also required. Bench trials are typically shorter in duration, and hence less costly for both the defendant and the state.

[82] In June 1998 the rate of incarceration per 100,000 of the general population was 1,245 for black people, 185 for white people, and 168 for South Asians. Howard League for Penal Reform, Fact Sheet 9, 2000.

the case that minority ethnic communities are under-represented at every level in the administration of justice, including the magistracy. Although in some urban areas ethnic lay Magistrates sit on the bench, they are still in a small minority.[83] There is an even lower proportion to be found amongst stipendiary Magistrates.[84] In the Crown Court, however, at least those covering inner-city areas, there are likely to be some jurors from black or Asian ethnic minorities.[85]

To recite these characteristics is not to infer that defendants belonging to racial minority groups are denied a fair trial in the Magistrates' courts. There is research, as well as much anecdotal evidence, to indicate that in the large majority of cases they are equitably treated. On the basis of Home Office commissioned research, ministers claimed that in contested cases black defendants were in fact less likely to be convicted than white defendants, both in the Magistrates' courts and the Crown Court. Nor did they accept that there was any difference in the use of custody between black and white male defendants in the Magistrates' courts and the Crown Court when other factors were taken into account.[86] Nevertheless, like many statistical

[83] A survey of lay Magistrates (excluding those in the Duchy of Lancaster) conducted in 1997 indicated that there were 753 lay Magistrates, 286 female and 467 male, from Afro-Caribbean and Asian ethnic minorities (2.9 per cent). The survey showed that overall 4.1 per cent of Magistrates classified themselves as belonging to an ethnic minority community. An increasing percentage of appointments of persons from ethnic minorities had been apparent in recent years, rising from 6 per cent in 1995 to 7.6 per cent in 1998. *Parl. Debates*, HL, 611, col. WA 46, 27 Mar. 2000.

[84] Since the unification of the stipendiary bench by Section 78 of the Access to Justice Act 1999, stipendiary Magistrates and metropolitan stipendiary Magistrates have been renamed District Judges (Magistrates' Courts). In March 2000 there were only two stipendiary Magistrates from the Asian community (1.9 per cent). *Parl. Debates*, HL, 611, ibid.

[85] The Royal Commission on Criminal Justice recommended in 1993 that in exceptional cases where there was a racial dimension, provided that compelling reasons could be advanced for such a course, it should be open to either the defence or the prosecution to argue that a multi-racial jury was required containing up to three people from ethnic minority communities. *Report*, Cm. 2263, *op. cit.*, p. 207. In its final response in 1996 the Government said that, while the proposal would remain under consideration, there was concern that it would depart fundamentally from the principle that a jury should as far as possible be chosen at random from a cross-section of the population as a whole. In April 2000, prompted by a Parliamentary Question from the author, the Government had looked at the issue again, and decided to give active consideration to the recommendation. *Parl. Debates*, HL, 612, col. WA 123, 20 Apr. 2000.

[86] Letter dated 14 Jan. 2000 from the Parliamentary Under-Secretary of State at the Home Office, Lord Bassam of Brighton, addressed to the author and circulated to other peers in advance of the Committee stage of the Criminal Justice (Mode of Trial) Bill on 20 Jan. 2000. Copies of the letter and enclosures were also placed in the Library of the House.

analyses retrospectively brought to bear to support conflicting arguments on public policy issues, the validity both of the Howard League and the Home Office research findings could be challenged. In practice, experience shows that survey data tend to be used to defend or attack measures already decided upon for policy reasons.

In the course of the Lords debate, Lord Dholakia, one of the few peers of East African Asian origin,[87] a Magistrate as well as a Liberal Democrat front-bench spokesman, argued that the fundamental point was that many ethnic minorities still perceive, even if it is not the reality, that there is unfairness in the criminal justice system because the law, inevitably for reasons of history, is in the hands of predominantly white people. The Magistrates' courts were no exception.[88] Later in the same debate Lord Taylor of Warwick, a black barrister with a criminal practice, reinforced the point. Speaking from the Conservative benches, he claimed that some black and Asian defendants choose jury trial because they fear they will not get a fair hearing by Magistrates. To have the right to elect jury trial removed from them would only further reduce their faith in the system. At a time when a report by Sir William Macpherson highlighted ways of improving race relations between the police and ethnic minorities[89] the Bill could cast a shadow once more. If the right to elect jury trial was lost, it would be difficult to win it back.[90]

VII

Parliamentary rules do not allow the reintroduction in the same session of a Bill identical to one that has already been rejected. But if the

[87] Navnit Dholakia was born in Tanzania and came to Britain in 1956. Appointments followed with the National Committee for Commonwealth Immigrants, Community Relations Commission, and Commission for Racial Equality, 1966–94. Member: Parole Review Committee, 1987–8, and Sussex Police Authority, 1991–4. National Association for the Care and Resettlement of Offenders (NACRO): member of Council, 1984–; Chairman, Race Issues Advisory Council, 1989–; Vice-Chairman, 1995–8; Chairman, 1998–. Life peer, 1997. President, Liberal Democratic Party, 2000–.

[88] *Parl. Debates*, HL, 608, *op. cit.*, col. 1279.

[89] *The Stephen Lawrence Inquiry*, Cm. 4262-I, The Stationery Office, Feb. 1999. The terms of reference for Sir William Macpherson of Cluny, a retired High Court judge, were to inquire into the matters arising from the death of Stephen Lawrence 'in order particularly to identify the lessons to be learned for the investigation and prosecution of racially motivated crimes' (p. 6).

[90] *Parl. Debates*, HL, 608, *op. cit.*, col. 1288.

Bill is amended, however slight the alterations, it can be introduced again either in the same or the other House under its original title, to which the suffix 'No. 2 Bill' is appended. An interval is necessary to enable the departmental ministers and managers of government business collectively to decide on tactics after a Parliamentary reverse. If set on trying again, probably in the other House, the extent of any changes need to be agreed, legal advisers and draftsmen instructed, and whips consulted. All this takes time, and opens up an opportunity for further representations. Although Straw, in the thick of the fray, appeared to be firmly committed to persisting with the Bill, it was not certain that other ministers, more concerned with public presentation and the likelihood of confrontation with a sizeable group of their own back-benchers in the Commons, were equally determined.

In such a situation a pause for thought is sometimes a more effective device than outright opposition. A forum for dispassionate inquiry was conveniently to hand, since in December 1999 the Lord Chancellor had appointed Lord Justice Auld[91] to conduct a review of the practices and procedures of the criminal courts.[92] To take advantage of this situation, and to concentrate on an aspect that had received little attention either in the Parliamentary debate or public discussion, I wrote to the Home Secretary on 2 February suggesting that a way out of the difficulties presented by the defeat in the Lords would be for him to invite the Lord Justice to consider and report as soon as possible on what offences might be reclassified as triable summarily only in order to reduce the burden on the Crown Court. The introduction of the mode of trial legislation in the Commons might be deferred until the results of such an inquiry were known.

Although courteously worded, Jack Straw's reply held out little hope that this suggestion would be accepted.

[91] Sir Robin Auld was appointed as a Judge of the High Court of Justice, Queen's Bench Division, in 1987, and as Senior Presiding Judge for England and Wales, 1995–8. Lord Justice of Appeal since 1995. Member, and Chairman, Criminal Committee, Judicial Studies Board, 1989–91.

[92] On 14 Dec. 1999 the Lord Chancellor appointed Lord Justice Auld to conduct a review of the criminal courts. The terms of reference were to carry out 'An inquiry into the practices and procedures of, and the rules of evidence applied by, the criminal courts at every level, with a view to ensuring that they deliver justice fairly, by streamlining all their processes, increasing their efficiency and strengthening the effectiveness of their relationships with others across the whole of the criminal justice system, and having regard to the interests of all parties including the victims and witnesses, thereby promoting public confidence in the law'. The review was expected to last for twelve months. *Parl. Debates*, HL, 608, col. WA 26, 14 Dec. 1999.

Home Secretary Queen Anne's Gate, London SW1 9AT

23 February 2000

Dear David

Thank you for your letter of 2 February about the Government's proposals to reform mode of trial.

You suggested that we should ask Lord Justice Auld to consider, in the course of his review of the criminal courts, whether there is any scope for reducing the burden on the Crown Court by reclassifying some either-way offences as summary. No doubt there are either-way offences which are seldom tried in the Crown Court or committed there for sentence, and which—if they are—receive sentences which the magistrates could have imposed. But the criterion for reclassification is that there should be no risk to the interests of justice in *precluding* an offence from being dealt with in the Crown Court. That is a severe test, and although you say that the last reclassification in 1988 has not led to any insuperable problems, it did not in fact prove entirely straightforward. Taking a motor vehicle without consent was reclassified as a summary offence on the basis that it was generally disposed of, or could have been disposed of, summarily; but it later had to be conceded (with the introduction of 'aggravated vehicle taking') that there are some circumstances in which this offence ought after all to be dealt with in the Crown Court.

Reclassification of offences which cover a wide range of behaviour inevitably leads to questions about the adequacy of magistrates' sentencing powers. But if—which is a logical consequence of some of the proposals for reclassification—we were then to give magistrates the power to commit summary only offences for sentence in the Crown Court, this would have the effect of denying the defendant the right to argue for a Crown Court trial, as they will be able to do under our Bill. What we need to do, and what I am confident the Bill will do, is to ensure that cases which require jury trial receive it.

I think we always have to keep the classification of offences under review and I will do so. But I think it is a separate issue from a determination of venue in either-way cases.

I appreciate, as ever, your writing to me. If you would like to meet me I should be very pleased to do so—easiest for me (and probably for you) would be in my room in the Commons in the late afternoon or early evening. My Diary Secretary . . . can arrange . . .

I am copying this letter to Derry Irvine and Gareth Williams.

Yours ever

Jack

While replies to the numerous letters on policy matters addressed to ministers by Parliamentarians are normally drafted by civil servants, with the draft approved or amended by the minister before signature and despatch, no official would have presumed to make the offer contained in the penultimate paragraph. The invitation could only have come from Straw himself. The offer was taken up and the discussion at the meeting which followed went further than rehearsing the case for another reclassification scrutiny similar to the previous exercise in 1988. It afforded an opportunity to raise the possibility of more radical alternatives. The first was to examine current practice in the United States in order to establish whether the problems inherent in the either-way category could be eradicated by moving in the direction of a straightforward bipartite system of offences triable either summarily or on indictment, and where to draw the line between them. If adopted, the administration of such a system would be facilitated by the introduction of a unified court system, eliminating the organizational distinctions between the Crown Court and the Magistrates' courts. This would allow less serious offences to be tried by a new tribunal, possibly composed of a District Judge (formerly a stipendiary Magistrate) sitting with between two and four lay Magistrates drawn from the local community.

The Home Secretary said that he was 'not averse' to a three-tier system: trial by Magistrates for summary-only offences; trial by a stipendiary Magistrate or District Judge sitting with lay Magistrates for offences of intermediary seriousness; and trial by a Crown Court judge and jury for indictable offences. The current boundaries between the different categories of offence could also be reviewed. The key principle would be that for each offence category there should be only one mode of trial. A minute of the meeting would be forwarded to Lord Justice Auld.[93]

On 16 February 2000 there was a complementary initiative in the House of Commons when fifty-nine Government supporters put their names to an early-day motion put down by Robert Marshall-Andrews QC, a Labour MP and Crown Court Recorder. The wording was:

That this House congratulates the Government on the institution of a Review of Criminal Justice under the chairmanship of Sir Robin Auld; notes

[93] A draft minute of the discussion was sent to the author to comment upon before it was forwarded to Sir Robin Auld.

that the scope of the review includes mode of trial in either way offences; and calls upon the Government to postpone any legislation on this issue until at least the publication of this review.[94]

Although early-day motions have no legislative standing they function as a useful safety valve, enabling MPs to indicate what they really believe before the whips get at them. As a rule fewer than half of the signatories will vote against their own Government when it comes to a division on a Bill enforced by a strong whip.

The Parliamentary necessity that the No. 2 Bill should differ from the Bill withdrawn in the Lords was met by a substantial concession to the views of the Lord Chief Justice, whose support was vital to the Government's chances of getting the legislation through. This was to eliminate the requirement that in reaching their decision on mode of trial Magistrates should take account of the effect of a conviction on an accused person's livelihood or reputation. Both Bingham and the Magistrates' Association, important allies in the attempt to reform the mode of trial, had expressed concern about the potential discriminatory effect of this provision on those who had little or no reputation to lose, including members of racial minorities. It had been a key factor, however, in persuading the Royal Commission to recommend curtailing access to jury trial, and a reason which had frequently been called in aid by the Home Secretary in defending his proposals. Thus, in seeking to cement a new alliance, Straw had to accept the risk of weakening his ties with the old. By deleting the livelihood and reputation clause and substituting criteria relating to the seriousness and complexity of the offence, and the sentencing power of the court,[95] he supplied a fresh store of ammunition to his opponents.

With this important change the Second Reading debate on the Criminal Justice (Mode of Trial) (No. 2) Bill took place in the House of Commons on 7 March. The debate was a lengthy one, lasting for five and a quarter hours, and ended in three divisions. The first was on a reasoned amendment moved by Marshall-Andrews declining to give the Bill a Second Reading on the ground that it failed properly to safeguard or maintain the right to jury trial in either-way offences. Two hundred and fourteen members voted for the amendment, mainly Conservatives and Liberal Democrats but also twenty-nine Labour MPs. Many others abstained. The scale of the revolt, which

[94] Early Day Motion 406.

[95] *Parl. Debates*, HC, 345, col. 891, 7 Mar. 2000.

would have been fatal in previous Parliaments when the Government of the day enjoyed smaller overall majorities, still left Labour with a majority of just over one hundred.[96] On a second division, the House agreed to give the Bill a Second Reading by 315 votes to 188. The Liberal Democrats then called a third division to vote against a motion to commit the Bill to a special standing committee. This too was defeated, by a majority of 325 to 181.

In opening the debate, the Home Secretary had set the Bill in the context of the Government's programme to modernise the criminal justice system and improve confidence in it. Its purpose was to make the system more responsive to the needs of victims, witnesses, and the public at large, and those of defendants. He claimed that the proposal had received the unanimous backing of the Royal Commission in 1993, and enjoyed the active endorsement of the Lord Chief Justice and the vast majority of the High Court Bench, as well as the Magistrates' Association and all three police associations. While justified in its own right, the Bill would produce considerable savings of more than £120 million a year, representing resources which could be better used elsewhere in the criminal justice system.[97]

The Shadow Attorney General, Edward Garnier, followed from the Opposition Front Bench. His speech was more partisan, provoking continual interruptions. After some preliminaries, he accused Straw of 'persisting with this silly and unthinkable Bill', not because it would do good or because it was the right thing to do, but because if he were to withdraw it and pass the issue over to the Auld inquiry he would be seen as a weak Home Secretary, who had given way to the unelected House of Lords and to the fifty-nine of his colleagues who had signed the early-day motion criticizing his stance.[98] Garnier forecast that the Bill would add to the existing lack of confidence in the summary justice system on the part of ethnic minorities, and that hearings on venue would lead to dissatisfaction in the minds of many defendants. Nor should the House rely on the Government's 'unaudited assumptions' that the Bill would save money.[99]

In moving his amendment, Marshall-Andrews declared an interest. He had been a member of the Bar for thirty-three years, and a Recorder of the Crown Court with full powers of a Crown Court judge for eighteen years. In that time he had presided over many

[96] On the Question that the amendment be made, the House divided Ayes 214, Noes 315. Ibid., cols. 969–70, 7 Mar. 2000.

[97] Ibid., col. 886.

[98] Ibid., col. 902.

[99] Ibid., cols. 907–8.

criminal trials, sitting with Magistrates on appeals and committals for sentence. He had represented many defendants, as well as the police, serious crime squads, and regional crime squads. He had, he declared, 'met a lot of coppers, a lot of victims, and a lot of witnesses'.[100] The one abiding and passionate interest that he had in the Bill was that it should preserve the integrity, reputation, and fairness of the system he had served. With that experience, he had no hesitation in saying that the measure was one of the worst Bills to come before the House for many years:

> It will cause real and perceived injustice; it will cause immense delay and anxiety to victims, defendants and witnesses, and their families; and it will create vast expense.

He held that view in common with every institution and organization concerned with civil liberties.[101]

To the historian of criminal policy the most noteworthy contribution came from a former minister no longer in the mainstream of Government or Opposition politics. Michael Howard reminded the House that when he had considered the original proposal to restrict jury trial in February 1997 he had made it clear that he was putting it forward for consultation, and without commitment. In his statement at the time he had referred specifically to the provision of a right of appeal against a decision by Magistrates not to allow a case to go to the Crown Court. So it was hardly the new provision which Straw gave as a reason for his change of heart. If he had remained as Home Secretary after the 1997 general election, Howard said he would have tried to persuade his colleagues to accept and implement the proposal. He did not know whether he would have succeeded in doing so. Nevertheless that is what he would have tried to do for many of the reasons now put forward by Labour ministers in each House. Had the Mode of Trial Bill been introduced in its original form, including taking account of the effect of a conviction on the reputation and livelihood of a defendant, he would have voted for it. He was aware that it was a moot point whether his support would have caused more embarrassment to his friends on the Opposition front bench or to the Home Secretary, but that is what he would have done.[102] However, the deletion of that provision

[100] *Parl. Debates*, HC, 345, col. 917.
[101] Ibid., cols. 917–18.
[102] Ibid., col. 915.

from the No. 2 Bill, and the substitution of wording that would forbid the court to take any account of the circumstances of the accused, crippled the discretion that Magistrates could exercise and struck at the heart of the Bill. For that reason, he would vote with the Opposition against the Second Reading.[103]

VIII

Restricting access to jury trial remained a fiercely defended tenet of Government policy, despite the setback encountered in the Lords and the scale of opposition it encountered from its own backbenchers in the Commons. What had begun as a time- and hence cost-saving policy, an attempt to implement a relatively minor, if controversial, procedural change, had turned into a test of strength for ministers. The battlefield was ill chosen, not simply because of the lack of enthusiasm among so many of the Government's own troops, but because of the maladroit way in which the wording of the No. 2 Bill had been altered in transit from the Lords to the Commons.

As Howard's speech made clear, the substitution of new wording for the deleted reputation and livelihood proviso meant that the court, in deciding on the mode of trial, would no longer be able to take account of any circumstances, in particular previous convictions, which might be relevant in a given case. The revised wording of Clause 1 of the Bill read:

> . . . the court shall consider (a) the nature of the case; (b) any of the circumstances of the offence (but not of the accused) which appears to the court to be relevant.

This formulation, although unsuccessfully challenged in a powerfully reasoned speech in Standing Committee by the former Attorney General, Sir Nicholas Lyell,[104] had the unexpected consequence of jeopardizing the support of the Home Secretary's most influential claimed supporter, the Lord Chief Justice. In an exchange of letters, subsequently deposited in the Library of the House, Straw argued that it was not the intention to change the courts' present practice any further than required by the removal of

[103] Ibid., col. 917.

[104] Parliamentary Under-Secretary of State, Department of Health and Social Security, 1986–7; Solicitor General, 1987–92; Attorney General, 1992–7.

the defendant's power of election. The question was whether excluding the accused's circumstances from consideration would have the unintended effect of preventing Magistrates from directing to the Crown Court cases which ought properly to be tried there. He did not think it would, but suggested that if there were doubts on the subject they could be dispelled by issuing clarification in the Mode of Trial guidelines.[105]

Further discussion of Bingham's concerns was remitted to a meeting with the Home Secretary scheduled to take place on 6 April. In the event, the meeting was postponed and not rearranged since on 19 April it was announced from 10 Downing Street that the Queen had approved the appointment of Bingham as the Senior Lord of Appeal in Ordinary, being succeeded as Lord Chief Justice by Lord Woolf. Both appointments were to take effect on 6 June 2000.[106] Woolf's views on the mode of trial issue were not on record, but it was unlikely that he would wish to dissociate himself from the stance taken by his predecessor after testing judicial opinion.

The relatively technical distinctions between the types of case that would be included or excluded from consideration by the Magistrates became a running sore for the Government throughout the Committee and remaining stages of the Bill. The wording, in particular the distinction between the relevant circumstances of the offence, but not of the offender, was subjected to a degree of disputatious scrutiny normally reserved for the most arcane of scholarly scripts. Despite the disproportionate amount of Parliamentary time consumed by the Mode of Trial (No. 2) Bill in the Commons, the Government's majority ensured that no changes were made. The Bill was short, with only one substantial clause. Three consequential clauses authorized some necessary amendments and repeals to existing legislation, and the method of bringing the measure into force once enacted, and confined its extent to England and Wales.

[105] Letter addressed to Lord Bingham of Cornhill from the Home Secretary, 21 Mar. 2000. In a letter to Sir Nicholas Lyell dated 21 Aug. 2000 the Prime Minister added another reason. 'The difficulty with giving the courts such a wide-ranging discretion' [i.e. taking into account all the circumstances of the case] he wrote, 'is that it would create a perception that defendants would be treated differently on the basis of their social or economic standing in society.'

[106] In addition, Lord Phillips of Worth Matravers, a Lord of Appeal in Ordinary, was appointed to succeed Lord Woolf as Master of the Rolls, and Sir Richard Scott, Vice-Chancellor, as a Lord of Appeal in Ordinary in succession to Lord Phillips.

Yet the intensity of opposition provoked by the Bill, on the Government side of the House as well as on the Conservative and Liberal Democrat benches, meant that consideration in Standing Committee took up four half-day sessions, with virtually full-day sessions on the floor of the Commons at Second Reading on 7 March and at Third Reading on 25 July. On the latter occasion the debate was curtailed by a timetable motion (or guillotine), a procedural device limiting the further proceedings on the Bill to five hours. After a vote against the timetable motion, won by the Government by 311 votes to 170,[107] the debate continued until 10.51pm when the Government won a second division by a reduced majority of 282 votes to 199.[108]

The debate resumed in the House of Lords after a foreshortened Summer Recess. The few weeks remaining before the end of the session and the Opening of Parliament, for what was likely to be the final session before a general election, was a time for completing consideration of any legislation still outstanding. The most urgent and controversial, if not the most far-reaching in its scope and intended effects, was the Criminal Justice (Mode of Trial) (No. 2) Bill. The Second Reading was moved by the Attorney General on 28 September 2000.

Even for an advocate of Williams's calibre it was an uphill task. His preliminary remarks did not convey any sense of optimism as to the outcome. Many of those due to speak in the debate, he said, were his personal and professional friends. He anticipated that they would feel unable to support the Bill. He recognized that their motives were honourable, but he questioned their conclusions.[109] As the five-hour-long debate unfolded this pessimistic forecast proved to be accurate. Out of a total of twenty-one speakers who followed the Attorney General's opening speech, no more than three peers on the Government benches supported the Bill, reinforced by a solitary cross-bencher putting forward the views of the Magistrates' Association. All the remaining speakers were opposed, sometimes vehemently so.[110] Although neither Bingham nor Woolf was present, judicial experience, and strongly expressed criticisms, were contributed by two retired Lords of

[107] *Parl. Debates*, HC, 354, cols. 986–8, 25 July 2000.

[108] Ibid., cols. 1018–22.

[109] *Parl. Debates*, HL, 616, col. 961, 28 Sep. 2000.

[110] The two most outspoken Labour critics in the previous debates in Dec. 1999 and Jan. 2000, Baroness Kennedy of the Shaws QC, and Baroness Mallalieu QC, were joined by Lord Brennan QC. In his former capacity as Chairman of the Bar Council he had been the signatory of the letter addressed to MPs and peers at an earlier stage in the controversy.

Appeal,[111] and a previous Master of the Rolls, Lord Donaldson of Lymington. Donaldson's speech was particularly influential since he was one of the very few to have changed his mind on the issue. In the January debate he had aligned himself with Bingham; but since then two factors had caused him to change sides. The first was the new provision which forbade the court to take account of the circumstances of the accused when considering the seriousness of the offence. This went much further than removing the false emphasis given to those factors in the original Bill. Secondly, like many other speakers, he entertained:

> grave doubts about the Government's motives in putting forward the Bill at this time. Why not wait for Lord Justice Auld's recommendations? What on earth is the hurry?[112]

The answer to this question, although not given in the debate, was that the proposal to limit access to jury trial had been included in the explicitly 'tough on crime' passage in the Queen's speech at the start of the session. It had nothing to do with the considered programme of law reform of which the pragmatic reviews by Auld on the criminal courts and John Halliday on sentencing policy were part. Originally seen as a relatively minor, although potentially controversial, procedural change, ministers had restricted their freedom to manoeuvre by giving it undue prominence in their priorities for legislation, and then promoting it vigorously in the media. The choice of the Police Federation Conference for its unveiling exemplified the wider audience at which the 'tough on crime' message was aimed. Consequently, changing the mode of trial became subsumed into the Government's overall presentational imperative. Although such a tactic ensures maximum immediate publicity it can lead to unpredictable political endings.

The outcome of the Lords debate in September 2000 was a foregone conclusion. The only matter of interest was the magnitude of the defeat which the Government had so unnecessarily brought upon itself. In the event it went down by more than two to one: 184 voted to amend the motion that the Bill be read a second time, leaving out 'now' and substituting 'this day six months'. With no more than eighty-eight peers voting not content, the Bill was effectively lost.[113]

[111] Lords Ackner and Simon of Glaisdale.

[112] *Parl. Debates*, HL, 616, col. 1012, *op. cit.*

[113] Ibid., cols. 1033–4.

8

Community Penalties: Enforcement and Structural Change

I

No better example can be found in the Parliament elected in 1997 of the interaction between the Government's promotional and managerial imperatives than its policies towards community penalties. Ministers became convinced that the public perception of non-custodial penalties for persons convicted of less serious criminal offences was generally one of undue lenience. As the enforcement agency, the Probation Service was seen as being oriented more towards rehabilitating offenders in the community than towards ensuring punishment for their misdeeds and protecting potential victims from further offending. Enforcement, especially in the context of returning offenders to court for breaching the terms of their orders, was criticized as being deficient: characteristically too reluctant and too slow, with wide variations in different parts of the country.

The centrality of non-custodial penalties in the practical operation of the criminal justice system as a whole, and the morale of probation officers, seldom received more than perfunctory acknowledgement. In 1997, the year in which Labour came to power, some 140,000 offenders were sentenced to community penalties by the courts, compared with 93,100 sentenced to immediate custody. The latter statistic was the highest for over fifty years, indicating the tide of more punitive opinion influencing sentencing practice. The following year saw a marked upward trend in the numbers of both offenders sentenced to community penalties, 149,400, and those sentenced to immediate custody, 100,600.[1] In 1998 the number of offenders sentenced to immediate custody for all offences was 71 per

[1] Home Office, *Criminal Statistics, England and Wales, 1998*, Cm. 4649, The Stationery Office, 2000, p. 19. The actual statistics of numbers sentenced to immediate custody were 93,093 in 1997 and 100,566 in 1998. The numbers sentenced to community penalties were 139,990 in 1997 and 149,388 in 1998.

cent higher than in 1993. In the same year the average prison population reached 65,298, an increase of 47 per cent since 1993, and the highest level recorded in modern times. The growth was primarily due, not to increases in the overall numbers of offenders being sentenced, but to increases in custody rates (i.e. the proportion of convicted offenders sent to prison) and in sentence lengths.[2]

Less than a decade earlier, during the late 1980s and early 1990s, seen in retrospect as a high-water mark of rational policy-making, overt efforts had been made to ease what was identified as a looming crisis of prison overcrowding by shifting the emphasis in sentencing towards punishment in the community as an alternative to custody.[3]

Painstaking consultation had carried the higher judiciary along, although a number of flaws, notably the treatment of multiple offences and previous convictions in the new sentencing regime and the method of calculating unit fines, offered scope to hostile critics in the magistracy and some traditionalists in the higher courts who were opposed to the whole approach embodied in the Criminal Justice Act 1991. While the defects were soon remedied in an amending Criminal Justice Act in 1993,[4] a significant strand of public opinion, relatively

Table 11. *Type of sentence or order,*[a] *1993–8, England and Wales*

	1993	1994	1995	1996	1997	1998
Immediate custody[b]	58,700	69,800	79,500	85,300	93,100	100,600
Community sentences[c]	114,800	129,600	129,900	132,700	140,000	149,400

[a] Excluding fines, absolute and conditional discharges.

[b] Unsuspended imprisonment, detention in a young offender institution, secure training orders (in 1998), and detention under Section 53 of the Children and Young Persons Act 1933.

[c] Probation orders, supervision orders, attendance centre orders, combination orders, and curfew orders.

Source: Home Office, *Criminal Statistics, England and Wales, 1998*, Table 7A. Statistics to the nearest hundred.

[2] Home Office: Research, Development and Statistics Directorate, *Research Findings No. 94*, 1999, p. 1.

[3] See *Responses to Crime*, Vol. 2, Ch. 5, 'The Quest: Punishment in the Community', 1987–90, pp. 209–54.

[4] See *Responses to Crime*, Vol. 3, Ch. 1, 'The Criminal Justice Act 1993', pp. 3–36.

dormant until roused, was sceptical about the validity and effectiveness of what had been redesignated as punishment in the community. Although the Probation Service Act 1993 consolidated the powers of the Secretary of State to ensure the proper discharge by probation committees of the duties imposed on them by statute,[5] and to make rules regulating community service orders and the supervision of persons subject to probation orders,[6] they were treated in practice as reserve powers and little or no use was made of them.[7] All that was needed to activate the latent antipathy was a signal from the new Government. Nor did the managerial imperative leave the Probation Service with any chance of avoiding the drive towards modernisation.

The scope was extensive. The majority of all sentences imposed by the courts were served in the community, either in whole or in part. Where a custodial term of imprisonment was followed by a period on licence, subject to statutory entitlement and good behaviour, prisoners released on parole would be under the supervision of the Probation Service. Many more would be subject to supervision having been sentenced to community penalties by the courts, in the shape of probation orders, community service orders, or a combination of the two. A much smaller, although not insignificant, number were under voluntary post-release supervision each year. Some detailed statistics for the period 1993–8 are set out in Table 12.

When the plans for reorganizing the Probation Service were being drawn up in 1998, nearly 130,000 offenders were under supervision in the community as a result of court orders. A further 23,573 were under post-release supervision. About 17,000 people were employed by the Probation Service, of whom some 7,000 were trained and qualified probation officers.[8]

II

Government policy towards the reform of probation was two-pronged: structural and procedural. No statement of intention was

[5] Probation Service Act 1993, Section 11(1). [6] Ibid., Section 26.

[7] In reply to Parliamentary Questions the Home Office confirmed that no use had been made of the powers contained either in Sections 11(1) or 26 of the Probation Service Act 1993 in the most recent five-year period for which information was available. *Parl. Debates*, HL, 616 (5th ser.), col. WA 90, 27 July 2000.

[8] On 30 June 1999 there were 7,182 qualified probation officers (full-time equivalents) in post. *Parl. Debates*, HL, 609, col. WA 49, 3 Feb. 2000.

Table 12. *Supervision by the Probation Service, 1993–8, England and Wales*[a]

	1993	1994	1995	1996	1997	1998
Persons under statutory supervision in the community sentenced to non-custodial penalties (court orders)	96,563	107,257	107,333	110,274	115,622	129,784
Persons under statutory post-release supervision by the Probation Service	15,038	16,251	16,566	17,035	19,408	22,726
Persons under voluntary post-release supervision by the Probation Service[b]	2,978	2,438	1,733	1,446	1,242	860
All post-release supervision[c]	17,981	18,648	18,267	18,465	20,642	23,573

[a] Number of persons under supervision in England and Wales on 31 December annually.
[b] Excludes voluntary post-release supervision beyond three years.
[c] Each person is counted once only in the total even if subject to several types of supervision at the year-end.

Source: Home Office, *Probation Statistics, England and Wales, 1998*, Table 5.3.

included in the 1997 general election Manifesto, although in the immediate post-election period a variety of initiatives were canvassed to toughen up the public image of community penalties. One of the least plausible, which was seriously considered before being set aside, was a merger between the Prison Service and the Probation Service.

Soon after the new ministers had arrived at the Home Office a Prisons-Probation Review was set up to look at ways in which such integration could improve efficiency and performance. The stated aims were: to identify how the two services might work together in developing programmes designed to reduce the likelihood that many offenders would reoffend; to prepare prisoners for release and resettlement in the community; and to share resources, information, and knowledge about reducing offending and protecting the public.[9] The internal report of the review was followed by a consultation document entitled *Joining Forces to Protect the Public: Prisons-Probation* in August 1998. A close textual interpreter[10] noted that the language used in *Joining Forces* indicated that reforming the Probation Service had become part of New Labour's wider mission to modernise British society, and to find a form of politics—a third way[11]—between, or rather beyond, the statism of the left and the market-worship of the right. Even in this timely context ideology gave way to pragmatism when faced with the practical implications of attempting to fuse two services with such distinct and deeply engrained cultures. As a result of the consultation process, the Home Secretary decided that the services should not be combined but, in a slippery phrase, 'should retain their separate identities while using complementary methods to achieve . . . common goals'.[12]

Behind the management jargon was the reality that the prison system was dominated by the need for security and the control of offenders in custody. Escapes or serious disturbances, as previous governments had found to their cost, could be highly damaging politically. The Probation Service, on the other hand, was primarily concerned with the supervision and guidance of less serious offenders

[9] Home Office, *Joining Forces to Protect the Public: Prisons-Probation*, Aug. 1998, p. 4.

[10] M. Nellis, 'Towards "the Field of Corrections": Modernizing the Probation Service in the Late 1990s', 33 *Social Policy and Administration*, No. 3, Sept. 1999, p. 303. Dr Nellis is a Lecturer in Criminal Justice Studies at the University of Birmingham.

[11] The bible of the 'Third Way' is A. Giddens, *The Third Way: The Renewal of Social Democracy*, Polity Press, Cambridge, 1998. Professor Anthony Giddens has been Director of the London School of Economics since 1997. For a useful discussion of the significance of the political discourse of the Third Way, see N. Fairclough, *New Labour, New Language?*, *op. cit.*, p. 9.

[12] Criminal Justice and Court Services Bill, *Explanatory Notes*, [HC Bill 91], p. 2, para. 6. Explanatory notes, prepared by the sponsoring Government department in order to assist readers of the Bill and inform debate in Parliament, had been recommended by the Select Committee on Modernisation of the House of Commons in a report on the legislative process: HC 190, Session 1997–98. The proposal was subsequently adopted by both Houses. The notes do not form part of the Bill and are not endorsed by Parliament.

sentenced to community penalties, or those released on licence from custody. Although there were areas of overlap, the essential tasks were different, and called for different skills.

After this unsettling start the objectives of public policy towards probation were divided into three strands: more rigorous enforcement of community sentences; reorganization of the existing fifty-four separate probation services into a national service based in forty-two local areas; and hiving off the responsibilities of the Probation Service for Family Court work to a new Children and Family Court Advisory and Support Service (CAFCASS). Whereas the second and third of these policies required primary legislation, the first had hitherto been regarded as a matter of Probation Service practice, negotiated and agreed with the Home Office, and incorporated in national standards.

The enforcement of probation or community service orders was described by the Chair of the Association of Chief Officers of Probation (ACOP) as being the:

> unsentimental edge of community supervision that brings down a sanction on an offender who can't or won't adhere to the terms of their court order or the conditions of their release from prison.

In his opening address to the Association's Annual General Meeting in April 2000 he said that enforcement for the Probation Service was like waiting lists for hospitals, detection rates for the police, and examination results for schools, adding:

> like police, doctors, and teachers, probation staff have had their fair share of public berating from the Secretary of State and wagging of ministerial fingers.[13]

This pertinent remark referred to a speech by Jack Straw to the same audience the previous year. Then the Home Secretary had used the platform to challenge the Probation Service to strengthen the enforcement of court orders and post-custody licences so as to improve public and political confidence in community sentences. In the intervening period the Home Office had taken administrative action by amending the national standards so that two, rather than three, missed appointments without good reason (described as

[13] G. Dobson, opening statement on 'Improving Enforcement' at the Annual General Meeting of the Association of Chief Officers of Probation, Barbican, London, 11 Apr. 2000.

'unacceptable absences') would result in the offender being returned to the court.[14] At their AGM in the Spring of 2000 the Chief Officers repeated that the commitment of the Probation Service to the proper enforcement of court orders was unambiguous. Straw's comments had been taken to heart and two large-scale audits commissioned as part of an urgent action plan to improve enforcement. All fifty-four services had taken part and the results of the first audit, published in July 1999, confirmed the widely held view that performance in dealing with the minority of offenders who repeatedly failed to comply with the terms of their orders and licences was 'variable and in many cases unacceptable'.

The audit findings, based on a study of supervision in more than 10,000 cases, were fed back without delay to probation areas and good practice advice disseminated with a view to improving performance. The second national audit reported on how practice had changed after six months. The independent researchers concluded that while the results gave 'no room for complacency', it was fair to say that over the country as a whole the second round results showed 'considerable improvements' in the way in which the Probation Service set appointments and dealt with absences. The fact that the audit showed 'such marked improvement' indicated that the Service was 'capable of delivering tougher enforcement'.[15] Twelve months after the Home Secretary's strictures, the Minister of State, Paul Boateng,[16] was congratulating the same audience on shifting the culture of the Service so profoundly within such a short space of time. In contrast with the assumptions on which ministers had relied, the second audit showed that 92.5 per cent of offenders subject to probation orders, community service orders, and on licence, had either

[14] The revised national standards for the supervision of offenders in the community took effect from 1 Apr. 2000. They set out the requirements for the supervision and conduct of offenders and the procedures on non-compliance. In Probation Circular 24/00 the Probation Unit of the Sentencing and Correctional Policy Directorate at the Home Office gave guidance on the enforcement of orders under the new national standards. Discretion to depart from the standards, for example by reducing the frequency of contact or not taking breach action, could be exercised only with the authority of a manager.

[15] *Improving Enforcement—The Second ACOP Audit*, C. Hedderman and I. Hearnden, Criminal Policy Research Unit, South Bank University, London, Mar. 2000, p. 6. HM Inspectorate of Probation approved the design of the audit and validated the findings.

[16] Opposition front-bench spokesman on Treasury and Economic Affairs, 1989–92; on Legal Affairs, 1992–7. Parliamentary Under-Secretary of State, Department of Health, 1997–8; Minister of State, Home Office, 1998–2001.

complied with their order or licence or been returned to court for breach proceedings.[17]

By then, however, the die was cast. Internally generated change was not enough to serve the Government's purpose of demonstrating the full extent of its concern to protect the public from reoffending. Besides, the legislative steamroller had already begun its ponderous progress through Parliament. Adversarial politics meant that there was little realistic possibility of halting it altogether. If handled tactically, however, there might be opportunities to alter its course during its journey towards the statute book.

III

The symbolic, more than the practical, impact of the changes lay behind the intention of ministers to change the names of the Probation Service and the orders made by the court. The initial proposal to 'rebrand' the Probation Service as the Community Punishment and Rehabilitation Service attracted resentment within the Service and widespread ridicule. Lord Hurd of Westwell, adding an authoritative voice to the protests, remarked that:

> not much good is done in the real world by altering the labels on people's official notepaper and on their office doors.

If the Government was determined to alter the 'respected and accepted' name of the Probation Service, could they not find something crisper and less clumsy?[18]

Since the proposed title had been chosen personally by Straw from a short list submitted by Home Office officials, it was a tribute to him that he listened to the criticism and agreed to substitute a less emotive alternative: the National Probation Service for England and Wales.[19] It was that title which appeared in the Criminal Justice and Court Services Bill introduced in the House of Commons on 15 March 2000.

Two decades earlier similar motivation had prompted a Conservative Government to delete the words 'and After-Care' from the formal title

[17] *Parl. Debates*, HL, 612, col. WA 182, 3 May 2000.

[18] *Parl. Debates*, HL, 608, col. 1323, 24 Jan. 2000.

[19] No Home Office functions in the field of criminal justice have been devolved to the National Assembly for Wales. A Crime Reduction Director was appointed to be answerable to the National Assembly.

of the Probation Service.[20] The reason then given was that the reference to after-care, which had been added by the Criminal Justice Act 1967, was no longer appropriate. It emphasized one aspect of the Service's work at the expense of other functions which it was undertaking. It was claimed that the reversion to the original name had the support at the time of all the main Probation Service organizations and the Magistrates' Association.[21] The same could not be said of the response of the representative organizations in 2000 to the Labour Government's intention to redesignate probation orders as community rehabilitation orders, community service orders as community punishment orders, and combination orders as community punishment and rehabilitation orders.

Both the clumsiness to which Hurd and others had objected in the renaming of the Probation Service, and a stubborn refusal to abandon the penal overtones, were demonstrated in the nomenclature. As the Penal Affairs Consortium pointed out, far from clarifying public confusion about community sentences the names sounded so similar that they were likely to increase confusion. Moreover, it was misleading to select names which suggested that probation orders contained no element of punishment, and community service orders contained no element of rehabilitation. It was the considered view of the forty-one organizations represented in the Consortium that the changes would 'do nothing to increase public confidence in community sentences or public understanding of their content, nature or effectiveness'.[22]

The Association of Chief Officers of Probation[23] and the National Association of Probation Officers (NAPO), as well as the Magistrates' Association and the Justices' Clerks' Society, were among the organizations directly affected by the proposed changes in the names of the orders. Each was opposed. In its representations on the Bill, NAPO argued that the term 'probation order' had international resonance and recognition, pointing out that in the post-Communist era many Eastern European countries were setting up probation services with

[20] Criminal Justice Act 1982, Section 65.

[21] *Parl. Debates*, HL, 614, col. WA 59, 26 June 2000.

[22] *Comments by the Penal Affairs Consortium on the Criminal Justice and Court Services Bill*, 29 June 2000, p. 2.

[23] ACOP believed that the public would continue to refer verbally to probation whatever changes were made. Public opinion research commissioned from MORI by the Association confirmed that the word was not a liability. *Probation 2000*, Annual Report of Chief Officers of Probation, 1999–2000, p. 9.

probation orders on the British model. The same point was developed eloquently by Vivien Stern, for two decades Director of NACRO, and an internationally respected authority:[24]

> The new name for community service orders is even worse; that is, community punishment order. At one blow, the name change destroys the ethos and meaning of a sanction which was invented here in Britain and spread all around the world. The essence of a community service order is 'service'. It is a measure which brings into the sentencing framework an element of reparation, restitution, paying back to the community, and putting offenders in a position to rebuild their relationship with the community and awakening in them a sense of social obligation.
>
> At its best, it shows offenders that there are people worse off than themselves. It shows offenders that they can help people and be valued for it. Sometimes they voluntarily carry on with the community service work once the order is completed. It shows those being helped that offenders are people, too, and can do good as well as ill. It is a penalty with enormous possibilities for development. Once it becomes a community punishment order, it loses all that meaning.[25]

The dispute over retitling the Probation Service and the relevant orders went deeper than the linguistic fashions of contemporary politics. In the context of criminal justice, community penalties serve three functions: to punish offenders for their criminal acts; to protect society in the future by rehabilitating offenders; and to divert as many offenders as possible from custodial sentences in order to curtail the growth in the prison population. In the late 1980s and early 1990s the third of these objectives had been a significant influence in policy-making, if not always explicitly proclaimed. Since then, under governments formed by each of the two main political parties, resort to community penalties as a means of controlling the size of the prison population went into sharp decline. Rehabilitation had also often proved an ephemeral goal. Perceptions were all-important, and the demonstrable public perception was that probation was a soft option and that imprisonment was the proper penalty for a wide range of crimes. The narrowing of the gap between the use of immediate custody and community sentences as disposals of the courts is

[24] Director, NACRO, 1977–96. Member: Youth Training Board, 1982–8, Committee on the Prison Disciplinary System, 1984–5. Secretary General, Penal Reform International, 1989–. Visiting Fellow, Nuffield College, Oxford, 1984–91; Senior Research Fellow, International Centre for Prison Studies, King's College, London, 1997–. Life peer, 1999.

[25] *Parl. Debates*, HL, 614, col. 1300, 3 July 2000.

an indicator of how perceptions can influence not only the thrust of public policy but also sentencing practice.

The organizational structure devised for the reformed Probation Service raised questions of accountability and control. In place of the existing fifty-four separate probation services would be a National Probation Service, headed by a National Director, and directly accountable to the Home Secretary.[26] It would be based on forty-two local areas coterminous with those of the police and the Crown Prosecution Service. Each probation area would have a compact board consisting of a chairman, a chief officer, and not less than five other members.[27] Although such boards would be responsible for the employment of all staff, apart from the chief officer, the use of their powers to provide the relevant services in their areas would be constrained within a defined statutory framework. The chief officer and all the members (except for a judge appointed by the Lord Chancellor) were to be appointed by the Home Secretary and could be removed by him. Unlike police authorities or Magistrates' committees, the 'chairpeople' (as Straw described them) of the probation committees would also be appointed by the Secretary of State.[28]

The Criminal Justice and Court Services Bill specified the functions and responsibilities of the local boards, and empowered the Secretary of State to issue directions as to how they should be fulfilled. If he was not satisfied by the performance of a local board, which appeared to be failing or offering poor value for money, he could replace it and substitute other management arrangements. The premises occupied by the local board and its staff would be centrally owned on behalf of the National Probation Service, and the board would be unable to borrow money without the approval of the Secretary of State.

In reply to criticisms of the centralization of power in the hands of ministers, and for operational purposes their departmental officials, it was argued that the new arrangements represented a clearer form of accountability. In a candid letter addressed to a front-bench

[26] Eithne Wallis, Chief Probation Officer for Oxfordshire and Buckinghamshire, was appointed as National Director designate of the Probation Service of England and Wales with effect from 18 Sep. 2000.

[27] So far as practicable, regulations were to provide for the persons appointed to be representative of the local community in the board's area, and to live or work (or to have lived or worked) in that area. Schedule 1, Section 2(6), Criminal Justice and Court Services Act 2000.

[28] *Parl. Debates*, HC, 347 (6th ser.), col. 227, 28 Mar. 2000.

Opposition speaker after the Lords' debate on the Second Reading of the Bill, the Parliamentary Under-Secretary of State claimed that:

Under the current arrangements Probation Committees are accountable to nobody for the performance of their services. I have seen a wide and inexplicable variation in standards of performance and efficiency achieved by different Committees, and the statutory independence of the Committees has, frankly, made it very difficult for us to take effective action to improve the standards of poorly performing services.

In the future there will be a direct line of accountability from local boards, through the National Director, to the Home Secretary and through him to Parliament. Where large sums of public money are being spent on a service which is of legitimate public interest—as work with offenders most certainly is—it is right that there should be proper arrangements for the oversight and accountability of that service.[29]

Such a justification for the virtual nationalization of what had been for more than a century a local service answerable to magistrates sitting in the courts before whom the offenders appeared,[30] and maintaining close links with the local authorities in the area, did scant justice to the deep roots of the previous arrangements. What is more, the assumption of central control and powers of patronage represented a conspicuous volte-face. When in Opposition, Straw had insisted:

I want justice to be locally tailored, which is one reason why we are convinced of the need to have locally accountable Crown Prosecutors in place of the present, monolithic nationalised system . . .[31]

His deputy as Home Office spokesman on the Opposition frontbench in the Commons, Alun Michael, berated the concept of central appointments to police authorities as 'a highly damaging move which would make the police more remote from the communities

[29] Letter dated 11 July 2000 from Lord Bassam of Brighton, Parliamentary Under-Secretary of State at the Home Office, to Baroness Blatch. A copy of the letter was placed in the Library of the House of Lords.

[30] The concept of probation was developed during the second half of the nineteenth century as the jurisdiction of the Magistrates' courts was extended. In 1887 the Probation of First Offenders Act enabled courts to release first offenders on probation, but without any systematic supervision. Twenty years later it was followed by the Probation of Offences Act 1907. See G. Mair, 'Community Penalties and the Probation Service', *The Oxford Handbook of Criminology*, 2nd edition, Oxford University Press, 1997, pp. 1198–200.

[31] *Parl. Debates*, HC, 284, col. 925, 4 Nov. 1996.

they serve'.[32] An early-day motion signed by over 150 Labour MPs on 11 January 1993 stated that any attempt to introduce nominated boards of the Home Secretary's own choosing would do 'terrible damage to accountability and public confidence'.[33] As Leader of the Opposition, Tony Blair called on the Prime Minister to drop the Home Secretary's:

> disastrous proposals to remove the local say for local people in their policing. Mr Clarke wants to replace it with a system of centralised bureaucratic boards. A popular voice in local policing is far preferable to control by ministerial appointees . . . We need more, not less, local accountability.[34]

The explicit rejection of these beliefs by ministers once in office may have been partly motivated by the aim to promote more effective practice in supervising offenders nationally. But changing ideology also played a part. In criminal policy, as in other areas of public administration, the demands of modernisation called for models of central control, rather than delegated authority and local accountability.

IV

The restructuring of the Probation Service provided a timely opportunity to create a new service directed towards meeting the specialized needs of children and families involved in the court system, principally in civil proceedings. Hitherto the only non-criminal type of work undertaken by the Probation Service was handled by the Family Court Welfare Service (FCWS), staffed by personnel charged with looking after the interests of children in divorce or other legal disputes between their parents. Some of the work was undertaken in partnership with the voluntary sector funded through partnership grants from local probation services. That area of responsibility was scheduled to cease in April 2001 when three existing agencies, the FCWS, the Guardian ad Litem[35] and Reporting Officer Service, and the Children's branch of the Official Solicitor's Department, were

[32] Press Release from Alun Michael MP, Shadow Minister for Home Affairs, 6 Nov. 1992.

[33] House of Commons, Early Day Motion 1130, *Police Forces*, 11 Jan. 1993.

[34] The Labour Party, *News Release*, PR 291/93, 12 Jan. 1993.

[35] A guardian *ad litem* is a person appointed to defend an action or other proceeding on behalf of a minor or a person under a disability.

due to merge into a new agency called the Children and Family Court Advisory and Support Service for England and Wales (CAFCASS).[36] Unwieldy though the full title was, the acronym CAFCASS had a resonance which led to it being accepted far more readily than the other changes in name.

The proposal for a unified service had been the subject of an earlier consultation paper[37] and encountered little or no hostility when it was announced. Since the proceedings would be non-criminal the guiding precept would be fairness to the parties rather than punitiveness. As such the new model probation officers, shorn of their historic mission to advise, assist, and befriend, were no longer regarded as the most appropriately equipped professional staff for a family court welfare service.[38]

The innovation of CAFCASS was politically uncontroversial, receiving relatively little attention when the Criminal Justice and Court Services Bill was considered by Parliament in the 1999–2000 legislative session. From his experience as a long-serving former Law Officer, however, Sir Nicholas Lyell warned that, while non-party political, the merger might not be easily accomplished. There was a significant difference in culture between court welfare officers and guardians *ad litem*. The welfare officers dealt with the day-to-day work of particular courts and were mostly employees of the Probation Service or under contract to it, whereas guardians *ad litem* largely worked freelance. The Lord Chancellor's Department, to which responsibility for the new service was being passed, would need to be sensitive in moulding the component services together. The whole issue of child care, when dealt with in the courts, and of family breakdown which is so often the cause of court proceedings, was 'hugely contentious and known to lead to many complaints'.[39]

[36] The Guardian ad Litem and Reporting Officer Service was the responsibility of the Department of Health. After being joined to the Family Court Welfare Service and the Children's branch of the Official Solicitor's Office to form a new non-departmental public body, CAFCASS would become part of the Lord Chancellor's responsibilities, including annual funding.

[37] *Support Services in Family Proceedings: Future Organization of court welfare services*, Department of Health, Home Office, Lord Chancellor's Department, and Welsh Office, 1998.

[38] See S. M. Cretney, 'Court Welfare: Radicalism or Gradualism', October [1998] *Fam. Law*, 575. Dr Cretney was a Law Commissioner, 1978–83. Professor of Law, 1984–93, and Dean of the Faculty of Law, 1984–8: University of Bristol. He has been a Senior Research Fellow of All Souls College, Oxford since 1993.

[39] *Parl. Debates*, HC, 347, cols. 256–7, 28 Mar. 2000.

At the heart of some of the most difficult cases was the conflict that could occur between the views or desires of a child and decisions on where his or her best interests lay.

Safeguarding the welfare of children was the aim of another part of the same Bill. Although it was simply described in the Queen's Speech as 'preventing unsuitable persons from working with children', a wide gap existed between this unexceptionable declaration of intent and devising a workable scheme. The previous Government had published two consultation documents before the 1997 election outlining an approach which was initially to be confined to convicted sex offenders.[40] By the time the Criminal Justice and Court Services Bill was introduced three years later the prohibited category had expanded to include persons who had come to notice, either when working with children or by commission of an offence against a child.[41] Where an individual was identified as being unsuitable to work with children he or she would be disqualified from applying for or accepting such work, or to offer any services that involved it. There would be criminal penalties for breach. It would also be an offence for any person to offer the opportunity to work with children to an individual whom they knew to be subject to disqualification from such work.

Although a need 'to strike the right balance between providing protection for vulnerable members of society and protecting the freedoms of individuals' had been recognized in the 1996 consultation document,[42] libertarian concerns had receded into the background by the end of the decade. Authoritarian policies were often justified on the ground that they would be tested in local pilot schemes before national implementation. An example of an extended time-scale in the Criminal Justice and Court Services legislation was compulsory drug-testing, of both offenders and alleged offenders, at various points in their contact with the criminal justice system. The new powers allowed for drug-testing in three separate situations. The first was after a suspect in police detention had been charged with certain acquisitive or drugs offences. The second was when a court was considering passing a community sentence on a convicted offender aged

[40] *Sentencing and the Supervision of Sex Offenders: A Consultation Document*, Home Office, Cm. 3304, June 1996, and *Sex Offenders: A Ban on Working with Children*, Home Office and Scottish Office, Jan. 1997.

[41] The Bill included a definition of the circumstances under which an individual would be deemed to have committed an offence against a child, and listed the offences.

[42] *Sentencing and the Supervision of Sex Offenders*, *op. cit.*, para. 75.

eighteen and over. The third was when a prisoner over the age of eighteen and convicted of certain offences was due to be conditionally released on licence. These proposals differed significantly from the Drug Treatment and Testing Order (DTTO) introduced by the Crime and Disorder Act 1998. Before making a DTTO, in association with a community sentence, the court was required to obtain the offender's consent.[43] There was no compulsion.

While the evidence linking crime with drug misuse, particularly heroin and cocaine/crack, was compelling, so was the urgent need for more extensive facilities for treatment. The Government estimated that when in place a compulsory testing scheme would cost more than £45 million per year, comprising £22.6 million for testing arrestees, £7.8 million for testing persons subject to community sentences, and £15.1 million for testing pre-release prisoners. Yet if the resources for treatment were not available it is hard to see what constructive outcome would result. Indeed the impact, on bail decisions for example, could be negative. If a court was informed of positive drug tests, but lacked immediate access to assessment and treatment services, it would remand more defendants to drug-ridden prisons. This could only be counter-productive to the aim of reducing drug-related crimes. Even a short period in custody often results in loss of accommodation and/or employment, which significantly increase the likelihood of reoffending.

Replying to these criticisms, the Government was conciliatory. Ministers accepted that in some parts of the country the demand for drug treatment services exceeded the current availability. The problem was acknowledged and action was being taken to address it. A recruitment campaign, conducted jointly with the Department of Health, aimed at securing a further 700 drug workers by April 2001. Consideration was also being given to setting up a National Treatment Agency, which would have a crucial role in the future development of drug treatment services. In addition to overseeing a pooled national treatment budget, it could become involved in the direct commissioning of residential rehabilitation places, together

[43] An interim evaluation of the effectiveness of Drug Treatment and Testing Orders in three pilot areas was published by the Home Office Research, Development, and Statistics Directorate in 1999. See P. J. Turnbull, *Drug Treatment and Testing Orders: Interim Evaluation*, Research Findings No. 106, Home Office, 1999. Assessment of suitability for a Drug Treatment and Testing Order is presented to the court in a pre-sentence report. Courts must be satisfied that offenders are dependent on drugs and would benefit from treatment.

with setting minimum standards for quality and outcomes from treatment services and inspecting against these standards.

The time-scale for the introduction of compulsory drug-testing was protracted. The intention was to pilot schemes at no more than three sites for a period of two years, starting in the Spring of 2001. The pilot programmes would be evaluated, and were not expected to result in an unmanageable rise in demand for treatment services. If more widespread drug-testing was rolled out from April 2003, it was hoped that progress in the interval would have gone a long way towards closing the gap between demand and supply in the drug treatment sector.[44] What this meant in practice was that the Criminal Justice and Court Services Bill, as a collection of measures bearing on a variety of criminal justice issues, had been utilized as a convenient vehicle, as such Home Office Bills had often been before, for statutory powers which would be needed when new schemes were introduced at some time in the future.

V

In the mechanics of probation reform two changes aroused the most deeply felt objections by the Probation Service. Although contained in separate legislation both were aimed at strengthening sanctions against breaches of community orders. One had merited inclusion in the list of 'tough on crime' initiatives foreshadowed in the Queen's Speech in November 1999. This was a requirement for social security benefits to be withdrawn or reduced for failure by an offender, having received a prior warning, to comply with the conditions of a community order.[45]

Later in the session, a related offence attracting automatic imprisonment was included in the Criminal Justice and Court Services Bill. Where there was a second unacceptable failure within twelve months to comply with the terms of a community order, an offender would be referred back to the Magistrates' court for breach proceedings. If found to be in breach of a specified order to which the warning

[44] Information contained in letters sent to Baroness Stern and Lord Dholakia by Lord Bassam of Brighton on 11 July 2000, and placed in the Library of the House of Lords.

[45] The commentary that follows draws on the author's article, 'Loss of Benefit: A Misplaced Sanction', [2000], Crim. L.R. 661. Reproduced with permission.

provisions applied, an offender aged eighteen or above must then be sentenced to up to three months' imprisonment. Should the court take the view that it was resentencing for the original offence, it would impose a longer period of imprisonment. Where the court found the circumstances of the case to be exceptional, or where the breach involved an offender under the age of eighteen, then the existing discretionary sanctions available to the court would apply without incurring the new presumption of imprisonment. A similar duty was placed on the Crown Court.

Each of these novel sanctions, loss of benefit and mandatory imprisonment for breach, was intended to be both exemplary and coercive. When introducing the Government's programme for the legislative session 1999–2000, Tony Blair accepted that some of the measures designed to cut crime might be opposed on civil liberty grounds. He justified this with the glib comment:

> the civil liberty that is most prized by British citizens is the freedom to go about their daily lives free from crime and harassment and, when crimes are committed, for the perpetrators to be properly punished.[46]

Soon after, when introducing a 148-page composite Bill making important changes to the system of child support, pensions, and social security, the Secretary of State for Social Security, Alastair Darling, was even more explicit about the coercive intent of a proposed breach of probation sanction so unexpectedly, and inappropriately, inserted into his Bill. Asked whether removing benefits would encourage rehabilitation or whether it would lead to reoffending because people's circumstances had become more difficult, Darling replied that the remedy in such cases lay in the hands of the person who breaks a probation order. He declared:

> People are not required to live in poverty or to lose their benefit. They are required to do only what the court tells them to do. If they are not willing to do that, they can have no cause for complaint.[47]

Since any references to additional penalties, punishment, or sanctions would jeopardize the proposal under the Human Rights Act 1998 the Government opted for a description straight out of *Yes, Minister*. It was, ministers pronounced, 'additional benefit conditionality'. No mention was made of the fact that in parallel, but otherwise unrelated,

[46] *Parl. Debates*, HC, 339, col. 27, 17 Nov. 1999.
[47] *Parl. Debates*, HC, 342, col. 161, 11 Jan. 2000.

legislation a mandatory term of imprisonment would be the unavoidable consequence of precisely the same conduct, failure to comply with the terms of a community order after one prior warning, unless there were exceptional circumstances. Neither then nor later did ministers attempt to explain what the relationship would be between the two sanctions.

In the form in which the Child Support, Pensions, and Social Security Bill was introduced, and passed through all its stages in the Commons, the loss of benefit sanction would be for a fixed period to be set in regulations. It would commence as soon as the relevant benefit office received notification from the Probation Service that, on the basis of information that a person had failed to comply with the requirements of a community order, the person had been referred to the Magistrates' court for breach proceedings. In the first instance, it was intended that the measure should be piloted in separate areas of England and Wales in order to test the effectiveness of the links between Social Security Offices and the Probation Service, and also to assess the behavioural impact on offenders. For the duration of the pilot schemes the sanction period would be set at four weeks, and would apply to unemployed offenders subject to probation orders, community service orders, and combination orders. The targeted age range was between eighteen and fifty-nine, and the affected benefits were the Jobseeker's Allowance (JSA), Income Support (IS), and the JSA equivalent of certain training allowances (TAS). Housing benefit would not be withdrawn. In certain defined circumstances, benefits might be reduced rather than withdrawn.

One of the main objections to the concept of forfeiting benefit was that it trespassed on territory that properly belonged to the courts. Probation is part of a judicial process, and community penalties are criminal sentences supervised by a statutory Service. It is open neither to the Secretary of State for Social Security, nor any other minister, to hijack court orders as a 'tough on crime' gesture in an otherwise unrelated Bill. They are penal, not administrative sanctions, which are and should remain entirely separate from eligibility for social security benefits based on need.

The most conspicuous departure from judicialized proceedings in the original version of the Child Support, Pensions, and Social Security Bill was that the withdrawal or reduction of benefit would precede the court hearing. Disentitlement would be triggered whenever a probation officer decided that an offender should be referred back to the court for failure to comply with the requirements of a community sentence. The anticipated involvement of the procurator-fiscal in the Scottish procedure indicated that this would be effectively the first stage in a prosecution: the laying of information before a court after a second unacceptable absence. It would then be for the court to establish the facts and decide whether or not the conditions of the order have been breached, and if so, to impose a proportionate penalty.

The initial claim, frequently repeated by ministers, that about 30,000 offenders in England and Wales were returned to court as a result of breach proceedings,[48] was revised downwards to 28,500 while the Bill was before Parliament. What had not been disclosed in the earlier statistic was that in about 400 cases no sentence was given for breach.[49] A later analysis carried out by the Inner London Probation Service showed that subsequent information led to 751 out of about 5,500 cases in Inner London (around 13.65 per cent) either being withdrawn before a court hearing or being refused after a hearing. The reasons for withdrawal were varied, but the commentary suggested that many were not proceeded with because the evidence about the unacceptability of absences or other forms of non-compliance was not strong enough to hold up in court.[50] In these circumstances, the Bill provided that any benefit payments which would have been made but for the sanction should be made retrospectively.

Retrospective reimbursement on these lines would be wholly inadequate compensation, and points up the error of combining civil sanctions and criminal proceedings. Another criticism is that the decision to initiate breach proceedings should not imply a presumption of guilt sufficient to attract an automatic penalty in the form of benefit loss. The Government's reply, that receipt of benefit is often subject to conditions and that reported breaches of community sentences are sufficient grounds to activate benefit sanctions, did not meet these criticisms. Still less convincing were the assumptions that

[48] In Scotland about 12,400 people were sentenced to community service orders or probation orders in 1998, about 4,000 of whom were subject to proceedings for breach. See Child Support, Pensions, and Social Security Bill, *Explanatory Notes* [HL Bill 54], p. 116.

[49] *Parl. Debates*, HC, 344, col. 864W, 22 Feb. 2000. The revised total of 28,500 was for England and Wales in the calendar year 1998, i.e. before the revised national standards came into effect.

[50] *Breach Proceedings*, Inner London Probation Service, Mar. 2000, unpublished.

the threat of being brought back to the court would 'send a signal' to offenders that they must not breach their orders, and that the signal would be received and acted upon. The proposal made no allowance for such unreceptive categories as the dyslexic, those with learning difficulties, the elderly, nor the mentally disordered, who presented little risk to the public but were at high risk of breach. The reality of much probation work with offenders, characterized as one step back for every two steps forward, was ignored. In effect loss of benefit was a conspicuous example of 'gesture politics', disregarding the dictates of both practical experience and legal rights.

The notion of sending signals by way of legislation was bolstered by an argument based on good citizenship, or rather on bad citizenship, where the rights and responsibilities of the citizen were abused. To breach an order of the court, the contention went, was to break a contract between the offender and the state. References recurred in the Parliamentary debates to offenders who were subject to a community order being a chronic menace to a local community, terrorizing or vandalizing housing estates, and generally making the lives of residents a misery. But to describe this deplorable state of affairs as breaching a contractual relationship was a misleading caricature. A contract must be between parties who know that they are entering into a relationship with one another. It is a species of agreement whereby an obligation is created by the parties to it, not a unilateral declaration by one party in the ignorance of the other. The unthinking adoption of imagery which to some members of the Government, or their political advisers, seemed to be no more than a convenient rhetorical device was in fact a debasement of public dialogue and a misleading distortion of legal relationships.

VI

Effective enforcement is a desirable objective in the penal system. The Probation Service and the Home Office had already taken action to strengthen the enforcement of community orders and ensure conformity with national standards. Further legislation was pending to this end. It was a mistake to attempt to interfere with these measures by the addition of an ill thought out administrative sanction that would lead to offenders who might be trying, however slowly or fitfully, to establish themselves in a local community suddenly finding that they had no money. A high proportion would be drug or alcohol misusers for whom the court had decided that a period under supervision offered the best hope of overcoming their addiction, consequently reducing the likelihood of reoffending. For such people, as for many others, whether caused by impoverishment, recklessness, or resentment, reoffending is often impulsive and irrational. Since deterrence depends on a rational calculation of the chances of detection and the severity of punishment, it will be least effective in such circumstances.

A racial perspective was also brought out in the representations of the Commission for Racial Equality (CRE). The Commission believed that, should the proposal be implemented, it would operate to the relative disadvantage of ethnic minorities who, if serving a community sentence, were more likely than their white counterparts to be in receipt of benefits. The CRE was concerned to note that withdrawal of benefits would follow an alleged, not a proven, breach. In a letter to the Secretary of State for Social Security the acting Chairman of the Commission pointed out an apparent inconsistency with the aims of the Race Relations (Amendment) Bill which was currently before Parliament. That Bill extended the Race Relations Act 1976 to those functions of public authorities currently not covered by legislation. A policy which in its application operated to the disadvantage of a particular racial group, that was proportionately less able to comply with the conditions or requirements of the policy, would be unlawful unless it could be justified. The CRE asked the Secretary of State to consider whether justification for the proposed measure outweighed its likely disproportionate impact on ethnic minorities.[51]

The likelihood that the populist-inspired new penalty would be discriminatory in a wider sense was self-evident. If two offenders, one employed and with earnings, the other unemployed and on benefit, possibly joint defendants charged with the same offence, were brought back to court and resentenced for breach of their community orders, the offender whose benefits were withdrawn or reduced would suffer an additional penalty. Article 14 of the European Convention on Human Rights expressly prohibits discrimination on the ground of status, which includes financial status. Article 6 (right

[51] Letter from Hugh Harris, Acting Chairman, Commission for Racial Equality, to Rt. Hon. Alastair Darling, Secretary of State for Social Security, 28 Mar. 2000. Quoted with permission.

to a fair trial) could also be relevant to any challenges which might follow once the Human Rights Act 1998 came into force in the Autumn of 2000.

These arguments, particularly the prospect of a double penalty for the poor and the unemployed, and the fact that benefits would be withdrawn or reduced by administrative action in advance of a court hearing to establish whether or not the terms of a community order had been breached, were deployed in a series of debates in the Lords. At Committee stage a cross-party amendment to leave out the relevant clauses[52] was supported by speakers in all parts of the House, other than on the Government benches. Even there the voices of some doubters were heard. In order to give ministers time for reconsideration the amendments were not pressed to a vote in Committee, but were put down again in a narrower form for further debate on Report. On 27 June 2000 the House gave its verdict. By a majority of 170 to 116 a series of amendments in the names of the same sponsors as at the previous stage were carried against the Government.[53] The effect was to defer the imposition of the loss of benefit sanction until after a court had made a determination that an offender had failed to comply with the conditions of a community sentence. It was the minimum requirement to conform with the rule of law and habits of legality.

The next step owed as much to the intricacies of managing government business as to the merits of the argument. Although ministers could use their majority in the Commons to reverse the defeat and send the Bill back again to the Lords, the process would take time. The long Summer Recess was imminent and the legislative programme behind schedule. A last-minute measure aimed at preventing disorderly English football supporters from travelling to Europe for international matches in the Autumn added to the backlog of uncompleted legislation.[54] Moreover, the Government front bench in the Lords, and the Chief Whip in particular, were aware of a degree of

[52] The amendment was moved by the author, supported by Earl Russell (Lib. Dem.), Baroness Kennedy of the Shaws (Lab.), and the Bishop of Lincoln.

[53] *Parl. Debates*, HL, 614, cols. 848–51, 27 June 2000.

[54] The Football (Disorder) Bill received its First Reading in the Commons on 13 July 2000 and passed through all stages in both Houses in two weeks, receiving Royal Assent on 28 July 2000. Amendments made in the Lords ensured that powers under the Act to impose banning orders, or to detain people for enquiries about their involvement in violence or disorder, would expire one year after coming into force, unless Parliament renewed them by an affirmative resolution. In any event, the powers would expire two years after coming into effect.

unhappiness on their own side over the loss of benefit provision. In Parliamentary politics such mundane factors can sometimes achieve a change of course more readily than displays of eloquence or the weight of informed opinion.

The outcome was a negotiated concession. The Government agreed that on Third Reading it would accept further amendments drafted by Parliamentary Counsel and tabled in the names both of the Departmental minister, Baroness Hollis of Heigham,[55] and myself. These gave effect to the decision of the House that no action should be taken to withdraw or reduce social security benefits until a court had made a determination that there had been a failure to comply with the conditions of a community order. The amendments went further in two respects.

The first was that in reaching its determination the court should be satisfied that the failure to comply with the requirements of the order should be 'without reasonable excuse', wording which appeared in the concurrent criminal justice legislation[56] and met a particular concern expressed by Baroness Kennedy. Secondly, once notified by the Probation Service that a breach had been proven, the Benefits Agency would be empowered to take the appropriate administrative action, subject to a provision for repayment if the offender successfully appealed the court's finding of a breach.[57] Although the main ground for objection had been met, by ensuring that there would be no departure from the maxim of no penalty without law, the revised wording still left the dependent defendant worse off than the earning defendant. Thus the new wording might not be the last word on the controversy.

[55] Academic appointments at the University of East Anglia, 1967–90; Dean, School of English and American Studies, 1988–90. Councillor, Norwich City Council, 1968–91 (Leader, 1983–8); Norfolk County Council, 1981–5. Member: Regional Economic Planning Council, 1975–9; Press Council, 1989–90. Commissioner, English Heritage, 1988–91. Life Peer, 1990. Parliamentary Under-Secretary of State, Department of Social Security, 1997–2001.

[56] Criminal Justice and Court Services Bill, Clause 48(3) of HL Bill 83.

[57] *Parl. Debates*, HL, 615, cols. 1110–11, 19 July 2000. The Lords' amendments were accepted by the House of Commons after a short debate the following week (*Parl. Debates*, HC, 354, cols. 819–22, 24 July 2000), and the Child Support, Pensions, and Social Security Act received the Royal Assent on 28 July 2000.

VII

The presumption of imprisonment contained in Clause 48 (originally Clause 46) of the Criminal Justice and Court Services Bill combined two features which had received the most forthright criticism, inside and outside Parliament. The first was mandatory sentences of imprisonment whereby the punishment is prescribed by law irrespective of the degree of culpability of the offender and the consequences of the harm done. This is familiar ground which has been traversed several times in the previous volumes of *Responses to Crime*, as well as in earlier Chapters of this volume. The second objection of principle was the use of custody as a penalty for breach of a community order where the original offence which had led to the making of the order had not been sufficiently serious, in the opinion of the court, to attract a custodial sentence. In addition, there was the unexplained relationship between loss of social security benefit for failure to comply with the conditions of a community order, and the term of imprisonment that the same individual could expect to incur under the provisions of the Criminal Justice and Court Services Bill which was under consideration in the Commons while the House of Lords was occupied with the Child Support, Pensions, and Social Security legislation.

In both instances a warning would have to be issued by the supervising officer before the offender was referred back to the court for breach proceedings. The form of the warning for breach of a qualifying community order was spelt out in considerable detail in the Commons Bill. It would be necessary: to record the circumstances of the failure; to establish that the failure was unacceptable (i.e. without reasonable excuse); and to inform the offender that if within the next six or (as appropriate) twelve months he again failed to comply with any requirement of the order, he would be liable to be brought before a court. Should there be a further failure, unless there were exceptional circumstances the court would then be bound to impose a custodial sentence of up to a maximum of three months' imprisonment on an offender aged eighteen or over. Where the court found the circumstances of the case to be exceptional, or if the offender was under the age of eighteen, the existing discretionary sanctions available to the court would apply without the presumption of imprisonment.[58]

[58] Criminal Justice and Court Services Bill, *Explanatory Notes*, [HC Bill 91], p. 21, para. 115.

Although the intention of the two measures was the same, the scope of the mandatory penalty of imprisonment was wider. In the Criminal Justice and Court Services Bill as published, six orders to which the new scheme would apply were listed. They were: community rehabilitation orders (formerly probation orders); community punishment orders (formerly community service orders); community punishment and rehabilitation orders (formerly combination orders); curfew orders; exclusion orders; and drug abstinence orders. In Standing Committee in the Commons the Government amended the Bill to disapply the statutory warning scheme to failed drug tests undertaken as a requirement of a drug abstinence order, or a drug abstinence condition of another order.[59]

In making heartfelt representations against the mandatory sentence of imprisonment for a second unacceptable failure to comply with the conditions of a community sentence the Probation Service, through both its Chief Officers and the National Association (NAPO), argued that this aspect of practice had hitherto been governed by national standards, and there was evidence from the recent audits of rising levels of enforcement being achieved without recourse to legislation. The requirement which the Bill laid on the courts to impose a custodial sentence for such a failure was a cause of great concern. The Service believed that the measure would add very considerably to the prison population, the work-load of the courts, the police, and the Crown Prosecution Service, and would result in custodial terms for many offenders. On second thoughts, ministers had removed drug abstinence orders, or drug abstinence conditions in other orders, from the legislation because of a recognition that addicts rarely give up drugs at once, but that the habit diminishes on a gradual scale.

It was the experience of the Probation Service that the same logic applied to those being supervised under probation and combination orders, when changes in attitudes and behaviour are achieved gradually and over a considerable period of time. To imprison offenders on their second unacceptable failure would undermine the capacity of the Service to achieve lasting change in the behaviour of persistent offenders, which requires patience and perseverance to achieve results. The courts understood this, and were well able to decide on

[59] *Parl. Debates*, HC, Standing Committee G, cols. 230–1, 2 May 2000.

the most suitable disposal, judged on the merits of each individual case.[60]

If implemented, it was likely that the proposed new procedure would undermine the value, and possibly the use, of community sentences as penal sanctions. Magistrates' courts have to deal with a wide range of offenders, including many with personality difficulties and disadvantages which affect their ability to comply with community sentences. As a consequence, the inevitable increase in the prison population could be expected to reflect disproportionately social disadvantage and special needs. Chief Probation Officers believed that both the costs and negative effects of the measure had been seriously underestimated.[61]

Ministers spoke a different language in reply. The scrupulous reasoning based on professional experience was not answered, but met with assertions. A new catch-phrase 'certainty of outcome' was added to the often repeated insistence that the enforcement of community sentences must be strengthened. The Minister of State with responsibility for prisons and probation at the Home Office, Paul Boateng, set the tone when winding up the debate on Second Reading of the Criminal Justice and Court Services Bill in the House of Commons:

> We must strengthen enforcement. It is vital that the Probation Service deliver to courts and to sentencers a sentence that is so administered as to command public support and confidence. In order to have credible community sentences, the present inconsistencies and failures in dealing with breaches must be addressed.
>
> In relation to the points made by Liberal Democrat Members, those matters must be dealt with in the context of a clear understanding that some offenders have chaotic and disordered lives. However, those offenders must realise that that chaos cannot be allowed to continue—leading as it invariably does to increased and repeated offending in a vicious cycle. We need a clear and focused legal framework to restore order to that chaos. Order can be restored only when there is an understanding that breaches will lead to imprisonment. There are no two ways about it and there is no soft or easy answer. It must be understood that community sentences are not meant to

[60] Extracts from enclosure to a letter to the author from J. Roberts, Chief Probation Officer for Hereford and Worcester, 18 July 2000, later circulated to certain members of the House of Lords before the Committee stage of the Criminal Justice and Court Services Bill on 2 and 4 Oct. 2000. Jenny Roberts was chair of the Association of Chief Officers of Probation 1991–2.

[61] Ibid.

be a soft option. When someone fails to take advantage of the opportunity that a community sentence offers, he will go to prison.[62]

To have the intended impact such a policy must have a deterrent effect. Coincidentally an authoritative report, readily accessible to policy-makers, was to hand. A comprehensive survey and analysis of recent studies concerning criminal deterrence and sentence severity had been commissioned by the Home Office in September 1997 and was published in 1999.[63] The work had been carried out at the Institute of Criminology at Cambridge and the authors included two of the most eminent of contemporary criminologists. Andrew von Hirsch, before migrating to Cambridge, had been a Professor at the School of Criminal Justice at Rutgers University in the United States, and was author of a seminal work on *Censure and Sanctions* as well as other influential publications on sentencing and criminal justice. Anthony Bottoms, Wolfson Professor of Criminology, had been Director of the Cambridge Institute from 1984 to 1998. At the request of the Home Office the survey concentrated on sentencing policies, and in particular on the possible deterrent effects of increasing sentence severity.[64]

Noting that a salient issue in the debate on sentencing policy was whether penalty levels should be substantially increased, particularly with respect to the use and duration of imprisonment, the authors said that no one could give a confident answer to the question 'Would raising sentence levels improve general deterrence?' Any answer would have to give explicit recognition to the uncertainties involved.[65] One consequence of the subjective nature of deterrence was that changes in the likelihood or severity of punishment would only affect it if certain preconditions were satisfied. These included: recognition by the offender that the probability of conviction or the severity of punishment had changed; that he must take the altered risks into account when deciding whether to offend; that he must believe there to be a non-negligible likelihood of being caught; and, if caught, that the

[62] *Parl. Debates*, HC, 347, col. 288, 28 Mar. 2000.

[63] A. von Hirsch, A. E. Bottoms, E. Burney, and P.-O. Wikström, *Criminal Deterrence and Sentence Severity: An Analysis of Recent Research*, University of Cambridge Institute of Criminology, Hart Publishing, Oxford and Portland, Oregon, 1999. Andrew von Hirsch is Honorary Professor of Penology and Penal Law at the University of Cambridge; Elizabeth Burney is a Research Fellow at the Institute of Criminology; and Per-Olof Wikström is a University Lecturer in the Sociology of Crime. Anthony Bottoms was knighted in 2001 for services to criminology.

[64] Ibid., p. 1.

[65] Ibid., p. 41.

altered penalty would apply to him. Finally, and most conjectural, a potential offender must be willing to alter his conduct in the light of a perceived change in the certainty or severity of punishment. If, for example, his life-style depended on a supply of drugs, and offending was the means of financing active drug use, then enhanced certainty or severity of punishment was unlikely to make him desist.[66]

Although the density of the narrative, and the circumspect style of presenting the results of the survey, avoided the risks of embarrassing tabloid headlines, the report did nothing to endorse ministerial confidence in the deterrent effect of harsher sanctions on criminal offending. Having explained that it was not their remit to offer specific policy recommendations, the authors went on to list a number of considerations bearing on the question of whether large overall increases in penalty levels would be advisable for the sake of enhanced deterrence.[67] If applied to commonplace middle-level offences, such as burglary, higher sentence levels would involve heavy financial costs, raising issues of competing priorities for public expenditure. Other consequences would be the social effects of holding in custody significant proportions of young males in socially excluded groups, a phenomenon which the USA was already experiencing.[68] While there was no definitive answer to the question of whether, and to what extent, substantial increases in the use and duration of custody could enhance marginal deterrence, the findings of recent studies 'diminished the plausibility of expecting any large deterrent benefits'.[69] Of particular interest to readers of the report participating in, or commenting upon, the criminal process was a warning that singling out certain types of crime for enhanced punishment for deterrent ends would be a potential source of conflict with the principles of proportionality in sentencing.

VIII

After the Second Reading of the Criminal Justice and Court Services Bill, which took place in the House of Lords before the Summer

[66] Ibid., p. 7. Treatment held out better prospects. Research evaluating drug treatment and testing orders showed that although some offenders had not received a lot of treatment, the average weekly amount spent on drugs fell from £400 to about £30. Home Office Research, Development, and Statistics Directorate, *Research Findings, No. 106*, *op. cit.*, p. 3.

[67] von Hirsch *et al.*, ibid., pp. 48–9.

[68] Ibid., p. 48.

[69] Ibid.

Recess,[70] the Committee and subsequent stages were delayed until the House resumed in the Autumn. As a result, business managers in both Houses, faced with an unusually heavy legislative programme, were under the same constraints of time as had helped to bring about the concession on benefit loss. Once again, a cross-party alliance of four peers[71] tabled amendments to delete the clause which would empower the Government to require the courts to impose custodial sentences on offenders who, after one warning, had failed to comply with the conditions and procedures attached to a community order. Faced with a repeat of the earlier debates on loss of benefit, and the likelihood of a similar outcome, Home Office ministers were more conciliatory. What was equally important was that the recess allowed time for interventions behind the scenes.

Shortly after he had succeeded Lord Bingham as Lord Chief Justice,[72] Lord Woolf had raised with the Home Secretary personally his reservations about the implications for sentencing policy of a mandatory sentence of imprisonment for breaching a community order. The Probation Service was convinced that the policy would be counter-productive if implemented, and there were unmistakable signs of dissent on the government benches in the Lords. Ministers were in a quandary. They acknowledged that 'much of the criticism of the enforcement proposals was directed at the mandatory nature of the presumption of imprisonment'.[73] They maintained that the objective was:

> not to imprison many extra offenders but, rather, to improve compliance with community sentences and enhance the credibility of those sentences both with sentencers and the general public.[74]

Once again, the justification rested on the perceived 'need to send out a strong message that community sentences cannot be ignored or treated lightly by offenders subject to them'; leading to the conclusion

[70] *Parl. Debates*, HL, 614, cols. 1284–341, 3 July 2000.

[71] Lord Windlesham (Con.), Lord Dholakia (Lib. Dem.), Baroness Stern (Ind.), and the Bishop of Lincoln.

[72] On 18 Apr. 2000 Lord Bingham of Cornhill was appointed as the Senior Lord of Appeal in Ordinary in succession to Lord Browne-Wilkinson, and Lord Woolf as Lord Chief Justice of England and Wales. Lord Phillips of Worth Matravers succeeded Lord Woolf as Master of the Rolls. Lord Bingham and Lord Woolf took up their appointments on 6 June 2000.

[73] Letter to the author from Lord Bassam of Brighton, Parliamentary Under-Secretary of State, Home Office, 13 Sep. 2000.

[74] Ibid.

that these prerequisites called for 'the introduction of a more rigorous and consistent enforcement regime'.[75]

All the skills of tactical withdrawal were marshalled to devise a formula that would retain an appearance of consistency with these objectives whilst meeting, at least in part, the objections of the critics. The stratagem adopted was to keep the clause, but to revise it in such a way as to permit greater judicial discretion in sentencing without jettisoning the sacrosanct objective of certainty of outcome. The Attorney General, Lord Williams of Mostyn, one of the most accomplished ministerial debaters, was chosen for this delicate task when Parliament resumed after the recess. At Committee stage on 4 October he moved a series of Government amendments to Clause 48 of the Bill. He explained them in the following terms:

> . . . where an offender is aged 18 or over and is subject to a community order to which the statutory warning provisions apply, having found the breach to have occurred, the court would first decide whether or not, notwithstanding the current breach, the offender's response to the sentence as a whole was such that it was likely that the order would be successfully completed. If the court took that view—in other words, successful completion likely—it would allow the order to continue; and it would be under a duty to punish the breach by imposing a community punishment order, a curfew order, or, where the appropriate age applied, an attendance centre order.
>
> If the court does not believe that there is a likelihood that the order would be successfully completed, there would be a requirement to impose a custodial sentence, other than in exceptional circumstances.[76] If the original offence itself was punishable by imprisonment, a prison sentence would be imposed for the original offence. If the original offence was not so punishable, the prison sentence would be limited to not more than three months.

[75] Ibid.

[76] The 'exceptional circumstances' proviso originated from the automatic sentence of life imprisonment for a second serious offence unless there were 'exceptional circumstances relating to either of the offences or to the offender . . .'. Section 2 of the Crime (Sentences) Act 1997 is now consolidated in the Powers of Criminal Courts (Sentencing) Act 2000, Section 109. It did not apply directly to the other two categories of mandatory sentence in the same Act: a minimum of three years' imprisonment for a third conviction for domestic burglary, or a minimum of seven years' imprisonment for a third class A drug trafficking conviction. For both of these two categories of offence the minimum sentence was automatic, unless there were specific circumstances relating 'to any of the offences or to the offender' which would make it unjust to impose the prescribed custodial sentence. The meaning and scope of 'exceptional circumstances' was further construed by the Court of Appeal, Criminal Division, in *R.* v. *Offen* and other cases, reported with an acerbic commentary by Dr David Thomas at [2001] Crim. L.R. 63.

The existing exclusion—that is, those who are under 18 and those who fail to comply with a requirement to refrain from using Class A drugs—would remain.

As in the original wording, the presumption would also be displaced where there were exceptional circumstances to justify it. In dealing with these cases, the courts would be obliged to impose one of the alternative community sentences as a penalty for breach or resentence for the original offence, if thought appropriate.[77]

Williams concluded by saying that he believed the amendments were a 'proportionate, reasoned and reasonable response' to the criticisms which had been made. Speaking for himself, he was grateful, 'because the consequences of listening to them and trying to engage in a reasonable debate had brought a better outcome'.[78]

The effect of the changes, which were accepted by a Committee of the Whole House with a sense of relief, was to restore a measure of discretion to the courts when dealing with breaches of community orders. In his first speech in the Lords since taking up his appointment as Lord Chief Justice in the Summer, Lord Woolf acknowledged that the proposal was much more satisfactory than what had previously been contained in the Bill. However, both in its original form and in that now proposed, the clause raised an issue of principle.[79] In its original form Clause 48 had the disadvantage that, although designed to give non-custodial sentences more credibility when conditions were breached, it was likely in practice to lead to the opposite result. Probation officers would be more reluctant than they should be to give warnings, or to bring offenders back to court. Woolf continued by asking:

What is the evidence that magistrates or judges are being unduly lenient when offenders are brought back before the courts for a breach of a condition imposed on a custodial sentence? That is not the impression of probation officers with whom I have discussed the matter. If we are treating offenders unduly leniently, training plus guideline decisions from senior judges can produce the required result. Why place a judge in the entirely artificial situation of having to impose an artificial sentence of imprisonment?

The new provision requires the court, if it is not satisfied that a community sentence can be completed, still to impose a sentence of imprisonment. What are the requirements with regard to that sentence of imprisonment? The court must ask itself what would be the sentence if the offender had just

[77] *Parl. Debates*, HL, 616, cols. 1605–6, 4 Oct. 2000.
[78] Ibid., col. 1606.
[79] Ibid., col. 1608.

been convicted. But that is not the situation. A period of time would have elapsed before the sentence would have been imposed. Secondly, the sentencer has to consider what decision he would have imposed when the matter was originally before him. But that is putting the sentencer in an entirely artificial position. His intention at the time was not to impose a sentence. So he is asked to go through a hoop which serves no purpose.

Then, the court is being asked to impose imprisonment in some circumstances for an offence in relation to which no imprisonment could be imposed. A sentence of imprisonment is imposed for that offence in substitution for the means of disposal in the community which had originally been imposed. It is justified on the basis: 'Ah, but the offender has since committed a breach of the order that was made'. But imposing imprisonment in those circumstances is still imposing a sentence for the original offence. If Parliament had previously said that the proper sentence was not imprisonment, is it right, as a matter of principle, to impose imprisonment because the community sentence that was imposed has not been complied with?[80]

Broadening his censure, Woolf accepted that great improvements had been made by the legislation which the Bill sought to amend, the Powers of Criminal Courts (Sentencing) Act 2000. That Act, he claimed, had brought together legislation spread across numerous Acts of Parliament, and the resulting consolidation was very much a step to be commended. Yet now, once again, the mistakes of the past were being repeated by trying to deal piecemeal with particular problems which had been identified, frequently without conducting the investigations that should have been carried out to see whether amendments to what had so recently been consolidated in that Act were justified. He ended with a resounding warning which deserves to be reproduced verbatim, and should be pinned up as a standing reminder in the rooms occupied by Home Office ministers and their advisers:

Complexity is a menace in any system of justice. What we are constantly doing is increasing that complexity. We have reduced the complexity in the civil justice system. That has assisted the administration of justice. What is being done now, and what has been done over the preceding years, is to move in the opposite direction with regard to the criminal justice system. I respectfully suggest to noble Lords that that process should be avoided unless an overwhelming case is made out to move in the other direction. As far as concerns this amended Clause 48, I know of no such case.[81]

80 Ibid., cols. 1609–10.

81 Ibid., col. 81. Clause 48 of the Bill amending the Powers of Criminal Courts (Sentencing) Act 2000 (breach of requirements of community orders) was enacted as Section 53 of the Criminal Justice and Court Services Act 2000 (breach of community orders: warning and punishment).

IX

The Criminal Justice and Court Services Bill received the Royal Assent and was enacted shortly before the end of the Parliamentary Session 1999–2000. Together with the Crime and Disorder Act 1998, these two measures achieved the most extensive remodelling of the institutions and process of criminal justice since the Criminal Justice Act of 1991. Despite the size of the Labour majority in the Commons, neither measure passed into law without protracted and detailed legislative scrutiny. The Standing Committee in the House of Commons met seven times in April and May 2000 and debated 190 amendments. Thirty-one were made, as were seven of the nine new clauses tabled. (See Tables 13 and 14.) At Report stage on the floor of the House, a further three new clauses and 113 amendments were made. As Table 14 shows, all the changes were made by the Government, often to improve the drafting. A small number are likely to have resulted from Opposition concerns, either arising in the course of debate, or as a result of negotiation.

In the Lords, where the Government had no overall majority and was unable to enforce such stringent whipping, ministers were in a weaker position. If they could persuade the Liberal Democrat peers of the merits of their proposals, they could defeat the Conservative Opposition.

Table 13. *Criminal Justice and Court Services Bill 1999–2000: House of Commons Standing Committee, hours of sitting*

	Morning (hrs/mins)	Evening (hrs/mins)
4 April 2000	2.30	–
6 April	1.53	–
11 April	2.27	2.11
13 April	1.52	–
18 April	0.49	2.32
2 May	–	2.48
9 May	1.29	–
Total time:		18 hours, 52 minutes

Source: Public Bill Office, House of Commons.

Table 14. *Criminal Justice and Court Services Bill 1999–2000: new clauses (NC) and amendments tabled in the House of Commons*

	(a) No. tabled: New Clauses	No. tabled: Amendments	(b) No. made: New Clauses	No. made: Amendments	of (b) Govt. NCs	of (b) Govt. amdts.	of (b) Opp. NCs	of (b) Opp. amdts.	of (b) Other MPs: NCs	of (b) Other MPs: amdts.
Standing Committee	9	190*	7	31	7	31	0	0	0	0
Report stage	17	190†	3	113	3	113	0	0	0	0

* 39 amendments were withdrawn: in the case of 37 of these, this followed debate in the Committee.
† 5 amendments were withdrawn; in the case of 4 of these, this followed debate.

Source: Public Bill Office, House of Commons.

But cross-party alliances, particularly on issues of principle, could be attractive to independent peers as well as to the main opposition parties. The outcome was that the Government was defeated seven times during the progress of the Bill through the House. Most of these amendments were rejected when the Bill was returned to the Commons, although the intention of some survived, usually with the original wording revised by the government draftsman. In all, 418 amendments and nine new clauses were made in the Lords, the Bill having been scrutinized for a total of twenty-three hours and thirty-five minutes (see Tables 15 and 16). When it was all over, the Home Secretary was magnanimous enough to remark:

> It will . . . never be possible to accommodate every proposal to modify a Bill, but I cannot think of any legislation which I have introduced which has not been improved by Parliament—and the Criminal Justice and Court Services Bill was no exception.[82]

In addition to creating two new national services, the National Probation Service for England and Wales, and the Children and Family Court Advisory and Support Service (CAFCASS), the Criminal Justice and Court Services Act 2000 set up an integrated system designed to prevent unsuitable people from working with children; provided statutory penalties for breach of community orders; and took powers for the compulsory drug-testing of offenders, or alleged offenders, at various points in their contact with the criminal justice system. Sentencing reforms included the abolition of detention in a Young Offender Institution (YOI) and custody for life for offenders between

Table 15. *Criminal Justice and Court Services Bill 1999–2000: House of Lords, hours of sitting*

Stage	Date	hrs/mins
Committee Stage	2 October 1999	6.45
	4 October 1999	7.40
Report Stage	31 October 1999	8.02
Third Reading	8 November 1999	1.08
Total time:		23 hours, 35 minutes

Source: Public Bill Office, House of Lords.

[82] Personal letter to the author from Rt. Hon. Jack Straw, 6 Dec. 2000.

Table 16. *Criminal Justice and Court Services Bill, 1999–2000: new clauses and amendments tabled in the House of Lords*

	No. tabled New clauses	No. tabled Amendments	No. made New clauses	No. made Amendments
Committee Stage	25	322	6	192
Report Stage	10	122	0	83
Third Reading	5	147	3	143
Total	40	591	9	418

By whom tabled:

	Government New clauses	Government Amendments	Opposition New clauses	Opposition Amendments	Other members New clauses	Other members Amendments
Committee Stage	6	189	16	101	3	32
Report Stage	0	77	10	48	0	6
Third Reading	3	138	2	8	0	1
Total	9	404	28	157	3	39

Source: Public Bill Office, House of Lords.

the ages of eighteen and twenty-one.[83] Following abolition, all defendants aged eighteen or over at the time of sentencing, who had received a custodial sentence, would be sentenced to either determinate sentences of imprisonment or to life imprisonment.[84]

The Act also introduced politically sensitive changes in the way tariffs are set for juveniles found guilty of serious offences and sentenced to detention at Her Majesty's pleasure. In future, tariffs would be set by the trial judge in open court, in the same way as for adults subject to discretionary life sentences applicable in all cases except convictions for murder.[85] This change, long resisted by successive Governments, was necessary to bring the law and sentencing practice relating to the most serious offences, including murder, committed by young people below the age of eighteen into line with the decision of the European Court of Human Rights in *T* v. *United Kingdom* and *V* v. *United Kingdom*.[86] Since that Court had concluded that ministers should not set tariffs for juveniles sentenced to detention at Her Majesty's pleasure, the change was irresistible.

A further change, on the face of it a minor one, chimed with an emergent current of penal opinion. The Act removed a requirement

[83] Custody for life is the fixed penalty for murder committed by a person aged between the ages of eighteen and twenty-one: Criminal Justice Act 1982, Section 8(1). Detention at Her Majesty's pleasure is the fixed penalty for children and young persons between the ages of ten and eighteen who have been convicted in the Crown Court of murder or manslaughter: Children and Young Persons Act 1933, Section 53(1). For a review of the issues raised by mandatory sentencing for murder and other serious crimes, and the increasing significance of decisions by the European Court of Human Rights on domestic law and practice, see *Responses to Crime*, Vol. 3, Chapter 9, 'Life Sentences: The Defects of Duality', pp. 331–84.

[84] Early in 2001 these provisions had not yet been implemented, nor were they expected to be brought into force for some time ahead. Letter from Lord Bassam of Brighton, Parliamentary Under-Secretary of State, Home Office, 22 Feb. 2001.

[85] On 13 March 2000 the Home Secretary made a statement in the House of Commons describing the legal and administrative changes necessary to abide by the findings of the European Court of Human Rights in the case of Thompson and Venables. *Parl. Debates*, HC, 346, cols. 21–4, 13 Mar. 2000.

[86] (2000) 30 EHRR 121, decided on 16 Dec. 1999. The applications by Thompson and Venables were heard together. They were the boys, aged ten at the time, convicted of the murder of a two-year-old child, James Bulger. The unanimous conclusion of the European Court of Human Rights was that there had been a violation of Article 5(4) of the Convention due to the absence of any judicial review of the continuing legality of the applicants' detention. A tariff of fifteen years, fixed by the Home Secretary to satisfy the requirements of retribution and deterrence, was set aside in judicial review proceedings reaching the House of Lords in its appellate capacity. In a fresh review after the Strasbourg judgment, the Lord Chief Justice, Lord Woolf, substituted a tariff of eight years, the same as the original recommendation by the trial judge. His subsequent practice statement is printed as an Appendix to this Chapter.

that a police reprimand or final warning could be given to a young offender only at a police station. The effect of the repeal was that these sanctions could be utilized at conferences attended by parents, police, and youth workers, as well as, if they wished, the victim or victims of the offence. Restorative cautioning, as it became known, could thus take place in settings less intimidating than a police station, such as the offices of a local Youth Offending Team (YOT). Police-led initiatives, pioneered by the Thames Valley Police and taken up by some other forces, were an innovative approach to the widespread blight of youth offending. Since its inception, the Youth Justice Board had stressed the importance of community participation in preventing reoffending, and reintegrating persistent young offenders into the community. Specific risk factors had to be addressed in a number of different ways, some of which involved victims as well as an offender's family and members of a YOT.

Conferencing is one of the few practical examples to be found in England or Wales of an alternative approach towards dealing with the consequences of criminal offending known as restorative justice. The general aim is to find ways of reconciling the interests of the victim, the offender, and the community in settings unlike court-rooms. Although there is no formal definition, restorative justice has been described succinctly as:

> a process whereby parties with a stake in a specific offence collectively resolve how to deal with the aftermath of the offence and its implications for the future.[87]

In England and Wales, a restorative conference will typically be attended by all of the parties affected by a crime at a meeting convened by a trained facilitator. Offenders are confronted with details about how their offending has affected the victim or victims, who may also be present.

[87] T. F. Marshall, *Restorative Justice: An Overview*, Restorative Justice Consortium, London, 1998, p. 5. Cited by Professor A. Ashworth in a lecture titled 'Is R.J. the way forward for criminal justice?', given at University College, London, in the series *Current Legal Problems*, 16 Nov. 2000. A leading academic authority on restorative justice is John Braithwaite, Professor of Law at the Australian National University, Canberra. For a recent publication, see J. Braithwaite, 'Restorative Justice: Assessing Optimistic and Pessimistic Accounts', in *Crime and Justice: A Review of Research*, Vol. 25, University of Chicago, 1999. Braithwaite also contributed an informative chapter on 'Restorative Justice' to *The Handbook of Crime and Punishment*, ed. M. Tonry, Oxford University Press, New York, 1998, pp. 323–44.

The movement, as seen by its protagonists, is an international one, with functional examples to draw on from Australia, New Zealand, and Canada. It has attracted some charismatic supporters who, while seldom speaking with one voice, have had to contend with criticisms of aiming too high and claiming too much. In practice, it is not easy to see how the communitarian principles of restorative justice can readily be reconciled with the bedrock requirements of the common law: the independence and impartiality of the judicial process; proportionality of penalties; consistency of outcomes; and compensating for wrongs done.[88] The media thrive on the drama and adversarial style of criminal justice, and are quick to categorize as 'soft on crime' any alternative procedures which do not convey strong elements of retribution and punishment. Faced with such sentiments, there can be little doubt how politicians would respond. For all that, restorative justice in its various manifestations, while still on a very limited scale, incorporates a genuinely reformist strain of idealism which is a heartening contrast to the pervasive pessimism characteristic of so many Western systems of criminal justice.

[88] See A. Ashworth, ibid., Lecture text, pp. 17–22.

APPENDIX

The practice statement printed below was made by Lord Woolf on 27 July 2000. It is reproduced with permission.

PRACTICE STATEMENT: LIFE SENTENCES FOR MURDER

This practice statement follows the decision of *Thompson and Venables* in the European Court of Human Rights on 16th December 1999. That Court concluded that Ministers should not set tariffs for juveniles sentenced to detention during Her Majesty's pleasure.

The Home Secretary, on 13th March 2000, made a statement to Parliament that legislation is to be laid before Parliament which will provide for tariffs for defendants under 18 years of age to be set by the trial Judge in Open Court as they are for adults subject to discretionary life sentences. It is proposed that tariffs will be appealable either by the Attorney General if believed to be unduly lenient, or by the defendant.

There are a large number of people, sentenced as juveniles, currently detained at Her Majesty's pleasure. The Home Secretary has proposed that I should undertake a fresh review of tariffs for these existing cases. Pending the necessary change in the law, there will also be fresh cases. The Home Secretary announced that until any legislation is enacted, he will set any *new* tariffs in accordance with my recommendation as to both existing and fresh cases. Before I make a recommendation to the Home Secretary, in both new and existing cases, I shall invite written representations from the detainees' legal advisers and also from the Director of Public Prosecutions who may include representations on behalf of victims' families.

I will take as my starting point the existing approach adopted in the case of adults sentenced to a mandatory life sentence. In the case of adults the usual length of tariff, or punitive term (which means the amount of time actually to be served by a person convicted or murder in order to meet the requirements of retribution and general deterrence) will be a period of *14 years* before the possibility of release arises for consideration at all.

In all these cases this term may be increased or reduced to allow for aggravating and mitigating features. Without seeking to be comprehensive, aggravating features will include:–

1. Evidence of a planned or revenge killing.
2. The killing of a child or a very old or otherwise vulnerable victim.
3. Evidence of sadism, gratuitous violence, or sexual maltreatment, humiliation or degradation before the killing.

4. Killing for gain (in the course of burglary, robbery, blackmail, insurance fraud, etc.).
5. Multiple killings.
6. The killing of a witness or potential witness to defeat the ends of justice.
7. The killing of those doing their public duty (police officers, prison officers, postal workers, fire-fighters, Judges etc.).
8. Terrorist, or politically motivated, killings.
9. The use of firearms or other dangerous weapons, whether carried for defensive or offensive reasons.
10. A record of serious violence.
11. Attempts to dismember or conceal the body.

Again, without seeking to be comprehensive, the following may normally be regarded as mitigating features:–

1. Age.
2. Sub-normality or mental abnormality.
3. Provocation (in a non-technical sense) or an excessive response to a personal threat.
4. The absence of an intention to kill.
5. Spontaneity and lack of pre-meditation (beyond that necessary to constitute the offence: e.g. a sudden response to family pressure or to prolonged and eventually insupportable stress).
6. Mercy killing.
7. A plea of guilty.
8. Hard evidence of remorse or contrition.

Before the first such cases are put before me to make a recommendation to the Home Secretary, it is appropriate for the general principles which will guide me in recommending tariffs to be made public. This is because it is right that the process by which tariffs are set should be open to public scrutiny. When making recommendations to the Home Secretary in such cases, I will announce my reasons in open court after taking into account any written representations I receive.

The approach set out above, which I intend to adopt, is based on that applied by judges and myself when establishing the tariff period to recommend to the Home Secretary in the case of all mandatory sentences for murder (i.e. where the sentence is life imprisonment in the case of an adult defendant).

9

Modernising Criminal Justice, 1997–2000

I

Loss of benefit and the presumption of imprisonment for breach of community orders, both moderated by amendments in the Lords, were shoots off the same stock. Such policies were rooted in a calculated attempt to demonstrate the responsiveness of Government to perceived public opinion, as well as its firmness and grasp. The degree of personal commitment on the part of the Prime Minister to policy issues on crime was displayed in a revealing memorandum sent to his policy advisers during a stay at Chequers over Easter 2000.[1] It was, one can surmise, a few days' respite for Blair, allowing time for reflection on the standing of the Government and the issues confronting it. These were identified in the memorandum as 'touchstone issues'. Each needed to be analysed and the correct policy response drawn up, 'but with a message which ties it all together'. Three of the five issues listed fell within the responsibilities of the Home Office. The first raised the possibility of a review of the law on self-defence as a result of the conviction of a farmer for murder after he had shot and killed a sixteen-year-old intruder at his home. The second was the pressing problem of how to handle the large numbers of asylum seekers, with an emphasis on their removal. The third item deserves quotation in full:

> (iii) On crime, we need to highlight tough measures: compulsory tests for drugs before bail, the PIU [Performance and Innovation Unit] report on the confiscation of assets; the extra number of burglars jailed under the 'three strikes and you're out'.
>
> Above all, we must deal now with street crime, especially in London. When the figures are published for the six months to April, they will show a

[1] The entire memorandum from the Prime Minister headed 'Touchstone Issues', signed TB, 29 Apr. 2000, was published verbatim in *The Times* on 17 July 2000. Although an inquiry was set up into how this and other documents had reached the press, its authenticity was subsequently confirmed. Extract reproduced by permission, © Times Newspapers Limited, 17 July 2000.

small—4 per cent—rise in crime.[2] But this will almost certainly be due to the rise in levels of street crime—mobile phones, bags being snatched. This will be worst in London. The Met Police are putting in place measures to deal with it; but, as ever, we are lacking a tough public message along with the strategy.

We should think now of an initiative, e.g. locking up street muggers. Something tough, with immediate bite which sends a message through the system. Maybe, the driving licence penalty for young offenders. But this should be done soon and I, personally, should be associated with it.

There can be no doubt that the constant demand from ministers and their political advisers for initiatives in response to events was a hallmark of public policy towards crime throughout the period of the Labour administration 1997–2001. A characteristic feature was the repeated emphasis on sending messages by way of legislation or administrative action, sometimes addressed to unaware or unreceptive target audiences. The question arises whether such opportunistic activity was merely waves on the surface, or whether it merged into the wider and deeper currents determining the tides of criminal policy.

Volume 3 of *Responses to Crime* was sub-titled 'Legislating with the Tide'. One reviewer, originally sympathetic to the advent of Labour to office in May 1997,[3] suggested that a fourth volume covering the final years of the century should be sub-titled 'Turning of the Tide'. That 'prophetically optimistic' suggestion depended on a deliberate move away from the overtly penal orientation of the outgoing party of law and order. It was not to be. While the style and values of the incoming ministers and their advisers were markedly different from their predecessors, the primacy accorded to opinion polling and other thermometers of public attitudes ensured that there was no change in direction. Not only did the punitive tide fail to ebb: in some places on the coastline it flowed further up the shore.

Part of the cause can be attributed to the desire of certain leading members of the Administration to be seen as identifying personally with the reactions of the many people directly or indirectly suffering pain or frustration from the effects of criminal offending or anti-social

[2] When the official crime statistics were published they showed there had been an increase of 3.8 per cent in the number of offences recorded by the police in the twelve months to March 2000. Eighty-three per cent of these offences were against property, and 13 per cent were violent crimes. Home Office, *Statistical Bulletin*, 12/00, 18 July 2000, p. 1.

[3] Sir Louis Blom-Cooper QC in the *Times Literary Supplement*, 26 Dec. 1997.

behaviour. The more optimistic among them believed that social values and deviant behaviour could be changed by governmental intervention. 'By acknowledging the duty to care', Tony Blair affirmed in a Party Conference speech, 'we earn the right to be tough on crime.'[4]

Although essentially a soundbite, there was a strain of dogma in the phrase. For Blair, as for other architects of New Labour, socialism was no longer defined in terms of economics, but in terms of values. Its central idea was that individuals are socially interdependent. The state could do less if behaviour was so altered that responsibility could be devolved to communities and individuals.[5] Alongside this concept was a drive to modernise. In forthright terms the Lord Chancellor, Lord Irvine, declared:

> The Government was elected on a radical agenda to modernise this country. All its institutions and services are liable to scrutiny, and those that are out-of-date, inefficient, or unaccountable to the people, will not survive unchanged. Nothing is ruled out: from the constitution to the economy, from the Houses of Parliament to the courts, fundamental reforms are underway. Change will be made whenever this will strengthen the social fabric, and promote a fairer, more decent, and more inclusive society.[6]

On a lower key was the unannounced emergence of a new political caste. While senior ministers in previous Governments, both Conservative and Labour, had employed special advisers, their role in policy terms was seldom more than marginal. With few exceptions, the advisers were young and inexperienced, aspirants for a political career anxious to get a foot onto one of the lower rungs on the ladder to preferment. At the Home Office, officials with long memories cite Anthony Lester as being influential, particularly in the fields of race relations and discrimination, when he was Roy Jenkins's special adviser in his second term as Home Secretary between 1974 and 1976. Edward Bickham's spadework for Douglas Hurd during the crucial preparation of the ground for the reformist Criminal Justice Act 1991 was noted in an earlier volume of *Responses to Crime*.[7] Predominately, however, the advisers of that

[4] *Speech to Labour Party Conference*, Brighton, 27 Sep. 2000; Labour Party Press Release, p. 16.

[5] V. B. Bogdanor, 'The Nineties', *England 1945–2000*, Vol. 12 *Folio History of England*, The Folio Society, 2001. Vernon Bogdanor is Professor of Government at the University of Oxford and a Fellow of Brasenose College.

[6] *Modernising Justice*, Cm. 4155, The Stationery Office, December 1998, p. 2.

[7] See Vol. 2, 1993, at pp. 205, 213, 216, 223, and 289.

era directed their efforts inwards, to the Home Secretary and other ministers, as well as any officials who would give them the time of day. In the sphere of criminal policy, none approached the authority or access of Norman Warner when he accompanied Jack Straw to the Home Office in the immediate aftermath of the general election in May 1997.[8]

In several respects Warner was not typical of the new breed. He had been both an Under-Secretary in Whitehall and Director of Social Services for a populous county before joining Jack Straw while still in Opposition. He knew Whitehall from the inside and was accepted back by the tribe without difficulty. Before long he moved on to higher responsibilities as Chairman of the Youth Justice Board. In contrast, the majority of special advisers attached to Labour ministers, numbering seventy-nine in June 2000,[9] were oriented towards the effective presentation of centrally directed policy initiatives. Each day they received a 'message text' from the Press Office at 10 Downing Street designed to co-ordinate responses, and wherever possible to steer media coverage on selected issues. The extent of this often hectic activity was separate from, and additional to, the routine work of the departmental press and public relations offices, largely staffed by civil servants.

II

The institutional, as well as the political, culture in Whitehall was also changing. The Home Office experienced two new brooms in succession, both selected from outside the Department. Richard Wilson, a career civil servant, had experience of the Cabinet Office and the Treasury before becoming Permanent Secretary at the Department of the Environment in 1992. In 1994 he moved on to the Home Office, overseeing the critical period of transition to the new Government in 1997. When appointed the following year as Secretary of the Cabinet and Head of the Civil Service, his replacement was David Omand. Once again, the new Permanent Secretary

[8] See Chapter 3, n. 15.

[9] The total number of special advisers in post had increased from fifty-three in June 1997 to seventy-nine three years later. *Parl. Debates*, HL, 618 (5th ser.), col. WA 33, 25 Oct. 2000.

was a well regarded outsider, without previous experience of the Home Office.[10]

Soon after his arrival, Omand was struck by the difference it makes when the purpose of a Department is defined in terms of the outcomes it wants to secure, such as crime reduction, rather than concentrating on the effective administration of traditional services such as the police.[11] For the Home Office key objectives were identified and promoted. They were to reduce crime and the fear of crime; to dispense justice fairly; and to promote confidence in the rule of law. Delivery of these outcomes would not be within the capacity of the Home Office alone. Partners would be needed, in central Government, in local government, and in the voluntary or private sector.

Much effort was put into defining quantitatively the outcomes the Government wanted to see, and in ways of measuring progress towards those goals. One example was an attempt to set down what would be needed to deliver a 30 per cent reduction in vehicle crime over a five-year period, 1999–2004,[12] and other less precisely specified crime reduction targets. In the course of pursuing that strategy the Police Directorate of the Home Office was reorganized into a Crime Reduction and Policing Directorate, taking over crime prevention work and refocusing the existing strands of administration directed towards specifically police objectives, conditions of service, training, and information technology. The changes were seen by ministers as ways of assisting and incentivizing the police to deliver their part of the overall crime reduction strategy.

The trend towards interdepartmental working in Whitehall enabled the Home Office to enlarge its role as a social work department. Historically, its function had been essentially regulatory, with occasional forays into social policy such as responsibility for child care services, which were transferred to the Social Care Group of the

[10] Ministry of Defence: Assistant Under-Secretary of State (Management Strategy), 1988–91, Programmes, 1991–2; Deputy Under-Secretary of State (Policy), 1992–6. Director General, GCHQ, 1996–7. Knighted in 2000, and resigned due to ill health, Jan. 2001. Omand's successor as Permanent Secretary, John Gieve, also came from outside the Home Office. His previous appointment was Managing Director, Finance Regulation and Industry Directorate, HM Treasury.

[11] Letter from Sir David Omand to the author, 25 Sep. 2000.

[12] Home Office, *The Government's Crime Reduction Strategy*, Nov. 1999, published details of the strategy to reduce vehicle crime by over 300,000 offences a year at pp. 20–1.

then Department of Health and Social Security in 1971, and co-ordinating central Government aid to voluntary organizations. Under the new regime the emphasis on joint working meant that located within the Home Office were several units with staff drawn from other government departments, supplemented by secondments from the voluntary sector or local government. Examples were the Family Policy Unit; the Active Community Unit; the Race Equality Unit; the Human Rights Unit; and the Freedom of Information Unit.[13] As the reach of the Home Office expanded beyond its traditional core responsibilities for the police, prisons, criminal policy, fire services, and immigration, the established ways of formulating and implementing policies underwent a sea change. 'Joined-up government' was not simply a catch-phrase, but a factual description of the creation of a tripartite structure for the overall management of criminal justice in England and Wales.

By the year 2000 policy-making, planning, and budgeting were being carried out jointly by the Home Office, the Lord Chancellor's Department, and the Law Officers' Department, with ministers supported by single team of officials drawn from all three Departments. In March of that year the Permanent Secretaries of the Home Office and the Lord Chancellor's Department, accompanied by the Director of Public Prosecutions, appeared together for the first time in front of the Committee of Public Accounts (PAC) of the House of Commons as Accounting Officers responsible jointly and severally for the criminal justice system as a whole.[14]

While this display of togetherness was commended by the PAC, its subsequent Report concentrated on the practical steps needed to translate a slogan into reality. Three 'key conclusions' were drawn. The first was that while 'the independence of the various players in the criminal justice system' was fundamental to justice, it was 'entirely compatible' with them taking joint responsibility for achieving value for money from the substantial resources spent on criminal justice. Current performance in progressing criminal cases was 'not satisfactory' and needed to be improved through more concerted joint monitoring and management. Secondly, the criminal justice

[13] Letter from Sir D. Omand, *op. cit.*

[14] Sir David Omand and Sir Hayden Phillips were the Permanent Secretaries respectively of the Home Office and Lord Chancellor's Department, while David Calvert-Smith, as Director of Public Prosecutions, was accountable for the Crown Prosecution Service.

system was 'some way' from having the information base needed to enable people to work together to plan and manage the system effectively. As a matter of priority, the Departments should agree upon key data definitions and ensure that local agencies could move quickly to share basic data about criminal cases on compatible computer systems. Thirdly, the pilot initiatives to expedite the handling of criminal cases by the police and the Crown Prosecution Service had shown that 'step-change improvements' could be achieved by effective joint working.[15]

In concluding the hearing, the chairman remarked diplomatically that all of the Committee of Public Accounts reports were a balance of criticism and lesson learning. He forecast that 'this one is going to be more lesson learning than criticism'.[16] Lessons were already being learned across Whitehall as the new systems approach was applied to the joint management (a description preferred to administration) of criminal justice by the Home Office, the Lord Chancellor's Department, and the Attorney General's Department. For the first time, it was possible to model the impact of changes in the law, or police activity, or reoffending behaviour programmes, on the disparate elements of criminal justice, including the work-load of the courts and the size of the prison population. Some of the changes were common across the Civil Service and reflected forces outside the control of Government. They included the phenomenal expansion of information and communications technology, the increasing international dimension of much of the work, especially as regards Europe, and the rising expectations of members of the public as to the quality and responsiveness expected from public services.[17] Others were geared more specifically towards reducing offending and increasing public safety.

To pull the strands together, Omand had given the Department a mission: 'to help build a safe, just, and tolerant society', in which staff could take pride. Although the introduction of a mission statement for the whole of the Home Office was new, the practice of defining what it stood for, with a particular emphasis on striking a balance between the needs of the community and the rights of the individual, was not. Statements of aims and objectives had featured regularly in publications by the Home Office during more recent

[15] House of Commons Paper 298, Session 1999–2000: Committee of Public Accounts, Twenty-seventh Report, *Criminal Justice: Working Together*, 26 June 2000, p. v.

[16] David Davis MP; ibid., p. 15.

[17] Letter from Sir D. Omand, *op. cit.*

administrations. With the progression to more senior posts of staff who had become familiar with such concepts at earlier stages in their careers, advance planning and management by objectives were recognized as factors that were central to performance.

Since the advent of Labour to office in 1997, the insistence on modernisation and organizational change left no room for doubt that ministers, and the senior officials they appointed or promoted, created a working environment that was subtly different in its objectives and methods. One example was the virtual elimination of the traditional Home Office possessiveness which had previously inhibited closer working with the Law Officers' Department and the strengthened Lord Chancellor's Department.[18]

By the financial year 2000–1 all the work of the Home Office was reorganized according to seven aims. They ranged from the relative precision of attempting to regulate entry to and settlement in the United Kingdom to the vacuity of Aim 5:

> Helping to build, under a modernised constitution, a fair and prosperous society in which everyone has a stake, and in which the rights and responsibilities of individuals, families and communities are properly balanced.

Each of the aims was allocated an 'aim-owner' in the shape of a senior civil servant on the Permanent Secretary's Management Board who was responsible for delivering the relevant objectives and targets.

The Home Office Business Plan for 2000–1 published these aims, accompanied by short statements from the named officials responsible for their delivery.[19] Since the achievement of each aim

[18] For an account of the origins and growth of the Lord Chancellor's Department as a distinct department of government, see *Responses to Crime*, Vol. 2, pp. 32–44.

[19] The aims and aim-owners for 2000–1 were: Aim 1, Reduction in crime, particularly youth crime, and in the fear of crime; and the maintenance of public safety and good order (John Lyon). Aim 2, The delivery of justice through effective and efficient investigation, prosecution, trial, and sentencing, and through support for victims (Sue Street). Aim 3, Prevention of terrorism, reduction in organized and international crime, and protection against threats to national security (John Warne). Aim 4, The effective execution of the sentences of the courts so as to reduce reoffending and protect the public (Sue Street). Aim 5, Helping to build, under a modernised constitution, a fair and prosperous society in which everyone has a stake, and in which the rights and responsibilities of individuals, families, and communities are properly balanced (Carolyn Sinclair). Aim 6, Regulation of entry to and settlement in the United Kingdom in the interests of social stability and economic growth, and facilitation of travel by UK citizens (Stephen Boys Smith). Aim 7, To reduce the incidence of fire and related deaths, injury, and damage and to ensure the safety of the public through civil protection (Charles Everett). Home Office, *Business Plan 2000–2001*, pp. 5–24. John Warne acted as Permanent Secretary during the interregnum between Sir David Omand's resignation and the arrival of John Gieve as his successor in April 2001.

required co-operation across the Department as a whole, the Management Board had an incentive to manage collectively the delivery of all the aims, with a view to reducing the problems associated with traditional 'stove pipes' or 'baronies' within the Home Office.[20] There were also support directorates on Communication; Corporate Development; Corporate Resources; a European and International Unit; the Legal Adviser's Branch; a Planning, Finance, and Performance Group; the Private Office to support ministers and the Permanent Secretary in the discharge of their Parliamentary and Departmental duties; and the Research, Development, and Statistics Directorate.[21] The cumulative effect of all this activity, reinforced by exceptional pressure from asylum-seekers on the Immigration Service, was a small year-on-year increase in the total number of staff employed in the years 1998–9 and 1999–2000, with a substantial increase forecast for each of the following two years (see Table 17).

III

The changes in the ways of working at the Home Office were reflected across the criminal justice system as a whole. Over a wider canvas the Government's aims and objectives were incorporated in a

Table 17. *Home Office: staff numbers 1998–2002*

Staff numbers[a]	1998–9[b] outturn	1999–2000 outturn	2000–1 plans	2001–2 plans
Civil Service full-time equivalents	7,911	8,182	10,541	11,104
Overtime	438	429	434	434
Casuals	363	301	282	278
Total	8,712	8,912	11,257	11,816

[a] Staff numbers include secondees, largely from police and fire authorities. Staff employed by HM Prison Service, UK Passport Agency, Forensic Science Service, and the Fire Service College are excluded.

[b] The total of staff employed in 1998–9 was a reduction on the previous years due in part to one function being detached to become a Non-Departmental Public Body, and another a service authority.

Source: Home Office, *Annual Report 1999–2000*, Cm. 4605, The Stationery Office, 2000, p. 86.

[20] Letter from Sir D. Omand, *op. cit.*

[21] Home Office, *Business Plan 2000–2001*, pp. 25–36.

business plan aimed at those at local or national level with responsibility for directing, planning, and managing the delivery of criminal justice services over forty-two areas in England and Wales resulting from a reorganization designed to bring boundaries into line with one another. The plan covered the Lord Chancellor's Department (for the courts), and the Attorney General's Department (for the Crown Prosecution Service), as well as the Home Office.

This time there were two 'overarching aims' and eight objectives. The aims were 'to reduce crime and the fear of crime and their social and economic costs', and 'to dispense justice fairly and efficiently and to promote confidence in the rule of law'. The statements of aim were then refined into objectives with accompanying performance measures and targets. These were to reduce the level of actual crime and disorder; to reduce the adverse impact of crime and disorder on people's lives; to reduce the economic costs of crime; to ensure just processes and just and effective outcomes; to deal with cases throughout the criminal justice system with appropriate speed; to meet the needs of victims, witnesses, and jurors within the system; to respect the rights of defendants and to treat them fairly; and to promote confidence in the criminal justice system.[22]

The document had little to say about financial resources or costs, although it included a table indicating projected expenditure on each of the Criminal Justice System (CJS) objectives for 2000–1 (see Table 18), and another for planned spending over the same period analysed by department and service. The latter showed that well over half (59.0 per cent) of the total planned expenditure on criminal justice for England and Wales would go on the police. Sixteen per cent would go on prisons, 7.5 per cent on legal aid, 5.5 per cent on the courts, 4.5 per cent on probation services, and 2.5 per cent on the Crown Prosecution Service and Serious Fraud Office.[23]

Beyond the year 2000–1 the financial resources allocated to criminal justice depended on the outcome of the Government's overall Spending Review 2000, and the public expenditure plans for a three-year period from 2001–2 to 2003–4. In a foreword to the document, presented to Parliament by the Chancellor of the Exchequer in July 2000, the Prime Minister itemized four priorities for the

[22] *Criminal Justice System Business Plan 2000–2001*, published by the Home Office, Lord Chancellor's Department, and the Attorney General's Office, May 2000, pp. 3–4.

[23] Ibid., p. 6.

Table 18. *Criminal justice system, objectives and resources, 2000–1*

Indicative spending by CJS objectives[a] (£m in resource terms)

CJS objective	1 Level of crime and disorder	2 Impact of crime and disorder	3 Economic costs of crime	4 Just processes and just outcomes	5 Speed through CJS process	6 Needs of victims, witnesses, and jurors	7 Respect rights of defendants	8 Promote confidence	**Total**
CJS Service									
Police[b]	5,363.00			2,303.00	44.00			2.00	7,712.00
HO	153.00			203.00	16.00			14.00	386.00
CPS				178.05	118.69	15.62			312.36
SFO			17.79						17.79
Legal Aid[c]				200.84	200.84	200.84	200.84	200.84	1,004.20
Magistrates' courts[c]		40.13	40.13	40.13	40.13	40.13	40.13	40.13	280.91
Crown Court[c]				62.80	62.80	62.80	62.80	62.80	314.00
LCD[c]		0.68	0.68	13.49	4.18	13.49	13.49	13.49	59.50
Probation Service				567.00					567.00
Prison Service	239.00			1,873.00					2,112.00
Victims inc. Victim Support and Criminal Injuries Compensation						216.00			216.00
Total	5,755.00	40.81	58.60	5,441.31	486.64	548.88	317.26	333.26	12,981.76

[a] Attribution on the assumption that where expenditure contributes to more than one CJS objective the whole amount is allocated to the directly affected objective, not the indirectly affected ones (this applies particularly to objectives 2—fear of crime; 3—economic costs of crime; and 8—confidence in the CJS).

[b] Includes 6% police grant which relates to terrorism and organized crime.

[c] LCD costs are attributed equally to all of the objectives to which the Department contributes. Departments are developing their ability to attribute costs more accurately.

Source: Criminal Justice System Business Plan, 2000–2001, p. 6.

overall allocation of resources. They were 'improving education, health, transport and fighting crime'.[24] Crime reduction was emphasized as the overriding priority for Home Office services.

The Government rejected the idea that crime was inevitable. Targets had been set to reduce the crimes which people were believed to be most concerned about, namely having their homes or cars broken into. Accordingly, there would be substantial investment in programmes for crime reduction. Police spending plans would be increased so that by 2003–4 they were £1.6 billion higher than in 2000, with an extra £310 million rising to £540 million being invested each year in prisons and community punishments.[25] The cumulative result was that over the next three years Home Office spending was forecast to grow by an average of 6.4 per cent a year in real terms, from a total of £8,149 million in 2000–1 to £10,613 million in 2003–4.[26]

As part of the spending review, the Chancellor of the Exchequer announced a new reserve of £525 million over the three years 2001–2 to 2003–4 to be used to help deliver the objectives and targets set out in the latest CJS public service agreement. In November 2000 Lord Irvine, an influential member of the Ministerial Group on the Criminal Justice System, said that initial decisions on the use of the reserve would be made in the next few months.[27] He added that, alongside the new resources, the Government was working with the police, the Crown Prosecution Service, the courts, and probation and prison services towards 'an on-going programme of modernisation and reform', and was engaged in a number of important reviews of the criminal justice process. These included Sir Robin Auld's review of the criminal courts, and a review of the present sentencing framework, led by John Halliday, formerly Director of Criminal Justice Policy at the Home Office.[28]

[24] HM Treasury, *Prudent for a Purpose: Building Opportunity and Security for All*; 2000 Spending Review: New Public Spending Plans 2001–2004, Cm. 4807, The Stationery Office, July 2000.

[25] Ibid., p. 57.

[26] Ibid., p. 60.

[27] *Parl. Debates*, HL, 618 (5th ser.), col. WA 141, 7 Nov. 2000.

[28] Ibid. John Halliday had been Principal Private Secretary to the Home Secretary, 1980–3; Assistant Under-Secretary of State, Home Office, 1983–7; Under-Secretary of State DHSS; then Dept. of Health, 1987–90. Head, Criminal Department, Home Office, 1990–6; Director of Criminal Policy, 1996–8; Director of Criminal Justice Policy, 1998–2000; Director, Review of the Sentencing Framework, 2000–1.

IV

The adoption of objectives, aimed not simply at countering crime, but at reducing it by stated amounts, was an ambitious policy bordering on the audacious. Risks as well as benefits could result. A strong economy made possible the provision of additional financial, human, and IT resources to demonstrate that the modern approach depended upon more than words and exhortation. Since the Labour Government had come to office in 1997 the scale of structural reform had been extensive. Both the Probation Service and the Crown Prosecution Service had been reorganized to correspond with geographical police areas, with the intention that these three main agencies of criminal justice should in future co-operate with one another more effectively. A new system of youth justice had been devised and implemented which held out hopeful prospects. The enforcement of community orders had been strengthened. Other measures described in the previous Chapters had been introduced with the specific aim of reducing crime and protecting the public.

But what of policy outcomes? For a while, there were grounds for hope. In the year to March 1999 the underlying rate of recorded crime fell by 1.4 per cent. It was the sixth consecutive year in which all recorded crime had fallen, and the first time in the 1990s that recorded crimes of violence had fallen.[29] The number of offences of domestic burglary, both recorded and cleared up, had fallen every year between 1994 and 1998–9. In the following year to March 2000, despite the optimistic tone of the Government's Crime Reduction Strategy and annual business plans, the recorded crime statistics indicated an increase back to the 1997–8 level, with a 3.8 per cent increase in all offences. Domestic burglary in England and Wales showed a contrary trend, with a continued decline of 6.5 per cent on the previous year. The annual police statistics of burglaries from dwellings, however, indicated that in areas served by some of the larger police forces, notably the Metropolitan Police and the Thames Valley force, there were increases of between 5 and 15 per cent for 1999–2000, compared with the previous year.[30] The Home Office statistics on recorded violent crime also showed that in the twelve

[29] *The Government's Crime Reduction Strategy*, *op. cit.*, p. 6.

[30] HM Inspectorate of Constabulary, *Report of HM Chief Inspector of Constabulary, 1999–2000*, HC 895, The Stationery Office, 2000, p. 33, Figure 9 (corrected).

months ended March 2000 there had been a large increase: as much as 16.1 per cent on the previous year.[31]

For realistic planning, as opposed to the pursuit of political advantage, a longer span than year-on-year comparisons was required. Despite the short-term ups and downs, the underlying trends of criminal offending in England and Wales were high both by international standards and historically. Recorded crime had doubled since the 1980s and early 1990s, and was much higher than twenty years before. Demographic and economic factors were forecast to be adverse, with the statistical models showing that rates of property crime were likely to be powerfully influenced as the number of young men in a society increased, and also by economic factors such as consumption expenditure.[32]

Yet the intractability of human behaviour and the multifarious factors bearing on criminal offending made it hard to predict what the actual results would be. The extent of drug abuse, and its known connection with persistent acquisitive offending, was recognized as a particular problem. Proven outcomes were always likely to be the Achilles heel of New Labour's approach. No one could be certain whether the modernisation agenda of target-setting and performance indicators would lead to lasting improvement, or be followed through with sufficient drive and competence.

Even within the citadel, Norman Warner, by now an articulate Government supporter in the House of Lords as well as chairman of the Youth Justice Board, harboured doubts. Drawing on his previous experience as a senior Whitehall official, Warner observed in December 1999, more than two and a half years after Labour had come to office, that implementation strategies for new programmes were often weak. Civil servants seemed to think that policy and legislation was their job, rather than delivering results on the ground. Working across departmental organizational boundaries was not much better than in the 1970s, when a joint approach to social policy was afoot. In arguing for a change in civil service culture, he concluded wryly: 'Good management and implementation skills are not rewarded; digging ministers out of holes is.'[33]

[31] Home Office Statistical Bulletin, Issue 12/00, *Recorded Crime Statistics, England and Wales, April 1999 to March 2000*, 18 July 2000.

[32] *The Government's Crime Reduction Strategy*, *op. cit.*, p. 6. The number of young men, the age group most likely to become involved in criminal activity, was forecast to rise by 4 per cent over a three-year period from 1999.

[33] Letter to the Editor, *The Times*, 14 Dec. 1999.

Tools were at hand, but were of limited practical value to the new-style managers of crime reduction programmes. Techniques such as modelling certain types of crime, particularly the prevalent property offences of theft and burglary, had been developed which held out some interesting possibilities of prediction. Even so, guarded language was used. Models were not intended to give a full picture of what causes crime. Nor were they designed to explain crime, although they could help to identify certain pressures on crime trends and predict how such pressures might influence trends in the future.[34] For example, research showed that since 1945 the growth of property crime was 'intimately linked with growth in the economy'.[35]

The traditional instruments of crime control, the police, the courts, and the prisons, remained in the forefront of public policy as they had for generations. Police powers in the investigation of crime had been reorganized under the Conservatives by the Police and Criminal Evidence Act of 1984.[36] Although the total numbers in custody had moved inexorably upwards, the Prison Service had enjoyed a period of relative calm since the high-profile escapes from Whitemoor in September 1994 and Parkhurst in January 1995, which followed the riot and disturbances at Strangeways in April 1990. The exhaustive report on the Strangeways incident and its causes, by the then Lord Justice Woolf and Judge Stephen Tumim, was accompanied by recommendations which were of far-reaching significance.[37]

The privatization of prisoner escorts to and from the courts, and contracts for the design, construction, and management of a limited number of new private-sector prisons, had been accomplished without the dire consequences predicted by some opponents of private-sector

[34] Home Office Research Study 198, *Modelling and predicting property crime trends in England and Wales, A Research, Development, and Statistics Directorate Report*, 1999, p. 2.

[35] Home Office Research Study 195, *Trends in Crime Revisited, A Research, Development, and Statistics Directorate Report*, 1999, p. 15. Over the last half-century increasing wealth has been devoted to more stealable commodities, cars and electronic goods prominent amongst them: ibid., p. 16.

[36] See *Responses to Crime*, Vol. 2, pp. 185–92.

[37] *Prison Disturbances April 1990, Report of an Inquiry by Lord Justice Woolf (Parts I and II) and Judge Tumim (Part II)*, Cm. 1456, HMSO, London, 1991. The second part of this influential report examined the role of the prison service and the way prisons were run, reviewing what action should be taken to divert from prison those persons who did not need to be there.

participation in the penal system.[38] Overcrowding and impoverishment of regimes, particularly in the local prisons, continued to be a serious problem, although temporarily relieved by recourse to a technological innovation, the electronic tag. This device enabled selected prisoners to be released from custody early, subject to monitoring and curfew restrictions confining them to a particular address at particular times.

The Home Detention Curfew (HDC) scheme was introduced in England and Wales from January 1999. Medium-term prisoners serving sentences of three months or more, but less than four years, would be considered for release up to sixty days early. Most prisoners would be eligible for the scheme, subject to an assessment of risk, although certain categories would be excluded. Prisoners required to register on release under the Sex Offenders Act 1997 would be released on HDC only in exceptional circumstances, and with the personal approval of the Director General of the Prison Service.[39] Other ineligible categories were prisoners awaiting deportation or without a fixed address, and those who had failed to comply with a curfew order. The decision on release was taken by the prison governor, after consideration of an assessment of the risk of reoffending prepared by prison and probation staff, as well as the likelihood that the prisoner would comply with the curfew conditions on release.[40]

Although originally intended to ease the transition of prisoners from custody to the community, the HDC scheme proved to be an expedient instrument for moderating the most acute consequences of overcrowding. From 28 January 1999, when the scheme began, to 30 November 1999, 45,000 prisoners were eligible for HDC, of whom approximately 14,000 were released. The release rate of 31 per cent

[38] By January 2000 there were four private sector-managed establishments, and four DCMF establishments. The latter had been procured under the Public Finance Initiative (PFI) following Design, Construct, Manage, and Finance competitions. HM Prison Service, *Annual Report and Accounts, April 1999–March 2000*, HC 622, The Stationery Office, 2000, p. 76.

[39] Only three offenders required to register under the Sex Offenders Act 1997 were released between 1 Jan. 1999 and 1 Dec. 2000. Contrary to policy, in all three cases the releasing establishments failed to seek the consent of the Director General. Letter from Lord Bassam of Brighton, Parliamentary Under-Secretary of State, Home Office, 1 Dec. 2000. Section 65 of the Criminal Justice and Court Services Act 2000 excluded prisoners subject to the notification requirements of the Sex Offenders Act 1997 from the Home Detention Curfew Scheme altogether.

[40] Home Office Research, Development, and Statistics Directorate, *Research Findings No. 10: Home Detention Curfew—The first year of operation*, K. Dodgson and E. Mortimer, 2000, p. 2.

was less than the 50 per cent rate which had been expected. This indicated that a cautious approach had been taken toward risk assessment, which contributed to a politically defensible rate of successful completion of about 95 per cent. The most common reason for recall to prison was failure to comply with curfew conditions. Very few prisoners were recalled because they had reoffended, or posed a risk of serious harm to the public. Technical failures of either installation or monitoring were also at a low level.

A further extension of electronic monitoring[41] followed less than twelve months later. Power had been conferred on the courts as early as 1991 by the Criminal Justice Act of that year to impose a curfew order as a sentence in its own right on convicted defendants aged sixteen or over. The Act also provided for the electronic monitoring of an offender's whereabouts, or tagging as it became known, where the offender had expressed his willingness to comply with the requirements of the order.[42] Although when in Opposition the Labour front bench in the Commons initially rejected tagging out of hand,[43] a lengthy series of trials between 1995 and 1998 had shown substantially improved standards of technical reliability. Nevertheless, it was not until eight years after the authorizing legislation had been enacted that curfew orders with electronic monitoring were made available to all courts in England and Wales on 1 December 1999.

Between then and 20 November 2000, a total of 4,693 curfew orders with electronic monitoring were made. Of these, 424 (9 per cent) were revoked.[44] No figures were available centrally on the reasons for revocation: whether the offender had failed to conform to the terms of the order, or because of faults in the electronic equipment. In the early stages, both penologically and operationally, electronic monitoring

[41] Electronic monitoring (EM) is defined as a means of determining whether a person is present or absent from a particular place at any given time by the use of electronic equipment. EM projects were first brought into use in the United States and have since been adopted in many other countries.

[42] Section 12(6) of the Criminal Justice Act 1991 stated that before making a curfew order, 'the court shall obtain and consider information about the place proposed to be specified in the order (including information as to the attitude of persons likely to be affected by the enforced presence there of the offender)'.

[43] Roy Hattersley, then Opposition Deputy Leader and spokesman on Home Affairs, declared, 'Electric tagging would be a farce if it were ever implemented in this country. We have read encouraging reports in serious newpapers that, while the Government feel that they must save face by going ahead with the clauses, they have no intention of implementing the proposal . . .' *Parl. Debates*, HC, 181 (6th ser.), col. 160, 20 Nov. 1990.

[44] *Parl. Debates*, HL, 619, col. WA 119, 27 Nov. 2000.

had been an experiment with an uncertain outcome. But perseverance combined with technological advances meant that by the end of the year 2000 it had become an accepted and technically reliable method of dealing with low-risk offenders, many of whom would otherwise have been in prison. In this way tagging, one of the most innovative developments of the decade, grew up incrementally on the fringes of penal policy, attracting relatively little attention and diminishing antagonism.

V

Despite the fact that the Home Detention Curfew curtailed the rate of increase in the population in custody by an average of some 2,000 inmates, the pressure of numbers on the prisons continued throughout the late 1990s and into the new millennium. By September 2000 the total population in custody was close to 65,000 inmates, of whom some 11,100 were remanded in custody pending trial or sentence, and 53,200 were sentenced prisoners (see Table 19).[45] Thus, after a short period of respite, the prison population had returned to a level comparable to where it had been before the impact of HDC. A further factor which masked the underlying rate of growth was the plea before venue procedural change made possible by the Crime (Sentences) Act 1997 and implemented in October of that year. This had the effect of more offenders being sentenced in the Magistrates' courts, where the maximum sentence that could be imposed for a single offence was six months' imprisonment, rather than in the Crown Court, where sentence lengths would be longer.

The sharp increase in the female population in custody to 3,380 in September 2000 was a cause of particular concern. Over three decades the total number of women in prison had grown from less than a thousand in 1970 to a level that was estimated to reach about 4,000 by 2005. To contain the larger numbers, two new women's prisons were planned.

[45] To obtain a fuller picture of the total number of persons held in custody or detention in England and Wales by a court order, it is necessary to add the growing number of restricted patients detained in hospital under the mental health legislation. On 31 Dec. 1999 there were 2,857 patients in this category. The total represented a 4 per cent increase on the previous year, similar to the average yearly increase over a ten-year period. Home Office Statistical Bulletin 21/00, *Statistics of mentally disordered offenders 1999, England and Wales*, S. Johnson and R. Taylor, Nov. 2000, p. 1.

Table 19. *Population in Custody (England and Wales)*

	1995	1996	1997	1998	1999	(thousands) Sep. 2000
Remand, of which	11.4	11.6	12.1	12.6	12.5	11.1
male	10.9	11.1	11.5	11.8	11.8	10.4
female	0.49	0.54	0.60	0.7	0.75	0.69
Sentenced, of which	39.1	43.0	48.4	52.2	51.1	53.2
male	37.6	41.3	46.4	49.8	48.7	50.5
female	1.46	1.7	2.05	2.38	2.41	2.69
Other	0.62	0.63	0.57	0.55	0.57	0.70
Total	51.0	55.3	61.1	65.3	64.4	65.0

Source: Home Office, Research, Development and Statistics Directorate, *Prison Population Brief*, July and September 2000, Table 2. These figures are the annual averages (actuals), plus the September 2000 count. Components may not add up to totals because thay have been rounded independently.

In order to reassess the situation in the light of the known facts about the characteristics of female offenders, and the patterns of their offending, the Prison Reform Trust commissioned an independent inquiry into the use of imprisonment for women offenders. With Professor Dorothy Wedderburn[46] in the chair, the Committee produced a report as notable as an earlier publication, also sponsored by the Prison Reform Trust: the report of a Committee on the penalty for murder, chaired by Lord Lane.[47]

A cogent argument cited in support of the objective of reducing the number of women in custody was that imprisonment all too often had the effect of aggravating the problems which had led to their offending. Many of the women had been abused, as children or as adults, or both. Typically they had spent time in local authority care, and had little education. A high proportion suffered from

[46] Emeritus Professor of Industrial Sociology, University of London. Principal: Bedford College, 1981–5; Royal Holloway and Bedford New College, University of London, 1985–90. Senior Research Fellow, Imperial College of Science, Technology and Medicine, 1981–. Member, Government Committee on the Pay and Condition of Nurses, 1974–5; Royal Commission on the Distribution of Income and Wealth (part-time), 1974–8.

[47] For a discussion of this report, and the then Home Secretary's reaction to it, see *Responses to Crime*, Vol. 3, pp. 372–6.

mental health problems, one in five having received in-patient care in a psychiatric hospital in the year prior to their imprisonment. Fifty per cent of women prisoners take prescribed medication. Prison conditions can contribute to the inmates being more of a threat to themselves than to others. These considerations raised a question of public policy as to the extent to which prisons should be used to contain persons in need of mental health treatment.

Another perspective was the impact on the family. More than 60 per cent of women in prison are mothers, and 45 per cent had children living with them at the time of their imprisonment. The report estimated that the living arrangements of more than 8,000 children were affected each year as a result of the mothers' enforced absence.[48] Even quite short periods of a mother in custody have a disproportionate effect on their children. About 8 per cent are taken into local authority care, while others experience considerable insecurity in such care arrangements as their mothers are able to make from prison. The majority are looked after by other family members or friends. A significant contrast between men and women in prison is the way that mothers often attempt to maintain contact with their children and carers while in custody. For the vast majority of children, the absence of their mother in prison is the first time they are separated from her. This experience for children perpetuates a cycle of deprivation.[49] It also constitutes an ominous portent for the future.

The changes recommended by the Committee looked to one of the Government's own creations as a model. The antecedents and setting up of the Youth Justice Board were described in an earlier Chapter. It was subsequently adopted as a precedent for the Committee's main recommendation: the establishment of a National Women's Justice Board. The ambitious concept was of a new statutory body with its own budget and management structure, and powers to commission services from other relevant agencies, including the Probation Service, the Prison Service, the National Health Service, local authorities, and voluntary bodies. The remit would be to establish both a

[48] *Justice for Women: The Need for Reform*, the Report of the Committee on Women's Imprisonment, Prison Reform Trust, London, 2000, p. 9. The real numbers may be higher because some mothers do not reveal that they have children for fear that their children might be taken into local authority care.

[49] D. Wedderburn, 'Justice for Women: The Need for Reform', 132 *Prison Service Journal*, Nov. 2000, p. 33. This summary draws on Professor Wedderburn's informative article as well as the Report of the Committee on Women's Imprisonment.

network of local Women's Supervision, Rehabilitation, and Support Centres for female offenders serving community sentences, and a national system of geographically dispersed custodial units to replace the existing women's prison system.[50]

In the transition period it was envisaged that the new Board would take over from the Prison Service the running of the remaining custodial establishments and integrate them with the community centres, particularly in respect of rehabilitative services. While recognizing recent efforts by the Prison Service to pay greater attention to the particular needs of women offenders, the Committee concluded that even if and when additional resources were made available, the continuous rise projected in the numbers of women incarcerated would limit the scope for real improvements. Moreover, the culture of the Prison Service was still dominated by the male ethos. Hence the conclusion was that only radical structural reform could deal with the problems which had been identified.

The report of the inquiry was published in April 2000. Yet its recommendations received no mention in a consultation document outlining the Government's strategy for women offenders published six months later. Such reaction as there was by ministers was low-key. In May a courteous reference to the report was made in a reply by a Government Whip in the House of Lords to a Question about the female prison population asked by Lord Hurd in his capacity as chairman of the Prison Reform Trust.[51] In July the Director of the Trust met Tessa Jowell, the Minister responsible for the Women's Unit at the Cabinet Office, to discuss matters arising from the report. The Minister commented that she was particularly interested in the issues affecting the children of prisoners. A copy of the report had been passed to the Social Exclusion Unit.[52]

The preliminary Home Office response took the form of an acknowledgement by Paul Boateng, the Minister of State with responsibility for Prisons and Probation, to a letter from Dorothy Wedderburn enclosing a copy of the report. He described it as:

50 Summary of Recommendations, *Justice for Women: The Need for Reform*, *op. cit.*, p. 79.

51 *Parl. Debates*, HL, 612, cols. 922–3, 2 May 2000. Lord Bach welcomed the report as 'a major contribution to the thinking on the treatment of women in the criminal justice system'. Hurd retired as Chairman of the Prison Reform Trust the following year.

52 Letter from Tessa Jowell to Juliet Lyon, Director, Prison Reform Trust, 8 Aug. 2000.

an excellent and incisive analysis of many of the issues in relation to women offenders. The report makes a series of recommendations which we will consider carefully in developing further policy in this area.[53]

He agreed that the issue of social exclusion was a key priority for Government, which was determined to ensure that it was not passed down the generations. When women had offended already, the Government wanted to ensure that policy and practice were based on the evidence of what works to reduce reoffending, both for female and male offenders, whether serving community or custodial sentences.[54]

After an interval of two months, the Minister met Professor Wedderburn and the Director of the Prison Reform Trust to discuss the report and its recommendations. The meeting was attended by eight senior officials, including the Head of the Women's Policy Group at HM Prison Service headquarters. Boateng dismissed the central proposal to establish a National Women's Justice Board as 'not a runner'. He maintained that such a structure could not be justified because it represented unequal treatment. His analogy was with a National Black Justice Board, or something similar, to oversee work with offenders drawn from ethnic minority groups. He was, however, prepared to consider arguments for differential sentencing for those with primary care responsibilities, both women and men. The importance of developing more effective community sentences for women who do not represent a risk to the public was also discussed. The need for 'joined-up' services, improved resettlement, and better understanding of the needs of foreign national prisoners were all endorsed.

Despite the interest attracted by the report, some one hundred copies having been requested by the Prison Service alone, and the Minister of State's confirmation that all the recommendations it contained would be carefully considered, the overall reaction by the Government was disappointing. In particular no reference to the main proposal for a National Justice Board for Women appeared in the consultation paper on women offenders when it was published in the Autumn.[55] Nor was there any commitment to the importance of

[53] Letter from Rt. Hon. Paul Boateng to Professor Dorothy Wedderburn, 10 May 2000.

[54] Ibid.

[55] Home Office, *The Government's Strategy for Women Offenders*. The document was undated by administrative oversight, but was published on 12 Oct. 2000.

reducing the numbers of women in prison; nor to the over-use of remands in custody. On the need to strengthen the role of families, the document referred to the Sure Start programme, intended to give support to the most excluded young mothers, which might extend to those in custody.

In his introduction the Home Secretary remarked that the statistics on women and crime were striking, even to those who worked every day in the criminal justice system. Although only 17 per cent of known offenders were women, it was estimated that they accounted for some 900,000 recorded crimes in England and Wales each year. He accepted that because women were a relatively small minority of the offending population, the factors leading them to offend, or to reoffend, had been overlooked in the past. He did not subscribe to the 'all women offenders are victims' rhetoric, nor to the equally misguided view that women offenders were a lost cause.[56] What was needed was effective joint work by the Prison and Probation Services to prevent them reoffending, and a network of support for vulnerable women in the community both to prevent offending in the first place, and to help with the resettlement of ex-offenders. But on the reality of imprisonment, the conditions, the impact on families, and the future prospects resulting from the growing population of women inmates, he was silent.

Without reading too much into the minutiae of policy-making, the episode suggests that the prevailing orthodoxy—the concentration on generalizations and broad strategic objectives—served to inhibit thorough and open-minded consideration of comprehensive proposals put forward by a well qualified and non-political group after concentrated study. The era of independent advisory councils with expert knowledge had passed, being replaced by internal policy groups or single-person reviews. The comparison was unfavourable with the inception of community service orders as a constructive alternative to imprisonment nearly a quarter of a century before. That innovation owed much to the determination of another prominent woman social scientist and penal reformer, Barbara Wootton, chair of a sub-committee of the Advisory Council on the Penal System which had launched the proposal.[57]

[56] Ibid., p. 1.

[57] See *Responses to Crime*, Vol. 2, pp. 120–2.

VI

The connections between certain kinds of drug use and criminal behaviour[58] carried over into the prisons. In 1998 the Comprehensive Spending Review had allocated an additional £76 million to the Prison Service to develop and implement a strategy to reduce the availability and use of drugs over a three-year period, 1999–2002. By the end of the first year a treatment service framework was in place, providing a range of interventions from basic advice and counselling for all prisoners to intensive therapeutic programmes for those with the most serious addiction. The rate of positive random tests fell from 25 per cent in 1996–7 to 14.2 per cent in 1999–2000.[59]

Not all the performance targets set for the Prison Service resulted in the same levels of achievement. Out of a total of thirteen targets for 1999–2000, slightly less than half (six) were met, while seven were not met.[60] In his annual report for 1998–9, HM Chief Inspector of Prisons referred to some of the most critical inspection reports he had made during his tenure of office. Despite the fact that ministers and successive Directors General had made it abundantly clear that they were not prepared to tolerate the situation, conditions in at least three of the most important prisons in the system, Wormwood Scrubs and Wandsworth for adult male prisoners, and Feltham for young offenders, remained 'wholly unacceptable'.[61] At both Feltham and Wormwood Scrubs the Chief Inspector was disturbed to find that nothing had been done to improve the treatment and conditions of prisoners which his reports had condemned two years earlier. Particular attention was drawn to the 'appalling conditions in which the most vulnerable and impressionable juvenile remand prisoners were held at Feltham'. Unacceptable staff attitudes towards prisoners at both Wormwood Scrubs and Wandsworth also attracted scathing criticism. In commenting on such extreme examples of malpractice, the Chief Inspector wrote:

[58] T. Bennett, *Drugs and crime: The result of the second developmental stage of the NEW-ADAM programme*, Home Office Research Study 205, Research, Development, and Statistics Directorate, 2000, p. x.

[59] HM Prison Service, *Annual Report and Accounts, 1999–2000*, HC 622, The Stationery Office, 2000, pp. 10 and 32.

[60] Ibid., pp. 10–11.

[61] HM Inspectorate of Prisons for England and Wales, *Report of HM Chief Inspector of Prisons*, HC 548, The Stationery Office, 2000, p. 3.

responsibility for the treatment of and conditions for prisoners did not appear to feature as prominently in line management's list of priorities as one might reasonably expect.

At Feltham, at least, a follow-up inspection had disclosed considerable advances, and the promise of further improvements, following the personal intervention of the Director General.[62]

Such forthright criticisms by the Chief Inspector, Sir David Ramsbotham,[63] widely publicized in a series of detailed reports on inspections at individual establishments, as well as thematic reports and his annual report to Parliament, made him an uncomfortable public servant for ministers to live with. Yet his reports on the actual state of the prisons were an essential complement to the recitation of aims and overarching objectives set out in the official reports of the Prison Service. His unmistakable independence, allied with sophisticated communication skills, was such that, in the same way as his predecessor, Sir Stephen Tumim, Ramsbotham came to be seen as the conscience of the prison system. Consequently it may not have been an entire coincidence that for a time the continuation of a separate appointment as Chief Inspector of Prisons was in doubt. Shortly before the Summer Parliamentary recess in 2000, the Home Secretary undertook to publish a consultation paper setting out a choice of options for drawing the work of the prisons and the probation inspectorates closer together. The resulting document was issued the following month by Paul Boateng.

One of the options was to appoint the same person as both HM Chief Inspector of Prisons and Chief Inspector of Probation. This was possible under the existing legislation, although it had been discussed with neither of the two post-holders. A joint appointment, it was claimed, 'would provide overall strategic direction for the inspection of both services and strong oversight to ensure they were working in a co-ordinated way . . .'.[64] The document recognized that the two Inspectorates had a very different ethos, as did the two services. There was also a risk that a single Chief Inspector's responsibilities might become so wide that there would be insufficient contact

[62] Ibid., p. 4.

[63] Commanded UK Field Army, 1987–90; Adjutant General, 1990–3. Chmn, Hillingdon Hospital NHS Trust, 1995. HM Chief Inspector of Prisons, 1995–2001.

[64] *Inspecting the Work of the Prison and Probation Services: Options for the Future*, Option D, para. 14.

with practice on the ground to gain the confidence of the public or ministers. Yet the consultative text ended on a prejudgmental note:

> . . . the public has a right to expect that we do in fact have a coherent system either side of the prison gates which works to reduce re-offending and to ensure that governors and the Parole Board make decisions on release and supervision based on sound risk assessment and reports from prison and probation staff. A joint Chief Inspector could maintain the focus on these important objectives, which can otherwise fall through the net of two separate inspection systems. An independent and influential appointment covering both public services could give the inspectorates a powerful voice as the Government's cross-cutting strategies for reducing re-offending and moves towards more flexible sentencing are developed.[65]

The notion of merging the offices of Chief Inspector of Prisons and Chief Inspector of Probation attracted vehement criticism, especially evident in the House of Lords and the Probation Service. Both at Committee and Report stages of the Criminal Justice and Court Services Bill, the Lords debated a cross-party amendment to ensure that no such appointment could be made. All the existing forms of co-operation would remain unchanged. In its representations against a joint Chief Inspector, the Probation Service argued that it already co-operated closely with the Prison Service in the form of periodic joint inspections or thematic reviews carried out by the separate Inspectorates of Prisons and Probation. Recent examples were comprehensive reviews on life sentence prisoners and the preparation of prisoners for release and resettlement. This type of joint working was desirable and effective; it was likely to continue, and did not call for any legislative intervention.

The consultation document failed to take account of the fact that only about one-third of the work of the Probation Service overlaps with that of the prisons, whereas virtually all its work is linked to the courts or the police, or to both. The Probation Service also co-operates with health authorities in respect of drug use and mentally disordered offenders, as well as with local authorities, especially in the context of youth justice initiatives. The Association of Chief Officers of Probation (ACOP) agreed that there was merit in periodic joint inspections in each of these areas of probation work in the community, but pointed out that the consultation document:

[65] *Inspecting the Work of the Prison and Probation Services: Options for the Future*, Option D, para. 15.

> . . . provides no evidence of the benefits to the Prison Service of this proposal. ACOP believes it would be to the detriment of Probation, in that inspections would be driven by the larger organization, the Prison Service. The flexibility and choice of thematics, speed of response and focus on performance would, we believe, be lost if we were to become part of a much larger Inspectorate with a very different brief and culture to that of our own.[66]

The differences in culture between the two Services were indeed far more profound than the ill defined concept of 'cross-cutting strategies' for reducing reoffending and protecting the public. Security and discipline are at the heart of the Prison Service. The first task of the prison officer is to ensure that offenders sentenced to imprisonment remain in custody for the authorized period. The need to avoid disturbances, the most serious of which may lead to temporary loss of control, is formative of attitudes towards security and discipline. The Inspectorate is, and should be, primarily concerned with what happens inside the prisons. Are they secure? Do the conditions in which inmates are held correspond with what they are supposed to be? How effective are the precautions to prevent drugs being smuggled into, and then traded within, the establishment? Are the managers and prison officers properly carrying out the onerous tasks with which they are charged?

There is also a clear distinction between loss of liberty through imprisonment and the restrictions imposed by community sentences. Unlike the prisons, the Probation Service concentrates on rehabilitation in the community, drawing on local support and initiatives. Although a recognized degree of overlap exists, it is hard to escape the suspicion that the consultation document was, in part at least, an opportunity for ministers to rid themselves of a turbulent Chief Inspector. Providing this *bon mot*, Lord Hurd remarked that matters had not got as far as that in Whitehall; indeed could not get as far as that. But of a sense of irritation he had no doubt, and much evidence.[67] At Report stage the Government contention that the amendment was unnecessary and out of place failed to persuade. By 188 votes to 120 an amendment moved by the author was agreed.[68]

By the time the Lords' amendments were considered by the Commons the consultation period had ended. What the Home

[66] ACOP statement cited by the author in *Parl. Debates*, HL, 618, col. 834, 31 Oct. 2000.

[67] Ibid., col. 837.

[68] Ibid., cols. 846–8.

Secretary described as 'a helpful scheme'[69] had been suggested by five of HM Chief Inspectors (of Constabulary, the Crown Prosecution Service, the Magistrates' courts, and the Probation and Prison Services) 'to inspect practice across their boundaries systematically'. Only small minorities of respondents who had replied to the consultation document had been in favour either of the status quo, or the appointment of a single joint Chief Inspector for Prisons and Probation. Inspecting across boundaries, however slight the difference with existing practice, was therefore the face-saving option that Straw proposed to pursue. The appointment of Sir David Ramsbotham would be extended for a further eight months until the end of July 2001, the date on which Sir Graham Smith, HM Chief Inspector of Probation since 1992, would be retiring. Both Chief Inspector posts would be advertised in the New Year.

While insisting that nothing had been done by stealth to displace the incumbent Chief Inspector of Prisons, Straw acknowledged the anxieties expressed in the Lords.[70] He believed his proposal had dealt with them. Nevertheless the Conservative Opposition in the Commons voted against the Question that the House do disagree with the Lords' amendments, going down to defeat by 166 votes to 345.[71] When the Bill came back again to the Lords, however, the compromise was accepted with relief. The essential point had been won. Each service would continue to have its own Chief Inspector in the future.

VII

Few general statements of policy towards crime by ministers or other Government spokesmen since Labour came to power in 1997 omitted a mention of the victims. For both presentational and policy reasons sympathetic references to support for victims and witnesses was subsumed into the overall strategy. As an example, the wording of the second Home Office aim set out in its business plan for 2000–1 was 'The delivery of justice through effective and efficient investigation, prosecution, trial and sentencing, and through support for victims'.[72] More specifically, the objective of a better service for victims and witnesses was to be achieved (a) by ensuring that the public agencies of criminal

[69] *Parl. Debates*, HC, 356, col. 845, 14 Nov. 2000. [70] Ibid., col. 846.
[71] Ibid., cols. 850–4. [72] Home Office, *Business Plan 2000–2001*, p. 8.

justice adhered to the twenty-seven standards of service contained in the *Victim's Charter*; (b) by establishing support services for victims and witnesses in the Magistrates' courts to complement those already available in the Crown Court; (c) to implement procedural reforms intended to protect vulnerable or intimidated witnesses in court; and (d) to monitor and keep under review the system of making financial compensation for criminal injuries.

Chronologically, criminal injuries compensation had come first with the introduction in 1964 of a non-statutory scheme providing for *ex gratia* payments from public funds to be made to the victims of violent crime. In total, some £220 million was paid out in compensation to more than 230,000 victims or their dependants over the first twenty years. By the mid-1980s the annual cost had escalated sharply, rising from just under £40 million in 1984–5 to nearly £46 million in the following year, causing scepticism in Whitehall as to whether resources would continue to be available to fund the scheme at its current levels. As the number of victims receiving compensation had risen far more rapidly than the recorded increase in violent crime, the lower limit for claims was raised in order to concentrate resources on those injuries which substantially affected the well-being of the claimant.[73] But the number of applications continued to increase, at a rate faster than they could be processed. By 1987–8, the year in which the discretionary scheme was made statutory, there was a backlog of 78,087 applications waiting to be dealt with.

Although Parliament had legislated to provide for the setting up of a statutory system to administer compensation payments for criminal injuries as of right,[74] its implementation was postponed because of the long delays which had built up in the processing of applications under the discretionary scheme. By 1992–3 the number outstanding had reached 86,951, with an estimate for the following year rising to 94,200. The expenditure on compensation was expected to increase from £152.5 million to £170 million.[75] In these

[73] *Responses to Crime*, (1987), 'The Victims', pp. 30–1.

[74] Part VII of the Criminal Justice Act 1988 provided for the setting up of a statutory body to administer a scheme for the payment of compensation for criminal injuries. It was never implemented, and was repealed by the Criminal Injuries Compensation Act 1995.

[75] *Responses to Crime*, Vol. 3 (1996) contains a full description of the labyrinthine changes in the ways of compensating victims for criminal injuries in the 1990s, and the political and legal challenges that resulted. See ibid., Chapter 9, 'Compensation for Victims: A Disorderly Reform', pp. 433–77.

circumstances, after a further delay caused by a set-back in the courts, the Government switched to a system of fixed tariff payments related to the gravity of the injury. This replaced the more time-consuming and costly process of lawyers assessing each individual award on the basis of what the damages were likely to have been if awarded by a court.[76]

Apart from eligibility for compensation from public funds as a result of specific injuries resulting from a criminal offence, a victim may benefit from a compensation order made by the court and enforceable against an offender. Legal aid may also be available to enable victims with limited financial resources to take action in the civil courts to obtain compensation from an offender, or to protect them from a violent partner.

The emotional impact of a crime on the victim, whether or not it results in a prosecution reaching the courts, can be as great or greater than the material loss. Until the mid-1970s virtually no attention was paid to the human effects of crime and how they could be countered. In 1974 volunteers in Bristol began working with the police to provide emotional support and practical assistance to victims of theft, burglary, or assault who were referred to them by the police. From this original initiative a national network of local victim support schemes grew rapidly.[77] Before long volunteers were being recruited, trained, and supported by paid co-ordinators throughout the country. The range of offences was extended to cover the most serious, including murder and manslaughter, and the most intimate, domestic violence and sexual offences.

A quarter of a century later access to services helping victims to cope with the consequences of crime was on a national scale and had become an integral part of public policy. By 1999–2000 more than a million people (1,129,237) who had been affected by crime were offered help by Victim Support, the name by which the National Association of Victim Support Schemes is known.[78] In total there were 331 local schemes and branches in England, Wales, and Northern Ireland, of which forty-two were organized into eleven Area or County schemes. A national telephone helpline was based at the Head

[76] *Responses to Crime*, Vol. 3 (1996), pp. 461–3.

[77] Helen Reeves was appointed as Director of the NAVSS in 1980 and has contributed inspirational leadership as the chief executive over more than two decades. She was created a Dame in 1999. The author declares an interest as President of Victim Support, an honorary office, since 1992.

[78] Victim Support, *Annual Report*, 2000, p. 8.

Office in London. Ninety-three per cent of those who worked for Victim Support, a total of 15,609 people in 1998–9, did so in a voluntary capacity.[79] A recruitment drive to mark the Silver Jubilee Year was launched in the presence of The Queen and resulted in an initial response of nearly 6,000 potential volunteers. The most crucial element of this public/private partnership was the extent of public funding. By the financial year ended 31 March 2000 the Home Office grant for the services provided by Victim Support exceeded £15 million.[80]

The largest part of the funding was required to meet the cost of the newest service, the support of victims and witnesses attending criminal trials. Initially confined to some Crown Court centres, Victim Support pioneered the concept in the early 1990s of trained volunteers to provide emotional support and practical information about the court process. The then Lord Chief Justice, Lord Taylor of Gosforth, had been a stalwart enthusiast. One of his last public engagements before his resignation in 1996, and his untimely death the following year, was to preside at a Victim Support event held in the Crown Court at Newcastle-on-Tyne.

Research, as well as observation, validated the need of many victims of crime who are required to give evidence at a trial to be accompanied by a reliable person who can help with guidance and reassurance. There may be an opportunity to visit a court centre in advance so as to familiarize themselves with the layout of a court-room. Few victims know what is expected of them, nor what the procedure will be. It can be an intimidating experience to give a public airing of unpleasant events, including accusing another person of a crime, and the resultant fear that this may induce. Moreover, few victim-witnesses understand or are prepared for the ordeal of cross-examination.[81]

The Witness Service now operates in every Crown Court centre in England and Wales, and is currently being extended into every Magistrates' court, with a target date for completion of April 2002.[82]

[79] Ibid., p. 11. In addition there were over 900 paid staff to co-ordinate the activities of each local service and provide support and supervision for the volunteers.

[80] Ibid., p. 15. In addition to public funds, an audit in December 1999 showed that local Victim Support schemes were raising a total of about £2.5 million each year. Ibid., p. 16.

[81] See Victim Support, *Helping people cope with crime*, 1999, p. 13.

[82] By the end of March 2001 it was estimated that about 45 per cent of Magistrates' courts would be covered, well in excess of the Government target. 77 *VSM* (*Victim Support Magazine*), Winter 2001, p. 2.

In the year 1999–2000 some 126,106 people used the Crown Court Witness Service, a total very similar to that of the previous year. The majority of witnesses were referred by the Crown Prosecution Service (55 per cent of all persons supported), followed by victims called to give evidence (23 per cent), and victims' relatives and friends (18 per cent). The largest offence category was serious crimes of violence, such as murder or attempted murder, manslaughter, robbery, and assault (43 per cent). The second most frequently helped group by crime type was burglary and theft (11 per cent).[83]

The predominance of prosecution witnesses among those seeking support is a reminder of the risks they may face of intimidation or harassment by defendants, or those associated with defendants. A recent study has identified the significance of community-wide intimidation, real or perceived, comprising victim and non-victim witnesses, whose perception of the possibility of intimidation means that they are not prepared to come forward and give evidence to the police.[84] Specific instances of intimidation involving actual physical assaults or damage to property, intended to deter a person from reporting a crime or giving evidence in court, can lead to a community-wide form of intimidation. While the police may take special measures to protect high-risk individuals from life-threatening intimidation, it is a social evil if community-wide intimidation deters potential witnesses in particular locations from participating in the process of justice.

VIII

Recognition of the needs of victims and their crucial role as witnesses were among the unquestionable advances in the process of criminal justice in the closing years of the twentieth century. For a long time the impetus had been maintained by the voluntary movement. But the adoption of victims' interests by Government made possible a step-change, both in the scale of funding and the scope of public responses to private initiatives.

Other recognizable improvements were harder to identify. The system of youth justice had been transformed and held out promise for the future. A start had been made in setting up locally based crime and

[83] Victim Support, *Annual Report 2000*, p. 10.

[84] See N. R. Fyfe and H. McKay, 'Desperately Seeking Safety', *Brit. J. Criminol.* (2000) 40, 675–91 at 677.

disorder partnerships between the police, local councils, the health service, and voluntary organizations, with the specific aim of reducing the incidence of crime. The Crown Prosecution Service had got over its teething troubles and was delivering a higher, but not yet entirely adequate, standard of service. Delays between charging suspects and trial had been reduced substantially, if not yet achieving the targets set in 1997. Criminal legal aid was still in the throes of fundamental reorganization, and it was too early to say whether the fears of its most forthright critics would be justified. The enforcement of community penalties had been strengthened, and the Probation Service brought under more direct control by central Government.

And the prisons? The overall population in custody had increased by one-third over the preceding decade. At some establishments overcrowding was at intolerable levels, particularly in the older local prisons. Throughout the system there were too many examples of conditions and regimes failing to meet the required standards, some of them brought to light as a result of the vigilance of the Chief Inspector and his team. The demands of managerialism meant that much time was taken up in providing the data needed to monitor performance at a prison under no less than fifteen performance indicators and forty-two targets.[85] Meanwhile, the accelerating incarceration of women and the needs of unsentenced prisoners[86] raised special problems. The menace of drugs remained, in the prisons as in the wider community.

On procedural justice, expert reviews were in progress of the criminal courts and the sentencing framework which could lead to radical changes during the next Parliament. One independent-minded judge succeeded another as Lord Chief Justice, both well able to check any displays of arbitrary power by errant ministers. The Human Rights Act subtly altered the relationships between Parliaments, the executive, and the courts.[87]

[85] S. Bryans, 134 *Prison Service Journal*, March 2001, p. 9. The author was a serving prison governor writing in his capacity as a member of the National Executive Committee of the Prison Governors Association.

[86] HM Inspectorate of Prisons for England and Wales, *Unjust deserts: A Thematic Review by HM Chief Inspector of Prisons of the Treatment and Conditions for Unsentenced Prisoners in England and Wales*, Home Office, Dec. 2000.

[87] The Human Rights Act came fully into force on 2 Oct. 2000. It was effective in Scotland, Wales, and Northern Ireland earlier since under the terms of the Scotland Act 1998, the Government of Wales Act 1998, and the Northern Ireland Act 1998 the devolved institutions in those parts of the United Kingdom may not do anything which is incompatible with the Convention rights.

By the end of the twentieth century the characteristics of criminal justice policies were notably different from half a century earlier. The broadly bipartisan approach shared by the main political parties was no more than a faint memory, not always accurately recalled, of an era that had passed. Reliance on expertise was diminished, although still needed in the development of practical policies behind the scenes. Far more visible was the fiercely competitive day-by-day struggle for favourable media exposure. As the Prime Minister's 'touchstone issues' memorandum, quoted earlier in this Chapter, showed so clearly, the dominant thrust of policy-making by Government since 1997 had been the perceived need to maintain a constant flow of tough-sounding initiatives, calculated to inspire greater confidence in the criminal justice system on the part of the general public. The momentum of legislation quickened: five major or omnibus Bills on criminal justice receiving the Royal Assent in the 1997–2001 Parliament.[88] Plausible as the overall strategy had been in terms of electoral politics, the danger is that once institutionalized the consequences of opportunism may come to overshadow the often inconvenient aderence to the principles of justice and individual liberty. Dispensing justice is more than a rhetorical slogan: it should be accepted as an indispensable requirement at every stage in the criminal process.

[88] Crime and Disorder Act 1998, Access to Justice Act 1999, Youth Justice and Criminal Evidence Act 1999, Criminal Justice and Court Services Act 2000, Criminal Justice and Police Act 2001.

Index

NOTE: All references are to England and Wales unless otherwise stated